Stories
in *Verse*

Stories
in *Verse*

MAX T. HOHN
Editor

With a New Introduction by
JOHN GEHLMANN

TWELFTH PRINTING-1978
LIBRARY OF CONGRESS CATALOGUE
CARD NUMBER 61-3198
ISBN 0-672-73234-3 (PBK)
ISBN 0-672-73253-3X

Printed by permission of Bobbs-Merrill Co.

Calvert Education Services
Hunt Valley, Maryland 21031
USA

PRINTED IN THE UNITED STATES OF AMERICA
2003

Contents

PART ONE

Stories in Verse

Contents

PART TWO

Stories in Verse

Contents

Stories in Verse

To the Teachers Who
Will Use This Book

The publication of *Stories in Verse* in 1943 inaugurated "The Odyssey Texts in Types of Literature." This series of high-school texts is edited on the assumption that, at the secondary school level, division into types is an excellent way to teach appreciation of literature, because the satisfactory reading of each type of literature requires a special technique, and because for each type this special technique involves different factors which need to be clearly identified for both teachers and pupils. Therefore all volumes in this series are limited to a single type and are frankly *texts* designed for use by a *class* in a *school* where a *teacher teaches* and the *pupil learns*.

As the Odyssey Texts have increased in number over the past two decades, this original assumption has been substantiated by the warm welcome and increasing use accorded each successive volume. Evidently many teachers agree that pupils are most comfortable and cooperative and self-respecting in a frank pupil-teacher relationship, and that they are eager for the sense of clear purpose and achievement which comes from the *conscious* aim at mastery of definite knowledge or skills.

Stories in Verse

That the first volume in the Odyssey series should be a book of poetry was perhaps inevitable, for in no other field is the need for teaching of a reading technique more evident and compelling. Many, if not most, boys and girls of high-school age have concluded that the reading of poetry is a highbrow, silly, unintelligible, dull, valueless performance. The teacher cannot persuade these skeptics that they are mistaken if he simply allows them to "mess around with a lot of poems." To accomplish this important task of persuasion, he needs a textbook which clearly enumerates and teaches the values of poetry and thus develops enjoyment in the reading of this type of literature.

And it was equally inevitable that this first volume should be limited to *narrative* poetry. If a typical American youth is to learn to enjoy poetry, he must discover in it some relation to the life he lives, and to the things from which he already gets pleasure. In the early high-school years, a pupil of normal interests is not really capable of sharing adult emotional reactions to experience. Consequently he does not respond with enthusiasm to much lyric poetry; indeed, a great deal of this is "poison" to him. He reacts much more favorably to action, real or imagined. Therefore the poems he will enjoy most are narrative, not lyric; and his introduction to poetry should be limited to those poems which tell a story.

Stories in Verse is divided into two parts: Part One, in which serious intensive study of certain elements of good narrative poetry is carried on; and Part Two, in which more relaxed and leisurely reading of good poems changes this reading from a task to a pleasure.

In Part One, the first step has been to identify clearly the relevant elements of instruction, and to treat each in a separate section. There are three of these elements: narrative, word music, and imagery.

The first section treats the sources of enjoyment in narrative. The treatment is very simple, and each of these sources of pleasure is illustrated by a poem which classroom experience has proved satisfactory for the purpose.

In the second section the exposition moves from *story* to *verse* and treats the pleasure inherent in the musical quality of poetry. The argument is that by writing in poetic form the story-teller adds to the attractions of narrative the inexhaustible pleasures of music. Here again the treatment is very simple; but wherever the use of terms makes possible a kind of discussion that seems valuable, the terms have been given. If a concept is not in itself difficult, the name will not make it so; and to avoid the name is to handicap discussion needlessly.

The third section treats a matter of real difficulty: poetic imagery. This part of the exposition is an honest attempt to make imagery comprehensible to the average high-school pupil; many teachers have found the discussion exceedingly helpful in promoting the sensual awareness characteristic of the trained reader of poetry. If only because it is less familiar to the pupil than either narrative or word music, the subject of the imagery requires more attention. For this reason the organization is somewhat different, the progress is more gradual, and tested exercises have been included.

To round out the material in Part One, two brief sections provide instruction in the reading of two specialized sorts of poetry: ballads and blank verse. Unlike the first three sections, these are not fundamental to the plan of the book.

Part Two provides further reading experiences in which the student will apply the knowledge gained in Part One, firmly clinching it in his mind, and acquiring the ease and familiarity necessary for real enjoyment.

In Part Two, as in Part One, the poems have been selected for intrinsic merit and for proved pupil interest. The order in which they are arranged, though by no means haphazard, is not necessarily rigid. Those who like topical groupings will find numerous bases for rearrangement: humor, rides, dialect, patriotism, songs, theme. Various supplementary activities have been suggested: singing, dramatization, story writing, listening to records, reports to the class, vocabulary study.

The editorial material is of five kinds. A headnote tells the pupil what to expect in the poem that follows. Sidenotes are used to point out the particular features for which the poem was included, or to give help for a correct and effective reading. Endnotes give instructions for a second, more finished reading, or for class discussion, advanced work, or for vocabulary study. Footnotes explain historical and geographical references, and foreign and rare words. Finally, a glossary includes all difficult words that seem to be useful additions to the pupil's vocabulary. The superior pupil who tends to be annoyed by help which he does not need may well be mollified (privately) by a little judicious praise for his progress in reading poetry. This book was edited for the average pupil.

All the editorial material is designed with the expectation of oral reading of the poems. It is assumed that much of the class time will be devoted to this activity. Poetry must be read aloud. In its origin poetry was an oral art, and so it remains for the best poets today. As Archibald MacLeish puts it, "The ear is the poet's perfect audience, his only true audience." Rhythm is the fundamental poetic appeal for the typical high-school boy or girl, as for most other readers.

In all teaching of appreciation, and especially in the teaching of poetry, enthusiasm is contagious. Therefore the editorial material is deliberately written in a personal style, so that the editor's enthusiasm may reënforce the teacher's. It is hoped that the frequent appearance of the pronoun "I" is for this reason justified and will be found unobjectionable.

The "Postscript" contains a survey of epic poetry, and suggestions for further reading of narrative poems. Some teachers may wish to discuss epic poetry earlier and to carry the suggested reading about epic heroes along with the study of the text. This section also gives definitions of the types of poetry, for teachers who want definitions.

Stories in Verse

When *Stories in Verse* was published in 1943, Max T. Hohn, the editor referred to his colleagues, Rodney A. Kimball and John Gehlmann, as "really co-editors of this book." Because of the untimely death of Mr. Hohn in 1955, the task of preparing this revision has fallen to Mr. Kimball and me. Fortunately, so excellent was Mr. Hohn's editorial work and selection of poems that little change has been thought necessary—or desirable. In its new format it is still Mr. Hohn's book, which for almost twenty years has helped teachers open the doors of poetry to thousands of American high-school boys and girls, who, until they studied *Stories in Verse*, were sure poetry was just one of the minor errors of misguided adults.

John Gehlmann

Acknowledgments

The editor gratefully acknowledges the kindness of authors, agents, and publishers in giving permission to reproduce material in this anthology, as follows:

D. Appleton-Century Company: for "St. Swithin," from *Harp in the Winds* by Daniel Henderson.

Berman's Jewish House and Philip M. Raskin, editor: for "The Two Brothers" by Isaac Leib Peretz, translated by Jacob Robbins, from the *Anthology of Modern Jewish Poetry*.

William Rose Benét: for "Morgiana Dances," from his volume, *Man Possessed*; and to William Rose Benét and Dodd, Mead & Company for "Jesse James" and "The Skater of Ghost Lake," from the same volume.

Brandt & Brandt: for Stephen Vincent Benét's "The Mountain Whippoorwill," from *Ballads and Poems*, published by Farrar & Rinehart, Inc., copyright, 1918, 1920, 1923, 1925, 1929, 1930, 1931, by Stephen Vincent Benét: for the selection from *John Brown's Body*, published by Farrar & Rinehart, Inc., copyright, 1927, 1928, by Stephen Vincent Benét; and for Siegfried Sassoon's "Counter-Attack," from *Counter-Attack*, published by E. P. Dutton & Co., Inc., copyright, 1940, by Siegfried Sassoon.

The Clarendon Press: for ballads adapted from the *Oxford Book of Ballads*, published by the Clarendon Press at Oxford.

Elizabeth Coatsworth: for "A Lady Comes to an Inn."

Covici-Friede, Inc.: for lines from "Lapsus Linguae" by Keith Preston.

Curtis Brown, Lts.: for "Dunkirk" by Robert Nathan. Copyright by Robert Nathan.

Dodd, Mead & Company, Inc.: for "Jesse James" and "The Skater of Ghost Lake," from *Golden Fleece* by William Rose Benét; for lines from "The Spell of the Yukon," and for "The Cremation of Sam McGee," from *The Spell of the Yukon* by Robert Service; for lines from "The Great Lover," from *The Collected Poems of Rupert Brooke*, copyright, 1915, by Dodd, Mead & Company, Inc.: for lines from "A Vagabond Song," from *Poems* by Bliss Carman; for "Cerelle," from *Lanterns in the Dusk* by Margaret Bell Houston, copyright, 1930. Used by permission of the publishers.

Doubleday, Doran & Company, Inc.: for "Evening Prayer," from *Selected Lyrics* by Amelia Josephine Burr, copyright, 1927, by Doubleday, Doran & Company, Inc.; for the "Ballad of East and West," from *Departmental Ditties and Barrack Room Ballads*, by Rudyard Kipling, copyright, 1892, 1893, 1899, 1927. Reprinted by permission of Doubleday, Doran & Company, Inc., of Messrs. A. P. Watts & Son, London, and the executrix of Mr. Kipling.

Gerald Duckworth & Co., Ltd., London and Alfred

Acknowledgments

A. Knopf, Inc.: for "Matilda," from *Cautionary Tales for Children* by Hilaire Belloc.

E. P. Dutton & Co., Inc.: for "Pershing at the Front," "Tact," and "The Vizier's Apology," from *Lyric Laughter* by Arthur Guiterman; for "The Sands of Dee," and "The Three Fishers," from Everyman's Library edition of *Poems* by Charles Kingsley; for "The Man Hunt," from *The Vale of Tempe* by Madison Cawein; for a passage from the introduction to *Rama, the Hero of India* by Dhan Gopal Mukerji; for "Bête Humaine," from *Poems: 1916-1918* by Francis Brett Young. All published and copyrighted by E. P. Dutton & Co., Inc., New York.

Farrar & Rinehart, Inc.: for "Gamesters All," by DuBose Heyward, from *Carolina Chansons* by Hervey Allen and DuBose Heyward, copyright, 1922. Reprinted by permission of the publishers

Godwin Publishers: for "From This the Strength," from *Roll On, Pioneers* by Fred Lape.

Harcourt, Brace and Company, Inc.: for "Da Leetla Boy," "Da Wheestlin' Barber," and "Two 'Mericana Men," from *Selected Poems of T.A. Daly*; for "De Boll Weevil Song," from *The American Songbag* compiled by Carl Sandburg; for "Swimmers," from *Selected Poems and Parodies of Louis Untermeyer*. Reprinted by permission of the publishers.

Harper & Brothers: for "Old Christmas Morning," from *Lonesome Water* by Roy Helton; for "The True Story of Skipper Ireson," from *Star-Glow and Song* by Charles Buxton Going; for verses quoted from *The*

Acknowledgments

Alfred A. Knopf, Inc.: for "Matilda," reprinted from Hellaire Belloc's *Cautionary Tales for Children*, by permission of Alfred A. Knopf, Inc., and of Gerald Duckworth & Co., Ltd.; for "Concerning the Economic Independence of Women," reprinted from *In America* by John V. A. Weaver; and for "Sea Lullaby," reprinted from *Collected Poems of Elinor Wylie*, by permission of and special arrangement with Alfred A. Knopf, Inc., authorized publishers.

J. B. Lippincott Company for lines from "Smells," from *Chimney-smoke* by Christopher Morley; and for "My Sense of Sight," from *The Laughing Willow* by Oliver Herford.

The Macmillan Company: for "The Ballad of Cap'n Pye," "The Lady of the Tomahawk," "Lazybones," "The Means Massacre," and lines from "Crystal Moment," all from Robert P. Tristram Coffin's *Collected Poems*; for "Flannan Isle," "The Stone," and lines from "In a Restaurant," all from W. W. Gibson's *Collected Poems*; for "Simon Legree," from Vachel Lindsay's *Collected Poems*; for "Spanish Waters," from John Masefield's *Poems*; for "The Romney," from Harriet Monroe's *Chosen Poems*; for "The Ballad of Father Gilligan," from William Butler Yeats's *Collected Poems*. By permission of the publishers.

Virgil Markham: for "The Christ of the Andes," "How the Great Guest Came," and "The Right Kind of People," by Edwin Markham. Reprinted by permission.

Ruphine A. McCarthy: for "St. Brigid," from *The Harp of Life* by Denis A. McCarthy.

Stories in Verse

Juanita J. Miller: for Joaquin Miller's "Columbus" and "Kit Carson's Ride," by permission Juanita J. Miller.

Idella Purnell: for "A Shot at Night."

G. P. Putnam's Sons: for lines from "Unheralded," from *Any Spring* by Dorothy Aldis.

Random House, Inc.: for "Shameful Death," from *Selected Prose and Poetry* by William Morris.

Selma Robinson: for "Ballad of the Huntsman."

Edna Davis Romig: for "Forest Fire," from *Blue Hills* by Edna Davis Romig; Dorrance & Company, Inc., publishers.

The Rotarian, Chicago: for "Buck Fever," by Bert Cooksley.

William B. Ruggles: for "The Pioneer."

Charles Scribner's Sons: for lines from Alan Seeger's "I have a Rendezvous with Death"; and for "The Revenge of Hamish," from *The Poems of Sidney Lanier*.

Frederick A. Stokes Company: for "The Highwayman," and lines from "The Sign of the Golden Shoe," from the *Collected Poems* of Alfred Noyes, Volume I.

Rosalind B. Thayer: for "Casey at the Bat" by Ernest Thayer.

The University of Chicago Press: for "Poverty," from the *Panchatantra*, and "The Serpent and the Mouse," from *Golden Gloom*, both by Arthur W. Ryder, and both reprinted by permission of the The University of Chicago Press.

The University of Nebraska: for "Haying" by Ethel Romig Fuller. Reprinted by permission of the copyright

Acknowledgments

owners, Prairie Schooner, University of Nebraska.

The Viking Press, Inc.: for "The Creation" and passages from the author's preface to *God's Trombones* by James Weldon Johnson, copyright, 1927; and for "The Image," from *The Espalier* by Sylvia Townsend Warner. By permission of the publishers.

A. P. Watt & Son, London: for "The Ballad of East and West," from *Departmental Ditties and Barrack Room Ballads*, by Rudyard Kipling. Reprinted by permission of A. P. Watt & Son, of Doubleday, Doran & Company, Inc., and the executrix of Mr. Kipling.

For special courtesies the editor expresses his appreciation to Mr. William Rose Benét, Mr. Roy Helton, Miss Margaret Bell Houston, Miss Idella Purnell, Mr. Philip Raskin, Mrs. Edna Davis Romig, Mr. Burton E. Stevenson, Mrs. Ernest Lawrence Thayer, and Mr. Clement Wood.

To the Boys and Girls
Who Will Use This Book

I wish I could believe that every boy and girl who opens *Stories in Verse* will leap for joy at the chance to read a new collection of poems. Unfortunately my experience obliges me to admit that many high-school students are anything but enthusiastic about any book of poetry. And yet I am convinced that this does not need to be so. In fact, the chief reason for making this book is that I want to do something about the general indifference to poetry that exists among high-school pupils.

Why do you dislike reading poetry—if you do dislike it? Or, if you delight in reading verse, what are the reasons why you delight in it? Are not the reasons here the same as for your attitudes towards other things? Why do some people enjoy dancing, or tennis, or public speaking, while others are indifferent to these pursuits, or detest them? Why do opinions vary as to the pleasure to be found in attending symphony concerts, football games, automobile shows, air maneuvers? In general, don't you enjoy whatever you understand and get something out of? You like a thing if you know what it is all about; and you enjoy doing things that you do well enough to take pride in your skill. The principles undoubtedly hold for the reading of poetry as well as for other diversions, and this book has been planned to conform to these two principles.

You have a perfect right to ask, "What good is poetry? What has poetry to offer me in the form of entertainment or of mental or spiritual development? How will I be a happier person by studying this book?" *Stories in Verse* tries to help you answer these questions. It tries to help you discover the enjoyment to be found in the *music* of poetry and in the full *life of the senses* which is achieved through poetry and which makes us enjoy the beauty and loveliness and charm and grandeur of a world that to the unenlightened often appears dull and commonplace.

Stories in Verse is only a first book in the study of poetry; it is only a start. And, because for the beginner narrative poetry seems to me to be more enjoyable than lyric, I have limited the poems in this book to those which tell a story. (And I have opened the book with a section on the pleasures of reading *narrative*, which should lift to a more mature, adult level your ability to read stories.) But I hope that what you learn in this book will encourage you later to extend your reading to lyric poetry, which will open for you the door to some of the greatest utterances of the human heart.

Stories in Verse is divided into two parts. In Part One you will be made aware of the pleasures offered by the reading of narrative poetry. In Part Two you will put into practice what you have learned in Part One and thus become such a competent reader of narrative poetry that reading it will for you no longer be a task, but a delight. And your study of *Stories in Verse*, by making you a discerning, educated reader of narrative poetry, will, I hope, bring you an added pleasure, the pride which always attends the efficient use of a difficult skill. Such a program, I believe, will put at your command a wealth of pleasurable experience which you would not willingly have missed.

You will find that much is said about reading aloud. Verse, like music, is designed to appeal to the ear; therefore, to be fully appreciated, it must be heard. Perhaps, as a rule, you will want to read the poem once silently, to get the story, before you make use of the suggestions for oral reading. Then read it aloud as often as possible, till you know it well. Each poem has much to offer you, if you will take the trouble to become truly familiar with it. And experienced readers all agree that the greatest poems yield new values with every re-reading.

I sincerely hope that every boy and girl who uses this book may gain from it some understanding of the great joy which enriches the lives of those who love poetry and read it with appreciation and may thus bring unto his own life many hours of high delight.

Stories in *Verse*

Part One:

Sources of Pleasure in Narrative Poetry

Finding Enjoyment in Narrative

Since the selections in this book are *stories* in *verse*, they offer us double opportunity for enjoyment: (1) the pleasure to be found in a *story* well told, and (2) the special delight to be derived from the music of the *verse* form and the magic of the poet's imagination. In this first section of our book we are going to examine the kinds of pleasure to be found in the elements of *narrative*, whether the story be written in poetry or in prose. In later sections we shall explore the possibilities for added enjoyment when the story is presented in *poetic* form.

The elements of narrative are four in number: action, characters, setting, and theme. Each has its own special kind of pleasure to offer us if we are alert to our opportunities as we read.

ACTION

Of the four sources of pleasure to be found in a narrative, the one which first comes to mind is action. We all want a story to move. We like to escape from humdrum reality by experiencing vicariously* the thrills of romantic adventure. Or we like humorous incidents which bring a smile to our lips and relaxation to our minds. A story full of action, which is either dramatic or funny, is sure to be a general favorite. We all like *thrills* and *laughs*.

Particularly do we find our interest engaged if the action of the story takes the form of a *plot*. A plot is a series of interrelated incidents presenting two opposing forces engaged in a conflict. Every story must have action to be a story at all, but action does not necessarily involve conflict; hence, not every story has a plot. But if a story does have a plot and if the author handles the plot well—that is, if he arouses our sympathy for one of the combatants and our hop‹ that this one will win; and if, up to the last minute, he keeps us uncertain as to the outcome of the struggle—then he creates in our minds a state of *suspense*. This suspense most of us find particularly exciting and enjoyable.

In some stories the action is merely *suggested*. The author gives us the bare facts of his experience, and allows us to speculate on the story behind the facts. A classic example of this sort of writing is Washington Irving's "The Stout Gentleman." This is an amusing account of a mysterious traveler at an inn, who never actually appeared to Irving's view but who challenged

---

*Probably the word vicariously is new to you. I assume that you are interested in extending your vocabulary; and sometimes when a hard word seemed the best way of saying a thing, I have used it. On pages 560 to 573 is a glossary defining many unusual words found in this book. You should turn to this glossary whenever you find a word you do not know.

his curiosity and stimulated his imagination. When an author shares such an experience with us he offers us the opportunity to develop the suggested story by giving our imaginations free rein, and thereby to feel the *joy of creation*.

Thus we see that the action of a story may offer us at least four kinds of pleasure: (1) vicarious thrills, (2) laughs, (3) suspense, (4) the joy of literary creation.

CHARACTERS

But action is not the only source of enjoyment in a narrative; besides action, a story must have characters. Sometimes they are funny; sometimes they are noble and inspiring; sometimes they are horrible examples of what to avoid. From various types of characters cunningly portrayed, we increase our *understanding of human nature*. Indeed, for many readers the author's skill in presenting his characters is the greatest source of pleasure in the story.

SETTING

A third element in narrative is the setting. The author sets each story in a particular time and a particular place. Reading stories thus affords us the pleasure of traveling and obtaining *increased knowledge of many interesting places and historical periods*. For instance, in this book the poets re-create for us such settings as pirate haunts of the South Seas and the white magic of the Yukon.

THEME

A fourth source of enjoyment in some narratives is what we sometimes call a "theme."* This is the practical truth or the moral lesson, or the bit of philosophy, that the story was written to illustrate. Not all stories have themes in this sense, but those which do have them offer us *wisdom* with which we can strengthen our characters and become more worth-while persons, or *inspiration* to better living, which impels us to live up to our best selves – and we are always happiest when we are true to the ideals we cherish.

A good story, then, will thrill us by its action, amuse us by its humor, hold us in suspense concerning the outcome of the struggle in the plot, stimulate our imaginations to create the story behind the facts, increase our understanding of our fellow human beings, take us journeying to interesting places, or inspire us to lead better lives. It does not have to do all of these seven things, but it will do at least one of them. If we are to get the greatest satisfaction from our reading of narratives, we must be alert to all of these possibilities for enjoyment, and not miss any of them as we read.

For this first section of our book I have chosen seven stories in verse which illustrate these various sources of

---

* Some authors use the word *theme* to denote a story's central impression, or single effect, or main idea. In this sense all good stories have themes. In the present book, however, the word is used in the more restricted sense defined above.

pleasure. By reading these seven poems and the editorial helps, you will, I hope become more aware of the four elements in narrative, and be prepared to appreciate fully the story in any story poem.

THE GLOVE AND THE LIONS
Leigh Hunt

The pleasure we find in this little story is the vicarious thrill derived from the dash and vigor with which it is told. The author has made the action swift and dramatic. When you read it to the class, they should feel the speed and drama which have made this poem a popular favorite for three generations.

King Francis was a hearty king, and loved a royal sport,
And one day as his lions fought, sat looking on the court;
The nobles filled the benches, with the ladies by their side,
And 'mongst them sat the Count de Lorge, with one for
    whom he sighed:
And truly 'twas a gallant thing to see that crowning
    show,   5
Valor and love, and a king above, and the royal
    beasts below.

Ramped and roared the lions,
    with horrid laughing jaws;
They bit, they glared, gave
    blows like bears, a wind
    went with their paws;

Swift, vigorous action in the pit. Notice the short, snappy sentences. Bring out the wind *and* the whisking foam *in your reading.*

With wallowing might and stifled roar they rolled on
    one another,
Till all the pit with sand and mane was in a
    thunderous smother;   10
The bloody foam above the bars came whisking
    through the air;

Said Francis then, "Faith, gentlemen, we're better
    here than there."
De Lorge's love o'erheard the King, a beauteous
    lively dame,
With smiling lips and sharp bright eyes, which
    always seemed the same;
She thought, the Count my lover is brave as brave
    can be;   15
He surely would do wondrous things to show his
    love for me;
King, ladies, lovers, all look on; the occasion is divine;
I'll drop my glove to prove his love; great glory will
    be mine.

She dropped her glove, to prove his love, then
    looked at him and smiled;
He bowed, and in a moment leaped among the lions
    wild;   20
The leap was quick, return was quick, he has
    regained his place,
Then threw the glove, but not with love, right in the
    lady's face.
"By heaven," said Francis,
    "rightly done!" and he rose   A dramatic and forceful
    from where he sat;   ending; don't let your voice
                                 weaken.
"No love," quoth he, "but vanity, sets love a task like that."

---

1. This poem is based on a story of an event supposed to have occurred at the
   court of Francis I, king of France in the sixteenth century. Two other great
   poets, the Englishman, Robert Browning, and the German, Johann Christoph
   Freidrich Schiller, have written about this incident.

CASEY AT THE BAT
Ernest Lawrence Thayer

This story is a classic of American humor, known to all lovers of baseball. It was made famous by a popular American comedian, DeWolf Hopper, who recited it many hundreds of times in theaters all over the country; the poem is more definitely associated with him than with its author, who was a California newspaperman. Besides being humorous, it is dramatic, vivid, and rapid in its action.

The outlook wasn't brilliant for the Mudville nine that day:
The score stood four to two, with but one inning more to play,
And then when Cooney died at first, and Barrows did the same,
A pall-like silence fell upon the patrons of the game.

A straggling few got up to go in deep despair. The rest   5
Clung to the hope which springs eternal in the human breast;
They thought, "If only Casey could but get a whack at that –
We'd put up even money now, with Casey at the bat."

But Flynn preceded Casey, as did also Jimmy Blake,
And the former was a hoodoo, while the latter was a cake;   10
So upon that stricken multitude grim melancholy sat,
For there seemed but little chance of Casey getting to the bat.

But Flynn let drive a single, to the wonderment of all,
And Blake, the much-despiséd, tore the cover off the ball;
And when the dust had lifted, and men saw what had occurred,   15

There was Jimmy safe at second and Flynn a-hugging third.

Then from five thousand throats and more there rose a lusty yell;
It rumbled through the valley, it rattled in the dell;
It pounded on the mountain and recoiled upon the flat,
For Casey, mighty Casey, was advancing to the bat.   20

There was ease in Casey's manner as he stepped into his place;
There was pride in Casey's bearing and a smile lit Casey's face.
And when, responding to the cheers, he lightly doffed his hat,
No stranger in the crowd could doubt 'twas Casey at the bat.

Ten thousand eyes were on him as he rubbed his hands
          with dirt;   25
Five thousand tongues applauded when he wiped
          them on his shirt;
Then while the writhing pitcher ground the ball into his hip,
Defiance flashed in Casey's eye, a sneer curled Casey's lip.

And now the leather-covered sphere came hurtling
          through the air,
And Casey stood a-watching it in haughty grandeur there.   30
Close by the sturdy batsman the ball unheeded sped –
"That ain't my style," said Casey. "Strike one!" the umpire said.

From the benches, black with people, there went up
          a muffled roar,
Like the beating of the storm-waves on a stern and distant shore;
"Kill him! Kill the umpire!" shouted someone on the stand; 35
And it's likely they'd have killed him had not Casey raised his hand.

With a smile of Christian charity great Casey's visage shone;
He stilled the rising tumult; he bade the game go on;
He signaled to the pitcher, and once more the dun sphere flew;
But Casey still ignored it, and the umpire said, "Strike two!"   40

"Fraud!" cried the maddened thousands, and echo answered
        "Fraud!"
But one scornful look from Casey and the audience was awed.
They saw his face grow stern and cold, they saw his muscles strain,
And they knew that Casey wouldn't let that ball go by again.

The sneer has fled from Casey's lip, his teeth are
        clenched in hate;   45
He pounds with cruel violence his bat upon the plate.
And now the pitcher holds the ball, and now he lets it go,
And now the air is shattered by the force of Casey's blow.

Oh, somewhere in this favored land the sun is shining bright;
The band is playing somewhere, and somewhere
        hearts are light,   50
And somewhere men are laughing, and little children shout;
But there is no joy in Mudville – great Casey has struck out.

THE HIGHWAYMAN[*]
Alfred Noyes

The title of this poem may bring to your mind romantic tales of pioneer days in the Far West; highwaymen, stagecoaches, shipments of gold, maidens in distress, heroic cowboys, last-minute rescues. The particular highwayman of this story, however, lived in England, back in the seventeenth or the eighteenth century when the stagecoach was the sole means of travel there, and when many an Englishman lived as a daredevil outlaw preying on the stagecoaches and robbing the passengers of their money and valuables.

You will find this story of the highwayman and Bess, the landlord's fair daughter, an exciting tale mainly because it has a good **plot** *— a tense conflict between two opposing forces, which engages your interest by means of suspense. You will find yourself thinking, "The highwayman wins, he loses; no he wins; no, he loses..." This suspense is the essence of a well-constructed plot, and good plot is the most important element in many stories.*

PART ONE
I

The wind was a torrent of darkness among the gusty trees,
The moon was a ghostly galleon tossed upon cloudy seas,
The road was a ribbon of moonlight over the purple moor,
And the highwayman came riding—
    Riding—riding   ⁵
The highwayman came riding, up to
    the old inn-door

If you are alert, the very word highwayman *will suggest the two conflicting forces.*

* Reprinted by permission from *Collected Poems*, Vol. I, by Alfred Noyes. Copyright, 1906, by Frederick A. Stokes Company.

II

He'd a French cocked-hat on his forehead, a bunch of lace at
his chin,
A coat of claret velvet, and breeches of brown doeskin;
They fitted with never a wrinkle: his boots were up to the
thigh!
And he rode with a jewelled twinkle,   10
His pistol butts a-twinkle,
His rapier hilt a-twinkle, under the jewelled sky.

III

Over the cobbles he clattered and clashed in the dark inn-yard,
And he tapped with his whip on the shutters, but all was
locked and barred;
He whistled a tune to the window, and who should be
waiting there   15
But the landlord's black-eyed daughter,
Bess, the landlord's daughter,
Plaiting a dark red love-knot into her long black hair.

IV

And dark in the dark old inn-yard a stable-wicket creaked
Where Tim the ostler listened; his face was white and
peaked;   20
His eyes were hollows of madness, his hair like moldy hay,
But he loved the landlord's daughter, | The opposing force takes
The landlord's red-lipped | shape.
daughter,
Dumb as a dog he listened, and he heard the robber say—

V

"One kiss, my bonny sweetheart, I'm after a prize tonight,   25
But I shall be back with the yellow gold before the morning
      light;
Yet, if they press me sharply, and harry me though the day,
Then look for me by moonlight,
      Watch for me by moonlight,
I'll come to thee by moonlight, though hell should bar the way."   30

VI

He rose up in the stirrups; he scarce could reach her hand,
But she loosened her hair i' the casement! His face burnt like
      a brand
As the black cascade of perfume came tumbling over his
      breast;
And he kissed its waves in the moonlight,
      (Oh, sweet black waves in the moonlight!)   35
Then he tugged at his rein in the moonlight, and galloped
      away to the West.

PART TWO
I

He did not come in the dawning; he did not come at noon;
And out o' the tawny sunset, before the rise o' the moon,
When the road was a gypsy's ribbon, looping the purple moor,
A red-coat troop came marching—   40
      Marching—marching—
King George's men came marching,
      up to the old inn-door.

> The conflict is now unmistakably clear.

II

They said no word to the landlord, they drank his ale instead,
But they gagged his daughter and bound her to the foot of
    her narrow bed;
Two of them knelt at her casement, with muskets at their side!   45
There was death at every window;
    And hell at one dark window;
For Bess could see, through her casement, the road that *he*
    would ride.

III

They had tied her up to attention, with many a sniggering jest;
They had bound a musket beside her, with the barrel beneath
    her breast!   50
"Now keep good watch!" and they
    kissed her. She heard the dead
    man say—

> Is the struggle already over?

Look for me by moonlight;
    Watch for me by moonlight;
I'll come to thee by moonlight, though hell should bar the way!

IV

She twisted her hands behind her; but
    all the knots held good!   55

> No, there is still some hope for the outlaw.

She writhed her hands till her fingers were wet with sweat or blood!
They stretched and strained in the darkness, and the hours
    crawled by like years,
Till, now, on the stroke of midnight,
    Cold, on the stroke of midnight,
The tip of one finger touched it! The trigger at least was hers!   60

V

The tip of one finger touched it; she strove no more for the rest!
Up, she stood up to attention, with the barrel beneath her
      breast,
She would not risk their hearing; she would not strive again;
For the road lay bare in the moonlight;
      Blank and bare in the
      moonlight;   65

This stanza is a fine example of well-handled suspense.

And the blood of her veins in the moonlight throbbed to her
      love's refrain.

VI

Tlot-tlot; Tlot-tlot! Had they heard it? The horse-hoofs
      ringing clear;
Tlot-tlot, Tlot-tlot, in the distance? Were they deaf that they
      did not hear?
Down the ribbon of moonlight, over the brow of the hill,
The highwayman came riding,   70
      Riding, riding!
The red-coats looked to their priming! She stood up, straight
      and still!

VII

Tlot-tlot, in the frosty silence! *Tlot-tlot,* in the echoing night!
Nearer he came and nearer! Her face was like a light!
Her eyes grew wide for a moment; she drew one last deep breath, 75
Then her finger moved in the moonlight,
      Her musket shattered the moonlight,
Shattered her breast in the moonlight and warned him—with
      her death.

VIII

He turned; he spurred to the West; he
did not know who stood

The highwayman wins.

Bowed, with her head o'er the musket, drenched with her
own red blood! [80]

Not till the dawn he heard it, his face
grew grey to hear

But his escape has been at too great a cost; he hasn't really won.

How Bess, the landlord's daughter,
The landlord's black-eyed daughter,

Had watched for her love in the moonlight, and died in the
darkness there.

IX

Back, he spurred like a madman, shrieking a curse to the sky, [85]

With the white road smoking behind him, and his rapier
brandished high!

Blood-red were his spurs i' the golden noon; wine-red was
his velvet coat.

When they shot him down on the
highway,

He loses.

Down like a dog on the highway,

And he lay in his blood on the highway, with the bunch of
lace at his throat. [90]

* * * * *

X

And still of a winter's night, they say, when the wind is in the trees,
When the moon is a ghostly galleon tossed upon cloudy seas,
When the road is a ribbon of moonlight over the purple moor,

A highwayman comes riding—
Riding—riding— [95]
A highwayman comes riding, up to the old inn door.

XI

Over the cobbles he clatters and clangs in the dark inn-yard;
He taps with his whip on the shutters, but all is locked and barred;
He whistles a tune to the window, and who should be waiting there
But the landlord's black-eyed daughter, [100]
 Bess, the landlord's daughter,
Plaiting a dark red love-knot into her
 long black hair.

But, if you believe in ghosts, the highwayman-lover really wins, after all!

Other poems for those who need further study of a plot:

A LADY COMES TO AN INN
Elizabeth Coatsworth

Miss Coatsworth here shares with you a brief glimpse into a romantic, exciting, mysterious situation, which awakened her curiosity but did not satisfy it. What is on the printed page in this case is not complete; it is an unfinished fragment, a challenge to your own creative ability. The **suggested story** *may take root in your mind and eventually be completed there, if you find enjoyment—as who doesn't?—in setting your imagination free to interpret such brief glimpses into the realm of mystery and romance.*

Three strange men came to the Inn;
One was a black man pocked and thin,
One was brown with a silver knife,
And one brought with him a beautiful wife.

That lovely woman had hair as pale   5
As French champagne or finest ale,
That lovely woman was long and slim
As a young white birch or a maple limb.

Her face was like cream, her mouth was a rose,
What language she spoke nobody knows,   10
But sometimes she'd scream like a cockatoo
And swear wonderful oaths that nobody knew.

Her great silk skirts like a silver bell
Down to her little bronze slippers fell,
And her low-cut gown showed a dove on its nest   15

In blue tattooing across her breast.

Nobody learned the lady's name
Nor the marvelous land from which they came,
But still they tell through the countryside
The tales of these men and that beautiful bride.   20

Try to write—in prose or verse—an account from your own experience of some such glimpse into the lives of others. Perhaps you overheard a quarrel which promised drastic consequences, but you never learned what really happened; perhaps you saw a stranger receive a telegram which changed tears to smiles (or smiles to tears). Some of you may be inspired to write the story which "A Lady Comes To An Inn" suggests to you.

Other poems for those who need further study of suggested story:

THE LADY OF THE TOMAHAWK
Robert P. Tristam Coffin

Although in this poem there is plenty of action—swift, vivid action, related with a dash of wit—the main interest lies in the **character** *of Hannah Dustin; and the chief enjoyment to be found in reading and re-reading the story is a growing acquaintance with this amazing "lady of the tomahawk." When you begin to find as much interest in characters as in action, you are beginning to grow up in your reading of stories.*

Hannah was a lady,
   She had a feather-bed,
And she'd worked Jonah and the whale
   Upon the linen spread,
She did her honest household part   5
To give our land a godly start.

Red Injuns broke the china
   Her use had never flawed,
The ripped her goose-tick up with knives
   And shook the down abroad.   10
They took her up the Merrimac
With only one shirt to her back.

Hannah Dustin pondered
   On her cupboard's wrongs,
Hannah Dustin duly mastered   15
   The red-hot Injun songs.
She lay beside her brown new mates
Remembering the Derby plates.

She got the chief to show her
   How he aimed his blow   20
And cut the white man's crop of hair
   And left the brains to show.
The Lord had made her quick to learn
The way to carve or chop or churn.

The moon was on the hilltop,   25
   Sleep was on the waves,
Hannah took the tomahawk
   And scalped all twenty braves.
She left her master last of all,
And at the ears she shaved his poll.   30

Homeward down the river
   She paddled her canoe.
She went to her old cellar-place
   To see what she could do.
She found some bits of plates that matched,   35
What plates she could she went and patched.

She built her chimney higher
   Than it had been before,
She hung her twenty sable scalps
   Above her modest door.   40
She sat a-plucking new gray geese
For new mattresses in peace.

Make a list of adjectives which describe Hannah: *domestic*, *resourceful*, etc. (or nouns: *good housewife*, etc.). Defend each choice by citing the lines which justify it. Now select the one which seems to you to be the best one-word description of Hannah. After you have come to some conclusion in your mind about her, try to discover some general truths about human nature which Hannah's character illustrates. For instance, the fact that Hannah seems more deeply concerned about her Derby plates than about her own skin illustrates this general truth: "To many people certain cherished possessions are of almost incredible importance."

In which of the preceding poems have the characters increased your understanding of human nature? What did you learn, for instance, from the character of de Lorge's love, Casey, the landlord's daughter Bess, the lady who came to the inn? Make general statements of truth about human nature based upon these characters.

FOR THE AMBITIOUS STUDENT

Hannah Dustin is a real historic character, and Mr. Coffin's account of her noted exploit is substantially correct. She was born in 1657 in Haverhill, Massachusetts. The famous Indian raid occurred March 15, 1697. As Hannah left with her captors, she saw her house in flames; and one of the Indians took her week-old baby and brained it by knocking it against a tree. You might prepare an interesting report out of further details of Hannah Dustin's life. There is a good account in the *Dictionary of American Biography.*

Other poems for those who need further study of character:

SPANISH WATERS
John Masefield

Just as "The Lady of the Tomahawk" suggests by its title that its chief interest will be in character, so the title of this poem suggests that its chief interest will be found in **setting**. *Although it is a story of buried treasure, with all the implications of romantic adventure among the pirates of the Spanish Main, the center of interest, found in both the first and last lines, is the loud surf of Los Muertos. If you read the poem aloud several times, this surf will, I promise you, be beating and ringing in your ears, as it rings in the ears of the old, starving, half-blind beggar-musician who tells the story—and as it rings in the ears of many hundreds of readers who know and love this poem.*

Spanish waters, Spanish waters, you
    are ringing in my ears,
Like a slow sweet piece of music from
    the gray forgotten years;

> No action in this first stanza—nothing but the magic *beach.*

Telling tales, and beating tunes, and bringing weary thoughts to me
Of the sandy beach at Muertos, where I would that I could be.

There's a surf breaks on Los Muertos,
    and it never stops to roar,   5
And it's there we came to anchor, and
    it's there we went ashore,

> Notice how slowly the action is introduced, and how the setting is built up.

Where the blue lagoon is silent amid snags of rotting trees,
Dropping like the clothes of corpses cast up by the seas.

---

5 *Los Muertos*: islands off the southern coast of Cuba. *Los Muertos* is Spanish for "the dead (men)."

We anchored at Los Muertos when the dipping sun was red,
We left her half-a-mile to sea, to west of Nigger Head;   10
And before the mist was on the Cay, before the day was done,
We were all ashore on Muertos with the gold that we had won.

> A suggestion of story at last

We bore it through the marshes in a half-score battered chests,

> Note the vivid and ugly details. What effect do they have on you?

Sinking, in the sucking quagmires to the sunburn on our breasts,
Heaving over tree-trunks, gasping, damning at the flies and heat,   15
Longing for a long drink, out of silver, in the ship's cool lazareet.

The moon came white and ghostly as we laid the treasure down,
There was gear there'd make a beggarman as rich as Lima Town,
Copper charms and silver trinkets from the chests of Spanish crews,

> In a way all this is still setting. Why?

Gold doubloons and double moydores, louis d'ors and portagues,   20

Clumsy yellow-metal earrings from the Indians of Brazil,
Uncut emeralds out of Rio, bezoar stones from Guayaquil,
Silver, in the crude and fashioned, pots of old Arica bronze,
Jewels from the bones of Incas desecrated by the Dons.

> Here's a whole history packed into one line.

---

10 *Her*: the ship.   11 *Cay*: bay   16 *Lazareet*: ship's store-room.
18 *Lima* (lē´ mä) *Town*: Lima, capital of Peru, was once a city of fabulous wealth.
20 *double moydores*, *louis d'ors* and *portagues*: gold coins of various values.
22 *Rio*: Rio de Janeiro, capital and chief city of Brazil. *bezoar* (bè zôr) *stones*: stones used as an antidote for poison. *Guayaquil* (gwì-ä-kèl´): a gulf on the west coast of South America.
23 *Arica*: (ä rè´kä): a South American province.
24 *Incas*: an important, powerful, and highly civilized tribe of South American Indians. *Dons*: Spanish noblemen

We smoothed the place with mattocks, and we took and
    blazed the tree,   25
Which marks yon where the gear is hid that none will ever see,
And we laid aboard the ship again, and south away we steers,
Through the loud surf of Los Muertos | The surf again
    which is beating in my ears.

I'm the last alive that knows it. All the rest have gone their ways
Killer, or died, or come to anchor in the old Mulatas Cays,   30
And I go singing, fiddling, old and starved and in despair,
And I know where all that gold is hid, if I were only there.

It's not the way to end it all. I'm old and nearly blind,
And an old man's past's a strange thing, for it never leaves
    his mind.
And I see in dreams, awhiles, the beach, | It's the *beach* he dreams
    the sun's disc dipping red,   35 | of, more than the *gold.*
And the tall ship, under topsails, swaying in past Nigger Head.

I'd be glad to step ashore there. Glad to take a pick and go
To the lone blazed coco-palm tree in the place no others know,
And lift the gold and silver the has mouldered there for years
By the loud surf of Los Muertos which | Is it beating in yours yet?
    is beating in my ears.   40 | Would you like to go there?

Other poems for those who need further study of setting:

THE RIGHT KIND OF PEOPLE
Edwin Markham

In this poem, selected to illustrate emphasis upon **theme***, the poet's purpose is clearly to impress upon you a bit of philosophic truth—or, at least, something which the poet feels to be the truth.*

Gone is the city, gone the day,
Yet still the story and the meaning stay:
Once there was a prophet in the palm shade basked
A traveler chanced at noon to rest his mules.
"What sort of people may they be," he asked,   5
"In this proud city on the plains o'erspread?"
"Well, friend, what sort of people whence you came?"
"What sort?" the packman scowled; "why, knaves and fools."
"You'll find the people here the same," the wise man said.

Another stranger in the dusk drew near,   10
And pausing, cried, "What sort of people here
In your bright city where yon towers arise?"
"Well, friend, what sort of people whence you came?"
"What sort?" The pilgrim smiled with lifted head;
"Good, true, and wise."   15
"You'll find the people here are the same,"
The wise man said.

Can you state clearly the theme—the bit of truth or wisdom—for the sake of which the poet is telling the story? Do you accept the theme of this story as truth?

It not, why not?

Although none of the other poems in this book so far has been primarily a "theme" story, several of them have themes. State in one sentence the theme for each of as many of the preceding poems as you can.

Do you like stories which teach lessons or convey truths? If you have built up within yourself an antagonism toward stories of this type, try to get rid of it, for it will rob you of much pleasure and profit in your reading. Some of the greatest stories in the world (Aesop's fables, and the parables of Jesus, for instance) are frankly told to teach us profoundly important truths, which may add to our wisdom and even to our joy in life.

Other poems for those who need further study of theme:

To Summarize

Having studied these seven poems, you are able, I hope, to secure a fuller enjoyment from the four elements of narrative. You should now be aware that this enjoyment may come from the following sources:

1. **Action:**
   a. Thrills from speed and vigor
   b. Laughs from humor
   c. Suspense from conflict in plot
   d. Joy of creation from developing a suggested story
2. **Characters:**
   increased understanding of human nature
3. **Setting:**
   increased knowledge of geography and history
4. **Theme:**
   wisdom or inspiration

Finding Enjoyment
in the Music of Poetry

Now that we have learned the sources of pleasure that come from the narrative itself, let us go on to discover some of the ways our pleasure in these stories can be increased by the fact that they are written in the form of poetry. After we listen to a story in verse, the very first thing that we say about it is that it has a pleasing sound. It is quite obviously meant to be heard, and that is why we should always read it aloud. It will appeal to our ears in a way that a prose version does not; in short, it is musical. Among the musical devices available to the poet, two of the best are *rhythm* and the *repetition of sounds*.

RHYTHM

In ordinary speech the accents or stressed syllables come irregularly, without planning; in poetry, however, these stresses are carefully and cunningly arranged to appeal to our ears. In most of the poems of this collection the accents come at fairly regular intervals, an arrangement which gives each poem a "swing," or definite rhythm, which we can actually feel, almost as easily as we can keep time to a dance tune. Furthermore, poets try to make their rhythm patterns suit the moods of the stories they are telling: a short, tripping swing for a happy story; a slow, stately one for a tragedy. If you do not feel the rhythm in poems, if you cannot sense where the stresses come, you are missing one of the chief delights that most people derive from stories told in poetry.

You are able to see more clearly how the words of a poem are arranged in *regular patterns* of rhythm when stressed syllables are printed in capital letters. Here is one of the simplest patterns:

> She DROPPED her GLOVE, to PROVE his LOVE,
> te   TUM   te   TUM   te   TUM   te   TUM
> then LOOKED at HIM and SMILED
> te   TUM   te TUM te   TUM

Another interesting pattern moves with an exciting rush:

> And, SAVE his good BROADsword,
> te   TUM te te   TUM   te
> he WEAPon had NONE,
> te TUM te te TUM

> He RODE all unARMED,
> te   TUM te te   TUM
> and he RODE all aLONE
> te te   TUM te te

As this pattern suggests the rhythmical beat of a horse's hoofs, it is often used in poems describing famous rides. There are many different rhythmic patterns; but whatever the pattern, be sure not to lose the fun which comes from hearing the regular rhythmic swing of the lines, and bringing it out as you read them aloud.

However, in this kind of reading there is a certain danger: a too-regular rhythm soon becomes extremely monotonous. Furthermore, the sing-song reader tends to become completely absorbed in the swing of the poem, and so fail to follow the meaning of the lines. To prevent just such a monotonous, mechanical effect, the poet deliberately varies his rhythm; and when you read poetry, you must not only feel the basic rhythm, but you must also make the swung if the basic pattern yield to the poet's *variations*.

There are a least three ways in which the poet avoids this too-regular rhythmic swing of his lines:

(1) He sometimes changes the position of the accents:
> NObody LEARNED the LAdy's NAME.
>
> TUM te te　　TUM　　te TUM te　TUM

Do not read such a line regularly:
> NoBODy LEARNED the LAdy's NAME.
>
> te TUM te　　TUM　　te　TUM te　TUM

(2) He sometimes adds extra syllables:
> Nor the MARvellous LAND from WHICH they CAME
>
> te (te)　TUM te(te)　TUM　te　　TUM　te　TUM

(3) Sometimes the poet carries a thought right on past the end of one line and into the next:

> Hannah Dustin pondered
>   On her cupboard's wrongs,
> Hannah Dustin duly mastered
>   The red-hot Injun songs.

Such run-on lines are often a cause of trouble, because many young readers, although they may have learned that in prose the unit of thought is the sentence, fail to realize that this is true of poetry also. They assume that the line is the unit of thought in poetry. The error is not hard to explain. The capital letter at the beginning of the line, the rime at the end, and the fact that in much of the simpler poetry of childhood each line did happen to be a sentence—all these elements tend to make the reader treat the line as the unit of thought in poetry, and to make the careless reader read poetry line for line, instead of sentence for sentence, forgetting that in this one respect poetry is exactly like prose: the unit of thought is still the sentence. What nonsense you often get by reading line for line may be seen in the second stanza of the familiar "In Flanders Fields" by John McCrae:

> We are the dead. Short days ago
> We lived, felt dawn, saw sunset glow,
> Loved and were loved; and now we lie
> In Flanders fields.

Here is what a thoughtless reader will make out of it:

> We are the dead short days ago.
> We lived, felt dawn, saw sunset glow;

> Loved and were loved and now we lie
> In Flanders fields.

Such a reading, of course, makes absurd nonsense; what the author really wrote is beautiful sense:

> We are the dead. Short days ago we lived, felt dawn, saw sunset glow, loved and were loved; and now we lie in Flanders fields.

Thus in spite of the capital letters, and the rimes, and your established habits, you must keep your eye on the end of the punctuation. For even though the line is a rhythmical unit, it is not always a thought unit. And therefore, when the poem contains run-on lines, you must not pause or drop your voice where the poet has given no punctuation to indicate that you should do so.

To get the greatest pleasure from the rhythm of poetry, then you must read aloud to hear the underlying rhythmic pattern of the verse. But you must never let the reading become sing-song: give a natural emphasis to the syllables and words; do not distort the pronunciation just to make it fit some regular pattern of rhythm; and don't ever lose sight of the essential meaning of the sentences.

To make you conscious of the rhythm of poetry, two strongly rhythmic poems are here introduced for you to practice on. Reading aloud takes skill, and most of you will need practice before you can read well enough to feel the pleasure that comes to the expert.

Stories in Verse

HOW THEY BROUGHT THE GOOD NEWS FROM GHENT TO AIX
Robert Browning

Here is a good poem for those who may need some help in learning to feel rhythm. It tells an exciting story with a rush and force achieved by a steady, rapid rhythm that never for a second slows down. As Browning himself acknowledged, the situation is purely imaginary, having no basis at all in history, even though Ghent and Aix can be found on the map of Europe. Therefore, the greatest significance of the poem lies in the regular beat of the horses' hoofs, which pulses through every line. As you read it, give it the strong rhythmic swing that Browning meant it to have. For this one poem let the rhythm of the galloping horses come through with unbroken **regularity***. This may not be the perfect way to read a poem, but it is a good way to get started in developing a "feel" for rhythm.*

I SPRANG to the STIRrup, and JOris, and HE;
te TUM   te te TUM te   te TUM te te TUM

I GALloped, Dirck GALloped, we GALloped all THREE;
te TUM   te   te   TUM te   te TUM te   te   TUM

"Good SPEED!" cried the WATCH, as the GATEbolts unDREW;
   te   TUM   te te   TUM te te TUM te   te TUM

"Speed!" ECHoed the WALL to us GALloping THROUGH;
    te   TUM te   te   TUM   te te TUM te te   TUM

BeHIND shut the POSTern, the LIGHTS sank to REST ⁵
te TUM   te te TUM te   te   TUM   te   te TUM

And INto the MIDnight we GALloped aBREAST.
te TUM te te TUM te   te   TUM te te TUM

Not a WORD to each OTHer; we KEPT the great PACE
 te te TUM   te te TUM te te TUM   te   te   TUM

Neck by NECK, stride by STRIDE, never CHANGing our PLACE;
  te te TUM   te te   TUM   te te TUM te te   TUM

I turned in my saddle and made its girths tight,
Then shortened each stirrup, and set the pique right,   10
Rebuckled the cheek-strap, chained slacker the bit,
Nor galloped less steadily Roland a whit.

'Twas moonset at starting; but while we drew near
Lokeren, the cocks crew and twilight dawned clear;
At Boom, a great yellow star came out to see;   15
At Düffeld, 'twas morning as plain as could be;
And from Mecheln church-steeple we heard the half-chime,
So Joris broke silence with, "Yet there is time!"

At Aershot, up leaped of a sudden the sun,
And against him the cattle stood black every one,   20
To stare thro' the mist at us galloping past,
And I saw my stout galloper Roland at last,
With resolute shoulders, each butting away
The haze, as some bluff river headland its spray:

And his low head and crest, just one sharp ear bent back   25
For my voice, and the other pricked out on his track;
And one eye's black intelligence,—ever that glance
O'er its white edge at me, his own master, askance!
And the thick heavy spume-flakes which aye and anon
His fierce lips shook upwards in galloping on.   30

By Hasselt, Dirck groaned; and cried Joris, "Stay spur!
Your Roos galloped bravely, the fault's not in her,
We'll remember at Aix"—for one heard the quick wheeze
Of her chest, saw the stretched neck and staggering knees,
And sunk tail, and horrible heave of the flank,   35
As down on her haunches she shuddered and sank.

So, we were left galloping, Joris and I,
Past Looz and past Tongres, no cloud in the sky;
The broad sun above laughed a pitiless laugh,
'Neath our feet broke the brittle bright stubble like chaff;   40
Till over by Dalhem a dome-spire sprang white,
And "Gallop," gasped Joris, "for Aix is in sight!"

"How they'll greet us!"—and all in a moment his roan
Rolled neck and croup over, lay dead as a stone;
And there was my Roland to bear the whole weight   45
Of the news which alone could save Aix from her fate,
With his nostrils like pits full of blood to the brim,
And with circles of red for his eye-sockets' rim.

Then I cast loose my buffcoat, each holster let fall,
Shook off both my jack-boots, let go belt and all,   50

Stood up in the stirrup, leaned, patted his ear,
Called Roland his pet-name, my horse without peer;
Clapped my hands, laughed and sang, any noise, bad or good,
Till at length into Aix Roland galloped and stood.

And all I remember is—friends flocking round   55
As I sat with his head 'twixt my knees on the ground;
And no voice but was praising this Roland of mine,
As I poured down his throat our last measure of wine,
Which (the burgesses voted by common consent)
Was no more than his due who brought good news from
      Ghent.   60

ELDORADO
Edgar Allan Poe

You were asked to read the preceding poem with a strong, regular, rhythmic swing, so that you would not miss the galloping hoofbeats that Browning meant you to hear. But you may have found that the poem seemed monotonous when read that way, and probably you did not follow the story very well. No poem is really so completely regular, not even "How They Brought the Good News from Ghent to Aix."

Now, to observe the various ways in which a poet achieves **variation** *in rhythm, consider the following poem, written by a master craftsman. There is here, too, a definite rhythmic pattern, but Poe varies his lines with such skill that the poem never becomes monotonous. Read it aloud, stressing carefully the meaning of the lines. Give each word its natural pronunciation. And be particularly careful not to pause or drop your voice where there is no punctuation to halt you.*

GAIly beDIGHT,
TUM te te TUM

Even the first line is irregular.

A GALlant KNIGHT,
te TUM te TUM

The regular pattern for II. 1,2,4,5.

In SUNshine AND in SHADow,
te TUM te   TUM te TUM te

L1. 3 and 6 of each stanza have another pattern.

Had JOURneyed LONG,
te TUM te   TUM

Regular, like I. 2.

SINGing a SONG,   5   Like I. 1.
TUM te te TUM

In SEARCH of ELdoRAdo.
te TUM   te TUM te TUM te

But he grew old —
This knight so bold —
And o'er his heart a shadow   A run-on line; don't pause.
Fell as he found   10   Stress *fell*; don't pause.
No spot of ground
That looked like Eldorado.

And, as his strength   Stress *And*; don't pause.
Failed him at length,   Stress *failed*.
He met a pilgrim shadow.   15
"Shadow," said he,   Like I. 1
"Where can it be —
This land of Eldorado?"

"Over the mountains   Run-on line; don't pause.
Of the Moon,   20   One syllable short.
Down the Valley of the Shadow   Very irregular: stress *Down*, *Val-*, and *Shad-*.
Ride, boldly ride,"   Stress both *Ride* and *bold*.
The shade replied, —
"If you seek for Eldorado."   An extra syllable; stress *seek*.

State the theme of "Eldorado" in a sentence. Did the rhythm add to, or seem out of keeping with, the thought?

One of the most interesting examples of the poet's use of rhythm is "Spanish Waters" (see page 25). In this poem Masefield, by means of a very unusual rhythm, has given us the sound of the slow, steady beat of the surf on the shore of Los Muertos, and we should miss half the pleasure in reading this poem if we failed to hear what he wanted us to hear:

Spanish WAters, Spanish WAters, you are RINGing in my EARS,
 te te   TUM te   te te TUM te   te te   TUM te te te TUM
Like a SLOW sweet piece of MUsic from the GRAY forgotten YEARS;
 te te TUM   te   te te TUM te te te TUM   te te te TUM

What a loss it would be if we should read this poem:

SPANish WAters, SPANish WAters, YOU are RINGing IN my EARS,
TUM te TUM te   TUM te   TUM te TUM te TUM te TUMte TUM

The sad, slow, mournful recalling of a long-ago experience would be gone. And in its place would be a hippity-hop rhythm whose effect would be quite out of keeping with the story.

FOR THE AMBITIOUS STUDENT

Look at still other poems you have read. Using the same system (te TUM), see how many rhythm patterns you find, and note their effectiveness. See how the stiff, forthright rhythm of "The Lady of the Tomahawk," for example, helps to suggest Hannah's stern character.

REPETITION OF SOUNDS

In addition to making a poem swing, the poet can give it several other pleasurable musical effects. Three of these, all of which are based on the principle of repeating sounds, are rime (spelled thus to avoid confusion between rhyme and rhythm), alliteration, and refrain.

The most common repetition of sounds is the simple, yet effective, device of *rime*. Nobody drives along the American highways without encountering jingles like this: "JUST SPREAD... THEN PAT .... NOW SHAVE.... THAT'S THAT." Change the last phrase to read: "That's fine." See how flat the slogan falls! So also in poetry there is a pleasure in hearing the final sound repeated:

> Her great silk skirts like a silver <u>bell</u>.
> Down to her little bronze slippers <u>fell</u>.

Sometimes the rime comes not at the ends of two lines, but within a single line. This is called an *internal rime*:

> a. I'll drop my <u>glove</u> to prove his <u>love</u>; great
>   glory will be mine.
> b. "No love," quoth <u>he</u>, "but vani<u>ty</u>, sets love a
>   task like that."

Often two or more syllables are used to make the rime:

> a. With wallowing might and stifled roar they
>   rolled on one an<u>other</u>,

Till all the pit with sand and mane was in a
    thunderous <u>smother</u>.

b. To the <u>rhyming</u> and the <u>chiming</u> of the bells.

The second device in which the principle of repeated sounds is used is that of beginning stressed syllables with the same sound, a device called *alliteration*. Again the advertiser recognizes the appeal of this device: "<u>P</u>ower in the <u>P</u>inches," reads a gasoline slogan; "<u>S</u>ervice with a <u>S</u>mile," boasts a restaurant. And since the very earliest days of poetry, all poets have delighted in its use:

a. <u>S</u>ir Patrick <u>S</u>pens is the best <u>s</u>ailor
    That ever <u>s</u>ailed the <u>s</u>ea.

b. Nobody <u>l</u>earned the <u>l</u>ady's name
    Nor the marvellous <u>l</u>and from which they came.

c. <u>T</u>elling <u>t</u>ales, and beating <u>t</u>unes, and bringing
    weary <u>t</u>houghts to me.

d. But in her <u>w</u>eb she still delights
    To <u>w</u>eave the <u>m</u>irror's <u>m</u>agic sights.

The third and most obvious repeating device is the repetition of a whole phrase or a line. This is called a *refrain*. It is like an echo. It is something that the reader remembers having heard before and enjoys hearing again.

a. Three fishers went sailing <u>away</u> <u>to</u> <u>the</u> <u>West</u>,
   <u>Away</u> <u>to</u> <u>the</u> <u>West</u> as the sun went down.

b. "O Mary, go <u>and</u> <u>call</u> <u>the</u> <u>cattle</u> home,
   <u>And</u> <u>call</u> <u>the</u> <u>cattle</u> home,
   Across the sands of Dee!"

Sometimes the refrain is a sort of chant to be sung or recited by listeners as an accompaniment to the story-teller, as in these stanzas (the refrains are enclosed in parentheses):

Jesse James was a two-gun man,
       (Roll on, Missouri!)
Strong-arm chief of an outlaw clan,
       (From Kansas to Illinois!)
He twirled an old Colt forty-five,
       (Roll on, Missouri!)
They never took Jesse James alive.
       (Roll on, Missouri, roll!)

Jesse James was King of the Wes';
       (Cataracks in the Missouri!)
He'd a di'mon' heart in his lef' breas';
       (Brown Missouri rolls!)
He'd a fire in his heart no hurt could stifle;
       (Thunder, Missouri!)
Lion eyes an' a Winchester rifle.
       (Missouri, roll down!)

By means of rhythm and the three kinds of repetition just discussed—rime, alliteration, and refrain—the poet makes his subtle appeal to your ears. But he cannot succeed until you hear the sounds he put there for you to hear. This is the chief reason why you should read all the poems aloud. Much of their appeal is lost unless you do so. And you must learn to read them well—read them so that they sound the way the poets intended them to sound.

You must read a poem many times before its full beauty becomes clear to you. In the first reading, concentrate on the sense of the words, to get the story. When the story is clear, you are free to turn your attention to the lovely patterns the poet has woven with his words. His word-music will sing to your ears, and the emotional effect the poet is striving for through both his story and his sound effects will be greatly heightened for you. Never expect to enjoy a poem fully until you have read it several times. When your ear becomes tuned to the magic music of the best poetry, you will begin to experience new thrills in reading and listening.

HOW THE HELPMATE OF BLUE-BEARD MADE FREE WITH A DOOR

Guy Wetmore Carryl

You are probably already familiar with the legendary story of Blue-Beard and his inquisitive wife. But that will not prevent your liking this rollicking version, which retells the gruesome old tale for the purpose of making you laugh. The humor lies, not in the story, but in the very flippant treatment. What makes it flippant is its skipping rhythm and its deliberate over-use of rime. Never have you read a poem with more deliberately elaborate rimes. Each line has an internal rime hidden in it, and the even-numbered lines rime in pairs.

A maiden from the Bosphorus, with eyes as bright as
    phosphorus,
Once wed the wealthy bailiff of the Caliph of Kelat.
Though diligent and zealous, he became a slave to jealousy;
Considering her beauty 'twas his duty to be that.
When business would necessitate a journey he would
    hesitate,   5
But, fearing to disgust her, he would trust her with his keys,
Remarking to her prayerfully, "I beg you'll use them carefully.
Don't look what I deposit in that closet, if you please."
It might be mentioned casually, that blue as lapis-lazuli
He dyed his hair, his lashes, his mustaches and his beard,   10
And, just because he did it, he aroused his wife's timidity;
Her terror she dissembled, but she trembled when he neared.
This feeling insalubrious soon made her most lugubrious,

And bitterly she missed her elder sister Marie Anne:
She asked if she might write her to come down and spend a
      night or two; [15]
Her husband answered rightly and politely: "Yes, you can."
Blue-Beard, the Monday following, his jealous feelings
      swallowing,
Packed all his clothes together in a leather-bound valise,
Then, feigning reprehensibly, he started out ostensibly
By traveling to learn a bit of Smyrna and of Greece. [20]
His wife made but a cursory inspection of the nursery,
The kitchen and the airy little dairy were a bore,
As well as big or scanty rooms, and billiard, bath, and
      anterooms,
But not that interdicted and restricted little door.
For, all her curiosity awakened by the closet he [25]
So carefully had hidden and forbidden her to see,
This damsel disobedient did something inexpedient
And in the key-hole tiny turned the shiny little key.
Then started back impulsively, and shrieked aloud
      convulsively;
Three heads of maids he'd wedded—
      and beheaded—met her eye. [30]
And turning round much terrified, her darkest fears were verified,
For Blue-Beard stood behind her, come to find her on the sly.
Perceiving she was fated to be soon decapitated, too,
She telegraphed her brothers and some others what she feared.
And Sister Anne looked out for them in readiness to shout
      for them [35]
Whenever in the distance with assistance they appeared.
But only from her battlement she saw some dust that cattle meant.

The ordinary story isn't glory, but a jest.
But here's the truth unqualified: the husband wasn't mollified;
Her head is in his bloody little study with the rest! [40]

The Moral: Wives, we must allow, who to their husbands
        will not bow,
A stern and dreadful lesson learn when, as you've read,
        they're cut in turn.

You might enjoy holding a rime contest, as follows: Divide the class into two teams, and let everybody hunt the correct and complete internal rime in each line. The first person to find it wins a point for his team, unless he fails to point out the complete and correct rime, in which case the point is scored by the opponents.

SEA LULLABY
Elinor Wylie

*In this poem of the sea, the poet tells us the slightest of stories: a little boy drowns in the surf. But the story is strangely effective. The **alliteration** of the s sound is deliberate; you can almost hear the sea. Then also, the smooth, lazy rhythm, with its two marked stresses in a line, suggests the recurring surge of waves up a beach. Finally, the poet has added greatly to the music of the poem by perfect handling of rime. Is it any wonder that "Sea Lullaby" is considered a masterpiece of poetic art?*

The old moon is tarnished
With smoke of the flood,
The dead leaves are varnished
With color like blood,

> Begin slowly and quietly.

A treacherous smiler   5
With teeth white as milk,
A savage beguiler
In sheathings of silk,

> Emphasize the alliteration from here on, especially of *s*.

The sea creeps to pillage,
She leaps on her prey;   10
A child of the village
Was murdered today.

> Begin to read louder; emphasize the harsh consonants: *p*, *ch*, etc.

She came up to meet him
In a smooth golden cloak,
She choked him and beat him   15
To death, for a joke.

> The first two lines very smooth

> Very fast and explosive

Her bright locks were tangled,
She shouted for joy,
With one hand she strangled
A strong little boy.

Louder and faster

20

Now in silence she lingers
Beside him all night
To wash her long fingers
In silvery light.

Very slowly and quietly

THE SANDS OF DEE
Charles Kingsley

A brief but splendid example of the use of **refrain** *is "The Sands of Dee," which is based on a brief account of a drowning that Kingsley read in a newspaper. The story is similar to "Sea Lullaby," except that this time the victim of the sea is a young girl. The simplicity with which the story is told, the rich use of rimes and alliteration, and the many haunting refrains make this a deeply moving poem. As you read it, notice how often a word, phrase, or line is echoed in a refrain.*

"O Mary, go and call the cattle home,
  And call the cattle home,
  And call the cattle home
 Across the sands of Dee;"
The western wind was wild and dank with foam,   5
  And all alone went she.

The western tide crept up along the sand,
  And o'er and o'er the sand,   Note the variation in these
  And round and round the sand,   refrains.
 As far as eye could see.   10
The rolling mist came down and hid the land:
  And never home came she.

"Oh! is it weed, or fish, or floating hair—
  A tress of golden hair,
  A drownèd maiden's hair   15   More refrains with
 Above the nets at sea?   variations

Was never salmon yet that shone so fair
    Among the stakes on Dee."

They rowed her in across the rolling foam,
    The cruel crawling foam,   [20]
    The cruel hungry foam,
   To her grave beside the sea:
But still the boatmen hear her call the | See I. 1.
    cattle home
    Across the sands of Dee. | See I. 4.

THE MERMAID
Old Ballad

Long a favorite song for around-the-piano groups, this sailor ballad is effective mainly because of its strongly marked rhythm and its rollicking **refrain**. *I hope that it will become one of your favorites, too. Its story is easily understood if you remember that superstitious sailors regard the mermaid as a sign that trouble is on its way.*

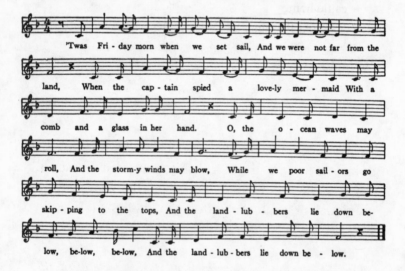

'Twas Fri-day morn when we set sail, And we were not far from the land, When the cap-tain spied a love-ly mer-maid With a comb and a glass in her hand. O, the o-cean waves may roll, And the storm-y winds may blow, While we poor sail-ors go skip-ping to the tops, And the land-lub-bers lie down be-low, be-low, be-low, And the land-lub-bers lie down be-low.

1.   'Twas Friday morn when we set sail,

      And we were not far from the land,

      When the captain spied a lovely mermaid,

      With a comb and a glass in her hand.

Chorus:

      O, the ocean waves may roll, and the stormy winds
         may blow,

      While we poor sailors go skipping to the tops,

And the land lubbers lie down below, below, below,
And the land lubbers lie down below.

2. Then up spake the captain of our gallant ship,
    And a well-spoken man was he:
    "I have married a wife in Salem town,
    And tonight she a widow will be."

3. Then up spake the cook of our gallant ship,
    And a red-hot cook was he:
    "I care much more for my kettles and my pots,
    Than I do for the depths of the sea."

4. Then three times around went our gallant ship,
    And three times around went she;
    Then three times around went our gallant ship,
    And she sank to the depths of the sea.

In reading or singing this song, let a few of the group recite the stanzas, while the rest come in strongly on the refrain. It might be fun to take individual parts: the narrator, the captain, the cook, and the chorus.

Other poems for those who need further study of the music of poetry:

To Summarize

This section is of course only the merest introduction to the word-music of poetry. But now that you have studied it, I think it is reasonable to hope that you will never be indifferent to these musical elements in a poem:

1. RHYTHM

    a. Regularity—for swing

    b. Variations—to avoid monotony

2. Repetition of sounds

    a. Rime

    b. Alliteration

    c. Refrain

Finding Enjoyment in Poetic Imagery

In the preceding sections you have learned the pleasures to be derived from stories in general and from the musical effects of poetry. Another element of poetry that can be equally delightful is known as imagery.

WHAT DO WE MEAN BY IMAGERY?

All that you learn of the world directly, that is, by your own experience, comes to you through your five senses: sight, hearing, taste, smell, and touch. These experiences are stored up in your mind as sense impressions, or "images." (I could have said "pictures"—probably shall, frequently enough; but I do not want you to lose sight of the many sounds, tastes, smells, and feels which are just as truly a part of your experience.) These stored up sense impressions are all called *images*.

Now when you want to tell someone else about some image which is in your mind, you use words to do so. You re-create in words the sense impression which is stored up in your memory and which you want to convey to him:

Sight— The photomap was an intricate pattern of *light and dark squares*.

Sound— In the study hall the boys *mumbled*, the girls *whispered*, and the seats *squeaked* constantly as bodies shifted.

Taste— The *sweet freshness* of the melon soothed his parched mouth and throat.

Smell— His mother's hands, with their *clean, soapy fragrance*, arranged his tie.

Touch— He squirmed uneasily as the woolen underwear *pricked and stung* him.

This re-creation in words of sense impressions is what we mean by *imagery*.

POETS EXCEL AT IMAGERY.

"Poetic imagery" has always been considered one of the chief features of good poetry. There are two reasons why the use of imagery is so frequently found in the work of creative artists, especially poets.

One reason is that the poet's five senses are much keener than yours and mine, and his mind much more alert. Usually he sees, hears, tastes, smells and feels much more intensely than we do. Assume, for example, that the sun is coming up outside my window. To me it may mean merely: "Time to get up!" Or I may feel vaguely: "Beautiful!" or "Startling!" But the poet observes the same sunrise much more intensely and accurately. His imagination moves at once into high gear. To him the sunrise is color, form, movement, splendor, significance. Whether by birth or by practice, the poet's mind and imagination are much more active than ours.

But the poet is set apart from ordinary people not merely by his superior powers of observation, but also by his superior skill in telling us about the things he has observed. Even if I were as sensitive to beauty as a poet, perhaps the best I could do to express in words my impression of, let us say, lovely autumn colors would be: "The gorgeous reds of the maples: don't they thrill you? And the blue asters: aren't they lovely?" But the poet, with his rare skill in words, says:

> The scarlet of the maples can shake me like a cry
> Of bugles going by.
> And my lonely spirit thrills
> To see the frosty asters like a smoke upon the hills.
> —Bliss Carman: "Vagabond Song"

When it is a sound image that the poet wishes to bring to life for us, he may choose his words so skillfully that the sound of the words themselves imitates the sound he wants you to hear. The name of this effect is terrifying indeed: *onomatopoeia*. But the thing itself is perfectly easy to appreciate. The are many single words which have little meaning beyond this magical power to suggest the sounds of the things they represent: *tinkle, whirr, buzz, murmur, skurr, plunk, chunking, clash, purr*. These are onomatopoetic words. Without any special poetic skill, we all use such words for their sounds; but the poet is able to produce onomatopoetic effects by putting together whole groups of words:

> Clang battle-axe, and clash brand!
> —Alfred, Lord Tennyson:
> "The Coming of Arthur"

Can you hear in these words the sound of the weapons? Or in the following lines, the two clearly distinguished tones of the whirring saw?

> And the saw snarled and rattled, snarled and rattled,
> As it ran light, or had to bear a load.
> —Robert Frost:
> "Out, Out—"

Indeed, this device may go beyond the single line, until a whole poem is made to sound like the thing it describes. As you remember, this is true of "Spanish Waters," "How They Brought the Good News from Ghent to Aix," and "Sea Lullaby." Thus the device called onomatopoeia is an additional means whereby the poet can use his skill with words to produce images of sound.

Imagery is generally associated with poetry, then, because of (1) the poet's superior powers of observation and (2) his superior skill in expressing his sense experiences in words.

THERE IS PLEASURE FOR YOU IN IMAGERY.
I have been at some pains to explain imagery, in
order that you may not miss the enjoyment it has to
offer you. One kind of pleasure we derive from
imagery is the pleasure of remembrance. This occurs
when the poet's image presents something which we
have previously experienced through our own senses.
Then the original sense experience returns to us in
imagination; and this recall in itself is a source of
satisfaction. Moreover, the poet often uses his power
of observation and his skill with language to create an
image so remarkably vivid and alive that his word-
picture sharpens our memories and rids them of their
original vagueness and fuzziness, thus greatly adding
to the pleasure of the remembrance. For most of us,
the following images offer that kind of pleasure:

> The cool kindliness of sheets, that soon
> Smooth away trouble; and the rough male kiss
> Of blankets.
> > —Rupert Brooke: "The Great Lover"

> The smell of coffee freshly ground, ...
> Or onions fried and deeply browned.
> > —Christopher Morley: "Smells"

> > Men and women at tables ...
> Eat steaks running with brown gravy,
> Strawberries and cream, éclairs and coffee.
> > —Carl Sandburg: "Child of the Romans"

The heady quavering of the violin
Sings through his blood.
          —Wilfred Gibson: "In a Restaurant"

I remember, I remember,
The fir trees dark and high;
I used to think their slender tops
Were close against the sky,
          —Thomas Hood: "Past and Present"

Another kind of satisfaction afforded by poetic images is the pleasure of novelty. This occurs when the poet re-creates in words something which is beyond the range of our previous sense experience. He has lived it, but we have not; thus the experience is novel, or new, to us. In this case the poet is extending the horizon of our experience by means of vivid images which have the charm of novelty. For many of us, the following images offer a novel experience:*

...I see birches bend to left and right
Across the line of straighter, darker trees.

                    —Robert Frost: "Birches"

....To be deep
Pillowed in silk and scented down.

                    —Alan Seeger: "I have a
                    Rendezvous with Death"

---

* Of course, whether the images here quoted are novel or familiar to you depends on your individual experience.

> And Aztec priests upon their teocallis
> Beat the wild war drums made of serpent's skin.
> > —Henry Wadsworth Longfellow:
> > "The Arsenal at Springfield"

> ...The musty reek that lingers
> About dead leaves and last year's ferns.
> > —Rupert Brooke: "The Great Lover"

> > He spies
> The horns of papery butterflies,
> Of which he eats, and tastes a little
> Of that we call the cuckoo's spittle.
> > —Robert Herrick: "Oberon's Feast"

These pleasures, then—of remembrance, perhaps heightened in vividness, and of novelty—are available to you in the imagery of poetry. Nor need they cease when the reading of the poem is concluded. The vivid imagery of the poet can sharpen your imagination, develop your own appreciation of beauty wherever you meet it, and increase the joy of your sense experiences throughout life.

BUT YOU MUST READ ACTIVELY.

As with rime or rhythm, it takes a wide-awake reader to enjoy the delights obtainable from poetic imagery. This is your responsibility. If you are determined to get the full pleasure from the poet's image, you will accept it as a stimulus to your own mind. Your own imagination will move into high gear; you will visualize the experience; and it will seem as vivid to you as it did to the poet. This is what he hopes his images may do; this is what they will do for you if you are the right kind of reader.

But you must be the right kind of reader. Let me show you what I mean. Consider these lines from Robert P. Tristram Coffin's "Crystal Moment":

> A buck leaped out and took the tide
> With jewels floating past each side.
> With his high head like a tree,
> He swam within a yard of me.

Now I have never seen a deer in the water. But when I read these lines with my imagination awake, as it should be, it is as if a little film were unrolling before my mind's eye, showing the smooth-flanked buck almost immersed in the water, antlered head thrust up to keep the nostrils free for air, cleaving the water so near me that I can see the two rows of ripples and bubbles quite distinctly. Because of its novelty and vividness, this mental moving picture is pleasurable. But this is true only because I actively exert my imagination as I read.

Now consider this passage at the end of Walter de La Mare's "The Listeners":

> Ay, they heard his foot upon the stirrup,
> And the sound of iron on stone,
> And how the silence surged softly backward,

When the plunging hoofs were gone.

This time not only the film but also the sound-track goes into action in my mind; by imagination I really hear the soft contact of stirrup and shoe leather, the hard ring of iron on stone, the dull thud of hoofs on the turf—yes, even the silence that smothers the echoes. But for the lazy or sleepy reader there is neither film nor sound-track. These things happen only if you read with an alert and active mind.

While we are discussing how to read images of sound, we should recall the device of onomatopoeia. You are not measuring up to the poet's expectations if you fail to observe this effect. In "How They Brought the Good News from Ghent to Aix" you are expected to hear the rhythm of galloping hoofs, so plainly imitated in the rhythm of the poem:

I galloped, Dirck galloped, we galloped all three.

And in "Sea Lullaby" you are expected to hear the swish and splash of sea water on sand:

Now in silence she lingers
Beside him all night
To wash her long fingers
In silvery light.

These effects are all carefully designed by the poet; don't miss them by poor reading.

Thus far I have given you examples only of sight and sound. But my advice to read alertly applies equally to images of taste, smell, and touch. The pleasant sense of touch that you experience when you get into a bed with freshly laundered linen should come vividly to mind when you read of

> The cool kindliness of sheets, that soon
> Smooth away trouble.

There should be so strong an impression of taste that your mouth begins to water when you read that

> Men and women at tables
> Eat steaks running with brown gravy.

And you should have an imaginary sensation of smell almost as strong as the real odor when you read of

> The musty reek that lingers
> About dead leaves and last year's ferns.

Do you see now what I mean by saying that you should read with an active imagination? The poet's superior observation and skill with words are lost on the lazy or sleepy reader. But to the reader with an alert mind they offer pleasures of remembrance and of novelty that greatly add to the joy of reading—and of living. When you learn to read poetry so well that you see with the poet's eyes, and hear with the poet's ears, you will have begun to achieve a fine and full life of the senses and to appreciate the keen joy of the spirit in the beauty of the world about us. Life would be a relatively stripped and barren thing without it.

EXERCISE:
LEARNING TO READ IMAGES ACTIVELY

Because imagery is probably the least familiar element of our study, I have chosen, largely from the poems you have already read, a series of images in order that you may now re-examine them actively with your teacher and your classmates. You are to discuss two aspects of each image:

(1) Decide which of the five senses is being appealed to in each image. Sometimes a given image appeals to several senses.

(2) Decide for yourself whether the image recalls an experience which you have had, or presents to you one that you have never had. If it is an old experience, does the image make your memory of it more vivid? Give the class some of the details that you recall.

a) Ramped and roared the lions.

b) The bloody foam above the bars came
    whisking through the air.

c) And when the dust had lifted, and men saw what
    had occurred,
    There was Jimmy safe at second and Flynn a-hugging third.

d) Ten thousand eyes were on him as he rubbed
>> his hands with dirt;
>> Five thousand tongues applauded when he
>> wiped them on his shirt.
>> Then while the writhing pitcher ground the
>> ball into his hip,
>> Defiance flashed in Casey's eye, a sneer
>> curled Casey's lip.

e) The sneer has fled from Casey's lip, his teeth
>> are clenched in hate;
>> He pounds with cruel violence his bat upon
>> the plate.

f) He'd a French cocked-hat on his forehead, a
>> bunch of lace at his chin,
>> A coat of claret velvet, and breeches of brown
>> doeskin.

g) Clumsy yellow-metal earrings from the
>> Indians of Brazil.

h) The sun's disc dipping red.

i) The moon came white and ghostly.

j) Till all the pit with sand and mane was in a
>> thunderous smother.

k) For one heard the quick wheeze of her chest.

l) We bore it through the marshes in a half-score
        battered chests,
  Sinking, in the sucking quagmires, to the
        sunburn on our breasts,
  Heaving over tree-trunks, gasping, damning at
        the flies and heat,
  Longing for a long drink, out of silver, in the
        ship's cool lazareet.

m) *Tlot-tlot; Tlot-tlot!* Had they heard it? The
        horse-hoofs ringing clear;
  Tlot-tlot, Tlot-tlot, in the distance? Were they
        deaf that they did not hear?

n) Have you felt the wool of the beaver,
  Or swan's down ever?

o) The squalling cat and the squeaking mouse,
  The howling dog by the door of the house.

p) My bed is waiting cool and fresh, with linen
  smooth and fair.

q) 'Twas a piteous sight to see, all around,
  The grain lie rotting on the ground.

IMAGERY IS HEIGHTENED BY COMPARISONS.

Poetry, we have said, is remarkable for its power to suggest images to the reader's mind. This suggestion is not always accomplished, however, by direct description.

Often, in trying to present an image to the reader, the poet will attempt to tell what it is like by drawing upon a second image in his mind, hoping to make the impression clearer or more vivid by the use of comparison.

The comparison may be expressed in any one of several different ways. For instance, the poet may say:

> The clouds in the sky were like lamb's wool.

He is trying to convey his on mental impression of the clouds to you by means of comparison with downy lamb's wool, and the word *like* is the sign of the comparison. Or he may use the word *as* (or *than*):

> The clouds in the sky were as soft and white as lamb's wool.

Frequently the comparison is set down without any word-of-comparison (*like, as, than*), and thus becomes much more compact:

> The sky was fleeced with lamb's wool clouds.

Or, finally, the poet may name the second image, without using any word at all to represent the original image:

> Lamb's wool floated softly in the blue sky.

In this case you are expected to see from the rest of the passage that the "lamb's wool" is not wool, but is really the fleecy clouds.

For ease in discussing these various formulas of comparison, you should know the commonly accepted names for them. Those containing *like* (*as, than*) are called *similes*; the shorter and more compact ones, without this word of comparison, are called *metaphors*. You may find it helpful to say that a simile is a comparison in which the likeness is *expressed* by some such word as *like, as, than*; whereas a metaphor is an *assumed* or *implied* comparison, without any such connecting word. Now and then a metaphor is the special kind in which a natural phenomenon is presented as if it were a person, or at least had some human characteristics. Such a metaphor has the special name of *personification*:

> Somewhere tonight ...the grim-lipped peaks
> Brood on a haggard land.
> —Lew Sarett: "Angus McGregor"

> With how sad steps, O Moon, thou climbst the skies!
> How silently, and with how wan a face!
> —Sir Philip Sidney: "Astrophel and Stella"

> Grief fills the room up of my absent child,
> Lies in his bed, walks up and down with me.
> —William Shakespeare: *King John*

Elinor Wylie's "Sea Lullaby" is really an extended personification, comparing the sea to a beautiful but bloodthirsty sort of witch.

All these kinds of comparisons—similes, metaphors, personifications—are called *figures of speech*, or *rhetorical figures*. As you can see, a figure of speech is a mode of expression which conveys the truth in a picturesque way, but is not a literal statement of truth. When the song-writer said, "Her neck is like the swan," he certainly did not want us to understand that her neck was as long and pliable as a swan's, or that it was covered with feathers. But the statement contains an essential truth which the reader is expected to perceive: Her neck is beautiful and graceful. This combination of literal falseness and underlying truth is the essential quality of figures of speech. (For this reason it is misleading to say that "Her neck is as slim as yours" is a simile; it is simply a sober, unimaginative statement of literal fact.)

BUT, AGAIN, YOU MUST READ ACTIVELY.

Like simple images, comparisons present a problem of successful reading. They will add to the effectiveness, in your mind, of the poet's images only if you clearly understand them. If you fail to understand, or perhaps even to perceive the comparison, you will miss much of the pleasure afforded by effective imagery, just as those who walk down the street without truly seeing anything miss most of the interest of the walk. Here, even more than with the simpler type of imagery discussed earlier, you must bring to your reading an alert and active mind. The poet says, for instance:

Then like popcorn in a shaker
The trees began to burst in bloom.
                    —Dorothy Aldis: "Unheralded"

What happens in your mind? Do you simply think of blossoming trees, and then read on to see what will happen among them? Since this is a visual image, you ought to visualize the thing, that is, really see it in your imagination: The brown, rather spindly branches of the apple tree, just beginning to put forth small green leaves to cover its winter nudeness, in a flash fleecing out into fluffy white blooms—overnight; as the dull, dry popcorn suddenly bursts into large white fluffs crowding each other in a narrow space, while you wink an eye. You are amazed at the speed of the change; you are dazzled by the gleaming whiteness; you may even get a hint of spring fragrance. I think that is what the poet wanted you to see; but I know there are many persons who do not perform this act of imagination. Of course, if you do not visualize as you read, the poet's visual images are lost on you.

In reading these comparisons, then, the skillful reader is sharply aware both of the original image, and of the secondary image compared with it, and senses clearly just what it is that makes the two alike. He does this with all poetic comparisons, whether they are used to illuminate images of sight, or of sound, taste, smell, or touch. Of course, this requires the full attention of his imagination!

Surely you will now agree that the reading of poetry

is a special technique that must be learned. But I hope
you are convinced, too, that the pleasure all this holds
out for you is richly worth the effort.

EXERCISE:
ANALYZING POETIC COMPARISONS

Whenever there is any danger of failure to
understand a comparison, it is well to analyze it. A
good way to do this is to use *a* and *b* as symbols: let *a*
represent the thing that "belongs in the story," and *b*
the secondary item brought in to be compared to it.
Remember that the *a* and the *b* are set together in
various ways:

> *a* is like *b*:
>> That stubborn fellow (*a*) is like a mule (*b*).
>
> *a* is as *b*:
>> That fellow (*a*) is as stubborn as a mule (*b*).
>
> *a* is *b*:
>> That stubborn fellow (*a*) is a mule (*b*).
>
> *b* (the *a* is not mentioned at all, but you know it
>> is—in this case—a man): The stubborn
>> mule! (*b*)

To be perfectly certain that you understand the
comparisons you read, you need to identify clearly the
a and *b*, and the quality of likeness which is referred
to or implied. For oral recitation, use the following
formula, filling the first blank with the *a*, the second
with the *b*, and the third with the quality of likeness:

The poet describes the _man_ by comparing him
with the _mule_ to bring out his _stubbornness_.

When you do this in writing, place the *a* and the *b* at
the left of a bracket, and the quality of likeness at the
right. If you wish, you may classify the comparison as
simile or metaphor in parentheses at the end:

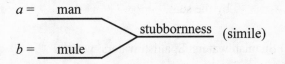

Note: this form is the one I shall use in this book to call
attention, now and then, to some comparison that might
either confuse you, or escape your notice altogether.

Now, carry out the following directions for each of
the comparisons given below:

(1) Analyze it, using the formula for written work,
    given above.
(2) Be prepared to discuss it with regard to two
    qualities: (a) In what essential ways are the two
    images similar? Are they sufficiently different
    otherwise? (b) Does the second image help you
    to see the original image more vividly?

a) That lovely woman had hair as pale
   As French champagne or finest ale.

b) But sometimes she'd scream like a cockatoo.

c) That lovely woman was long and slim
As a young white birch or maple limb.

d) Her great silk skirts like a silver bell
Down to her little bronze slippers fell.

e) Where the blue lagoon is silent amid snags of
rotting trees,
Dropping like the clothes of corpses cast up
by the seas.

f) Spanish waters, Spanish waters, you are
ringing in my ears,
Like a slow sweet piece of music from the
gray forgotten years.

g) The wind was a torrent of darkness among
the gusty trees.

h) The moon was a ghostly galleon tossed upon
cloudy seas.

i) The road was a ribbon of moonlight over the
purple moor.

j) A treacherous smiler
With teeth white as milk.

k) Maquoit Bay was a diamond's shine
Through the branches of the pine.

l) As pale as any orange flower,
   Cerelle. The gold-white sands
   Were like her hair, and drifting shells,
   White fairy shells, her hands.

m) His hair like moldy hay.

n) His face burned like a brand.

o) The irony of it cut me like steel.

p) The shore rocks rose, ugly and aged teeth
   Of earth.

q) The fog received
   Him in its arms.

r) The black cascade of perfume came tumbling
          over his breast.

s) They stretched and shook their wings, and
       folded them
   Feather by feather to their sides, like old
   Housewives storing their linen into drawers.

t) And sprang—as when an eagle high in
       heaven,
  Through the thick cloud, darts downward to
       the plain
  To clutch some tender lamb or timid hare,

Stories in Verse

So Hector, brandishing that keen-edged
               sword,
Sprang forward.

THE DESTRUCTION OF SENNACHERIB
George Noel Gordon, Lord Byron

More than 2500 years ago Sennacherib, king of Assyria, bent on conquering the Jews, came to Jerusalem, capital of Judah, and with his vastly superior army laid siege to the city. But so many of his men died of a pestilence that he had to lift the siege and withdraw, and Jerusalem was saved for the time. In the Bible (II Kings 18-19) you may read how the Baal-worshiping Assyrians lost 185,000 men in one night, slain by the Angel of the Lord.

This ancient story took root in Byron's imagination, and resulted in the following stirring stanzas. Two things, I think, account for the great popularity of this poem. One is its hypnotic rhythm. The other is its marvelously vivid **imagery***. As you read, watch for the signs of color, the gleams of sunlight and starlight, the stir and movement of the vast horde, and the awful silence of the dead multitude. The images and the accompanying* **figures of speech** *make a remarkable tapestry.*

The Assyrian came down like a
     wolf on the fold,
And his cohorts were gleaming
     in purple and gold;
And the sheen of their spears
     was like stars on the sea,
When the blue wave rolls
     nightly on deep Galilee.

1. *The Assyrian*: King Sennacherib.
2. *Cohorts*: bodies of troops.

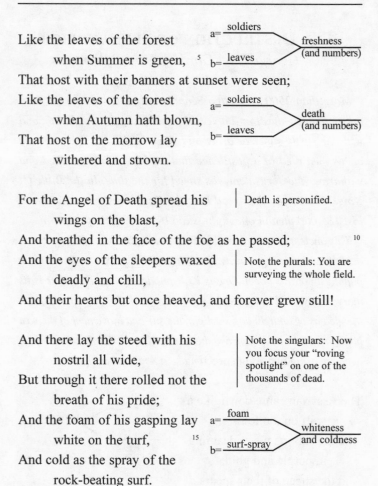

Like the leaves of the forest
  when Summer is green,   5
a= soldiers
b= leaves
freshness (and numbers)

That host with their banners at sunset were seen;

Like the leaves of the forest
  when Autumn hath blown,
a= soldiers
b= leaves
death (and numbers)

That host on the morrow lay
  withered and strown.

For the Angel of Death spread his
  wings on the blast,

Death is personified.

And breathed in the face of the foe as he passed;   10

And the eyes of the sleepers waxed
  deadly and chill,

Note the plurals: You are surveying the whole field.

And their hearts but once heaved, and forever grew still!

And there lay the steed with his
  nostril all wide,

Note the singulars: Now you focus your "roving spotlight" on one of the thousands of dead.

But through it there rolled not the
  breath of his pride;

And the foam of his gasping lay
  white on the turf,   15
a= foam
b= surf-spray
whiteness and coldness

And cold as the spray of the
  rock-beating surf.

And there lay the rider distorted and pale,

With the dew on his brow, and the
  rust on his mail;

Would dew form in a living brow?

And the tents were all silent, the banners alone,

The lances unlifted, the trumpet unblown.   20

---

8. *strown:* strewn; scattered
11. *waxed:* grew; became

And the widows of Ashur are loud in their wail,
And the idols are broke in the temple of Baal;
And the might of the Gentile,
    unsmote by the sword,
Hath melted like snow in the
    glance of the Lord!

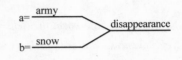

Did you construct the scene in your mind and see each detail as you read the poem? If not, you didn't really read the poem at all. Read it again, trying consciously to get the picture in your mind. Keep aware of the color and life in the first part, the silence and desolation that follow. This contrast is meant to stir your emotions. Are there appeals to any senses other than the sense of sight?

---

21. *Ashur*: Assyrian capital city.
22. *Baal*: heathen gods, served by idol-worship.
23. *Gentile*: anyone not a Jew; here, the Assyrian, King Sennacherib

A SHOT AT NIGHT
Idella Purnell

Here is a little poem that tells a brief incident with extraordinary effectiveness. You will find powerful visual and auditory **images**, *impressive* **figures of speech**, *and a disquieting power of suggestion. If, as you read, you get so strong an impression of a sudden burst of sound in the silent night, disturbing all the forms of life, that it seems for the moment the incident is happening again with you as a witness, and your nerves feel the grip of fear, then the reading process is truly successful.*

In addition to the compelling imagery, there are some fine sound effects here, so carefully handled that they are scarcely noticed.

A shot rings out upon the dreaming night.
Night shivers to pieces like a
     broken vase;   a= night   } shattering
     b= vase
The stars are spangled on the
     sky like lace;
The moon is shedding a terrible cold light;
And, like the crystal running of a stream   5
Of water flowing from a
     broken jar,   a= fear   } creeping
     b= water
Fear creeps across the earth,
     and every star
Stops moving, and a moment dulls the gleam
Of the ivory moon. The rustling boughs of trees
Are silent, and a rare and breathless chill
Falls on the world, and makes it very still.
Then the cocks crow, a watchdog barks ill ease   10
And is chorused by a hundred yapping curs.

Men turn in beds. A wind like
    weeping stirs.

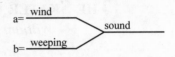

FOR THE AMBITIOUS STUDENT

In this poem, as in "A Lady Comes to an Inn" there is the suggestion of a thrilling story, not developed. Where did the shot come from? Who fired it? Was the aim true? What was the target? What example of high courage or sneaking cowardice is being enacted behind the curtain of darkness, buried in the soft-stirring silence of the chilly night? Why not write the story that occurs to you?

Stories in Verse

THE SKATER OF GHOST LAKE
William Rose Benét

Here is an eerie tale of a lovers' midnight rendezvous on a mysterious lake, ending in sinister tragedy. The poem is rich in **imagery**, *especially visual and auditory images. So vividly, indeed, are the sense impressions conveyed, that the alert, appreciative reader almost shivers with the cold —and shudders with dread.*

In reading it, then, try to see all that the poet put there—colors, lights and shadows, shapes, patterns on the ice, sweeping motion; and to hear all the whirrings, whispers, tinklings—a perfect orchestration of sounds, with fine **onomatopoetic** *effects. Note also the very appropriate* **figures of speech**. *All these devices deserve the most careful study.*

Ghost Lake's a dark lake, a deep lake
    and cold:

Visualize the scene: *deep, dark, black.*

Ice black as ebony, frostily scrolled;
Far in its shadows a faint sound whirrs;
Steep stand the sentineled deep,
    dark firs.

$a=$ firs $b=$ sentinels   erectness and silence

A brisk sound, a swift sound,
    a ring-tinkle-ring;

5   The faint sound of 1. 3 grows.

Flit-flit, —a shadow, with a stoop and a swing,
Flies from a shadow through the
    crackling cold.

Can you *hear* cold?

Ghost Lake's a deep lake, a dark lake
    and old!

Count up the repetitions of *dark lake* and *deep.*

Leaning and leaning, with a stride
    and a stride,

You should feel the skating rhythm.

— 84 —

Hands locked behind him, scarf blowing wide,   10
Jeremy Randall skates, skates late,
Star for a candle, moon for a mate. | Two more comparisons

Black is the clear glass now that he | Why all the *s* sounds?
    glides,
Crisp is the whisper of long lean strides,
Swift is his swaying, —but pricked ears hark.   15
None comes to Ghost Lake late after dark!

Cecily only, —yes, it is she!
Stealing to Ghost Lake, tree after tree,
Kneeling in snow by the still lake side,
Rising with feet winged,
    gleaming, to glide.   20

a= feet
b= birds
       winged

Dust of the ice swirls. Here is his hand,
Brilliant his eyes burn. Now, as was | Do eyes burn?
    planned,
Arm across arm twined, laced to his side,
Out on the dark lake lightly they glide. | The *l*'s suggest grace.

Dance of the dim moon, a rhythmical reel,   25
A swaying, a swift tune, —skurr of | Again the sound of the skates
    the steel;
Moon for a candle, maid for a mate,
Jeremy Randall skates, skates late.

Black as if lacquered the wide lake lies;
Breath is a frost-fume, eyes seek eyes; 30 | A metaphor

Souls are a sword-edge tasting the
    cold. | Hear the intricate pattern
Ghost Lake's a deep lake, a dark lake and old!   of sound.

Far in the shadows hear faintly begin
Like a string pluck-plucked of a violin, | Onomatopoeia
Muffled in mist on the lake's far bound,   35
Swifter and swifter, a low singing sound!

Far in the shadows and faint on the verge | Hear the *far, faint* echoes.
Of blue cloudy moonlight, see it emerge,
Flit-flit, —a phantom, with a swoop | Visualize the *phantom*.
    and a swing...
Ah! It's a night bird, burdened of wing!   40

Pressed close to Jeremy, laced to his side,
Cecily Culver, dizzy you glide.
Jeremy Randall sweepingly veers
Out on the dark ice far from the piers.

"Jeremy!" "Sweetheart?" "What do | Watch the quotation marks.
    you fear?"   45
"Nothing my darling, —nothing is here!"
"Jeremy!" "Sweetheart?" "What do you flee?"
"Something —I know not; something | Fear takes command.
    I see!"

Swayed to a swift stride, brisker of | Hear the rhythmic
    pace,   speed of flight.
Leaning and leaning, they race and they race;   50

Ever that whirring, that crisp sound thin
Like a string pluck-plucked of a violin;

Ever that swifter and low singing sound
Sweeping behind them, winding them round;
Gasp of their breath now that chill flakes fret;   55
Ice black as ebony, —blacker—
    like jet!

> See the black ice grow blacker. (How many times is it called black?)

Ice shooting fangs forth —sudden —
    like spears;

> Two comparisons

Crackling of lightning, —a roar in the ears!
Shadowy, a phantom swerves off from its prey ...
No, it's a night bird flit-flits away!   60

Low-winging moth-owl, home to
    your sleep!

> Hear the quiet echoes after the great noise of 1.58

Ghost Lake's a still lake, a cold lake and deep.
Faint in its shadows a far sound whirrs.
Black stand the ranks of its sentinel
    firs.

> The moving picture is over; the final chord is played, (Compare this stanza with the first.)

This poem has been presented as a study in poetic imagery, but it is equally interesting as a study in word-music, as the sidenotes indicate. Read it again, watching the rhythm and the highly skillful use of repetition of all kinds. Point out examples of alliteration, of repetition of single words, and of repetition of whole lines with slight variations in wording. This last is done with especially fine effect.

FOR THE AMBITIOUS STUDENT

"The Skater of Ghost Lake" is a very good example of suggested story. Readers who expect everything they read to be as clear and beyond dispute as a simple problem in addition will criticize the author of this poem for not providing answers to various bothersome questions; but in fairness we cannot complain if the story remains to the last somewhat mysterious and baffling — it's a ghost story, and a very good one, as you will agree, if you read it often enough to make it your own. I have read it a dozen times, and some questions even now remain unanswered in my mind. How did the lake get its name? What is the shadow that flies from a shadow? What is Jeremy afraid of? Is there a ghost, or is it only the moth owl? What is the whirring sound? If you would feel better having these questions answered, write out your own version of the story, clearing up these points and others that occur to you. It's your turn now!

Other poems for those who need further study of imagery:

To Summarize

It is probably true that imagery is not only the least familiar but also the most difficult subject of study in this book. However, after studying the explanations, the exercises, and the three poems in this section, you have now, I hope, reached the point where imagery is no longer a signal for work, but an invitation to pleasure. You have learned that

1. **IMAGERY IS THE RE-CREATION IN WORDS OF SENSE IMPRESSIONS OF**
   a. sight,
   b. sound (sometimes by *onomatopoeia*),
   c. taste,
   d. smell, and
   e. touch.

2. **POETS ARE ESPECIALLY SKILLFUL AT PROVIDING IMAGERY BECAUSE THEY HAVE**
   a. superior powers of observation, and
   b. superior skill in expressing their sense experiences in words.

3. **IMAGERY IS OFTEN HEIGHTENED BY COMPARISONS,**
   a. expressed (*similes*), or
   b. implied (*metaphors*).

4. **IMAGERY OFFERS YOU PLEASURES OF**
   a. remembrance (perhaps heightened by vividness), and
   b. novelty.

5. **IN ORDER TO REAP THESE PLEASURES, YOU MUST READ WITH AN ALERT MIND AND ACTIVE IMAGINATION.**

How to Read Ballads for Enjoyment

Among the most interesting of all story poems are the old ballads. These exciting tales of horror, murder, death, and cruel lovers have come down to us from a dim past when there were no books, movies, radios, or newspapers to thrill readers or listeners with the latest sensation or to provide them with escape from the humdrum realities of life. Our remote ancestors sat of an evening listening to minstrels, reciting these thrillers. No matter how often they heard them, they never tired of these exciting tales, and finally, after generations, even centuries, the stories were written down for our pleasure by people who searched for them through the countryside of England and Scotland, where the old legends were still being told.

In the hills, the lumber camps, and the ranch houses of our country, too, you can hear the ballads of our own people. Several fine collections of native American ballads have been made, and they also offer exciting reading.

So popular have the ballads always been, that many well-known poets have written imitation ballads which are among the best-loved poems in the language. The original ballads, however, are generally thought not to have been composed by any one poet, but rather to have reached their present form through constant additions and subtractions that were made as the familiar stories were retold.

The ballads have certain qualities of form and matter which set them off as a distinct type, and may give you some trouble as you first begin to read them. Ballads are not easy reading, but they are so exciting and so interesting that you can well afford the effort it takes to learn how to read them. A whole treasure chest of thrillers will be opened to your enjoyment when you have conquered the few difficulties in your path.

(1) The first of these difficulties arises from the fact that these old ballads are crude folk-poetry. You may find it difficult to fit the words of a line into a regular rhythm. This you must do, however, for the village folk recited or sang these stories to the accompaniment of music or dancing or both, and thus gave them a definite swing. You should swing them, too; and you must therefore be willing, when necessary, to depart from the natural stress of the words:

> Fair MARgaret WAS a PROUD laDY,
> The KING'S couSIN was SHE;
> Fair MARgaret WAS a RICH laDY,
> And VAIN as VAIN could BE.

In this respect, reading ballads is different from reading most other kinds of poetry.

(2) In the second place, you will find in the ballads a great deal of repetition, often of whole lines. As a rule, these refrains are merely a sort of chorus. They are a part of the oral rendering of the ballad, but not a part of the narrative proper. Do not let them get in the way of the story. In the old days they were probably chanted vigorously by the listeners as the narrator paused:

There were twa sisters sat in a bower;
Binnorie, O Binnorie!
There came a knight to be their wooer.
By the bonnie milldams of Binnorie.

He courted the eldest with glove and ring,
Binnorie, O Binnorie!
But he loved the youngest above anything.
By the bonnie milldams of Binnorie.

The eldest she was vexed sair,
Binnorie, O Binnorie!
And greatly envied her sister fair.
By the bonnie milldams of Binnorie.

For many of the ballads there are tunes to which they have been sung for centuries, and not till you actually sing them (solo for the story, chorus for the refrain) will you get the full flavor of the experience in the old shepherd's cottage the night the ballad singer happened by. I hope you and your classmates will be willing to give some of these old songs a real chance—story, rhythm, tune, and all.

(3) A third difficulty in reading ballads springs from the fact that all those that are very old belong not merely to a different time but also to a world quite different from ours. The behavior and the customs of the people in the ballads sometimes need explaining. You will find, for example, that these old ballads are full of superstition. To us in the twentieth century the superstitions are troublesome until we know the background of the ballads well enough to understand that the primitive people who made and sang these stories believed wholeheartedly in witches, fairies, ghosts, and black magic of all kinds. And so must we, for the time being!

(4) Since most of the old ballads that have come down to us were sung in the highlands of the Scottish border and have been recorded as they were sung there, they are in the Scotch dialect; and the pronunciation of certain words, as well as the unfamiliar spelling, has to be learned if the music of the old poetry is to be felt. To the ballad singers, *blood* rimed with Robin *Hood*, and both were pronounced quite differently from the way we say them now. *Mair* is the dialect word for *more*; *ain* is *own*; *gie* is *give*; etc. In most of the old ballads in this book I have modernized all the words except those whose old forms are necessary for the rhythm or the rime, but even these few will prove an obstacle to your enjoyment unless you master them. Footnotes explain these old forms.

(5) Finally, the narratives in the old ballads are often so highly condensed that we, who are unfamiliar with the stories, may have difficulty in understanding the poems.

Often great gaps are left in the action. Again, there is usually much rapid-fire dialogue, in which the speakers are not even introduced or named. These omissions did not bother the original listeners because, from long familiarity with the ballads, they knew the stories; but you as a newcomer, may be confused by the omissions until you have read the poems many times. You must learn to supply the gaps in the action, and to know just who is talking and in what circumstances:

> "O, where have you been, my long-lost love,
> This long seven years and more?"
> "O, I'm come to seek my former vows
> You granted me before."

> "O where hae ye been, Lord Randal, my son?
> "O where hae ye been, my handsome young man?"

> "I hae been to the wild wood; mother, make my
> bed soon,
> For I'm weary wi' hunting, and fain wad lie
> down."

If you persist until you have conquered these difficulties, you will find great enjoyment in these wonderful old stories. You will also read with added pleasure the more recent folk-ballads of our own country.

SIR PATRICK SPENS
Old Ballad

To start you in the reading of ballads I have selected the one which is perhaps the best-known of all the old folk story-poems. I have modernized most of the words to make it easier for you to read for the story and the "swing." Remember that ballads are technically pretty crude verse, and should not be read with the attention to the meaning which you must give to more literary poems. These poems were sung; and if you cannot give them a melody, you can at least give them a good swinging rhythm, even if you sometimes have to mispronounce some words or stress some that are unimportant.

In this ballad you will find the typical **ballad stanza***: four lines, the first and third lines having four stresses, the second and fourth lines having three stresses, and the second and fourth lines rhyming. As you read, mark the rhythm emphatically, as indicated in the first stanza below.*

1. THE SAILING

The KING sits IN DumFERling
    TOWN
  DrinkING the BLOOD-red WINE;
"O WHERE will I GET a GOOD saiLOR
  To SAIL this SHIP of MINE?"

Notice how the story begins without introduction.

Then up and spake an eldern knight
  Sat at the King's right knee.

5

Supply who. Often you need to do this; see 1.12

---

1. *eldern*: elderly

"Sir Patrick Spens is the best sailor
   That ever sailed the sea."

The King has written a broad letter,
   And signed it with his hand,   10
And sent it to Sir Patrick Spens,
   Was walking on the sand.

"To Noroway, to Noroway,
   To Noroway o'er the foam;
The King's daughtèr to Noroway,   15
   'Tis thou must take her home."

> Here is the *letter*. Note the typical ballad device of repetition —the poem is full of it.

The first line that Sir Patrick read,
   A loud laugh laughèd he;
The next line that Sir Patrick read
   The tear blinded his e'e.   20

"O who is this has done this deed
   And told the King of me,
To send me out, this time of year, | Winter
   To sail upon the sea?

"Be it wind or weet, be it hail or sleet,   25
   Our ship must sail the foam;
The king's daughtèr to Noroway,
   'Tis we must take her home."

---

9. *broad*: open, public —like broadcast.
20. *e'e*: eye. (Pronounce to rime with he.)
25. *weet*: wet

They hoisted their sails on Monday morn
   With all the speed they may;   30
And they have landed in Noroway
   Upon the Wodensday.

2. THE RETURN

"Make ready, make ready, my merry men all!
   Our good ship sails the morn."
"O say not so, my master dear,   35 | Watch the quotation marks.
   For I fear a deadly storm.

"Late, late yestreen I saw the new   Superstitious signs of bad
     moon   weather.
   With the old moon in her arm;
And I fear, I fear, my dear master,
   That we shall come to harm."   40

They had not sailed a league, a league,
   A league but barely three,
When the lift grew dark, and the wind blew loud,
   And gurly grew the sea.

The ropes the broke and the topmast snapt,   45
   It was such a deadly storm:
And the waves came over the broken ship
   Till all her sides were torn.

---

32. *Wodensday*: Wednesday.
37. *yestreen*: yesterday evening.
43. *lift*: sky
44. *gurly*: angry

"O where will I get a good sailòr
    To take the helm in hand,
Until I win to the tall topmast
    And see if I spy the land?" 50

"O here am I, a sailor good,
    To take the helm in hand,
Till you win up to the tall topmast, 55
    But I fear you'll ne'er spy land."

He had not gone a step, a step, | A favorite ballad device;
    A step but barely one, | see 11. 41-42
When a bolt flew out of the good ship's side,
    And the salt sea it came in. 60

"Go fetch a web of the silken cloth,
    Another of the twine,
And wrap them into our good ship's side,
    And let not the sea come in."

They fetched a web of the silken cloth, 65
    Another of the twine,
And they wrapped them into that good ship's side,
    But still the sea came in.

O loath, loath were our good Scots lords
    To wet their cork-heeled shoon; 70
But long ere all the play was played,
    Their hats they swam aboon.

---

72. *Their hats they swam aboon*: Their hats floated above them; i.e. the men were
    drowned.

And many was the feather bed
    That floated on the foam;
And many was the good lord's son   75
    That never more came home.

O long, long may the ladies sit
    With their fans into their hand,
Before they see Sir Patrick Spens
    Come sailing to the land.   80

O long, long may the ladies stand
    With their gold combs in their hair,
A-waiting for their own dear lords,
    For they'll see them no mair.

Half o'er, half o'er to Aberdour   85
    It's fifty fathom deep;
And there lies good Sir Patrick Spens,
    With the Scots lords at his feet!

---

84. *mair*: more

BABYLON
Old Ballad

This characteristic old ballad illustrates the use of refrain. Usually, when ballads are printed, the refrains are included in only the first and last stanzas; but in this ballad the refrain is printed in every stanza so that you will not forget to repeat it. While some able member of the class reads the story, the whole class may enjoy chanting the refrain.

There were three ladies lived in a bower —
    Eh, wow, bonnie!
And they went out to pull a flower
    On the bonnie banks o'Fordie.

They had not pulled a flower but one,   5
    Eh, wow, bonnie!
When up started to them a banished man
    On the bonnie banks o'Fordie.

He's taken the first sister by her hand,
    Eh, wow, bonnie!   10
And he's turned her round and made her stand
    On the bonnie banks o'Fordie.

"It's whether will you be a rank robber's wife,
    Eh, wow, bonnie!
Or will you die by my wee pen-knife?"   15
    On the bonnie banks o'Fordie.

7. *banished man*: outlaw

"It's I'll not be a rank robber's wife,
  Eh, wow, bonnie!
But I'll rather die by your wee pen-knife."
  On the bonnie banks o'Fordie.   20

He's killed this maid and he's laid her by,
  Eh, wow, bonnie!
For to bear the red rose company
  On the bonnie banks o'Fordie.

He's taken the second one by the hand,   25
  Eh, wow, bonnie!
And he's turned her round and made her stand
  On the bonnie banks o'Fordie.

"It's whether will you be a rank robber's wife,
  Eh, wow, bonnie!   30
Or will you die by my wee pen-knife?"
  On the bonnie banks o'Fordie.

"It's I'll not be a rank robber's wife,
  Eh, wow, bonnie!
But I'll rather die by your wee pen-knife."   35
  On the bonnie banks o'Fordie.

He's killed this maid and he's laid her by,
  Eh, wow, bonnie!

---

17. *rank*: proud, haughty, bold

For to bear the red rose company
  On the bonnie banks o'Fordie.   40

He's taken the youngest one by the hand,
  Eh, wow, bonnie!
And he's turned her round and made her stand
  On the bonnie banks o'Fordie.

Says, "Will you be a rank robber's wife,   45
  Eh, wow, bonnie!
Or will you die by my wee pen-knife?"
  On the bonnie banks o'Fordie.

"It's I'll not be a rank robber's wife,
  Eh, wow, bonnie!   50
Nor will I die by your wee pen-knife."
  On the bonnie banks o'Fordie.

"For in this wood a brother I hae;
  Eh, wow, bonnie!
And if you kill me, it's he'll kill thee"   55
  On the bonnie banks o'Fordie.

"What's thy brother's name? Come tell to me."
  Eh, wow, bonnie!
"My brother's name is Baby Lon."
  On the bonnie banks o'Fordie.   60

---

53. *hae*: have

"O sister, sister, what have I done!
    Eh, wow, bonnie!
O have I done this ill to thee!
    On the bonnie banks o'Fordie.

"O since I've done this evil deed,   65
    Eh, wow, bonnie!
Good shall never be my meed."
    On the bonnie banks o'Fordie.

He's taken out his wee pen-knife,
    Eh, wow, bonnie!   70
And he's twined himself of his own sweet life
    On the bonnie banks o'Fordie.

---

67. *meed*: reward.
71. *twined*: separated, deprived

THE IMAGE
Sylvia Townsend Warner

This is a modern ballad which has much of the flavor of the old ones. Note that most of the story is told through conversation. Note also that the foundation of the story is an old superstition: If some one wanted to kill an enemy by remote control, he would make an image of that person out of wax, clay, wood, or any other substance. Then he would stick pins, nails, or thorns into it, the theory being that the victim would suffer in corresponding places in his own body. Finally the image would be roasted or burned; and as it melted or finally crumbled, the victim died. This ancient form of magic is still practiced in widely separated parts of the world today.

"Why do you look so pale, my son William?
    Where have you been so long?"
"I've been to my sweetheart, Mother,
    As it says in the song."

see "Lord Randall," p 216

"Though you be pledged and cried to
    the parish   5
    'Tis not fitting or right
To visit a young maiden
    At this hour of night."

They had announced their engagement in the parish church.

"I went not for her sweet company,
    I meant not any sin,
But only to walk round her house
    And think she was within.   10

"Unbeknown I looked in at the window;
    And there I saw my bride
Sitting lonesome in the chimney-nook,   15
    With the cat alongside.

"Slowly she drew out from under her apron
    An image made of wax,
Shaped like a man, all stuck over
    With pins and with tacks.   20

"Hair it had, hanging down to its shoulders,
    Straight as any tow —
Just such a lock she begged of me
    But three days ago.

"She set it down to stand in the embers —   25
    The wax began to run.
Mother! Mother! That waxen image,
    I think it was your son!"

"'Twas but a piece of maiden's foolishness,
    Never think more of it.   30
I warrant that when she's a wife
    She'll have a better wit."

"Maybe, maybe, Mother.
    I pray you, mend the fire.
For I am cold to the knees   35
    With walking through the mire.

22. *tow*: flax

"The snow is melting under the rain,
    The ways are full of mud;
The cold has crept into my bones,
    And glides along my blood.   40

"Take out, take out my winding-sheet
    From the press where it lies,
And borrow two pennies from my | To keep the eyelids closed
    money-box | after death
    To put upon my eyes;

"For now the cold creeps up to my heart,   45
    My ears go Ding, go Dong:
I shall be dead long before day,
    For the winter nights are long."

"Cursèd, cursèd be that Devil's vixen
    To rob you of your life!   50
And cursèd be the day you left me
    To go after a wife!"

"Why do you speak so loud, Mother?
    I was almost asleep.
I thought the churchbells were ringing   55
    And the snow lay deep.

"Over the white fields we trod to our | He is still telling
    wedding, | his dream.

---

41. *winding sheet*: a sheet in which a corpse is wrapped.
49. *vixen*: shrew; female fox

She leant upon my arm —
What have I done to her that she
Should do me this harm?"   60

> Here he gets back to grim reality.

FOR THE AMBITIOUS STUDENT

Try to write the story which answers William's last question. Don't forget that you have heard only one side of the story.

EDWARD, EDWARD
Old Ballad

*In "Edward, Edward" I have left unchanged all the old spelling,
the poem being printed just as it was sung in the Scotch highlands.
When you have mastered the meaning and pronunciation of the old
Scotch words, you will discover that they add a certain pleasurable
effect to the poem. In most of the old ballads in this book, I have
modernized the language; but this time you may see and read an old
ballad in the original form.*

*The poem tells a horror story, the full force of which does not
explode until the last two lines. It employs several conventional ballad
devices: it is told by means of a question-and-answer dialogue
between a man and his mother; it is full of echoing repetitions; and
much of the story is suggested, not told. This conversation takes place
soon after the main action of the story has ended. That action you
have to reconstruct from the words of the speakers, and you will not
know the whole story until the last word is spoken, so well is the
suspense maintained by Edward's evasive answers. When you read it
a second time, its tragic horror is much clearer to you.*

"Why does your brand sae drop wi'
    blude,
    Edward, Edward?
Why does your brand sae drop wi' blude,
    And why sae sad gang ye, O?"
"O I hae killed my hawk sae gude,   5

> Do you suppose she already knows why?

---

1. *brand*: sword. *sae*: so. *blude*: blood.
4. *gang*: go.
5. *hae*: have. *gude*: good

Mither, mither;
O I hae killed my hawk sae gude,
And I had nae mair but he, O."

"Your hawk's blude was never sae red, | She doesn't believe him at all.
Edward, Edward;   ₁₀
Your hawk's blude was never sae red,
My dear son, I tell thee, O."
"O I hae killed my red-roan steed,
Mither, mither;
O I hae killed my red-roan steed,   ₁₅
That erst was sae fair and free, O."

"Your steed was auld, and ye hae got mair,
Edward, Edward;
Your steed was auld, and ye hae | His second story was
got mair; | no better than the first.
Some other dule ye dree, O."   ₂₀
"O I hae killed my father dear,
Mither, mither;
O I hae killed my father dear, | The truth at last
Alas, and wae is me, O!"

"And whatten penance will ye dree | She doesn't ask "Why did
for that?   ₂₅ | you do it?"
Edward, Edward?

---

8. *nae*: no.
16. *erst*: once; formerly.
17. *auld*: old. *mair*: more.
20. *dule*: grief. *dree*: suffer
24. *wae*: woe.
25. *whatten*: what.

Whatten penance will ye dree for that?
>   My dear son, now tell me, O."
"I'll set my feet in yonder boat,
>   Mither, mither;   30
I'll set my feet in yonder boat,
>   And I'll fare over the sea, O."

"And what will ye do wi' your towers and your ha',
>   Edward, Edward?
And what will ye do wi' your towers and your ha',   35
>   That were sae fair to see, O?"
"I'll let them stand till they doun fa',
>   Mither, mither; | If she wanted them for herself, she doesn't get them.
I'll let them stand till they doun fa',
>   For here never mair maun I be, O."   40

"And what will ye leave to your bairns and your wife,
>   Edward, Edward?
And what will you leave to your bairns and your wife,
>   When ye gang owre the sea, O?"
"The warld's room: let them beg through life,   45
>   Mither, mither; | In his despair he does not even care what happens to his own family.
The warld's room: let them beg
>   through life;
>   For them never mair will I see, O."

---

32. *fare*: go.
33. *ha'*: hall.
40. *maun*: must.

41. *bairns*: children.
44. *owre*: over.
45. *warld's*: world's

"And what will ye leave to your ain mither dear,
  Edward, Edward?   50
And what will ye leave to your ain mither dear,
  My dear son, now tell me, O?'
"The curse of hell frae me sall ye bear,
  Mither, mither;
The curse of hell frae me sall ye bear: 55
  Sic counsels ye gave to me, O!"

Do you think she had *counseled* him to kill his father?

---

49. *ain*: own.
53. *frae*: from. *sall*: shall.
56. *sic*: such.

GEARY'S ROCK
Lumberjack Ballad

Of the ballads created by Americans, some of the most interesting have come from the lumbercamps. "Back in the shanty, particularly on Saturday evenings, secure from the outer cold, — his supper stowed safely within him, the old iron stove throwing out its genial hat, and the mellowing ministrations of tobacco well begun, — the shanty-boy became story-teller and singer," says Franz Rickaby, who collected his **Ballads and Songs of the Shanty-Boy** *from the men who worked in the woods of Michigan, Wisconsin, and Minnesota during what Mr. Rickaby calls the "Golden Age of American Lumbering": 1870-1900. Most of the shanty-boy songs, like "Geary's Rock," are solos. In the camps they were sung by men known as "singers," who were highly popular with all the boys, and were allowed to remain on the crew because of their vocal abilities, even though some of them were exceedingly poor lumberjacks.*

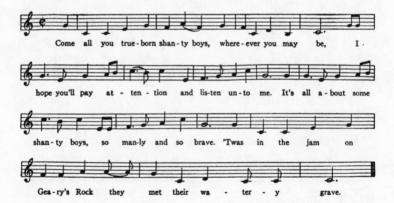

Come all you true-born shan-ty boys, where-ever you may be, I hope you'll pay at-ten-tion and lis-ten un-to me. It's all a-bout some shan-ty boys, so man-ly and so brave. 'Twas in the jam on Gea-ry's Rock they met their wa-ter-y grave.

Come all you true-born shanty-boys, wherever you may be,
I hope you'll pay attention and listen unto me.
It's all about some shanty-boys, so manly and so brave.
'Twas on the jam on Geary's Rock they met their watery
    grave.

'Twas on one Sunday morning as you shall quickly hear,   5
Our logs were piled up mountain-high, we could not
    keep them clear,
"Turn out, brave boys," the foreman cried, with a voice
    devoid of fear,
"And we'll break the jam on Geary's Rock and for
    Eagletown we'll steer."

Some of the boys were willing, while the others hid from
    sight.
For to break a jam on Sunday, they thought it was not right. 10
But six American shanty-boys did volunteer to go
To break the jam on Geary's Rock with their foreman,
    young Monroe.

They had not rolled off many logs before the boss to them
    did say,
"I would you all to be on your guard, for the jam will soon
    give way."
He had no more than spoke these words before the jam did
    break and go,   15
And carried away those six brave youths with their foreman,
    young Monroe.

Now when the news got into camp and attorneys came to
     hear,
In search of their dead bodies down the river we did steer,
And one of their dead bodies found, to our great grief and
     woe,
All bruised and mangled on the beach lay the corpse of
     young Monroe.   20

We took him from the water, smoothed back his raven-black
     hair,
There was one fair form amongst them whose cries did rend
     the air,
There was one fair form amongst them, a girl from Saginaw
     town,
Whose mournful cries did rend the skies for her lover that
     was drowned.

We buried him quite decently. 'Twas on the twelfth of May, 25
Come all you jolly shanty-boys, and for your comrade pray.
We engraved upon a hemlock tree that near his grave did
     grow —
The name, the age, and the drownding date of the foreman,
     young Monroe.

His mother was a widow living down by river side.
Miss Clark she was a noble girl, this young man's promised
     bride.   30
The wages of her own true love the firm to her did pay,
And liberal subscription she received from the shanty-boys
     that day.

She received their presents kindly and thanked them every
    one,
Though she did not survive him long, as you shall
    understand;
Scarcely three weeks after, and she was called to go,   35
And her last request was to be laid by her lover, young Monroe.

Come all you true-born shanty-boys, who would like to go
    and see
Two green mounds by the river bank where grows the
    hemlock tree;
The shanty-boys cut the woods all round. These lovers they
    lie low —
'Tis the handsome Clara Clark and her true love, brave
    Monroe.   40

FOR THE AMBITIOUS STUDENT

Besides the shanty-boy ballads, the lumberjacks
have made another important contribution to
American folk literature in the tall tales of *Paul
Bunyan*, which are still being told in the lumber
camps. Find a good collection of Paul Bunyan yarns
and select one to tell to the class. For a beginning, I
suggest "The Black Duck Dinner" from *Paul Bunyan*,
by James Stevens.

OLD CHRISTMAS
A Kentucky Mountain Ballad
Roy Helton

The final poem in this selection is another modern ballad, which has been worked out with great skill and sympathetic understanding of the type. In reading it, you must be careful to observe the quotation marks, and keep your imagination alert to perceive the dramatic story of a bloody feud behind the conversation. And remember that the ballad reader must not doubt for one moment that "spirits walk loose."

"Where you coming from, Lomey
    Carter,
    So early over the snow?
What's them pretties you got in your
    hand,
    And where you aiming to go?

| Sally Ann Barton opens the conversation. |
| Probably elder blossoms; see l. 27. |

"Step in, Honey. Old Christmas morning   5
    We hain't got nothing much;
Maybe a bite of sweetness and corn bread,
    A little ham meat and such.

"But come in, Lomey. Sally Ann Barton's
    Hungering after your face.   10

| Evidently Lomey had not visited Sally for some time. |

---

1. *Lomey*: Salome (a woman).
5. *Old Christmas*: January 6, formerly celebrated as Christmas, now usually called Epiphany of Twelfth Day. On Old Christmas Eve, according to Kentucky mountain superstition; spirits walk, elder bushes bloom, and animals kneel down to pray.

Wait till I light my candle up.
> Set down. There's your old place.

"Where you been, so early this morning?"
> "Grave yard, Sally Ann:

| Lomey speaks for the first time.

Up by the trace in the Salt Lick meadow
> Where Taulbe kilt my man."

15

| Sally Ann's husband Taulbe had killed Lomey's husband.

"Taulbe hain't to home this morning.
> Wisht I could scratch me a light:

Dampness gits in the heads of the matches;
> I'll blow up the embers bright."

20

"Needn't trouble. I won't be stopping:
> Going a long ways still."

"You didn't see nothing, Lomey Carter,
> Up on the grave yard hill?"

"What should I see there, Sally Ann Barton?"

25

> "Spirits walk loose last night."

"There was an elder bush a blooming
> While the moon still give some light."

"Yes, elder bushes they bloom, Old Christmas,
> And critters kneel down in their straw.

30

Anything else? Up in the grave yard?"
> "One thing more I saw:

"I saw my man with his head all bleeding
> Where Taulbe's shot went through."

---

15. *trace*: path, trail

"What did he say?" "He stooped and kissed me." ³⁵
    "What did he say to you?"

"Said Lord Jesus forgive your Taulbe;
    But he told me another word;
Said it soft when he stooped and | "Shoot!"
    kissed me;
    That was the last I heard." ⁴⁰

"Taulbe hain't come home this morning."
    "I know that, Sally Ann,
For I kilt him, coming down through the meadow
    Where Taulbe kilt my man.

"I met him up on the meadow trace ⁴⁵
    When the moon was fainting fast;
I had my dead man's rifle gun,
    And kilt him as he come past."

"I heard two shots." "'Twas his was second:
    He got me 'fore he died. ⁵⁰
You'll find us at daybreak, | "Spirits walk loose."
    Sally Ann Barton:
    I'm laying there dead at his side."

Stories in Verse: Part One

Other poems for those who need further study of ballads:

Old Ballads

Imitation Ballads

How to Read
Blank Verse for Enjoyment

Even when you have become experienced in the reading of ordinary riming poetry, you may sometimes still have trouble with the kind of poetry called *blank verse*. Since much of the world's greatest poetry is of this kind, it is surely worth your while to acquire some skill in reading it.

Blank verse is poetry consisting of ten-syllable, five-stress lines that do not rime. Notice: Blank Verse is poetry. Many pupils think at first that it is not poetry because there is no rime. But the essence of poetry is rhythm, not rime; and blank verse has rhythm. The standard line of blank verse has ten syllables and five stresses, the stresses coming on the even-numbered syllables. Here is a standard line:

To STRIVE, to SEEK, to FIND, and NOT to YIELD.
te TUM te TUM te TUM te TUM te TUM

But a ten-syllable, five-stress line — te TUM te TUM te TUM te TUM te TUM —repeated again and again with absolute regularity would be highly undesirable. If it did not completely prevent the communication of ideas by its hypnotic effect, it would be unbearably wearisome because of its monotony. As I have said before, the poet employs three devices to prevent such monotony:

(1) Variation in the position of stress in the line. As you observe, the normal position of the stresses is on the syllables 2, 4, 6, 8, 10; but often the natural accent of the words requires a change in the position of the stresses:

SHIVering LIKE a FRAGment OF the NIGHT.
TUM te te TUM te TUM te TUM te   TUM

In reading such a line, do not mispronounce the words for the sake of the swing of the rhythm, as you do in old ballads; but follow the natural accent of the words.

(2) Variation in the number of syllables. This is seldom accomplished by changing the number of accented syllables, but rather slipping in extra unaccented syllables:

Sweet HELen, MAKE me imMORtal WITH a KISS.
te TUM te TUM   te (te) TUM te   TUM te TUM

(3) Variation derived from run-on lines. These are especially common in blank verse. I think it is safe to say that in blank verse most of the lines run on, thus making a sharp pause within the

next line, at the point where the sentence ends:

> He bound them to the car, but left the head
> To trail in dust. And then he climbed the car,
> Took in the shining mail, and lashed to speed
> The coursers. Not unwillingly they flew.

When you are reading blank verse, the result of the line-by-line reading is especially disastrous because of the great number of run-on lines. Forget the capital letters, and keep your eye on the end punctuation. For even though the line is a rhythmical unit, it is not— except incidentally—a thought-unit. In blank verse, as in all other prose and poetry, the sentence is the unit of thought. And poetry, no matter what the type, should always be read with due regard for the thought.

All three kinds of variation are illustrated in this passage from "The Sign of the Golden Shoe," by Alfred Noyes:

> We had JUST SET our BRAZier SMOULderING,
>   te te TUM TUM te TUM te   TUM te TUM

> To KEEP the PLAGUE aWAY. MAny a HOUSE
> te TUM te   TUM te TUM TUM te te TUM

> Was MARKED with the RED CROSS. The BELLS TOLLED
>   te   TUM   te te TUM TUM   te TUM   TUM

> InCESSantLY. Nash CREPT inTO the ROOM
> te TUM te TUM te   TUM te TUM te TUM

SHIVering LIKE a FRAGment OF the NIGHT
TUM te te TUM te TUM   te TUM te   TUM

His FACE YELlow as PARCHment, AND his eyes
te TUM TUM te te   TUM te   TUM te TUM

BURNing.
TUM te

"The PLAGUE! He has TAKen it!" VOIces CRIED.
te   TUM   te te TUM te te   TUM te TUM

"THAT'S not the PLAGUE! The old CARrion-CROW is DRUNK;
TUM   te te   TUM   te te TUM tete TUM te TUM

But, STAND aWAY. What AILS you, NASH my LAD?"
te   TUM te TUM   te TUM te   TUM te TUM

THEN, through the CLAMour, as THROUGH a STORM at SEA,
TUM   te   te TUM te te   TUM te TUM te TUM

The MASter's VOICE, the VOICE of BEN, rang OUT,
te TUM te   TUM te TUM te TUM te TUM

"NASH!'"
TUM

(If this passage interests you, look up Alfred Noyes's *Tales of the Mermaid Tavern*, and read the whole poem. The book contains other good stories in verse besides this one.)

Variety within regularity, then, is the principle through which the poet avoids monotony in blank verse, and yet achieves the desired rhythmical effect.

It will cost you some practice to read blank verse properly. You have to avoid reading it so much like prose that the rhythm is completely lost; but you also have to avoid reading it with a sing-song, line-by-line rhythm that fails to bring out the meaning. It is rhythmical, and it does make sense. And much of it ranks with the finest poetry in the world.

OPPORTUNITY
Edward Rowland Sill

Here is a simple story in blank verse. Of course anyone can detect with the eye the difference between this poem and prose—the appearance on the page shows that it is verse, even before you notice that there is no rime. But you should detect the difference with your ear, too: if you do not feel the rhythm at once, re-read the poem—aloud, of course—until you feel it.

This I beheld, or dreamed it in a dream: —
There spread a cloud of dust along a plain;
And underneath the cloud, or in it
    raged

> Subject of *raged*? Don't stop; read on to *shields.*

A furious battle, and men yelled, and swords
Shocked upon swords and shields. A
    prince's banner

> Don't drop your voice.

5

Wavered, then staggered backward, hemmed by foes.
A craven hung along the battle's edge,
And thought, "Had I a sword of keener steel —
That blue blade that the king's son
    bears, — but this

> Don't drop your voice.

Blunt thing —!" he snapt and flung it from his hand,   10
And lowering crept away and left the field.
Then came the king's son, wounded,
    sore bestead,

> Series of adjectives runs into 1.13.

And weaponless, and saw the broken sword,
Hilt-buried in the dry and trodden sand,

---

7. *craven*: coward
11. *lowering*: looking sullen. (pronounce to rime with *towering*.)

And ran and snatched it, and with
    battle-shout   15 | Keep your voice up.
Lifted afresh he hewed his enemy down,
And saved a great cause that heroic day.

If you were unaware that this is a narrative with a theme, go back and read it again. Because the theme is the important thing, it doesn't matter whether the poet really experienced the incident or only dreamed it (line 1). Try to state this theme clearly, in your own words, in the manner of the "moral" at the end of an Aesop fable.

EVENING PRAYER
Amelia Josephine Burr

In the Sermon on the Mount, Christ said: "I tell you, love your enemies and pray for your persecutors, so that you may show yourselves true sons of your Father in Heaven." Here is a poem in blank verse which shows how hard it is to "pray for your persecutors." It is full of the pathos of little children in a war-torn world, and of the world's love and admiration for Albert, King of Belgium during the first World War. In reading it, a proper use of pauses is absolutely essential. Remember to read by sentences. And be sure that for each quotation you know just who is speaking.

You say there's only evil in this war —
That bullets drive out Christ? If you had been

> Note question mark. Observe pause.

In Furnes with me that night . .... what would you say,
  I wonder?
        It was ruin past all words,
Horror where joyous comfort used to be,   5
And not clean quiet death, for all day long

> These two fragments add up to exactly 10 syllables. The break gives a paragraph effect. No stop for five lines.

The great shells tore the little that remained
Like vultures on a body that still breathes.
They stopped as it grew dark. I looked about

> Watch the periods. Now go on for six lines.

The ghastly wilderness that once had been   10

---

3. *Furnes*: a Belgian city. (Pronounce as one syllable.)

A village street, and saw no other life
Except a Belgian soldier, shadowy
Among the shadows, and a little group
Of children creeping from a cellar school
And hurrying home. One older than the rest —   15
So little older! — mothered them all along
Till all at once a stray belated shell
Whined suddenly out of the gloom, and burst
Near by. The babies wailed and clung together,
Helpless with fear. In vain the little mother   20
Encouraged them — "But no! you mustn't cry,
That isn't brave, that isn't French!" At last
She led her frightened brood across the way
To where there stood a roadside Calvary
Bearing its sad, indomitable Christ —   25
Strange how the shells will spare just that! I saw
So many .....There they knelt, poor innocents,
Hands folded and eyes closed. I stole across | Watch full stops from here on.
And stood behind them. "We will say our prayer —
Our Father which art in heaven," she began,   30 | Don't stress *which*.
And all the little sobbing voices piped,
"Hallowed be thy Name." From down the road
The Belgian soldier had come near. I felt
Him standing there beside me in the dusk. | Broken line shows change of speakers.
"Thy kingdom come —"   35

---

24. *roadside Calvary*: a little shrine set up along the road as a place for devout
persons to pray. Such shrines were common in Europe.

"Thy will be done on earth
As it is in heaven." The irony of it | Slur the weak syllables.
Cut me like steel. If one could name this earth
In the same breath with heaven — what is hell?
Only a little child could pray like that.   40
"Give us this day our daily bread —" A pause.
There was no answer. She repeated it
Urgently. Silence yet. She opened wide
Reproachful eyes at them. Their eyes were open
Also, and staring at the shadowy shapes   45
Of ruin all around them. Now that prayer
Had grown too hard even for little children.
"I know — I know — but we must say the prayer,"
She faltered. "Give us this day our daily bread,
And — and forgive —" she stopped. 50 | Another change of speakers
"Our trespasses
As we forgive them who have
    trespassed against us." | A 12-syllable line. Say the weak syllables rapidly.
The children turned amazed, to see who spoke
The words they could not. I too turned to him,
The soldier there beside me — and I looked   55
Into King Albert's face ....I have no words
To tell you what I saw ....only I thought
That while a man's breast held a heart like that,
Christ was not — even here — so far away.

FROM THIS THE STRENGTH
Fred Lape

Here is a single, detached bit of experience, related in blank verse. You may think that throwing out the garbage is no fit subject for poetry, but wait till you see what the poet has done with it. I think what makes the experience impressive and memorable is the thought (hinted at in the title) that came to him as he watched the gulls.

In distribution of stresses, the lines of this poem vary. Do not try to force the stresses onto syllables 2, 4, 6, 8, 10, but let the natural accent of the words determine where the stresses come, there will be five stresses always.

The fog had made a twilight on the water.
The shore rocks rose, ugly and aged
    teeth

Of earth, discoloured at their bases where
The tide had ebbed. Upon their tops the gulls
Stood silently facing the hidden sea.   5

Two boys with garbage came to the land's edge.
The gulls rose in the mist, circling the boys,
Crying about their heads, gliding down air.
The boys leaned out and slung their
    load of waste

Over the rocks. Shrieking the gulls swept down.   10
Their bodies wove together by the cliff.
The strongest found the food. The
    others swung

(marginal note at line 2–3:) Keep right on to the middle of 1.4.

(marginal note at line 8–9:) Watch the periods.

(marginal note at line 12–13:) Full stop here. Then go on for four lines.

In circles waiting turn, or poised on water,
Beating their wings like butterflies, or clinging
To the wet rocks, let the slow roll of surf | Note the slowing up of the rhythm.

15

Surge under lifted wings. One gull flew out
With red meat in his bill. The fog received
Him in its arms; only the white tail shone,
A comet curving down the sphere of mist.
Two gulls settled upon the cliff again.

20

They stretched and shook their wings, and folded them | Sentence is three lines long.

Feather by feather to their sides, like old
Housewives storing their linen into drawers.

The boys went back. The gulls had cleaned the waste
And one by one soared off into the fog.

25

The ugly was consumed, gone to the bone, | Don't break the series: *bone, sinew, feather, wing, grace, strength.*

The sinew, feather, wing, to the sure grace
Of flight, the strength to beat against the air
And take the strong wind currents of the sky.

Note the appropriate sound effects in lines 8, 10, 15-16, 28-29. Try to bring these out as you read.

Point out five figures of speech that show how active was the poet's mind in taking possession of the material which observation brought to his attention.

To be sure that you have really understood the poem, state in your own words the poet's comment on the incident.

"OUT, OUT—"
Robert Frost

Here Robert Frost, America's poet of rural, outdoor life and master of blank verse, relates a boy's unhappy disaster, which fate decreed must bring his death. The language is simple and the sentences easy; yet the verses are most carefully worked out. All kinds of variety are used to full effect: short or long lines, shift in accent, shift in stops. But of course the story is the main interest.

The buzz-saw snarled and rattled in the yard | Onomatopoeia
And made dust and dropped stove-length sticks of wood,
Sweet-scented stuff when the breeze drew across it.
And from there those that lifted eyes could count
Five mountain ranges one behind the other   5
Under the sunset far into Vermont.
And the saw snarled and rattled, | Again the song of the saw
    snarled and rattled,
As it ran light, or had to bear a load.
And nothing happened: day was all but done.
Call it a day, I wish they might have said   10
To please the boy by giving him the half hour
That a boy counts so much when saved from work.
His sister stood beside them in her apron
To tell them "Supper." At the word, the saw,
As if to prove saws knew what supper meant,   15
Leaped out at the boy's hand, or seemed to leap —
He must have given the hand. However it was,
Neither refused the meeting. But the hand!
The boy's first outcry was a rueful laugh,

As he swung toward them holding up the hand [20]
Half in appeal, but half as if to keep
The life from spilling. Then the boy saw all —
Since he was old enough to know, big boy
Doing a man's work, though a child at heart —
He saw all spoiled. "Don't let him cut my hand off — [25]
The doctor, when he comes. Don't let him, sister!"

So. But the hand was gone already. | A 4-stress line. Is there a
The doctor put him in the dark of ether. | reason?

He lay and puffed his lips out with his breath.
And then — the watcher at his pulse took fright. [30]
No one believed. They listened at his heart.
Little — less — nothing! — and that ended it.
No more to build on there. And they, since they
Were not the one dead, turned to their affairs.

Robert Frost is noted for the conversational tone of his poems. Does his quiet, matter-of-fact tone in telling his story weaken its effectiveness?

The title of the poem is meant to suggest a passage from Shakespeare's *Macbeth*, in which the king, beset by difficulties and profoundly unhappy, comments on the brevity and the meaninglessness of human life by comparing it to a candle, a shadow, an actor, a tale told by an idiot:

"Out, out brief candle.
Life's but a walking shadow, a poor player
That struts and frets his hour upon the stage,
And then is heard no more; it is a tale
Told by an idiot, full of sound and fury,
Signifying nothing."

ACHILLES' REVENGE
From the Iliad
Homer
Translated by William Cullen Bryant

The following passage from Book XXII of Homer's famous epic, the Iliad, *as put into English by Bryant, will test your ability to read blank verse with enjoyment. As there are no helps at all, you will discover whether or not you can read this kind of poetry without assistance.*

This passage is near the end of the poem. While the Greek hero Achilles, son of Peleus, sulked in his tent like a willful child, his good friend Patroclus went out to fight the Trojans, and was killed by Hector, who took his armor. Now Achilles avenges his friend by killing Hector and dishonoring his corpse. If you want to read more of this stirring epic poem, the librarian will help you find the book.

He spake, and drew the keen-edged sword that hung,
Massive and finely tempered, at his side,   380
And sprang — as when an eagle high in heaven,
Through the thick cloud, darts downward to the plain
To clutch some tender lamb or timid hare,
So Hector, brandishing that keen-edged sword,
Sprang forward, while Achilles opposite   385
Leaped toward him, all on fire with savage hate,
And holding his bright buckler, nobly wrought,
Before him. On his shining helmet waved
The fourfold crest; there tossed the golden tufts
With which the hand of Vulcan lavishly   390

Had decked it. As in the still hours of night
Hesper goes forth among the host of stars,
The fairest light of heaven, so brightly shone,
Brandished in the right hand of Peleus' son,
The spear's keen blade, as, confident to slay   395
The noble Hector, o'er his glorious form
His quick eye ran, exploring where to plant
The surest wound. The glittering mail of brass
Won from the slain Patoclus guarded well
Each part, save only where the collar-bones   400
Divide the shoulder from the neck, and there
Appeared the throat, the spot where life is most
In peril. Through that part the noble son
Of Peleus drave his spear; it went quite through
The tender neck, and yet the brazen blade   405
Cleft not the windpipe, and the power to speak
Remained. The Trojan fell amid the dust.

(Here Achilles boasts of his revenge, and promises
to give Hector's body to the "foul dogs and birds of
prey." Hector begs for more honorable treatment, but
Achilles refuses, declaring that no sort of bribe would
alter his fixed purpose of revenge. The story
continues:)

Thus Hector spake, and straightway o'er him closed
The night of death; the soul forsook his limbs,
And flew to Hades, grieving for its fate, —   450
So soon divorced from youth and youthful might.
Then said the great Achilles to the dead: —

"Die thou; and I, whenever it shall please
Jove and the other gods, will meet my fate."

He spake, and plucking forth his brazen lance,   455
He laid it by, and from the body stripped
The bloody mail. The thronging Greeks beheld
With wonder Hector's tall and stately form,
And no one came who did not add a wound;
And, looking to each other, thus they said: —   460

"How much more tamely Hector now endures
Our touch than when he set the fleet on fire!"

Such were the words of those who smote the dead;
But now, when swift Achilles from the corpse
Had stripped the armor, ...   465
.....................…………..shamefully, he bored
The sinews of his feet between the heel
And ankle; drawing through them the leathern thongs
He bound then to the car, but left the head   490
To trail in the dust. And then he climbed the car,
Took in the shining mail, and lashed to speed
The coursers. Not unwillingly they flew.
Around the dead, as he was dragged along,
The dust arose; his dark locks swept the ground.   495
That head, of late so noble in men's eyes,
Lay deep amid the dust, for Jove that day
Suffered the foes of Hector to insult
His corpse in his own land.

Stories in Verse: Part One

Other poems for those who need further practice in reading blank verse:

Stories
in *Verse*

Part Two:

More Narrative Poems to Read for Enjoyment

THE CREMATION OF SAM MCGEE
Robert W. Service

*If "Casey at the Bat" has a rival in American humorous poetry,
here it is. "The Cremation of Sam McGee" is a general favorite,
though perhaps boys and men like it better than do the ladies,
who sometimes find Service's poems a little too rough-and-
ready for their taste. You will like the internal rime in the first half
of every line.*

> *There are strange things done in the midnight sun*
> > *By the men who moil for gold;*
> *The Artic trails have their secret tales*
> > *That would make your blood run cold;*
> *The Northern Lights have seen queer sights,*   5
> > *But the queerest they ever did see*
> *Was that night on the marge of Lake Lebarge*
> > *I cremated Sam McGee.*

Now Sam McGee was from Tennessee, where the cotton
    blooms and blows,
Why he left home in the South to roam 'round the Pole, God
    only knows.   10
He was always cold, but the land of gold seemed to hold him
    like a spell;
Though he'd often say in his homely way that "he'd sooner
    live in hell."

On a Christmas Day we were mushing our way over the
    Dawson Trail.

Talk of your cold! through the parka's fold it stabbed like a
    driven nail.
If our eyes we'd close, then the lashes froze till sometimes
    we couldn't see;   15
It wasn't much fun, but the only one to whimper was Sam
    McGee.

And that very night, as we lay packed tight in our robes
    beneath the snow,
And the dogs were fed, and the stars o'erhead were dancing
    heel and toe,
He turned to me, and "Cap," says he, "I'll cash in this trip, I
    guess;
And if I do, I'm asking that you won't refuse my last
    request."   20

Well, he seemed so low that I couldn't say no; then he says
    with a sort of moan:
It's the cursèd cold, and it's got right hold till I'm chilled
    clean through to the bone.
Yet 'tain't being dead — it's my awful dread of the icy grave
    that pains;
So I want you to swear that, foul or fair, you'll cremate my
    last remains."

A pal's last need is a thing to heed, so I swore I would not fail; 25
And we started on at the streak of dawn; but God! he looked
    ghastly pale.
He crouched on the sleigh, and he raved all day of his home
    in Tennessee;

And before nightfall a corpse was all that was left of Sam
McGee.

There wasn't a breath in that land of death, and I hurried,
horror-driven,

With a corpse half hid that I couldn't get rid, because of a
promise given;   30

It was lashed to the sleigh, and it seemed to say: "You may
tax your brawn and brains,

But you promised true, and it's up to you to cremate those
last remains."

Now a promise made is a debt unpaid, and the trail has its
own stern code.

In the days to come, though my lips were dumb, in my heart
how I cursed that load.

In the long, long night, by the lone firelight, while the
huskies, round in a ring,   35

Howled out their woes to the homeless snows — O God!
how I loathed the thing.

And every day that quiet clay seemed to heavy and heavier grow;

And on I went, though the dogs were spent and the grub was
getting low;

The trail was bad, and I felt half mad, but I swore I would
not give in;

And I'd often sing to the hateful thing, and it hearkened with
a grin.   40

Till I came to the marge of Lake Lebarge, and a derelict there lay;

It was jammed in the ice, but I saw in a trice it was called the
"Alice May."
And I looked at it, and I thought a bit, and I looked at my
frozen chum;
Then "Here," said I, with a sudden cry, "is my cre-ma-tor-e-um."

Some planks I tore from the cabin floor, and I lit the boiler
fire;   45
Some coal I found that was lying around, and I heaped the
fuel higher;
The flames just soared, and the furnace roared — such a
blaze you seldom see;
And I burrowed a hole in the glowing coal, and I stuffed in
Sam McGee.

Then I made a hike, for I didn't like to hear him sizzle so;
And the heavens scowled, and the huskies howled, and the
wind began to blow.   50
It was icy cold, but the hot sweat rolled down my cheeks,
and I don't know why;
And the greasy smoke in an inky cloak went streaking down
the sky.

I do not know how long in the snow I wrestled with grisly fear;
But the stars came out and they danced about ere again I
ventured near;
I was sick with dread, but I bravely said: "I'll just take a
peep inside.   55
I guess he's cooked, and it's time I looked"; . . .then the door
I opened wide.

And there sat Sam, looking cold and calm, in the heart of the
    furnace roar;
And he wore a smile you could see a mile, and he said:
    "Please close that door!
It's fine in here, but I greatly fear you'll let in the cold and storm—
Since I left Plumtree, down in Tennessee, it's the first time
    I've been warm."   60

There are strange things done in the midnight sun
    By the men who moil for gold;
The Artic trails have their secret tales
    That would make your blood run cold;
The Northern Lights have seen queer sights,   65
    But the queerest they ever did see
Was that night on the marge of Lake Lebarge
    I cremated Sam McGee.

FOR THE AMBITIOUS STUDENT

I wonder whether you would like to read some more poems by Robert W. Service, "The Canadian Kipling." "The Shooting of Dan McGrew" is, perhaps as well-known as "Sam McGee." Mr. Service's first book, *The Spell of the Yukon*, contains his most famous poems, many of which are about Yukon country, of which he writes:

It's the great, big, broad land 'way up yonder,
It's the forests where silence has lease;
It's the beauty that thrills me with wonder,
It's the stillness that fills me with peace."

"CURFEW MUST NOT RING TONIGHT"
Rose Hartwick Thorpe

Here is a thriller from your grandfather's old school reader. To some of you it will probably be only a literary curiosity, like the old-time melodramas that are periodically revived on the stage. Perhaps you have been fortunate enough to attend a performance of one of these, where the audiences are urged to hiss the villain and cheer the hero; such performances are often given at the many summer theaters flourishing these days. If you have, you may enjoy giving this "old favorite" an over-dramatic, exaggerated rendition — with gestures! But for many of you, the plot will pack a real thrill, if you take it seriously. The two opposing forces are Bessie and the sexton (or perhaps the curfew bell), and the object of the struggle is the life of Bessie's lover — no less!

Slowly England's sun was setting o'er the hilltops far away,
Filling all the land with beauty at the close of one sad day,
And the last rays kissed the forehead of a man and maiden fair, —
He with footsteps slow and weary, she with sunny floating hair;
He with bowed head, sad and thoughtful, she with lips all
    cold and white,   ⁵
Struggling to keep back the murmur, —
    "Curfew must not ring tonight."

"Sexton," Bessie's white lips faltered, pointing to the prison old,
With its turrets tall and gloomy, with its walls dark, damp,
    and cold,
"I've a lover in that prison, doomed this very night to die,   ¹⁰

---

7. *curfew*: a bell formerly rung in the evening as a signal for extinguishing fires

At the ringing of the Curfew, and no earthly help is nigh;
Cromwell will not come till sunset," and her lips grew
    strangely white
As she breathed the husky whisper: —
    "Curfew must not ring tonight."   15

"Bessie," calmly spoke the sexton, — every word pierced her
    young heart
Like the piercing of an arrow, like a deadly poisoned dart, —
"Long, long years I've rung the Curfew from that gloomy,
    shadowed tower;
Every evening, just at sunset, it has told the twilight hour;
I have done my duty ever, tried to do it just and right,   20
Now I'm old I will not falter, —
    "Curfew, it must ring tonight."

Wild her eyes and pale her features, stern and white her
    thoughtful brow,
As within her secret bosom Bessie made a solemn vow.
She had listened while the judges read, without a tear or sigh: 25
"At the ringing of the Curfew, Basil Underwood must die."
And her breath came fast and faster, and her eyes grew large
    and bright;
In an undertone she murmured: —
    "Curfew must not ring tonight."

With quick step she bounded forward, sprang within the old
    church door,   30
Left the old man threading slowly paths he'd trod so oft before;
Not one moment paused the maiden, but with eye and cheek aglow

Mounted up the gloomy tower, where the bell swung to and fro:
As she climbed the dusty ladder, on which fell no ray of light,
Up and up, — her white lips saying: —   35
   "Curfew must not ring tonight!"

She has reached the topmost ladder; o'er hangs the great, dark bell:
Awful is the gloom beneath her, like the pathway down to hell.
Lo, the ponderous tongue is swinging, — 'tis the hour of
      Curfew now,
And the sight has chilled her bosom, stopped her breath, and
      paled her brow.   40
Shall she let it ring? No, never! Flash her eyes with sudden light,
As she springs, and grasps it firmly, —
   "Curfew must not ring tonight!"

Out she swung — far out; the city seemed a speck of light below,
There 'twixt heaven and earth suspended as the bell swung to
      and fro,   45
And the half-deaf sexton ringing (years he had not heard the bell)
Sadly thought the twilight Curfew rang young Basil's funeral
      knell.
Still the maiden clung more firmly, and with trembling lips
      so white,
Said to hush her heart's wild throbbing: —
   "Curfew must not ring tonight!"   50

It was o'er, the bell ceased swaying, and the maiden stepped
      once more
Firmly on the dark old ladder where for hundred years before
Human foot had not been planted. The brave deed that she

had done
Should be told long ages after: as the rays of setting sun
Crimson all the sky with beauty, aged sires, with heads of white, [55]
Tell the eager, listening children,

     "Curfew did not ring that night!"

O'er the distant hills came Cromwell; Bessie sees him, and
     her brow,
Lately white with fear and anguish, has no anxious traces now.
At his feet she tells her story, shows her hands all bruised
     and torn; [60]
And her face so sweet and pleading, yet with sorrow pale
     and worn,
Touched his heart with sudden pity, lit his eyes with misty light:
"Go! Your lover lives," said Cromwell,

     "Curfew shall not ring tonight."

Wide they flung the massive portal; led the prisoner
     forth to die, — [65]
All his bright young life before him. 'Neath the darkening
     English sky
Bessie comes with flying footsteps, eyes aglow with love-
     light sweet;
Kneeling on the turf beside him, lays his pardon at his feet.
In his brave, strong arms he clasped her, kissed the face
     upturned and white, [70]
Whispered, "Darling, you have saved me, —

     "Curfew will not ring tonight!"

---

57. *Cromwell*: probably Oliver Cromwell, English general and statesman of the
    seventeenth century

LOCHINVAR
Sir Walter Scott

Here is another famous poem in the typical dashing rhythm of the beat of horses' hoofs. It is a favorite of millions because it tells an exciting incident with dash and vigor, and because everyone likes to see the brave hero win the girl of his choice. This poem is really the dramatic climax of a story which is left largely to your imagination.

O, young Lochinvar is come out of the west,
Through all the wide Border his steed was the best;
And, save his good broadsword, he weapons had none.
He rode all unarmed, and he road all alone.
So faithful in love, and so dauntless in war, 5
There never was knight like the young Lochinvar.

He stayed not for brake, and he stopped not for stone;
He swam the Eske river where ford there was none;
But, ere he alighted at Netherby gate,
The bride had consented, the gallant came late; 10
For a laggard in love, and a dastard in war,
Was to wed the fair Ellen of brave Lochinvar.

So boldly he entered the Netherby Hall,
Among bridesmen, and kinsmen, and brothers, and all.
Then spoke the bride's father, his hand on his sword 15
(For the poor craven bridegroom said never a word),
"O, come ye in peace here, or come ye in war,

---

2. *Border*: the border between England and Scotland.
7. *brake*: thicket

Or to dance at our bridal, young Lord Lochinvar?"

"I long wooed your daughter, my suit you denied; —
Love swells like the Solway, but ebbs like its tide; —   20
And now I am come, with this lost love of mine,
To lead but one measure, drink one cup of wine.
There are maidens in Scotland more lovely by far,
That would gladly be bride to the young Lochinvar."

The bride kissed the goblet; the knight took it up: 25
He quaffed off the wine, and he threw down the cup.
She looked down to blush, and she looked up to sigh,
With a smile on her lips, and a tear in her eye.
He took her soft hand, ere her mother could bar, —
"Now tread we a measure!" said young Lochinvar.   30

So stately his form, and so lovely her face,
That never a hall such a galliard did grace;
While her mother did fret, and her father did fume,
And the bridegroom stood dangling his bonnet and plume;
And the bride-maidens whispered, "'Twere better by far   35
To have matched our fair cousin with young Lochinvar."

One touch to her hand, and one word to her ear,
When they reached the hall door, and the charger stood near;
So light to the croupe the fair lady he swung,
So light to the saddle before her he sprung!   40

---

32. *galliard*: a gay, lively dance.
39. *croupe*: the back of a horse, just behind the saddle.

"She is won! We are gone! over bank, bush, and scaur;
They'll have fleet steeds that follow," quoth young
    Lochinvar

There was mounting 'mong Graemes of the Netherby clan;
Forsters, Fenwicks, and Musgraves, they rode and they ran;
There was racing and chasing on Cannobie Lee;   45
But the lost bride of Netherby ne'er did they see.
So daring in love, and so dauntless in war.
Have ye e'er heard of gallant like young Lochinvar?

FOR YOUR VOCABULARY

Two words applied to the bridegroom are *dastard*
and *craven*; both imply extreme cowardice. A dastard
is one who does *dastardly* deeds — that is, outrageous
deeds performed in a sneaking, *cowardly* manner. A
craven fellow (or you may just say a *craven*) is a faint-
hearted, *pusillanimous* chap, always in a state of fear.
Scott might also have called the poor bridegroom a
poltroon or a *recreant* (see page 419). On the other
hand, Lochinvar was *dauntless, bold, daring, gallant*.
Find in the dictionary the list of synonyms under the
word *brave*. Look up and bring to class the synonyms
listed under five other words. Are you sure you know
exactly what synonyms are?

41. *scaur*: rock.

LAZYBONES
Robert P. Tristram Coffin

Whenever you travel, you run into odd people. Come down to Maine and meet the Yanceys, who, as the poet says, "take the cake." They are good for a chuckle.

Of all the Tipsham lazybones
    The Yanceys took the cake,
Only in blueberry time
    Did Mother Yancey bake.

And then it was but six or so   5
    Pies that had the pip,
And the soggy bottom crust
    Would sink an iron ship.

The Yanceys boys went bare of foot
    Till the snowflakes flew,   10
And you could put in your right eye
    The corn Dan Yancey grew.

They were folks for whom the skies
    Were always low and murky.
They were always on hard-pan   15
    And poor as old Job's turkey.

One winter when the bay froze up
    From Whaleboat out to Ram,
The Yanceys did not have so much

---

15. *on hard-pan*: at the lowest level of poverty

As a knuckle-bone of ham. 20

They sat around their dying stove
　　And worried at the weather,
The neighbors went and got a cord
　　Of seasoned birch together.

They brought it to the Yancey home 25
　　Where seven tall sons sat
Round the last stick of their wood,
　　Crowding out the cat.

"Here you are, Dan Yancey, this
　　Will keep you for a spell." 30
They left the wood and went back home
　　Feeling pretty well.

But there was not a sign of smoke
　　From the Yancey flue
Going up that afternoon 35
　　On the Winter blue.

And when the dusk was coming on,
　　Dan came to Abel Leigh,
"Can't you send one of your boys
　　To saw my birch for me?" 40

No matter how queer people may be, they usually remind you of some one you know in your home town. Do you know any Yanceys in your part of the country?

THE THREE FISHERS
Charles Kingsley

"The Three Fishers" is a successful attempt to suggest the brooding danger in the lives of fishing folk a hundred years ago. The tragic tone of this poem is due not merely to the subject matter, but in large part also to the musical devices, especially the onomatopoetic last line of each stanza, and other repetitions. As you read the poem, try to feel the mood. Perhaps it will be even more effective to sing it to the tune given here, which, as Kingsley himself said, "enters into the real feeling of the words."

Three fish-ers went sail-ing a - way to the West, A-way to the West as the sun went down; Each thought on the wo-man who lov'd him the best, And the chil-dren stood watch-ing them out of the town; For men must work, and wo-men must weep, And there's lit-tle to earn, and man-y to keep, Though the har - bour bar be moan ———— ing.

Three fishers went sailing away to the West,
Away to the West as the sun went down;
Each thought on the woman who loved him the best,
And the children stood watching them out of the town;
For men must work, and women must weep,   5

And there's little to earn, and many to keep,
Though the harbour bar be moaning.

Three wives sat up in the lighthouse tower,
And they trimmed the lamps as the sun went down;
They looked at the squall, and they looked at the shower,   10
And the night-rack came rolling up ragged and brown.
But men must work, and women must weep,
Though storms be sudden, and waters deep,
And the harbour bar be moaning.

Three corpses lay out on the shining sands   15
In the morning gleam as the tide went down,
And the women are weeping and wringing their hands
For those who will never come home to the town;
For men must work, and women must weep,
And the sooner it's over, the sooner the sleep;   20
And good-bye to the bar and its moaning.

FOR THE AMBITIOUS STUDENT

"The Three Fishers" was made into a song by John
Hullah; the somber tone of the music adds to the effect of
the repetitions and deepens the mournful mood. Try a
musical interpretation for the class; if you cannot find the
whole composition, follow the melody as given here.

---

7. *harbour bar be moaning*: The sound of the rough sea breaking over the
   sandbank out at the mouth of the harbor is like a moaning.
11. *night-rack*: fog or mist rolling in from the sea at night.

THE WRECK OF THE HESPERUS
Henry Wadsworth Longfellow

Certainly one of the most famous and popular of the imitation ballads is this tragic story of shipwreck. Longfellow was obviously trying to make it sound just like the old ballads; so you must read it the same way. Keep the rhythm pattern regular, even if you have to shift some stresses. What lifts this poem above the commonplace is the poet's skill in making the story vivid through onomatopoeia and many effective similes. Read it with an alert imagination.

It was the schooner Hesperus,
    That sailed the wintry sea;
And the skipper had taken his little daughtèr,
    To bear him company.

Blue were her eyes as the fairy-flax,   5
    Her cheeks like the dawn of day,
And her bosom white as the hawthorn buds,
    That ope in the month of May.

The skipper he stood beside the helm,
    His pipe was in his mouth,   10
And he watched how the veering flaw did blow
    The smoke now West, now South.

Then up and spake an old Sailòr,
    Had sailed to the Spanish Main,
"I pray thee, put into yonder port,   15
    For I fear a hurricane.

8. *ope*: open   11. *veering flaw*: shifting gust of wind.

"Last night, the moon had a golden ring,
 And tonight no moon we see!"
The skipper, he blew a whiff from his pipe,
 And a scornful laugh laughed he.   20

Colder and colder blew the wind,
 A gale from the Northeast,
The snow fell hissing in the brine,
 And the billows frothed like yeast.

Down came the storm, and smote amain   25
 The vessel in its strength;
She shuddered and paused, like a frightened steed,
 Then leaped her cable's length.

"Come hither! "come hither! my little daughter,
 And do not tremble so;   30
For I can weather the roughest gale
 That ever wind did blow."

He wrapped her warm in his seaman's coat
 Against the stinging blast;
He cut a rope from a broken spar,   35
 And bound her to the mast.

"O father! I hear the church bells ring;
 Oh, say, what may it be?"
"'Tis a fog bell on a rock-bound coast!" —
 And he steered for the open sea.   40

"O father! I hear the sound of guns;
    Oh say, what may it be?"
"Some ship in distress, that cannot live
    In such an angry sea!"

"O father! I see a gleaming light;   45
    Oh say, what may it be?"
But the father answered never a word,
    A frozen corpse was he.

Lashed to the helm, all stiff and stark,
    With his face turned to the skies,   50
The lantern gleamed through the gleaming snow
    On his fixed and glassy eyes.

Then the maiden clasped her hands and prayed
    That savëd she might be;
And she thought of Christ, who stilled the wave,   55
    On the Lake of Galilee.

And fast through the midnight dark and drear,
    Through the whistling sleet and snow,
Like a sheeted ghost, the vessel swept
    Tow'rds the reef of Norman's Woe.   60

And ever the fitful gusts between
    A sound came from the land;
It was the sound of the trampling surf
    On the rocks and the hard sea-sand.

---

60. *Norman's Woe*: a reef in West Gloucester Harbor, Massachusetts

The breakers were right beneath her bows, 65
    She drifted a dreary wreck,
And a whooping billow swept the crew
    Like icicles from her deck.

She struck where the white and fleecy waves
    Looked soft as carded wool, 70
But the cruel rocks, they gored her side
    Like the horns of an angry bull.

Her rattling shrouds, all sheathed in ice,
    With the masts went by the board;
Like a vessel of glass, she strove and sank, 75
    Ho! ho! the breakers roared!

At daybreak, on the bleak sea-beach,
    A fisherman stood aghast,
To see the form of a maiden fair,
    Lashed close to a drifting mast. 80

The salt sea was frozen on her breast,
    The salt tears in her eyes;
And he saw her hair, like the brown seaweed.
    On the billows fall and rise.

Such was the wreck of the Hesperus, 85
    In the midnight and the snow!
Christ save us all from a death like this,
    On the reef of Norman's Woe!

Name three characteristics of this poem which you would find in the old ballads. Did any lines remind you directly of "Sir Patrick Spens"? Select five comparisons which helped you to see, hear, or feel what was happening. Mention four onomatopoetic words.

THE BALLAD OF THE OYSTERMAN
Oliver Wendell Holmes

Oliver Wendell Holmes, famous American humorist, wrote this poem to make you laugh. The chief source of its humor is its flippant treatment of typical ballad devices (ballad stanza, swift action, rapid-fire conversation) and a typical ballad subject (the death of two lovers). Since the old ballads were usually intensely serious, the absurdity of this silly story usually merits a laugh — at least, from those who know their ballads.

This poem would look more like a ballad if it were printed as most ballads are:

> It was a tall young oysterman
> Lived by the river-side,
> His shop was just upon the bank,
> His boat was on the tide.

When it is printed this way, you can readily see that it has regular ballad form.

If you can read this "ballad" so that it sounds funny to your classmates, you may consider your reading successful. Don't be afraid to overdo the reading a bit, especially the conversation.

It was a tall young oysterman lived by the river-side,
His shop was just upon the bank, his boat was on the tide;
The daughter of a fisherman, that was so straight and slim,
Lived over on the other bank, right opposite to him.

2. *tide*: the river

It was the pensive oysterman that saw a lovely maid,   5
Upon a moonlight evening, a-sitting in the shade;
He saw her wave her handkerchief, as much as if to say,
"I'm wide awake, young oysterman, and all the folks away."

Then up arose the oysterman, and to himself said he,
"I guess I'll leave the skiff at home, for fear that folks should
        see;   10
I read it in the story-book, that, for to kiss his dear,
Leander swam the Hellespont, —and | "I'm as good as Leander
        I will swim this here." | any day!"

And he has leaped into the waves, and crossed the shining stream,
And he has clambered up the bank, all in the moonlight gleam;
Oh! there were kisses sweet as dew, and words as soft as rain— 15
But they have heard her father's steps, and in he leaps again!

Out spoke the ancient fisherman, —"Oh, what was that, my
        daughter?"
"'Twas nothing but a pebble, sir, I threw into the water."
"And what is that, pray tell me, love, that paddles off so fast?"
"It's nothing but a porpoise, sir, that's been a-swimming past." 20

Out spoke the ancient fisherman: "Now bring me my harpoon!
I'll get into my fishing boat, and fix the fellow soon."
Down fell that pretty innocent, as falls a snow-white lamb;
Her hair drooped round her pallid | A famous (or perhaps
        cheeks, like seaweed on a clam. | infamous) simile

---

12. *Hellespont*: the Dardanelles, which are one to four miles wide. The reference
   is to an old Greek story, in which Leander nightly swam the Hellespont to
   visit his sweetheart.

Alas for those two loving ones! she waked not from her swound, [25]
And he was taken with the cramp, and in the waves was
    drowned;
But Fate has metamorphosed them, in pity of their woe,
And now they keep an oyster-shop for mermaids down below.

FOR YOUR VOCABULARY

The drowned heroine of this pathetic story had
pallid cheeks; therefore — using the noun from the
same root in place of the adjective — we may speak
of *pallor* of her face. Many adjectives ending in *–id*
have corresponding nouns in *–or*: *horrid* — *horror*,
rigid — *rigor*, *squalid* — *squalor*, *torpid* — *torpor*.
Write sentences (or, better yet, a paragraph or a little
story) using at least three such pairs of words.

ROBIN HOOD AND
THE BISHOP OF HEREFORD
Old Ballad

*One of the most romantic and exciting figures in all literature
is the outlaw-hero, Robin Hood, who, like most legendary
outlaws, endeared himself to the common folk by robbing the rich
in order to benefit the poor. His exploits are the subject of some
thirty popular ballads, sung for centuries over the length and
breadth of England, and the legend of his feats has grown until
there is hardly a village in England which does not claim some
part of this hero's adventures. All that we know of the real Robin
Hood comes from these few ballads, and people have long been
inventing all sorts of theories to explain him. But whether he was
a Saxon robber, a Norman nobleman in disgrace, or a
revolutionary leader, these merry adventures in Sherwood Forest
always provide a thrill or a chuckle. In the following ballad
Robin Hood is up to his familiar game of taking toll from a rich
and powerful Norman overlord, this time a Bishop.*

Come, gentlemen all, and listen a while;
    A story I'll to you unfold —
How Robin Hood servèd the Bishop,
    When he robbed him of his gold.

As it befell in merry Barnsdale,   5
    And under the green-wood tree,
The Bishop of Hereford was to come by,
    With all his company.

"Come, kill a ven'son," said bold Robin Hood,
    "Come, kill me a good fat deer;   10
The Bishop's to dine with me today,
    And he shall pay well for his cheer.

"We'll kill a fat ven'son," said bold Robin Hood,
    "And dress it by the highway-side,
And narrowly watch for the Bishop,   15
    Lest some other way he should ride."

He dressed himself up in shepherd's attire,
    With six of his men also;
And the Bishop of Hereford came thereby,
    As about the fire they did go.   20

"What matter is this?" said the Bishop;
    "Or for whom do you make this a-do?
Or why do you kill the King's ven'son,
    When your company is so few?"

"We are shepherds," said bold Robin Hood,   25
    "And we keep sheep all the year;
And we are disposed to be merry this day,
    And to kill of the King's fat deer,"

"You are brave fellows," said the Bishop,
    "And the King of your doings shall know;   30
Therefore make haste, come along with me,
    For before the King you shall go."

"O pardon. O pardon," says bold Robin Hood,
    "O pardon, I thee pray!
For it never becomes your lordship's coat   35
    To take so many lives away."

"No pardon, no pardon!" the Bishop says;
    "No pardon I thee owe;
Therefore make haste, come along with me,
    For before the King you shall go."   40

Robin set his back against a tree,
    And his foot against a thorn,
And from underneath his shepherd's coat
    He pulled out a bugle horn.

He put the little end to his mouth,   45
    And a loud blast did he blow,
Till threescore and ten of bold Robin's men
    Came running all in a row;

All making obeisance to bold Robin Hood;
    —'Twas a comely sight for to see: 50
"What matter, my master," said Little John,
    "That you blow so hastily?"

"O here is the Bishop of Hereford,
    And no pardon we shall have."
"Cut off his head, master," said Little John,   55
    "And throw him into his grave."

"O pardon, O pardon," said the Bishop,
    "O pardon, I thee pray!
For if I had known it had been you,
    I'd have gone some other way."   60

No pardon, no pardon!" said Robin Hood;
    "No pardon I thee owe;
Therefore make haste, come along with me,
    For to merry Barnsdale you shall go."

Then Robin has taken the Bishop's hand   65
    And led him to merry Barnsdale;
He made him to stay and sup with him that night,
    And to drink wine, beer, and ale.

"Call in the reckoning." Said the Bishop
    "For methinks it grows wondrous high."   70
"Lend me your purse, Bishop," said Little John,
    "And I'll tell you by-and-by."

Then Little John took the Bishop's cloak,
    And spread it upon the ground,
And out of the Bishop's portmanteau   75
    He told three hundred pound.

"Here's money enough, master," said Little John,
    "And a comely sight 'tis to see;

---

72. *tell*: reckon up; calculate.   76. *told*: counted.

It makes me in charity with the Bishop,
    Though he heartily loveth not me."   80

"So now let him go," said Robin Hood;
    Said Little John, "That may not be;
For I vow and protest he shall sing us a mass
    Before that he go from me."

Robin Hood took the Bishop by the hand,   85
    And bound him fast to a tree,
And made him to sing a mass, God knows,
    To him and his yeomanry.

Then Robin Hood brought him through the wood
    And causèd the music to play,   90
And he made the Bishop to dance in his boots,
    And they set him on his dapple-grey,
And they gave the tail within his hand —
    And glad he could so get away!

JOHNNIE ARMSTRONG
Old Ballad

In this ballad we find as hero another outlaw, a bold border bandit. Like Robin Hood, such an outlaw tends, with time, to become a romantic rascal, and the sympathy of the people seems to turn in his favor. In this particular case we are doubly inclined to favor the hero and victim of this tragic story, as the victor does not play fair.

This ballad is based on fact; it describes the fate of a member of a powerful family, the Armstrongs, who had long been plundering the border country between England and Scotland. In 1530 James V of Scotland decided to get rid of this chief offender against law and order, and he was not any too nice about doing it.

You will have little difficulty with this story, as it is told in a straight-forward, conventional manner, with only one gap in the narrative.

There dwelt a man in fair Westmoreland,
 Johnnie Armstrong men did
   him call;
He had neither lands nor rents coming in,
 Yet he kept eight score men in
   his hall.

> Most of the nobles owned great tracts of land yielding large incomes. Not so Johnnie!

He had horse and harness for them all,
 Goodly steeds were all milk-white;
O the golden bands about their necks,
 And their weapons, they were all alike.

5

News then was brought unto the king
    That there was such a one as he,   10
That livèd like a bold outlaw,
    And robbed all the north country.

The king he wrote a letter then,
    A letter which was large and long;
He signèd it with his own hand,   15
    And he promised to do him no wrong.

When this letter came Johnnie unto,
    His heart was as blithe as birds on the tree:
"Never was I sent for before any king,
    My father, my grandfather, nor none but me.   20

"And if we go the king before,
    I would we went most orderly;
Every man of you shall have his scarlet cloak,
    Laced with silver laces three.

"Every one of you shall have his velvet cloak,   25
    Laced with silver lace so white;
O the golden bands about your necks,
    Black hats, white feathers, all alike."

By the morrow morning at ten of the clock,
    Towards Edinborough gone was he,   30
And with him all his eight score men;
    Good Lord, it was a goodly sight for to see!

30. *Edinborough*: Edinburgh, capital of Scotland

When Johnnie came before the king,
    He fell down on his knee;
"O pardon, my sovereign liege," he said,   35
    "O pardon my eight score men and me."

"Thou shalt have no pardon, thou traitor strong,
    For thy eight score men nor thee;
For tomorrow morning by ten of the clock,
    Both thou and them shall hang on the gallow-tree."   40

But Johnnie looked over his left shouldèr,
    Good Lord, what a grievous look looked he!
Saying, "Asking grace of a graceless face—
    Why, there is none for you nor me."

But Johnnie had a bright sword by his side,   45
    And it was made of the mettle so free,
That had not the king stept his foot aside,
    He had smitten his head from | *He* is Johnnie; *his*, the King's.
    his fair body.

Saying, "Fight on, my merry men all,
    And see that none of you be ta'en;   50
For rather than men shall say we were hanged,
    Let them report how we were slain."

Then, God knows, fair Edinborough rose,
    And so beset poor Johnnie round,

---

46. *of the mettle so free*: of such excellent metal. (Today the word mettle means spirit.)
50. *ta'en*: taken

That fore score and ten of Johnnie's best men   50
    Lay gasping all upon the ground.

Then like a madman Johnnie laid about,
    And like a madman then fought he,
Until a false Scot came Johnnie behind,
    And ran him through the fair body.   55

Saying, "Fight on, my merry men all,
    I am a little hurt, but I am not slain;
I will lay me down for to bleed a while, | In reality, he is dying.
    Then I'll rise and fight with you again."

News then was brought to young | The scene shifts to his castle;
    Johnnie Armstrong,   60 | his son takes up the feud.
    As he stood by his nurse's knee,
Who vowed if e'er he lived to be a man,
    On the treacherous Scots revenged he'd be.

BINNORIE
Old Ballad

When two women love the same man, there is apt to be trouble. This old ballad of jealousy in love (often called "The Twa Sisters"), sung and recited in scores of versions the world over, has thrilled listeners for generations. You, too, will like this murder poem, which, like the best short stories, saves its climax for the very last line.

There were two sisters sat in a bower;
    Binnorie, O Binnorie!
There came a knight to be their wooer.
    By the bonnie milldams of Binnorie.

He courted the eldest with glove and ring,   5
But he loved the youngest above anything.

The eldest she was vexèd sair,
And greatly envied her sister fair.

Upon a morning fair and clear,
She cried upon her sister dear: 10

"O sister, sister, take my hand,
And we'll see our father's ships to land."

2, 4. These refrains are to be read throughout the whole poem, although, to save
    space, they are printed in the first and last stanzas.
7. *sair*: sore. i.e., greatly.

She's taken her by the lily hand,
And led her down to the river-strand.

The youngest stood upon a stone, [15]
The eldest came and pushed her in.

"O sister, sister, reach your hand!
And you shall be heir of half my land."

"O sister, I'll not reach my hand,
And I'll be heir of all of your land." [20]

"O sister, reach me but your glove!
And sweet Williàm shall be your love."

"Sink on, nor hope for hand or glove!
And sweet Williàm shall be my love!"

Sometimes she sank, sometimes she swam, [25]
Until she came to the miller's dam.

Out then came the miller's son,
And saw the fair maid floating in.

"O father, father, draw your dam!
There's either a mermaid or a swan." [30]

The miller hastened and drew his dam,
And there he found a drowned womàn.

You could not see her waist so small,
Her girdle with gold was broidered all.

You could not see her lily feet,   35
Her golden fringes were so deep.

You could not see her yellow hair
For the strings of pearls that were twisted there.

You could not see her fingers small,
With diamond rings they were covered all.   40

And by there came a harper fine,
To harp to the king when he should dine.

And when he looked that lady on,
He sighed and made a heavy moan.

He's made a harp of her breast-bone,   45
Whose sound would melt a heart of stone.

He's taken three locks of her yellow hair,
And with them strung his harp so rare.

He went into her father's hall,
And there was the court assembled all.   50

He laid his harp upon a stone,
And straight it began to play alone.

"O yonder sits my father, the King,
and yonder sits my mother, the Queen;

"And yonder stands my brother Hugh,
and by him my William, sweet and true." [55]

But the last tune that the harp played then—
  Binnorie, O Binnorie!
Was, "Woe to my sister, false Helèn!"
  By the bonnie milldams o' Binnorie.

 This ballad offers a fine opportunity for some exciting choral reading. There are five solo parts: the narrator, the elder sister, the younger sister, the miller's son, the talking harp. And there is a refrain for the whole group.

BARBARA ALLEN
Old Ballad

In Part One of this book you read "Geary's Rock," a native American ballad of the lumber camps. Now you may read one of the oldest and most popular of the English ballads as it is actually sung today in parts of this country. The text and the tune given here are found in Carl Sandburg's **The American Songbag,** *a book you would enjoy. This version of the story of "hard-hearted Barbara Allen," strangely enough, varies but little from that sung centuries ago in the border country of England, a remarkable fact when you remember that these stories were never seen in print by the people who sang them, but were passed on by word of mouth from generation to generation. The romantic ending of this story must have appealed greatly to ballad audiences, for you find it again and again in other ballads about true lovers. Here then is a present-day American example of ancient folk-balladry. I wonder whether people will still sing it five hundred years hence.*

In Lon-don Ci-ty where I once did dwell, there's where I got my learn-ing, I fell in love with a pret-ty young girl, her name was Bar-ba-ra Al-len.

In London City where I once did dwell, there's where I got
      my learning,
I fell in love with a pretty young girl, her name was Barbara Allen.
I courted her for seven long years, she said she would not have me;
Then straightway home as I could go and liken to a dying.

I wrote her a letter on my death bed, I wrote it slow and
      moving;   5
"Go take this letter to my old true love and tell her I am dying."
She took the letter in her lily-white hand, she read it slow
      and moving;
"Go take this letter back to him, and tell him I am coming."

As she passed by his dying bed she saw his pale lips quivering;
"No better, no better I'll ever be until I get Barbara Allen." 10
As she passed by his dying bed, "You're very sick and
      almost dying,
No better, no better you will ever be, for you can't get Barbara Allen."

As she went down the long stair steps she heard the death
      bell toning,
And every bell appeared to say, "Hard-hearted Barbara Allen!"
As she went down the long piney walk she heard some small
      birds singing,   15
And every bird appeared to say, "Hard-hearted Barbara Allen!"

She looked to the East, she looked to the West, she saw the
      pale corpse coming
"Go bring them pale corpse unto me, and let me gaze upon them.

---

4. *liken to a dying*: get set to die.
18. *them*: She must be looking for Willie among the dead.

Oh, mama, mama, go make my bed, go make it soft and narrow!
Sweet Willie died today for me, I'll die for him tomorrow!"   [20]

They buried Sweet Willie in the old church yard, they buried
    Miss Barbara beside him;
And out of his grave there sprang a red rose, and out of hers
    a briar.
They grew to the top of the old church tower, they could not
    grow any higher,
They hooked, they tied in a true love's knot, red rose around
    the briar.

FOR THE AMBITIOUS STUDENT

You might find and play for the class the Victor
recording of this ballad, sung by Royal Dadmun.

CERELLE
Margaret Bell Houston

"You can't put a square peg in a round hole," is an old saying. In this modern ballad we have a tender story of a romantic cowboy and his lovely bride, which illustrates just such a theme. Like many of the old ballads, this one is told simply, briefly, with much of the story left for your imagination to fill out. The author has described the bride, Cerelle, not directly, but in a series of comparisons. Only by reading these figures of speech with an alert imagination will you see why she never could have fitted into the hard life on a ranch. When you understand Cerelle, you will be deeply moved by her tragedy.

There was a score of likely girls
Around the prairieside,
But I went down to Galveston
And brought me home a bride.

A score or more of handsome girls, 5   What he meant by *likely*.
Of proper age and size,
But the pale girls of Galveston
Have sea-shine in their eyes.   We call it glamour.

As pale as any orange flower,
Cerelle. The gold-white sands   10
Were like her hair, and drifting shells,
White fairy shells, her hands.

I think she liked my silver spurs,
A-clinking in the sun.

She'd never seen a cowboy till   15
I rode to Galveston.

She'd never known the chaparral,
Nor smell of saddle leather,
Nor seen a round-up or a ranch,
Till we rode back together.   20

Shall I forget my mother's eyes?
"Is this the wife you need?
Is this the way to bring me rest
From forty men to feed?"

Cerelle — I think she did her best   25
All year. She'd lots to learn.
Dishes would slip from out her hands
And break. The bread would burn.

And she would steal away at times
And wander off to me.   30   She was aware of her own
And when the wind was in the south   failure and, of course,
She'd say, "I smell the sea!"   terribly homesick.

She changed. The white and gold   See II. 10-12
     grew dull
As when a soft flame dies,
And yet she kept until the last   35   She dies.
The sea-shine in her eyes

                    * * * * *

---

17. *chaparral*: desert shrubs

There are (I make a husband's boast)
No stronger arms than Ann's.
She has a quip for all the boys,
And sings among the pans.

This time he marries a
likely girl.

40

At last my mother takes her rest.
And that's how things should be.
But when the wind is in the south
There is no rest for me.

If you liked "Cerelle," you may enjoy reading an old ballad, "Lord Thomas and Fair Annet," which presents a similar situation. But that story is tragic and bloody, not tender and sad.

MAUD MULLER

John Greenleaf Whittier

Some poems suit the popular fancy so well that they become as familiar as certain pictures (like "Whistler's Mother") or certain musical pieces (like Schubert's "Serenade"). "Maud Muller" is one of these universal favorites.

It is a sad story told to demonstrate the ever-popular theme that in marriage love is more important than any considerations of rank, wealth, or family pride. In it you will find these famous, often-quoted lines:

> *For of all sad words of tongue or pen*
> *The saddest are these: "It might have been!"*

Maud Muller on a summer's day
Raked the meadow sweet with hay.

Beneath her torn hat glowed the wealth
Of simple beauty and rustic health.

Singing, she wrought, and her merry glee   5
The mock-bird echoed from his tree.

But when she glanced to the far-off town,
White from its hill-slope looking down,

The sweet song died, and a vague unrest
And a nameless longing filled her breast,—   10

A wish, that she hardly dared to own,
For something better than she had known.

The Judge rode slowly down the lane,
Smoothing his horse's chestnut mane.

He drew his bridle in the shade 15
Of the apple-trees, to greet the maid,

And asked a draught from the spring that flowed
Through the meadow across the road.

She stopped where the cool spring bubbled up,
And filled for him her small tin cup, 20

And blushed as she gave it, looking down
On her feet so bare, and her tattered gown.

"Thanks!" said the Judge; "a sweeter draught
From a fairer hand was never quaffed."

He spoke of the grass and flowers and trees, 25
Of the singing birds and the humming bees;

Then talked of the haying, and wondered whether
The cloud in the west would bring foul weather.

And Maud forgot her brier-torn gown,
And her graceful ankles bare and brown; 30

And listened, while a pleased surprise
Looked from her long-lashed hazel eyes.

At last, like one who for delay
Seeks a vain excuse, he rode away.

Maud Muller looked and sighed: "Ah me!   35
That I the Judge's bride might be!

"He would dress me up in silks so fine,
And praise and toast me at his wine.

"My father should wear a broadcloth coat;
My brother should sail a painted boat.   40

"I'd dress my mother so grand and gay,
And the baby should have a new toy each day.

"And I'd feed the hungry and clothe the poor,
And all should bless me who left our door."

The Judge looked back as he climbed the hill,   45
And saw Maud Muller standing still.

"A form more fair, a face more sweet
Ne'er hath it been my lot to meet.

"And her modest answer and graceful air
Show her wise and good as she is fair.   50

"Would she were mine, and I today,
Like her, a harvester of hay;

"No doubtful balance of rights and wrongs,
Nor weary lawyers with endless tongues,

"Bit low of cattle and song of birds,   55
And health and quiet and loving words."

But he thought of his sisters proud and cold
And his mother, vain of her rank and gold.

So, closing his heart, the Judge rode on,
And Maud was left in the field alone.   60

But the lawyers smiled that afternoon,
When he hummed in court an old love-tune;

And the young girl mused beside the well
Till the rain on the unraked clover fell.

He wedded a wife of richest dower,   65
Who lived for fashion, as he for power.

Yet oft, in his marble hearth's bright glow,
He watched a picture come and go;

And sweet Maud Muller's hazel eyes
Looked out in their innocent surprise.   70

Oft, when the wine in his glass was red,
He longed for the wayside well instead;

And closed his eyes on his garnished rooms
To dream of meadows and clover-blooms.

And the proud man sighed, with a secret pain,   75
"Ah, that I were free again!

"Free as when I rode that day,
Where the barefoot maiden raked her hay."

She wedded a man unlearned and poor,
And many children played round her door.   80

But care and sorrow, and childbirth pain,
Left their traces on heart and brain.

And oft, when the summer sun shone hot
On the new-mown hay in the meadow lot,

And she heard the little spring brook fall   85
Over the roadside, through the wall,

In the shade of the apple-tree again
She saw a rider draw his rein;

And, gazing down with timid grace,
She felt his pleased eyes read her face.   90

Sometimes her narrow kitchen walls
Stretched away into stately halls;

The weary wheel to a spinet turned,
The tallow candle an astral burned,

And for him who sat by the chimney lug, 95
Dozing and grumbling o'er pipe and mug,

A manly form at her side she saw,
And joy was duty and love was law.

Then she took up her burden of life again,
Saying only, "It might have been." 100

Alas for maiden, alas for Judge,
For rich repiner and household drudge!

God pity them both! and pity us all,
Who vainly the dreams of youth recall.

For of all sad words of tongue or pen 105
The saddest are these: "It might have been!"

Ah, well! for us all some sweet hope lies
Deeply buried from human eyes;

And, in the hereafter, angels may
Roll the stone from its grave away! 110

93, 94. *spinet, astral*: She imagined that her spinning wheel became a lovely
piano, and her cheap candle a beautiful lamp.

FOR THE AMBITIOUS STUDENT

The famous word, "It might have been," suggest a story. If Maud and the Judge had married, how do you think the marriage would have prospered? Try your hand at some episode in this "might-have-been" story. Both Bret Harte and F. P. Adams have done so in verse; you may enjoy looking up their poems.

FOR YOUR VOCABULARY

If the pronunciation of the word *draught* bothers you, remember that it is an old form of the word *draft*; then you will pronounce it correctly. As for the spelling, don't worry; just use *draft*. The spelling of many words has been similarly simplified: *plow for plough, color* for *colour, program* for *programme.* Can you name others? Which spelling do you prefer? Can you name words now in the process of simplification through (or should I say *thru*?) usage? What is your attitude toward "simplified spelling"? What are your reasons for your attitude?

IN SCHOOL-DAYS

John Greenleaf Whittier

Sometimes a poet gives us great pleasure by taking us back to familiar scenes and awakening in us happy memories. This poem has long been a great favorite because all of its readers have been to school, many even to a little one-room country school like that described here; and the imagery in the poem brings to them pictures which take them back to their childhood. To you also it may bring memories of your grade-school days. Notice that Whittier, like many of our early poets, uses his last stanza to bring out the full meaning and significance of the slim little story he has told.

Still sits the schoolhouse by the road,
    A ragged beggar sunning;
Around it still the sumachs grow,
    And blackberry vines are running.

Within, the master's desk is seen,   5
    Deep scarred by raps official;
The warping floor, the battered seats,
    The jack-knife's carved initial;

The charcoal frescoes on its wall;
    Its door's worn sill, betraying   10
The feet that, creeping slow to school,
    Went storming out to playing!

Long years ago a winter sun
    Shone over it at setting;

Lit up its western window-panes, [15]
    And low eaves' icy fretting.

It touched the tangled golden curls,
    And brown eyes full of grieving,
Of one who still her steps delayed
    When all the school were leaving. [20]

For near her stood the little boy
    Her childish favor singled:
His cap pulled low upon a face
    Where pride and shame were mingled.

Pushing with restless feet the snow [25]
    To right and left, he lingered; —
As restlessly her tiny hands
    The blue-checked apron fingered.

He saw her lift her eyes; he felt
    The soft hand's light caressing, [30]
And heard the tremble of her voice,
    As if a fault confessing.

"I'm sorry that I spelt the word:
    I hate to go above you,
Because," — the brown eyes lower fell,— [35]
    "Because, you see, I love you!"

Still memory to a gray-haired man
    That sweet child-face is showing.

Dear girl! the grasses on her grave
    Have forty years been growing!   40

He lives to learn, in life's hard school,
    How few who pass above him
Lament their triumph and his loss,
    Like her, — because they love him.

THE PIED PIPER OF HAMELIN
A Child's Story
Robert Browning

The story of the Pied Piper, as you probably know, is based on some obscure incident which has faded into legend; perhaps it was a Children's Crusade. But in Hameln, Germany, the tourist is still shown the various places where the events of the story are supposed to have occurred.

Robert Browning wrote this version to amuse the son of a friend, with no idea that it would ever become famous. But in the hands of a poet as gifted as Browning the old German legend became a poem charming, amusing, and emotionally appealing. Browning's imagery is occasionally startling: the Mayor's eye was like "a too-long opened oyster"; the Piper's eye "twinkled like a candle-flame where salt is sprinkled"; the children following the piper were chattering and running "like fowls in a barnyard when barley is scattering." To make us not only see but also hear both the rats and the children, Browning makes good use of onomatopeia:

> And the muttering grew to a grumbling;
> And the grumbling grew to a mighty rumbling;
> And out of the houses the rats came tumbling.

* * * * *

> There was a rustling that seemed like a bustling
> Of merry crowds jostling at pitching and hustling;
> Small feet were pattering, wooden shoes clattering...

Stories in Verse

These quotations also illustrate Browning's delight in playing with rimes; in this poem you will find many a rime that must have made the poet chuckle: obese — robe ease; council — gown sell; silence — mile hence; *and the pretty bad one at the end:* from mice — promise.

I

Hamelin Town's in Brunswick,
  By famous Hanover city;
The river Weser, deep and wide,
Washes its wall on the southern side;
A pleasanter spot you never spied;   5
  But, when begins my ditty,
Almost five hundred years ago,
To see the townsfolk suffer so
  From vermin, was a pity.

II

Rats!   10
They fought the dogs and killed the cats,
  And bit the babies in the cradles,
And ate the cheeses out of the vats,
  And licked the soup from the cooks' own ladles,
Split open the kegs of salted sprats,   15
Made nests inside men's Sunday hats,
And even spoiled the women's chats
  By drowning their speaking
  With shrieking and squeaking
In fifty different sharps and flats.   20

III

At last the people in a body
  To the Town Hall came flocking:
"'Tis clear," cried they, "our Mayor's a noddy;
  And as for our Corporation — shocking
To think we buy gowns lined with ermine   25
For dolts that can't or won't determine
What's best to rid us of our vermin!
You hope, because you're old and obese,
To find in the furry civic robe ease?
Rouse up, sirs! Give your brains a racking   30
To find the remedy we're lacking,
Or, sure as fate, we'll send you packing!"
At this the Mayor and Corporation
Quaked with a mighty consternation.

IV

An hour they sat in council,   35
  At length the Mayor broke silence:
"For a guilder I'd my ermine gown sell,
  I wish I were a mile hence!
It's easy to bid one rack one's brain-
I'm sure my poor head aches again,
I've scratched it so, and all in vain.   40
Oh for a trap, a trap, a trap!"
Just as he said this, what should hap
At the chamber door but a gentle tap?
"Bless us," cried the Mayor, "what's that?"
(With the Corporation as he sat,

---

24. *Corporation*: governing body of a city.

Looking little though wondrous fat;
Nor brighter was his eye, not moister
Than a too-long-opened oyster,   50
Save when at noon his paunch grew mutinous
For a plate of turtle green and glutinous)
"Only a scraping of shoes of a rat
Makes my heart go pit-a-pat!"

V

"Come in!" — the Mayor cried, looking bigger: 55
And in did come the strangest figure!
His queer long coat from heel to head
Was half of yellow and half of red,
And he himself was tall and thin,
With sharp blue eyes, each like a pin,   60
And light loose hair, yet swarthy skin,
No tuft on cheek nor beard on chin,
But lips where smiles went out and in;
There was no guessing his kith and kin:
And nobody could enough admire   65
The tall man and his quaint attire.
Quoth one: " It's as my great-grandsire,
Starting up at the Trump of Doom's tone,
Had walked this way from his painted tombstone!"

VI

He advanced to the council-table: 70
And, "Please your honors," said he, "I'm able,
By means of a secret charm, to draw

---

68. *Trump of Doom*: trumpet blown to announce the Day of Judgment.

All creatures living beneath the sun
That creep or swim or fly or run,
After me so as you never saw!
And I chiefly use my charm   75
On creatures that do people harm,
The mole and toad and newt and viper;
And people call me the Pied Piper."
(And here they noticed round his neck   80
   A scarf of red and yellow stripe,
To match with his coat of the self-same cheque;
   And at the scarf's end hung a pipe;
And his fingers, they noticed, were ever straying
As if impatient to be playing   85
Upon his pipe, as low it dangled
Over his vesture so old-fangled .)
"Yet," said he, "poor piper as I am,
In Tartary I freed the Cham,
   Last June, from his huge swarms of gnats;   90
I eased in Asia the Nizam
   Of a monstrous brood of vampire-bats:
And as for what your brain bewilders,
 If I can rid your town of rats
Will you give me a thousand guilders?"   95
"One? fifty thousand!"—was the exclamation
Of the astonished Mayor and Corporation.

---

79. *Pied*: clad in a coat of two or more colors in blotches.
86: *pipe*: an instrument now obsolete, consisting of a hollow cylinder blown
   from the end. It was commonly held in the left hand, leaving the right hand
   free for beating the tabor, which was often used with the pipe.
89,91. *Cham, Nizam*: titles of Asiatic rulers.

VII

Into the street the Piper stept,
  Smiling first a little smile,
As if he knew what magic slept   100
  In his quiet pipe while;
Then, like a musical adept,
To blow the pipe his lips he wrinkled,
And green and blue his sharp eyes twinkled,
Like a candle-flame where salt is sprinkled;   105
And ere three shrill notes the pipe uttered,
You heard as if an army muttered;
And the muttering grew to a grumbling;
And the grumbling grew to a mighty rumbling;
And out of the houses the rats came tumbling.   110
Great rats, small rats, lean rats. brawny rats,
Brown rats, black rats, gray rats, tawny rats,
Grave old plodders, gay young friskers,
  Fathers, mothers, uncles, cousins,
Cocking tails and pricking whiskers,   115
  Families by tens and dozens,
Brothers, sisters, husbands, wives—
Followed the Piper for their lives.
From street to street he piped advancing,
And step for step they followed dancing,   120
Until they came to the river Weser,
  Wherein all plunged and perished!
—Save one who, stout as Julius Caesar,
Swam across and lived to carry
  (As he, the manuscript he cherished)   125

---

102. *adept*: a skilled person; an expert

To Rat-land home his commentary:
Which was, "At the first shrill note of the pipe,
I heard a sound as of scraping tripe,
And putting apples, wondrous ripe,
Into a cider-press's gripe: 130
And a moving away of pickle-tub-boards,
And a leaving ajar of conserve-cupboards,
And a drawing corks of train-oil-flasks,
And a breaking the hoops of butter-casks:
And it seemed as if a voice   135
    (Sweeter far than by harp or by psaltery
Is breathed) called out, "Oh rats, rejoice!
    The world is grown to one vast drysaltery!
So munch on, crunch on, take your nuncheon!   140
Breakfast, supper, dinner, luncheon!'
And just as a bulky sugar-puncheon,
All ready staved, like a great sun shone
Glorious scarce an inch before me,
Just as methought it said, "Come, bore me!"
    —I found the Weser rolling o'er me."   145

VIII

You should have heard the Hamelin people
Ringing the bells till they rocked the steeple.
    "Go," cried the Mayor, " and get the long poles,

---

123. *Julius Caesar*: At one time stout-hearted Julius Caesar is said to have
    escaped from a captured ship, swimming with one hand and the other
    holding his commentaries up out of the water for safekeeping.
138. *Drysaltery*: a place of business selling salted food products.
139. *nuncheon*: noon luncheon

Poke out the nests and block up the holes!
Consult with carpenters and builders,   150
And leave our town not even a trace
Of the rats!"—when suddenly up the face
Of the Piper perked in the market-place,
With a, "First, if you please, my thousand guilders!"

XI

A thousand guilders! The Mayor looked blue;   155
So did the Corporation too.
For council dinners made rare havoc
With Claret, Moselle, Vin-de-Grave, Hock;
And half the money would replenish
Their cellar's biggest butt with Rhenish.   160
To pay this sum to a wandering fellow
With a gypsy coat of red and yellow!
"Beside," quoth the Mayor with a knowing wink,
"Our business was done at the river's brink;
We saw with our eyes that vermin sink,   165
And what's dead can't come to life, I think.
So, friend, we're not the folks to shrink
From the duty of giving you something for drink,
And a matter of money to put in your poke;
But as for the guliders, what we spoke   170
Of them, as you very well know, was in joke.
Beside, our losses have made us thrifty.
A thousand guilders! Come, take fifty!"

158,160. *Claret, Moselle, Vin-de-Grave, Hock, Rhenish*: various kinds of wine.
160. *butt*: large cask.

X

The Piper's face fell, and he cried,
"No trifling! I can't wait, beside! 175
I've promised to visit by dinner time
Bagdat, and accept the prime
Of the Head-Cook's pottage, all he's rich in,
For having left, in the Caliph's kitchen,
Of a nest of scorpions no survivor: 180
With him I proved no bargain-driver,
With you, don't think I'll bate a stiver!
And folks who put me in a passion
May find me pipe after another fashion."

XI

"How?" cried the Mayor, "d'ye think I brook 185
Beign worse treated than a Cook?
Insulted by a lazy ribald
With idle pipe and vesture piebald?
You threaten us, fellow? Do your worst,
Blow your pipe there till you burst! 190

XII

Once more he stept into the street
And to his lips again
Laid his long pipe of smooth straight cane;
And ere he blew three notes (such sweet

---

169. *poke*: a bag, a pocket
170. *pottage*: a thick soup or stew
182. *bate a stiver*: abate (lessen) my demand by the amount of a stiver (about two cents)
185. *brook*: put up with; endure.

Soft notes as yet musician's cunning   195
Never gave the enraptured air)
There was a rustling that seemd like a bustling
Of merry crowds justling at pitching and hustling;
Small feet were pattering, wooden shoes clattering,
Little hands clapping and little tongues chattering,   200
And, like fowls in a farm-yard when barley is
    scattering,
Out came the children running.
All the little boys and girls,
With rosy cheeks and flaxen curls,
And sparkling eyes and teeth like pearls,   205
Tripping and skipping, ran merrily after
The wonderful music with shouting and laughter.

XIII

The Mayor was dumb, and the Council stood
As if they were changed into blocks of wood,
Unable to move a step, or cry   210
To the children merrily skipping by,
—Could only follow with the eye
That joyous crowd at the Piper's back.
But how the Mayor was on the rack,
And the wretched Counicl's bosoms beat,   215
As the Piper turned from the High Street
To where the Weser rolled its waters
Right in the way of their sons and daughters!
However, he turned from South to West,

---

214. *on the rack*: in torture

And to Koppelberg Hill his steps addressed,   220
And after him the children pressed;
Great was the joy in every breast.
"He never can cross that mighty top!
He's forced to let the piping drop,
And we shall see our children stop!"   225
When, lo, as they reached the mountain-side,
A wondrous portal opened wide,
As if a cavern was suddenly hollowed;
And the Piper advanced and the children followed,
And when all were in to the very last,   230
The door in the mountain-side shut fast.
Did I say all? No! One was lame,
And could not dance the whole of the way;
And in after years, if you would blame
His sadness, he was used to say,—   235
"It's dull in our town since my playmates left!
I can't forget that I'm bereft
Of all the pleasant sights they see,
Which the Piper promised me.
For he led us, he said, to a joyous land,   240
Joining the town and just at hand,
Where waters gushed and fruit-trees grew
And flowers put forth a fairer hue,
And everything was strange and new;
The sparrows were brighter than peacocks here,   245
And their dogs outran our fallow deer,
And honey-bees had lost their stings,
And horses were born with eagle's wings:

And just as I became assured
My lame foot would be speedily cured,   250
The music stopped and I stood still,
And found myself outside the hill,
Left alone against my will,
To go now limping as before,
And never hear of that country more!"   255

XIV

Alas, alas for Hamelin!
   There come into many a burgher's pate
   A text which says that heaven's gate
   Opes to the rich at as easy rate
As the needle's eye takes a camel in!   260
The Mayor sent East, West, North, and South,
To offer the Piper, by word of mouth,
   Wherever it was men's lots to find him,
Silver and gold to his heart's content,
If he'd only return the way he went,   265
   And bring the children behind him.
But when they saw 'twas a lost endeavor,
And Piper and dancers were gone forever,
They made a decree that lawyers never
   Should think their records dated duly   270
If, after the day of the month and year,
These words did not as well appear,
  "And so long after what happened here
   On the Twenty-second of July,

---

257. *burgher's pate*, citizen's head.
259. See Luke 18.25.

Thirteen hundred and seventy-six:" 275
And the better in memory to fix
The place of the children's last retreat,
They called it, the Pied Piper's Street-
Where any one playing on pipe or tabor
Was sure for the future to lose his labor. 280
Nor suffered they hostelry or tavern
    To shock with mirth a street so solemn;
But opposite the place of the cavern
    They wrote the story on a column,
And on the great church-window painted 285
The same, to make the world acquainted
How their children were stolen away,
And there it stands to this very day.
And I must not omit to say
That in Transylvania there's a tribe 290
Of alien people who ascribe
The outlandish ways and dress
On which their fathers and mothers having risen
Out of some subterraneous prison 295
Into which they were trepanned
Long time ago in a mighty band
Out of Hamelin town in Brunswick land,
But how or why, they don't understand.

281. *suffered*: permitted.
290. *Transylvania*: a part of Rumania
296. *trepanned*: lured

XV

So, Willy, let me and you be wipers ³⁰⁰
Of scores out with all men-especially pipers!
And, whether they pipe us free from rats or fróm mice,
If we've promised them aught, let us keep our promise!

---

300. *Willy*: Willy Macready (son of the famous actor William Macready) for
whom the poem was written.

KING JOHN AND
THE ABBOT OF CANTERBURY
Old Ballad

Nearly all the old English ballads tell sad or violent stories, But here is one with a happy ending. It follows one of the oldest of all plots: someone is forced to solve a three-fold riddle to save his life. Read how the Abbot of Canterbury is saved from this predicament.

An anicent story, I'll tell you anon
Of a notable prince, that was callèd King John;
And he rulèd England with main and with might,
For he did great wrong, and maintained little right.

And I'll tell you a story, a story so merry,   5
Concerning the Abbot of Canterbury;
How, for his house-keeping and high renown,
They rode post for him to fair London town.

An hundred men, the King did hear say,
The Abbot kept in his house every day;·   10
And fifty gold chains, without any doubt,
In velvet coats waited the Abbot about.

"How now, Father Abbot, I hear it of thee
Thou keepest a far better house than me,
And for they house-keeping and high renown,
I fear thou work'st treason against my crown."   15

---

11. *chains*: men wearing the gold chains

"My liege," quoth the Abbot, " I would it were known,
I never spend nothing, but what is my own;
And I trust your Grace will do me no deere
For spending of my own true-gotten gear."   20

"Yes, yes Father Abbot, thy fault it is high,
And now for the same thou needest must die;
For except thou canst answer me questions three,
Thy head shall be smitten from thy bodie.

"And first," quoth the King, "when I'm in this stead,   25
With my crown of gold so fair on my head,
Among all my liege-men so noble of birth,
Thou must tell me to one penny what I am worth.

"Secondly, tell me, without any doubt,
How soon I may ride the whole world about.
And at the third question thou must not shrink,
But tell me here truly what I do think."   30

"O, these are hard questions for my swallow wit,
Nor I cannot answer your Grace as yet:
But if you will give me but three weeks' space,
I'll do my endeavor to answer your Grace.   35

"Now three weeks' space to thee will I give,
And that is the longest time thou hast to live;
For if thou dost not answer my questions three,
Thy lands and they livings are forfeit to me."   40

---

19. *deere:* harm; injury
25. *stead:* the proper or appointed place of a person; a seat (in this case, the throne.)

Away rode the Abbot all sad at the word,
And he rode to Cambridge and Oxenford;
But never a doctor there was so wise,
That could with his learning an answer devise.

Then home rode the Abbot of comfort so cold,
And he met with his shepherd a-going to fold: 45
"How now, my lord Abbot, your are welcome home;
What news do you bring us from good King John?"

"Sad news, sad news, shepherd, I must give;
That I have but three days more to live:
For if I do not answer him questions three,   50
My head will be smitten from my bodie.

"The first is to tell him there in that stead,
With his crown of gold so fair on his head,
Among all his liege-men so noble of birth,
To within one penny of what he is worth.   55

"The second, to tell him, without any doubt,
How soon he may ride this whole world about:
And at the third question I must not shrink,
But tell him there truly what he does think."

"Now cheer up, sire Abbot, did you never hear yet,   60
That a fool he may learn a wise man wit?

42. *Oxenford:* Oxford

Lend me horse, and serving-men, and your apparel,
And I'll ride to London to answer your quarrel.

"Nay frown not, if it hath been told unto me,
I am like your lordship, as ever may be: 65
And if you will but lend me your gown,
There is none shall know us at fair London town."

Now horses and serving-men thou shalt have,
With sumptuous array most gallant and brave;
With crozier, and miter, and rochet, and cope,   70
Fit to appear 'fore our Father the Pope."

"Now welcome, sire Abbot," the King he did say,
"'Tis well thou'rt come back to keep thy day,
For if thou canst answer my questions three,
They life and they living both savèd shall be.   75

"And first, when thou seest me here in this stead,
With my crown of gold so fair on my head,
Among all my liege-men so noble of birth,
Tell me to one penny what I am worth."

"For thirty pence our Savior was sold   80
By the false Judas, as I have been told;
And twenty-nine is the worth of thee,
For I think thou art one penny worser then he."

---

71. *crozier, miter, rochet, cope:* parts of a bishop's apparel

The King he laughed, and swore by St. Bittel,
"I did not think I had been worth so little!   85
—Now secondly tell me, without any doubt,
How soon I may ride this whole world about."

"You must rise with the sun, and ride with the same,
Until the next morning he riseth again;
And then your Grace need not make any doubt,   90
But in twenty-four hours you'll ride it about."

The King he laughed, and swore by St. John,
"I did not think it could be gone so soon!
-Now from the third question thou must not shrink,
But tell me here truly what I do think."   95

"Yea, that shall I do, and make your Grace merry:
You think I'm the Abbot of Canterbuty;
But I'm his poor shepherd, as plain you may see,
That am come to beg pardon for him and for me."

The King he laughed, and swore by the Mass,   100
"I'll make thee Lord Abbot this day in his place!"
"Now nay, my liege, be not in such speed,
For alack I can neither write, nor read."

Four nobles a week, then, I will give thee
For this merry jest thou hast shown unto me: 105
And tell the old Abbot when thou comest home,
Thou hast brought him a pardon from good King John."

FOR YOUR VOCABULARY

Except and *accept* are often misused by the unwary. *Except* is usually a prepostion: Everyone *except* Mary came early. *Accept* is a verb meaning *to receive* or *to answer* an invitation favorably: We *accept* your kind invitation with pleasure,

Other similar "pair" words that are often confused are *quite, quiet*; *whether, weather*; *affect, effect*; *resemble, reassemble*; *counsel, council*; *alley, ally*; *allsuion, illusion; emigrate, immigrate; eligible, illegible*; and the triplets *statue, stature, statute*. Use each of these pairs of words in a sentence which brings out meanings clearly. Do you know any other such pairs?

LADY ISABEL AND THE ELF-KNIGHT
Old Ballad

In practically every country of Europe this story was told and retold. It has one of the best surprise endings of all the ballads.

There came a bird out of a bush,
    On water for to dine,
And sighing sore, says the king's daughter,
    "O woe's this heart of mine!"

He's taken a harp into his hand,   5
    He's harped them all asleep,
Except it was the king's daughter,
    Who one wink could not get.

He's leaped upon his berry-brown steed,
    Taken her on behind himsel'   10
Then both rode down to that water
    That they call Wearie's Well.

"Wade in, wade in, my lady fair,
    No harm shall thee befall;
Oft times have I watered my steed   15
    With the waters of Wearie's Well."

The first step that she steppèd in,
    She steppèd to the knee;

---

1. *bird:* The bird whose song apparently causes the lady such woe may be the
elfin-knight in disguise. If so, in line 5 he assumes the shape of a man.

And sighing says this lady fair,
    "This water's not for me."   20

"Wade in, wade in, my lady fair,
    No harm shall thee befall;
Oft times have I watered my steed
    With the waters of Wearie's Well."   25

The next step that she steppèd in,
    She steppèd to the middle;
"O," sighing says this lady fair,
    "I've wet my golden girdle."

"Wade in, wade in, my lady fair,   30
    No harm shall thee befall;
Oft times have I watered my steed
    With the waters of Wearie's Well."

The next step that she steppèd in,
    She steppèd to the chin;   35
"O," sighing says this lady fair,
    "I'll wade no farther in."

"Seven king's daughters I've drowned there,
    In the water of Wearie's Well,
And I'll make you the eighth of them,   40
    And ring the common bell."

"Since I am standing here," she says,
    "This dreadful death to die,

One kiss of your comely mouth
      I'm sure would comfort me." ⁴⁵

He leaned over his saddle bow,
      To kiss her cheek and chin;
She's taken him in her arms two,
      And thrown him headlong in.

"Since seven king's daughters ye've drowned there, ⁵⁰
      In the water of Wearie's Well,
I'll make you bridegroom to them all,
      And ring the bell mysel'."

LORD RANDAL
Old Ballad

In this ballad, as in "Edward, Edward," there is nothing but a brief dialogue between a mother and her son; yet between the lines, with their haunting refrains, you will sense the tragic scene in the forest that took place just before this conversation began. You may enjoy reading this ballad with the old words and spelling, just as it has come down to us. After you have read it silently, try reading it orally: be sure to express in your voice the increasing concern of the mother, and the corresponding despair of the son.

"O where hae ye been, "Lord Randal, my son?
O where hae ye been, my handsome young man?"—
"I hae been to the wild wood; mother, make my bed soon,
For I'm weary wi' hunting and fain wad lie down."

"Where gat ye your dinner,Lord Randal, my son?"   5
Where gat ye your diner, my handsome young man?"—
"I dined wi' my true- love; mother, make my bed soon,
For I'm weary wi' hunting and fain wad lie down."

"What gat ye to your dinner, "Lord Randal, my son?"
What gat ye to your dinner, my handsome young man?"   10
"I gat eels boil'd in broo'; mother, make my bed soon,
For I'm weary wi' hunting and fain wad lie down."

---

4. *wad*: would
11 *broo*`: broth

What became of your bloodhounds, Lord Randal, my son?
What became of your bloodhounds, my handsome young
      man?"—
"O they swell'd and they died; mother, make my bed soon, [15]
For I'm weary wi' hunting and fain wad lie down."

"O I fear ye are poison'd, Lord Randal, my son!
"O I fear ye are poison'd,my handsome young man!"—
"O yes! I am poison'd; mother, make my bed soon,
For I'm sick at the heart, and I fain wad lie down." [20]

FOR THE AMBITIOUS STUDENT

Get the Victor record of "Lord Randal" as sung by
John Charles Thomas, and play it for the class.

ANGUS MCGREGOR
Lew Sarett

Here is tragedy reduced to it's simplest terms, and told in ballad form, with many effective comparisions . Angus probably thought of himself as a trapper or prospector. But I call him a sportsman, because, in pitting himself against nature, he refused the advantage of ax, dirk, gun, or compass. He thought he was waging a fair contest; but he lost...

Angus McGregor lies brittle as ice, | A simple comparison
With snow tucked up to his jaws,
Somewhere tonight where the hemlocks moan
And crack in the wind like straws. | Another simile

Angus went cruising the woods last month,   5
With a blanket-roll on his back,
With never an ax, a dirk, a gun,
Or a compass in his pack.

"The hills at thirty below have
        teeth;
McGregor," I said, " you're daft   10
To tackle the woods like a simple child."
But he looked at me and laughed.

a= the cold
b= teeth
sharpness

He flashed his teeth in a grin and said:
"The earth is an open book;

a= earth
b= book
?

I've followed the woods for forty years,   15
I know each cranny and crook.

"I've battled her weather, her winds, her brutes,
I've stood with them toe to toe;
I can beat them back with my naked fist
And answer them blow for blow."   20

Angus McGregor sleeps under the stars,
With an icicle gripped in his hand,
Somewhere tonight where the | The *peaks* are personified.
    grim-lipped peaks
Brood on a haggard land.

Oh, the face of the moon is dark | Also personified are *moon,*
    tonight,   25 | *wind,* and *wolves.*
And dark the gaunt wind's sigh;
And the hollow laughter troubles me
In the wild wolves' cry.

FOR THE AMBITIOUS STUDENT

The kind of struggle that pits a man against some force of nature is common in plot stories. One of these that much resembles "Angus McGregor" is Jack London's short story, "To Build a Fire." In that story the man had a dog as ally; but he lacked Angus's forty years of experience, and the cold he faced was not thirty, but seventy-five degrees below zero.

HOW THE GREAT GUEST CAME
Edwin Markham

In the New Testament, Matthew 25: 34-40, Christ was preaching to his disciples, telling them of the Judgment Day:

Then shall the King say unto them on his right hand, Come , ye blessed of my Father, inherit the Kingdom prepared for you from the foundation of the world:

For I was an hungred, and ye gave me meat: I was thirsty, and ye gave me drink: I was a stranger, and ye took me in: Naked, and ye clothed me: I was sick, and ye visited me: I was in prison, and ye came unto me.

Then shall the righteous answer him, saying, Lord, when saw we thee an hungred, and fed thee? or thirsty, and gave thee drink?

When saw we thee a stranger, and took thee in? or naked, and clothed thee?

Or when saw we thee sick, or in prison, and came unto thee?

And the King shall answer and say unto them, Verily I say unto you, Inasmuch as ye have done it unto one of the least of these my brethen, ye have done it unto me.

With these memorable words in mind, read this story by Edwin Markham.

I

Before the Cathedral in grandeur rose,
At Ingelburg where the Danube goes;
Before its forest of silver spires
Went airily up to the clouds and fires;
Before the oak had ready a beam,   5

While yet the arch was stone and dream—
There where the altar was later laid,
Conrad, the cobbler, plied his trade.

II

Doubled all day on his busy bench,   10
Hard at his cobblng for master and hench,
He pounded away at a brisk rat-tat,
Shearing and shaping with pull and pat,
Hide well hammered and pegs sent home,
Till the shoe was fit for the Prince of Rome.   15
And he sang as the threads went to and fro:
"Whether 'tis hidden or whether it show,
Let the work be sound, for the Lord will know."

III

Tall was the cobbler, and gray and thin,
And a full moon shone where the hair had been.   20
His eyes peered out, intent and afar,
As looking beyond the things that are.
He walked as one who is done with fear,
Knowing at last that God is near.
Only the half of him cobbled the shoes: 25
The rest was away for the heavenly news.
Indeed, so thin was the mystic screen
That parted the Unseen from the Seen,
You could not tell, from the cobbler's theme,
If his dream were truth or this truth were dream.   30

IV

It happened one day at the year's white end,
Two neighbors called on their old-time friend;
And they found the shop, so meager and mean,
Made gay with a hundred boughs so green.
Conrad was stitching with face ashine,   35
But suddenly stopped as he twitched a twine:
"Old friends, good news! At dawn today,
As the cocks were scaring the night away,
The Lord appeared in a dream to me,
And said, "I am coming your Guest to be!"   40
So I've been busy with feet astir,
Strewing the floor with branches of fir.
The wall is washed and the shelf is shined,
And over the rafter the holly twined.
He comes today, and the table is spread   45
With milk and honey and wheaten bread."

V

His friends when home: and his face grew still
As he watched for the shadow across the sill.
He lived all the moments o'er and o'er,
When the Lord should enter the lowly door—   50
The knock, the call, the latched pulled up,
The lighted face, the offered cup.
He would wash the feet where the spikes had been;
He would kiss the hands where the nails went in;
And then at the last would sit with Him   55
And break bread as the day grew dim.

VI

While the cobbler mused, there passed his pane
A beggar drenched by the driving rain,
He called him in from the stony street
And gave him shoes for his bruiséd feet.   60
The beggar went and there came a crone,
Her face with wrinkles of sorrow sown.
A bundle of fagots bowed her back,
And she was spent with the wrench and rack.
He gave her his loaf and steadied her load   65
As she took her way on the weary road.
Then to his door came a little child,
Lost and afraid in the world so wild,
In the big, dark world. Catching it up,
He gave it the milk in the waiting cup,   70
And led it home to its mother's arms,
Out of the reach of the world's alarms.

VII

The day went down in the crimson west
And with it hope of the blesséd Guest,
and Conrad sighed as the world turned gray: 75
"Why is it, Lord, that your feet delay?
Did You forget that this was the day?"
Then soft in silence a Voice he heard:
"Lift up your heart, for I kept my word.
Three times I came to your friendly door;   80
Three times my shadow was on your floor.
I was the beggar with bruiséd feet;
I was the woman you gave to eat;
I was the child on the homeless street!"

— 223 —

ABOU BEN ADHEM
Leigh Hunt

Even more famous then "How the Great Guest Came," "Abou Ben Adhem" presents a variation on the same theme. This time an angel appears in a vision and teaches that love for mankind is love for God.

Abou Ben Adhem (may his trible increase!)
Awoke one night from a deep dream of peace,
And saw, within the moonlight in his room,

> He saw an *angel* making the *moonlight* look *like a lily in bloom.*

Making it rich, and like a lily in bloom,
An angel writing in a book of gold:—   5
Exceeding peace had made Ben Adhem bold,
And to the Presence in the room he said,
"What writest thou?"— The vision raised its head,
And, with a look made of all sweet accord,
Answered, "The name of those who love they Lord."
"And is mine one?" said Abou. "Nay, not so,"   10
Replied the angel. Abou spoke more low,
But cheerily still; and said, "I pray thee, then,
Write me as one that loves his fellow-men."

The angel wrote, and vanished. The next night
It came again, with a great wakening light,   15
And showed the name whom love of God had blessed,

> (He showed the names of those blessed by their love of God.)

And lo! Ben Adhem's name led all the rest.

BUCK FEVER
Bert Cooksley

If you read this short poem with full appreciation of its vivid imagery, you will share with the speaker in the poem an unforgettable experience, and perhaps you will sympathize with his feeling, expressed so dramatically in the last line.

Since early dawn, through manzanita brush,
    Across the rock streams and shallows, working up
To toplands, where the giant redwoods crush
    Their green lips to the new moon's spilling cup;
Since dawn we marked his tracks and trailed him down
    Far groves and clearings, fields and vales, until,   5
Breasting a summit, we beheld his crown
    Lifted a moment on a neighbor hill.

Stealthily then, our hearts aflame, we made
    Our way across to him, silent as death,
On hands and knees and stomachs—half afraid   10
    To let out or draw in a single breath;
And then we saw him all, thrice twenty feet
    Away—no more!—like something in a dream,
One hoof upraised, his satin flanks abeat,
    From out his nostrils brief, white clouds of steam.   15

My gun was up, I had perfect sight,
    My finger wrapped the trigger as if wired...
"A lifetime's chance," they said in camp that night:
    But I say no man living could have fired!

1. *manzanita:* a California shrub

BÊTE HUMAINE*
Francis Brett Young

Here, as in the poem immediately preceding, is a sharp, vivid little picture for you to visualize clearly, and an idea for you to ponder. If you think it would have been cruel to shoot the buck in "Buck Fever," where do you draw the line between a killing which seems wrong and one which does not? Some people, like the author of "Bête Humaine," would condemn the slaughter of any harmless creature. The best poetic expression of this theme will be read later in "The Rime of the Anicent Mariner," by Samuel Taylor Coleridge, which is reserved as the poem most worthy to close this volume.

Riding through Ruwu swamp, about sunrise,
I saw the world awake; and as the ray
Touched the tall grasses where they sleeping lay,
Lo, the bright air alive with dragonflies:
With brittle wings aquiver, and great eyes   5
Piloting crimson bodies, slender and gay.
I aimed at one, and struck it and it lay
Broken and lifeless, with fast-fading dyes...

Then my soul sickened with a sudden pain
And horror, at my own careless cruelty,   10
That in an idle moment I had slain
A creature whose sweet life it is to fly:
Like beasts that pray with tooth and claw...
      Nay, they
Must slay to live, but what excuse had I?   15

---

* *Bête Humaine*: human beast (French)

TACT

Arthur Guiterman

Into his volume, Lyric Laughter, *Guiterman has packed both fun and sense. You will enjoy his keen sense of humor. "Tact," included from that collection, is a little theme poem whose point will escape you unless you read carefully the statements of both the "sayers of sooth." I like the way the Sultan orders the execution of the first soothsayer.*

The Sultan was vexed by a dream
    That had troubled his slumbers;
For, feasting on lobsters and cream
    With half-ripened cucumbers
And lying with head to the South   5
    Give the Night Mare full power:
He dreamed that the teeth of his mouth
    Tumbled out in a shower!
So, calling a sayer of sooth
    To interpret the vision,   10
He charged him to utter the truth
    With unflinching precision.

"Oh, Fountain of Justice and fear
    Of the infidel foeman,
The vision," expounded the seer,   15
    "Is of dolorous omen;
For Allah who governs this ball,—
    May his favor restore you!—
Decress that your relatives all
    Shall drop dead right before you!"   20

The Sultan leaped up in a fit
    Of devouring fury.
He stayed not to issue a writ
    Or impanel a jury,
But, "Shorten this fellow!" he said,   25
    "And be rapid about it!"
So off went the soothsayer's head;
    He was wiser without it.

One sage in the discard, they sent
    To the mosque for another,   30
An augur of wilier bent
    Than his innocent brother.
"Now Allah be honored and praised!"
    Cried this shrewdest of mages,
"And high let your banner be raised,   35
    For the vision presages
That long shall your Majesty thrive
    Like the fertile plantations;
So long that my Lord shall survive
    E'en his youngest relations!"   40

The gratified Sultan expressed
    His delight beyond measure;
The prophet went home with a chest
    Overflowing with treasure.
Which proves,—'tis a principle still,   45
    Let the blunt-spoken weigh it—
A person may say what he will
    If he knows how to say it.

FOR YOUR VOCABULARY

I think you will benefit by a study of the word *infidel* (I.14). It consists of three parts: a prefix *in-*, a root or stem *fid-*, and a suffix *-el*. The root *fid-* means *belief* or *faith*. You find it in another word with the same root, *fidelity*, meaning faithfulness. Perhaps that is why so many dogs are called *Fido*! The word *infidel* means a non-believer, *i.e.* a person not of the same faith.

The prefix *in-* in this case means *not*. Other common words with this prefix are *in-accurate, in-sane, il-legible, im-movable, ir-reverent*. (Note how the *n* changes before *l, m, r*.) Make a list of at least ten words which begin with *in- (il-, im-, ir-)* meaning not. Define *antonym*.

MATILDA
Who Told Lies, and was Burned to Death
Hilaire Belloc

You must remember having read a famous fable by Aesop, called "Wolf! Wolf!" Here you will read a modern story on the same theme, by a clever English poet. In this poem the author is not to be taken seriously, although the poem is most effective when read with great earnestness. Give strong emphasis to the captialized words, and read in a very solemn, moral tone of voice. Pretend you are a prim and proper old lady trying to make little Mary and Peter stop telling fibs!

Matilda told such Dreadful Lies, | Don't fail to sound shocked.
It made one Gasp and Stretch one's Eyes;
Her Aunt, who, from her Earliest Youth,
Had kept a Strict Regard for Truth,
Attempted to believe Matilda: 5
The effort very nearly killed her, | Make it rime.
And would have done so, had not She | Watch all run-on lines.
Discovered this Infirmity.
For once, towards the Close of Day,
Matilda, growing tired of play,   10
And finding she was left alone,
Went tiptoe to the Telephone
And summoned the Immediate Aid
Of London's Noble Fire-Brigade
Within an hour the Gallant Band   15 | Louder and faster
Were pouring in on every hand,
From Putney, Hackney Downs, and Bow

With Courage high and Hearts a-glow
They galloped, roaring through the Town,
"Matilda's House is Burning Down!"   20
Inspired by British Cheers and Loud
Proceeding from the Frenzied Crowd,
They Ran Ladders through a Score
Of windows on the Ball Room Floor;
And took Peculiar Pains to Souse   25
The Pictures up and down the House,
Until Matilda's Aunt suceeded | Ease up slowly.
In showing them they were not needed;
And even then she had to Pay
To get the Men to go Away!   30

* * * * *

It happened that a few Weeks later
Her Aunt was off to the Theatre | Make it rime.
To see that Interesting Play
The Second Mrs. Tanqueray.
She had refused to take her Niece   35
To hear this Entertaining Piece:
(A Deprivation Just and Wise | Show your approval in
To punish her for Telling Lies.) | your voice.
That Night a Fire *did* break out—
You should have heard Matilida Shout!   40
You should have heard her Scream and Bawl,
And throw the window up and call
To the People passing in the Street—
(The rapidly increasing Heat

Encouraging her to obtain   45
 Their confidence) but all In Vain!
For every time She shouted, "Fire!"
They only answered, "Little Liar!"
And therefore when her Aunt returned,
Matilda, and the House, were

       Burned.   50

> Read it as if you felt that she
> got just what she deserved.

FOR THE AMBITIOUS STUDENT

Why not memorize this poem and give it as a humorous skit, with gestures? Other simliar moral tales by Belloc that you would enjoy are "Jim," "Godolphin Horne, who was cursed with the Sin of Pride, and became a Boot-Black," and "George, who played with a Dangerous Toy, and suffered a Catastrophe of Considerable Dimensons."

THE TWO WIVES
A New England Legend
Daniel Henderson

Ghost stories are "scary" only if read effectively. Here is a brief thriller which is meant to give the listener a shock. Put into your voice a good "graveyard tone."

Jonathan Moulton lost his wife—
Neighbors said he took her life.
Did he poison or strangle or smother?
Howsoever, he married another.
A shy and unsuspicious thing,   5
She wore his first wife's wedding ring.

Asleep she lay where the first wife's head
Had pillowed itself on that fateful bed,
But she woke at midnight shivering:
A cold hand plucked at her marriage ring,   10
And a voice at her ear had a graveyard tone:
"Give the dead her own!" | Slowly; stress each word.

Jonathan woke at his young bride's scream.
Up he sprang and brought in candles,
But ghostly wives have elfin sandals. 15 | She disappeared so suddenly.
He swore to his bride it was just a dream,
He lifted her hand in the candle gleam.
"I'll wager my all that it's still on."
But—Lord ha'e mercy!—the ring was gone!

THE STONE
Wilfrid Wilson Gibson

*The poet tells this story with simplicity and directness. He also
makes a skillful use of repetitions that give the poem a haunting
musical quality and help to sustain the mood of tragedy and doom
which pervades the story. The best reading of this poem will be
simple and direct, but will not neglect the music in the refrains.*

"And will you cut a stone for him,
To set above his head?
And will you cut a stone for him—
A stone for him?" she said.

Three days before, a splintered rock   5
Had struck her lover dead—
Had struck him in the quarry dead,
Where, careless of the warning call,
He loitered, while the shot was fired—
A lively stripling, brave and tall,   10
And sure of all his heart desired...
A flash, a shock,
A rumbling fall...
And, broken 'neath the broken rock,
A lifeless heap, with face of clay,   15
And still as any stone he lay,
With eyes that saw the end of all.

I went to break the news to her:
And I could hear my own heart beat

With dread of what my lips might say;   20
But some poor fool had sped before;
And, flinging wide her father's door,
Had blurted out the news to her,
Had struck her lover dead for her,
Had struck the girl's heart dead in her,   25
Had struck life, lifeless, at a word,
And dropped it at her feet:
Then hurried on his witless way,
Scarce knowing she had heard.

And when I came, she stood alone—   30
A woman, turned to stone:
And, though no word at all she said,
I knew that all was known.

Because her heart was dead,
She did not sigh nor moan.   35
His mother wept:
She could not weep. | Stress: *she*
Her lover slept:
She could not sleep. | Stress: *she*
Three days, three nights;   40
She did not stir:
Three days, three nights,
Were one to her,
Who never closed her eyes
From sunset to sunrise,   45
From dawn to evenfall—
Her tearless, staring eyes,

That, seeing naught, saw all.

The fourth night when I came home from work,
I found her at my door.   50
"And will you cut a stone for him?"
She said: and spoke no more:
But followed me, as I went in,
And sank upon a chair;
And fixed her grey eyes on my face,   55
With still, unseeing stare.
And, as she waited patiently,
I could not bear to feel
Those still, grey eyes that followed me,
Those eyes that plucked the heart from me,   60
Those eyes that sucked the breath from me
And curdled the warm blood in me,
Those eyes that cut me to the bone,
And pireced my marrow like cold steel.

And so I rose, and sought a stone;   65
And cut it, smooth and square:
And, as I worked, she sat and watched,
Beside me, in her chair,
Night after night, by candlelight,
I cut her lover's name: 70
Night after night, so still and white,
And like a ghost she came;
And sat beside me, in her chair,
And watched with eyes aflame.
She eyed each stroke,   75

And hardly stirred:
She never spoke
A single word:
And not a sound or murmur broke
The quiet, save the mallet-stroke.   80

With still eyes ever on my hands,
With eyes that seemed to burn my hands,
My wincing, overwearied hands,
She watched, with bloodless lips apart,
And silent, indrawn breath: 85
And every stroke my chisel cut,
Death cut still deeper in her heart:
The two of us were chiselling,
Together, I and death.

And when at length the job was done,   90
And I had laid the mallet by,
As if, at last, her peace were won,
She breathed his name: and, with a sigh,
Passed slowly through the open door:
And never crossed my threshold more.   95

Next night I laboured late, alone
To cut her name upon the stone. | Stress: *her*

FOR YOUR VOCABULARY

One of the suffixes, or endings, you most frequently
find on words is *-less*, meaning "without." In this

poem alone there were these: *careless, lifeless, tearless, bloodless*. Here are three endings which mean "full of": *-ful* e.g., *careful; -some*, e.g., *troublesome; -ous*, e.g., *wondrous*. Make words with one or more of these various endings out of each word in the following list: *beauty, color, faith, loath, pity, soul, tooth.*

ANNABEL LEE
Edgar Allan Poe

A genius in using words to produce musical effects, Edgar Allan Poe is at his best in "Annabel Lee." It is sheer music from begining to end. Into the very words themselves Poe has incorporated a musical accompaniment to his story: therefore, as you read, remember that you are both narrator and musician. Your task as musician will not be difficult, for even the poorest reader must find some music in the lyric beauty of these lines. But don't become so hypnotized by the mournful music in the poem that you lose sight of the deeply moving story and its changing moods: the tenderness and wonder in the heart of the lover as he speaks of his dead sweetheart, his bold—almost defiant—assertion that neither heaven nor hell can separate him from his loved one, and the peace that comes from the spiritual reunion with his beloved at the end.

It was many and many a year ago,
    In a kingdom by the sea
That a maiden there lived whom you may know
    By the name of *Annabel Lee*;
And this maiden she lived with no other thought   ⁵
    Than to love and be loved by me.

I was a child and *she* was a child,
    In this kingdom by the sea,
But we loved with a love that was more than love—
    I and my *Annabel Lee*—   ¹⁰
With a love that the winged seraphs of heaven
    Coveted her and me.

And this was the reason that, long ago,
    In this kingdom by the sea,
A wind blew out of a cloud, chilling   15
    My beautiful *Annabel Lee*;
So that her highborn kinsmen came
    And bore her away from me,
To shut her up in a sepulchre
    In this kingdom by the sea.   20

The angels, not half so happy in heaven,
    Went envying her and me—
Yes!—that was the reason (as all men know,
    In this kingdom by the sea)
That the wind came out of the cloud by night,   25
    Chilling and killing my *Annabel Lee*,

But our love it was stronger by far than the love
    Of those who were older than we—
    Of many far wiser than we—
And neither the angels in heaven above,   30
    Nor the demons down under the sea,
Can ever dissever my soul from the soul
    Of the beautiful *Annabel Lee*;

For the moon never beams, without bringing me dreams
    Of the beautiful *Annabel Lee*;   35
And the stars never rise, but I feel the bright eyes
    Of the beautiful *Annabel Lee*;
And so, all the night-tide, I lie down by the side
Of my darling—my darling—my life and my bride,

In the sepulchre there by the sea— [40]
In her tomb by the sounding sea.

FOR YOUR VOCABULARY

In line 11 Poe used the word *seraphs*. Instead of this English form, he might have used the Hebrew plural, *seraphim*, which is often found with its companion word, *cherubim*. (Did you ever hear anyone say "cherubims"? Why there is no such word?) In English we have many words with both foreign and English plural forms. Look up in the dictionary the plurals of *gladiolus*, *narcissus*, *formula*, *vertebra*, *curriculum*, *memorandum*, *appendix*, *index*, *bandit*, *beau*.

BALLAD OF THE HUNTSMAN
Selma Robinson

A heartless girl lightly rejecting her devoted lover is a common story in the early ballads. In this brief modern poem that same old story, with a sudden and gruesome ending, is again dramatically presented. There are only two speakers—the girl and her lover. If you remember to watch the quotation marks, you will always know who is speaking.

When you read it aloud, use two tones of voice to indicate the two speakers. You can do much with your voice to give an impression of their characters.

And "No" she answered to his plea;
    "We never can be wed
Though you ask me a hundred times," said she.
    "Or a thousand times?" she said.

"Oh , then, farewell my golden dear,   5
    Farewell my stony-hearted.
I shall go away, far, far fom here."
    Said she: "It's time you started."

"I shall go away with my bag and my gun
    To hunt and forget," said he.   10
"I shall put my woven jacket on | He continues.
    And my boots that lace to the knee."

"It's time you left and I wish you luck.
    If you bag a grouse or a pheasant

Or a spotted quail," she said, "or a duck,   15
  Bring one to me for a present."
"Each time I aim into the blue
  Of the sky or the brown of the marsh,
I shall think I point my gun at you,"
  Said he, and his voice was harsh.   20

A day and a week and a month went by
  And again he stood at her door,
Pale and worn, with his cap awry,
  And stained were the clothes he wore;

Stained was his coat of woven wool   25
  And stained his boots of calf.
" But I've brought you a gift, my beautiful,"
  And he began to laugh.

"That's neither grouse nor spotted quail
  That you hide from me," she said.   30
"Any why is your face so pale, so pale, | She continues.
  And why are your hands so red?"

"Nor grouse nor quail nor duck I give,"
  He said, and spread apart
His hands, and there like a crimson sieve   35
  He offered his riddled heart.

A BALLAD OF MARJORIE
Dora Sigerson

Rarely do you find a ballad composed entirely of conversation, in which every word is within quotation marks. But here is one. There is a continuous alternation of questions and answers, with not a single "she asked," or "he answered." The story is tragic; it involves the simple emotions— love, horror, regret, sorrow; it is written in the standard ballad stanza pattern. The ending will come as a surprise.

"What ails you that you look so pale.
    O fisher of the sea?"
"'Tis for a mournful tale I own,
    Fair maiden Marjorie."

Majorie speaks.
Watch the quotes.

"What is the dreary tale to tell,   5
    O toiler of the sea?"
"I cast my net into the waves,
    Sweet maiden Marjorie.

"I cast my net into the tide
    Before I made for home: 10
Too heavy for my hands to raise,
    I drew it through the foam."

"What saw you that you look so pale,
    Sad searcher of the sea?"
"A dead man's body from the deep   15
    My haul had brought to me!"

"And was he young, and was he fair?"
    "Oh, cruel to behold!
In his white face the joy of life
    Not yet was grown a-cold."   20

"Oh, pale you are, and full of prayer
    For one who sails the sea."
"Because the dead looked up and spoke,
    Poor maiden Marjorie."

"What said he, that you seem so sad,   25
    O fisher of the sea?"
(Alack! I know it was my love, | She speaks to herself.
    Who fain would speak to me!)

"He said: 'Beware a woman's mouth— | The fisherman quotes
    A rose that bears a thorn.' "   30 | the corpse.
"Ah, me! these lips shall smile no more | Her own lips, of course.
    That gave my lover scorn." | She considers her coldness
                              | the cause of his suicide.

"He said: 'Beware a woman's eyes;
    They pierce you with their death.' "
"Then falling tears shall make them blind   35
    That robbed my dear of breath."

"He said: 'Beware a woman's hair—
    A serpent's coil of gold.' "
"Then will I shear the cruel locks
    That crushed him in their fold."   40

"He said: 'Beware a woman's heart
    As you would shun the reef.' "
"So let it break within my breast,
    And perish of my grief." | "So let my heart break."

"He raised his hands; a womans name   45
    Thrice bitterly he cried.
My net had parted with the strain;
    He vanished in the tide."

"A woman's name! What name but mine,
    O fisher of the sea?"   50
"A woman's name, but not your name,
    Poor maiden Marjorie."

Do you think the knowledge conveyed in the last two lines will make Marjorie's grief easier, or harder to bear?

Point out the four comparisons in the speeches of the dead man. Do they add to the effectiveness of his warnings?

If this ballad seems pleasantly musical, the effect is due in part to the alliteration. Point out several striking examples.

THE COURTIN'
James Russell Lowell

*In some modern poems, dialect helps to create the "local color"
or "flavor" of a situation, much as do the obsolete words in the old
Scottish ballads. Among the first writers in America to use dialect was
James Russell Lowell. "The Courtin'," composed in the language of
a typical Yankee farmer, has become an American classic.*

*In reading this poem of Huldy and her boyfriend Zekle, the first thing
you must do, of course, is to make sure the meaning of the dialect
words. An easy way to dispose of this difficulty is for each member of
the class to be responsible for clearing up the dialect in one stanza. Or
each pupil may bring a list of the words he cannot work out for himself,
and have the others help him to an understanding of these before the
poem is read in class. Many words which look queer will be quite
understandable if spoken aloud; in this matter of dialect the ear is
much more helpful than the eye. Use a nasal Yankee twang if you can.
If you develop the ability to read dialect easily, you will come to look
upon it not merely as a difficulty to be overcome but as a device which
adds materially to your pleasure in reading.*

God makes sech nights, all white an' still
    Fur'z you can look or listen,
Moonshine an' snow on field an' hill,
    All silence an' all glisten.

Zekle crep' up quite unbeknown
    An' peeked in thru the winder,
An' there sot Huldy all alone,
    'ith no one nigh to hender.

5

A fireplace filled the room's one side
    With half a cord o' wood in—   10
There warn't no stoves (tell comfort died)
    To bake ye to a puddin'.

A wa'nut logs shot sparkles out
    Towards the pootiest, bless her,
An' leetle flames danced all about   15
    The chiny on the dresser.

Agin the chimbley crook-necks hung,
    An' in amongst 'em rusted
The ole queen's-arm thet gran'ther Young
    Fetched back f'om Concord busted.   20

The very room, coz she was in,
    Seemed warm f'om floor to ceilin',
An' she looked full ez rosy agin
    Ez the apples she was peelin'.

'Twas kin' o' kingdom-come to look   25
    On sech a blessèd cretur;
A dogrose blusin' to a brook
    Ain't modester nor sweeter.

He was six foot o' man, A 1,
    Clear grit an' human natur';   30
None couldn't quicker pitch a ton
    Nor dror a furrer straighter.

---

17. *crook-necks*: squashes   19. *queen's-arm*: a musket
25. *kingdom-come*: heavenly

He'd sparked it with full twenty gals,
    Hed squired 'em, danced 'em, druv 'em,
Fust this one, an' then thet by spells—   35
    All is, he couldn't love 'em.

But long o' her his veins 'ould run
    All crinkly like curled maple;
The side she breshed felt full o' sun
    Ez a south slope in Ap'il.   40

She thought no v'ice hed sech a swing
    Ez hisn in the choir;
My! when he made Ole Hunderd ring
    She *knowed* the Lord was nigher.

An' she'd blush scarlit, right in prayer,   45
    When her new meetin'-bunnet
Felt somehow thru' its a crown a pair
    O' blue eyes sot upun it.

Thet night, I tell ye, she looked *some*!
    She seemed to 've gut a new soul,   50
For she felt sartin-sure he'd come,
    Down to her very shoe-sole.

She heered a foot, an' knowed it tu,
    A-raspin' on the scraper,—

---

32. *dror a furrer*: draw a furrow; to plow
43. *Ole Hunderd*: the tune to which the Doxology ("Praise God from whom all blessings flow") is usually sung

All ways to once her feelin's flew
    Like sparks in burnt-up paper.   55

He kin' o' l'itered on the mat,
    Some doubtfle o' the sekle;
His heart kep' goin' pity-pat,
    But hern went pity Zekle.   60

An' yit she gin her cheer a jerk
    Ez though she wished him furder,
An' on her apples kep' to work,
    Parin' away like murder.

"You want to see my Pa, I s'pose?"   65
    "Wal... no... I come dasignin'"—
"To see my Ma? She's sprinklin' clo'es
    Agin tomorrer's i'nin'."

To say why gals act so or so,
    Or don't 'ould be presumin';   70
Mebby to mean *yes* an' say *no*
    Comes nateral to women.

He stood a spell on one foot fust,
    Then stood a spell on t'other,
An' on which one he felt the wust   75
    He couldn't ha' told ye nuther.

---

58. *sekle*: sequel, that which is to follow

Says he, " I'd better call agin";
 Says she, "Think likely, Mister";
Thet last word pricked him like a pin,
 An'... Wal, he up an' kist her.   80

When Ma bimeby upon 'em slips,
 Huldy sot pale ez ashes,
All kin' o' smily roun' the lips
 An' teary roun' the lashes.

For she was jes' the quiet kind   85
 Whose naturs never vary,
Like streams that keep a summer mind
 Snow-hid in Jenooary.

The blood clost roun' her heart felt glued
 Too tight for all expressin'   90
Tell mother see how metters stood,
 An' gin 'em both her blessin'.

Then her red come back like the tide
 Down to the Bay o' Fundy,
An' all I know is they was cried   95
 In meetin' come nex' Sunday.

In many ways Huldy and Zekle are typical human beings. Try to state at least three truths of human nature that are illustrated in this poem. Analyze the simile in lines 85-89, and then make a generalization about human nature from this comment about Huldy.

---

94. *Bay o' Fundy*: a bay between Nova Scotia and New Brunswick noted for its swift 70-foot tides.
95. *they was cried*: Their engagement was announced in church.

Stories in Verse

DA WHEESTLIN' BARBER
T.A.Daly

America is often called the Melting Pot because so many races and nationalites are here molded into one great people. Naturally, when these various peoples came to America, they spoke the new language with their own dialects.

On the sidewalks of New York, Daly listened to these new Americans, and in many a humorous poem recorded the dialects he heard. Most of his poems are in the Italian dialect, which he has employed expertly. Daly is a poet for eveyone—his poems are about common, everyday affairs of life. And the dialect seems always to intensify the tone of the story, whether it is humorous, or sad, or patriotic, as the three peoms that follow here will show. In the first of them the amusing anecdote of the whistling barber is told with sure skill.

Las' night you hear da op'ra?
>   Eef you was uppa stair
An' eef you know Moralli
>   You mebbee saw heem dere.
Moralli? He's a barber,   5
>   But verra bright an' smart,
An' crazy for da op'ra;
>   He knows dem all by heart.
He's alla tima wheestlin',
>   An' often you can find   10
Jus' from da tune he wheestles
>   W'at thoughts ees een hees mind.
Eef you would ask a question,

— 252 —

Da answer you would gat
Ees notheeng but som' music— ¹⁵
Ha! w'at you theenk of dat?

Las' week hees wife Lucia—
Fine woman, too, is she—
She gave to heem som' babies,
Not only wan, but three! ²⁰
Eef to your shop som' neighbors
Should breeng sooch news to you
Eet sure would jus'excite you
To say a word or two;
But dessa Joe Moralli, ²⁵
Dees music-crazy loon,
He never stopped hees wheestlin'—
But justa changed hees tune.
Dees answer from hees music
Was all dat dey could gat; ³⁰
"Trio from "Trovatore."
Ha! w'at you theenk of dat?

He nevva stopped hees wheestlir'
Dat " Trovatore" tune,
Not even w'en he's dreenkin' ³⁵
Weeth frands een da saloon.
He wheestled eet dat evenin'
W'en home he went to see
Hees granda wife, Lucia,
An' leetla babies three. ⁴⁰

But w'en he stood bayfore dem
    He was so full weeth dreenk,
He looked upon dose babies
    An' wheestle— W'at you theenk?
O! den da tune he wheestled   45
    Was—how-you-call-eet?—"pat";
"Sextetta from Lucia."
    Ha! w'at you theenk of dat?

DA LEETLA BOY

T.A.Daly

In this poem Daly employs his skill at dialect to stir our sympathy deeply by a pathetic story. A father speaks brokenly—

Da spreeng ees com'; but oh, da joy
    Eet ees too late!
He was so cold, my leetla boy,
    He no could wait.

I no can count how manny week, 5
How manny day, dat he ees seeck;
How manny night I seet an' hold
Da leetla hand dat was so cold.
He was so patience, oh, so sweet!
Eet hurts my throat for theenk of eet; 10
An' all he evra ask ees w'en
Ees gona com' da spreeng agen.
Wan day, wan brighta sunny day,
He see, across da alleyway,
Da leetla girl dat's livin' dere 15
Eed raise her window for da air,
An' put outside a leetla pot
Of—w'at-you-call?—forgat-me-not.
So smalla flower, so leetla theeng!
But steell eet mak' hees hearta seeng: 20
"Oh, now, at las' ees com' da spreeng!
Da leetla plant ees glad for know
Da sun ees com' for mak' eet grow.

So, too, I am grow warm and strong."
So lika dat he seeng hees song.   25
But, ah! da night com' down an' den
Da weenter ees sneak back agen,
An' een da alley all da night
Ees fall da snow, so cold, so white,
An' cover up da leetla pot   30
Of—w'at-you-call?—forgat-me-not.
All night da leetla hand I hold
Ees grow so cold, so cold, so cold!

Da spreeng ees com'; but oh, da joy
        Eet ees too late!   35
He was so cold, my leetla boy,
        He no could wait.

TWO 'MERICANA MEN

T.A.Daly

Here we see the Melting Pot at work. This is a grand patriotic poem—a bit of real Americanism—done with just the right dash of humor.

Beeg Irish cop dat walk hees beat
    By dees peanutta stan',
First two, t'ree week w'en we are meet
    Ees call me "Dagoman."
An' w'en he see how mad I gat,   5
    Wheech, eesa pleass heem, too,
Wan day he say; "W'at's matter dat,
    Ain't 'Dago'name for you?
Dat's 'Mericana name, you know,
    For man from Eetaly;   10
Eet ees no harm for call you so,
    Den why be mad weeth me?"
First time he talka deesa way
    I am too mad for speak,
But nexta time I justa say: 15
    "All righta Meester Meeck!"

O! my, I nevva hear bayfore
    Sooch langwadge like he say;
An' he don't look at me no more
    For mebbe two, t'ree day.   20
But pretta soon agen I see
    Dees beeg poleecaman

Dat com' an' growl an' say to me:
    "Hello, Eyetalian!
Now, mebbe so you gon' deny   25
    Dat dat'sa name for you."
I smila back an' mak' reply:
    "No, Irish, dat'sa true."
"Ha! joe," he cry, "you theenk dat we
    Should call you 'Merican?"   30
"Dat's gooda 'nough," I say, "for me,
    Eef dat's w'at you are, Dan."

So now all times we speaka so
    Like gooda 'Merican:
He say to me, "Good morna, Joe,"   35
    I say, "Good morna, Dan."

FOR THE AMBITIOUS STUDENT

Memorize and give one of the Daly poems in this book, or if you would like to read further, get *Selected Poems of T.A.Daly* and choose some other example of his use of dialect. Some poems in which he has succesfully used an Irish brogue are in this volume.

THE CREATION
James Weldon Johnson

God's Trombones *is a series of sermons in verse by one of America's greatest Negro poets. "The Creation," the first sermon, tells with great earnestness and wonderful imagery the familiar Bible story found in the first chapter of Genesis. The author is trying to give us an authentic reproduction of the style of the sermons preached by the best Negro preachers, who, he says, "were all saturated with the sublime phraseology of the Hebrew prophets and steeped in the idioms of King James English, so when they preached and warmed to their work they spoke another language, a language far removed from traditional Negro dialect."*

"The old-time Negro preacher of parts," writes Mr. Johnson, "was above all an orator, and in good measure an actor. He knew the secret of oratory, that at bottom it is a progression of rhythmic words more than it is anything else...He preached a personal and anthropomorphic God, a sure-enough heaven and a red-hot hell. His imagination was bold and unfettered. He had the power to sweep his hearers before him; and so himself was often swept away. At such times his lanuage was not prose but poetry."

Make your reading sympathetic; above all, don't make it comic. Note that there are no quotation marks enclosing the speeches of God.

And God stepped out on space,
And He looked around and said:
I'm lonely—
I'll make me a world.

And far as the eye of God could see   5
Darkness covered everything,

Blacker than a hundred midnights
Down in a cypress swamp.

Then God smiled,
And the light broke,   10
And the darkness rolled up on one side,
And the light stood shining on the other,
And God said: That's good!

Then God reached out and took the light in His hands,
And God rolled the light around in His hands   15
Until He made the sun;
And He set the sun a-blazing in the heavens.
And the light that was left from making the sun
God gathered it up in a shining ball
And flung it against the darkness,   20
Spangling the night with the moon and stars.
Then down between
The darkness and the light
He hurled the world;
And God said: That's good!   25

Then God himself stepped down—
And the sun was on His right hand,
And the moon was on His left;
The stars were clustered about His head,
And the earth was under His feet.   30
And God walked, and where He trod
His footsteps hollowed the valleys out
And bulged the mountains up.

Then He stopped and looked and saw
That the earth was hot and barren.   35
So God stepped over to the edge of the world
And He spat out the seven seas—
He batted His eyes, and the lightnings flashed—
He clapped His hands, and the thunders rolled—
And the waters above the earth came down,   40
The cooling waters came down.

Then the green grass sprouted,
And the little red flowers blossomed,
The pine tree pointed his finger to the sky,
And the oak spread out his arms,   45
The lakes cuddled down in the hollows of the ground,
And the rivers ran down to the sea;
And God smiled again,
And the rainbow appeared,
And curled itself around His shoulder.   50

Then God raised His arm and He waved His hand
Over the sea and over the land,
And He said: Bring forth! Bring forth!
And quicker than God could drop His hand,
Fishes and fowls   55
And beasts and birds
Swam the rivers and the seas,
Roamed the forests and the woods,
And split the air with their wings.
And God said: That's good!   60

Then God walked around,
And God looked around
On all that He had made.
He looked at His sun,
And He looked at His moon,   65
And He looked at His little stars;
He looked on His world
With all its living things,
And God said: I'm lonely still.

Then God sat down—   70
On the side of a hill where He could think;
By a deep, wide river He sat down;
With His head in His hands,
God thought and thought,
Till He thought: I'll make me a man!   75

Up from the bed of the river
God scooped the clay;
And by the bank of the river
He kneeled Him down;
And there the great God Almighty   80
Who lit the sun and fixed it in the sky,
Who flung the stars to the most far corner of the night,
Who rounded the earth in the middle of His hand;
This Great God,
Like a mammy bending over her baby,   85
Kneeled down in the dust
Toiling over a lump of clay
Till He shaped it in His own image;

Then into it He blew the breath of life,
And man became a living soul.   90
Amen. Amen.

FOR THE AMBITIOUS STUDENT

If you liked "The Creation," you would enjoy several other poems from the same volume, *God's Trombones*. Get it and read one or two to the class. Most of these have been recorded by the author himself. If you can obtain the records, you will hear these sermons as they were meant to be rendered.

DE BOLL WEEVIL
American Negro Ballad

When a group of Negros in the South start to sing, they are apt to break into this song setting forth the destructive powers of the little insect pest, the boll weevil, whose depredations on the cotton fields of the South are said to have caused a loss greater than the total cost of the War between the states. It is small wonder, then, that the Southern sharecroppers looked upon this little fellow as their arch-enemy, and sang endless variations of this popular ballad. For the following version I have taken stanzas from various sources and arranged and modified them so that they make a fairly smooth story. The tune is adapted from Carl Sandburg's **American Songbag.**

Oh, de boll weevil am a little black bug,
    Come from Mexico, dey say.
Come all de way to Texas,
    Jus' a-lookin' for a place to stay,
Jus' a-lookin' for a home, jus' a lookin' for a home. [5]

De first time I seen de boll weevil,
    He was settin' on de square.
De next time I seen de boll weevil,
    He had all of his fam'ly dere,
Jus' a-lookin' for a home, jus' a- lookin for a home.   10

Boll weevil say to his wife:
    "Bettah stan' up on yo' feet,
Look way down in Mississippi,
    At de cotton we's got to eat,
De whole night long, de whole night long."   15

Boll weevil say to de lightnin' bug:
    "Can I get up a trade wid you?
If I was a lightnin' bug,
    I'd work de whole night through,
De whole night long, de whole night long."   20

De farmer take de boll weevil,
    An' he put him in de hot san';
De weevil say, "Dis is mighty hot,
    But I'll stand it like a man.
Dis'll be my home, dis'll be my home."   25

De farmer take de boll weevil
    An' he put him in a lump of ice.
De weevil say to de farmer,
    "Dis is mighty cool an' nice,
Dis'll be my home, dis'll be my home."   30

---

7. *square*: The top of the cotton-boll

De farmer take de boll weevil
    An' he put him in paris green;
De weevil say to de farmer,
    "Best bed I ever seen;
Dis'll be my home, dis'll be my home."   35

Boll weevil say to de farmer:
    "You can ride in dat Fohd machine.
But w'en I get through wid yo' cotton,
    Can't buy no gasoline,
Won't have no home, won't have no home."   40

Boll weevil say to de doctah:
    "Beetah pull out all dem pills.
W'en I get through wid de farmer,
    Can't pay no doctah's bills.
I have a home, I have a home."   45

Boll weevil say to de preacher:
    "Beetah close up dem church doors,
W'en I get through wid de farmer,
    Can't pay de preacher no mo.
I have a home, I have a home."   50

De merchant got half de cotton,
    De boll weevil got de res'—
Didn't leave de farmer's wife
    But one ol' cotton dress.
An' it's full of holes, an' it's full of holes.   55

De farmer say to de merchant,
    "We's in an awful fix;
De boll weevil et all de cotton up
    An' left us only sticks.
We's got no home, oh, we's got no home."   60

De farmer say to de merchant:
    "I want some meat an' meal!"
"Get away f'm here, yo` son-of-a-gun,
    Yo' got boll weevils in yo' fiel';
Deys got yo' home, dey's got yo' home."   65

Boll weevil say to de farmer,
    "I wish you all is well!"
Farmer say to de boll weevil:
    "I wish you wuz in hell!
I'd have a home, I'd have a home."   70

THE EMPEROR

Tu Fu

Translated from the Chinese by E. Powys Mathers

Most of you have seen some exquisite pieces of porcelain so delicate your mother has said, "Be careful! Don't handle that." This fragile loveliness is a quality that you will find in Chinese poetry. The little poem following is such a piece, delicate, beautiful, with a touch of the humor and wisdom which we think of as typically Chinese.

On a throne of new gold the Son of the Sky is sitting
    among his Mandarins. He shines with jewels and
    is like a sun surrounded by stars.

The Mandarins speak gravely of grave things: but the
    Emperor's thought has flown out by the open win-
    dow.   5

In her pavillion of porcelain the Empress is sitting among
    her women. She is like a bright flower among leaves.

She dreams that her beloved stays too long at council,
    and wearily she moves her fan.   10

A breathing of perfumed air kisses the face of the Em-
    peror.

1. the Son of the Sky: the Emperor of China
2. Mandarins(man'da-rinz): public officals of high rank, entitled to wear
    distinguishing buttons on their hats.
7. porcelain: a fine pottery, commonly called china.

"My beloved moves her fan, and sends me a perfume
   from her lips."

Towards the pavilion of porcelain walks the Emperor,   15
shining with his jewels; and he leaves his grave Man-
   darins to look at each other in silence.

FOR THE AMBITIOUS STUDENT

This is the first of a few poems in Part Two of this book which are translated from foreign languages. Although a poem necessarily loses some of its excellence in translation, I have included these few to remind you of the great storehouses of literature in languages other than English. Perhaps this one example of Chinese poetry will arouse in you a desire to read some more Chinese poems. If you find any others that you like, bring them to class and read them to your classmates.

FROM THE PANCHATANTRA

Anonymous

Translated from the Sanskrit by Arthur W. Ryder

*The **Panchatantra** (The Five Books) is one of the world's famous old collections of stories, like **Aesop's Fables** and the **Arabian Nights**. It is written in Sanskrit, the language of ancient India. Inserted into the stories at many points are bits of Hindu wisdom and philosophy in verse. Some of these have a slight thread of narrative, like the two that follow.*

I. POVERTY

A beggar to the graveyeard hied
And there "Friend corpse, arise, " he cried;
"One moment lift my heavy weight
Of poverty; for I of late
Grow weary, and desire instead   5
Your comfort; you are good and dead."
The Corpse was silent. He was sure
'Twas better to be dead than poor.

II. THE SERPENT AND THE MOUSE

Within a basket tucked away
In slow starvation's grim decay,
A broken-hearted serpent lay.

But see the cheerful mouse that gnaws
A hole, and tumbles in his jaws   5
At night—new hope's unbidden cause!

Now see the serpent, sleek with meat,

Who hastens through the hole, to beat
From quarters cramped, a glad retreat!

So fuss and worry will not do;   10
For fate is somehow muddling through
To good or bad for me and you.

FOR THE AMBITIOUS STUDENT

Besides the *Panchatantra*, India has produced several other famous books. One of the world's great narrative poems is the *Ramayana*, the epic story of the Hindu hero, Rama. This great hero-story has been put into English prose for young Americans by Dhan Gopal Mukerji, an Indian scholar who was educated in America and lived here. In the introduction to his book, *Rama, the Hero of India*, Mr. Mukerji says:

> "In India itself there is not a Hindu who can not tell you from memory the story of Rama. Though but ten percent of the population of India can read and write, yet there is hardly a Hindu who is ignorant of the *Ramayana*. From babyhood on we hear our epics. First our mothers, then our minstrels recite the heroic tales of the ancient times. And as we grow up we learn to recite it for our own pleasure."

A good way for you to start to build an understanding of our neighbors in India would be to read the story of Rama, as Mr. Mukerji told it.

THE ERLKING

Johann Wolfgang von Goethe

Translated from the German by Sir Walter Scott

*Probably you are already familiar with this famous story. The Erkling (**der Erlkönig***) is the king of the elves, who works mischief and ruin to children. This time his victim is a small boy who is nestled in the arm of his father, riding swiftly home through the woods on a cold, stormy night. Though the father spurs his horse to its utmost effort, the erlking is not to be cheated his prey.*

O who rides by night thro' the woodland so wild?
It is the fond father embracing the child;
And close the boy nestles within his loved arm
To hold himself fast, and to keep himself warm.

"O father, see yonder! see yonder!" he says;⁵
"My boy, upon what dost thou fearfully gaze?"
"O, 'tis the Erlking with his crown and shroud."
"No, my son, it is but a dark wreath of the cloud."

$|$ The Erlking speaks.

"O come and go with me, thou loveliest child;
By many a gay sport shall thy time be beguiled; ¹⁰
My mother keeps for thee full many a fair toy,
And many a fine flower shall she pluck for my boy."

"O father, my father, and did you not hear
The Erlking whisper so low in my ear?"
"Be still, my heart's darling— my child, be at ease; ¹⁵

It was but the wild blast as it sung thro' the trees."

"O wilt thou go with me, thou | The Erlking
    loveliest boy?
My daughter shall tend thee with care and with joy;
She shall bear thee so lightly thro' wet and thro' wild,
And press thee, and kiss thee, and sing to my child." 20

"O father, my father, and saw you not plain
The Erlking's pale daughter glide past thro' the rain?"
"O yes, my loved treasure, I knew it full soon;
It was the gray willow that danced to the moon."

"O come and go with me, no longer | The Erlking
    delay, 25
Or else, silly child, I will drag thee away."
"O father! O father! now, now keep your hold,
The Erlking has seized me—his grasp is so cold!"

Sore trembled the father; he spurr'd thro' the wild,
Clasping close to his bosom his shuddering child;
He reaches his dwelling in doubt and in dread,
But, clasp'd to his bosom, the infant was dead.

FOR THE AMBITIOUS STUDENT

Set to effective music by Schubert, "The Erlking" is well-known as a popular concert song. Perhaps some one in the class can bring to school the recording by Ernestine Schumann-Heink or the one by Sigrid

Onegin. The music adds much to the dramatic horror of the tragedy.

It is interesting to hear this poem read by four pupils, one for each of the three characters and one for a narrator. The narrator speaks the first and last stanzas, and the two words, "he says," in line 5.

KITTY OF COLERAINE

Anonymous

The Irish are noted for their light-hearted blarney, and here we get a taste of it. Just as in "Bluebeard," the deliberate, over-use of rime contributes to the fun. Some of the rimes are not apparent until you give the Irish pronunciation, so you'll have to polish up your brogue. Notice, too, as you read, that the story is told with a lilting swing that just suits its gay nonsense.

As beautiful Kitty one morning was tripping
     With a pitcher of milk for the fair of Coleraine,
When she saw me she stumbled, the pitcher down tumbled,
     And all the sweet buttermilk watered the plain.
"Oh, what shall I do now? 'Twas looking at you now!   5
     I'm sure such a pitcher I'll ne'er see again.
'Twas the pride of my dairy. Oh, Barney McCleary,
     You're sent as a plague to the girls of Coleraine."

I sat down beside her, and gently did chide her
     That such a misfortune should give her such pain;   10
A kiss then I gave her, and before I did leave her
     She vowed for such pleasure she'd break it again.
'Twas the haymaking season—I can't tell the reason—
     Misfortunes will never come single, 'tis plain!
For very soon after poor Kitty's disaster   15
     The devil a pitcher was whole in Coleraine.

BARNEY O'HEA
Samuel Lover

Here is another poem with an Irish lilt and Irish wit. Sure and the Irish are the great ones for a bit of blarney and the smooth tongue and the impudent grin!

Now let me alone, though I know you won't,

> For two stanzas she gives Barney some good advice.

    Impudent Barney O'Hea!
    It makes me outrageous
    When you're so contagious,
And you'd better look out for the stout Corney Creagh;   5
    For he is the boy
    That believes I'm his joy,
So you'd better behave yourself, Barney O'Hea!
    Impudent Barney,
    None of your blarney,   10
    Impudent Barney O'Hea!
I hope you're not going to Bandon Fair,
For indeed I'm not wanting to meet you there,
    Impudent Barney O' Hea!
    For Corney's at Cork,   15
    And my brother's at work,
And my mother sits spinning at home all the day,
    So no one will be there
    Of poor me to take care,
So I hope you won't follow me, Barney O' Hea!   20
    Impudent Barney,

---

5. Rime with line 2.

None of your blarney,

Impudent Barney O'Hea!

But as I was walking up Bandon
    Street,

Just who do you think that myself
    should meet,

Now she tells the reader how well Barney accepted her advice!

25

But impudent Barney O'Hea!

He said I looked killin',

I called him a villain,

And bid him that minute get out of the way.

He said I was joking,   30

And grinned so provoking,

I couldn't help laughing at Barney O'Hea!

Impudent Barney,

None of your blarney,

Impudent Barney O'Hea!   35

He knew 'twas all right when he saw me smile,

For he was rogue up to ev'ry wile,

Impudent Barney O'Hea!

He coaxed me to choose him,

For if I'd refuse him   40

He swore he'd kill Corney the very next day;

So, for fear 'twould go further,

And just to save murther,

I think I must marry that madcap, O'Hea!

         45

Bothering Barney,

'Tis he has the blarney

To make a girl Mistress O'Hea.

THE CROPPY BOY*
A Ballad of '98
William B. McBurney

The age-old struggle of Ireland for indepenence from England has offered many opportunities to the tellers of tales, whether in poetry or prose. Here is a dramatic incident related in old ballad form, with much conversation and rapid action. An Irish boy, about to join the Irish rebels, goes to his priest's house for confession, little suspecting what awaits him there.

"Good men and true! in this house who dwell,
To a stranger *bouchal*, I pray you tell
Is the Priest at home? or may he be seen?
I would speak a word with Father Green."

"The Priest's at home, boy, and may be seen;   5
'Tis easy speaking with Father Green;
But you must wait, till I go and see
If the holy Father alone may be."

The youth has entered an empty hall—
What a lonely sound had his light foot-fall!   10
And the gloomy chamber's chill and bare,
With a vested Priest in a lonely chair. | He is dressed in his priestly robes.

Croppy: one of the Irish rebels of '98, who wore their hair cut close to the head (cropped). In the year 1798, the Irish revolted against the English, with battles at New Ross, Wexford, and other towns.
2. *bouchal* : young man (Irish).

The youth has knelt to tell his sins.
"*Nomine Dei*," the youth begins:
At "*mea culpa*" he beats his breast, 15
And in broken murmurs he speaks the rest.

The Boy begins the ritual of confession.

"At the siege of Ross did my father fall,
And at Gorey my loving brothers all.
I alone am left of my name and race;
I will go to Wexford and take their place. 20

"I cursed three times since last Easter
     Day—
At Mass-time once I went to play;
I passed the churchyard one day in haste,
And forgot to pray for my mother's rest.

He confesses his minor sins.

"I bear no hate against living thing; 25
But I love my country above my King.
Now, Father! bless me, and let me go
To die, if God has ordained it so."

He puts Ireland ahead of the English King.

The Priest said nought, but a rustling noise
Made the youth look above in wild surprise; 30
The robes were off, and in scarlet there
Sat a yeomen captain with fiery glare,

With fiery glare and with fury hoarse,

---

14. *Nomine Dei*: in the name of God (Latin).
15. *mea culpa*: through my fault (Latin).
32. *yeoman*: a member of the Yeomanry, a British volunteer cavalry force.

Instead of blessing, he breathed a curse:
"'Twas a good thought, boy, to come here and shrive; 35
For one short hour is your time to live.

"Upon yon river three tenders float;
The Priest's in one, if he isn't shot;
We hold his house for our Lord the King,
And— 'Amen,' say I—may all traitors swing!" 40

At Geneva barrack that young man died,
And at Passage they have his body laid.
Good people who live in peace and joy,
Breathe a prayer and a tear for the Croppy boy.

THE BALLAD OF FATHER GILLIGAN
William Butler Yeats

The old ballads were full of the supernatural activities of creatures like witches, elves, and fairies, all of them wicked. In this modern imitation ballad by a great Irish poet, one of God's good angels miraculously helps Father Gilligan in his hour of need.

The old priest Peter Gilligan
Was weary night and day;
For half his flock were in their beds, | There must have been a
Or under green sods lay. | plague.

Once, while he nodded on a chair, | 5
At the moth-hour of eve,
Another poor man sent for him, | To administer the last rites
And he began to grieve. | of the church

"I have no rest, nor joy, nor peace,
For people die and die"; | 10
And after cried he, "God forgive!
My body spake, not I!"

He knelt, and leaning on the chair
He prayed and fell asleep;
And the moth-hour went from the fields, | 15
And stars began to peep.

They slowly into millions grew,
And leaves shook in the wind;

---

6. *moth-hour*: twilight

And God covered the world with shade,
And whispered to mankind.   20

Upon the time of sparrow-chirp,
When moths came once more,
The old priest Peter Gilligan
Stood upright on the floor.

"Mavrone, mavrone! the man has died   25
While I slept on the chair";
He roused his horse out of its sleep,
And rode with little care.

He rode now as he never rode,
By rocky lane and fen;   30
The sick man's wife opened the door:
"Father! you come again!"   But this is his first
                                    appearance!

"And is the poor man dead?" he cried.
"He died an hour ago."
The old priest Peter Gilligan   35
In grief swayed to and fro.

"When you were gone, he turned and died
As merry as a bird."   The man's sins had been
                                   forgiven, and he died in
The old priest Peter Gilligan   peace
He knelt him at that word.   40

---

21. *Time of sparrow-chirp*: dawn
25. *Mavrone*: alas (Irish; literally, my grief).

"He who hath made the night of stars
For souls who tire and bleed,
Sent one of His great angels down
To help me in my need.

"He who is wrapped in purple robes, 45
With planets in His care,
Had pity on the least of things
Asleep upon a chair."

St. Brigid
Denis McCarthy

Both the legends and the true stories dealing with the saints of the Church are fascinating reading. Doubtless you know some of them, such as the legend of St. George and the dragon, or of St. Patrick and the snakes. Closely rivalling St.Patrick in the hearts of all good Irishmen is sweet St. Brigid (or Bridget). In the following poem her story is told with historical accuracy, and with a characteristic Irish twist to the language.

Brigid, the daughter of Duffy, she wasn't like other young things,
Dreaming of lads for her lovers, and twirling her bracelets and rings;
Combing and coiling and curling her hair that was black as the sloes,
Painting her lips and her cheeks that were ruddy and fresh as the rose.
Ah, 'twasn't Brigid would waste all her days in such follies
     as these—   5
Christ was the Lover she worshipped for hour after hour on her knees;
Christ and His Church and His poor,—and 'twas many a mile
     that she trod
Serving the loathsome lepers that ever were stricken by God.

Brigid, the daughter of Duffy, she sold all her jewels and gems,
Sold all her finely-spun robes that were braided with gold to the
     hems;   10
Kept to her back but one garment, one dress that was faded and old,
Gave all her goods to the poor who were famished with
     hunger and cold.
Ah, 'twasn't Brigid would fling at the poor the hard word
     like a stone—

Christ the Redeemer she saw in each wretch that was ragged
    and lone;
Every wandering beggar who asked for a bite or a bed   15
Knocked at her heart like the Man who had nowhere to shelter
    His head.

Brigid, the daughter of Duffy, she angered her father at last.
"Where are your dresses, my daughter? Crom Cruach! You wear
    them out fast!
Where are the chains that I bought you all wrought in red gold
    from the mine?
Where the bright brooches of silver that once on your bosom
    would shine?"   20
Ah' but 'twas he was the man that was proud of his name and his race,
Proud of their prowess in battle and proud of their deeds in the chase!
Knew not the Christ, the pale God Whom the priests from
    afar had brought in,
Held to the old Gaelic gods that were known to Cuchulain and Finn.

Brigid, the daughter of Duffy, made answer, "O father," said she,   25
"What is the richest of raiment, and what are bright jewels to me?
Lepers of Christ must I care for, the hungry of Christ must I feed;
How can I walk in rich robes when His people and mine are
    in need?
Ah, but 'twas she didn't fear for herself when he blustered
    and swore,
Meekly she bowed when he ordered his chariot brought to
    the door;   30

18. *Crom Cruach*: the chief idol of pagan Ireland.
24. *Cuchulain, Finn*: see pages 549-550

Meekly obeyed when he bade her get in at the point of his sword,
Knowing whatever her fate she'd be safe with her Lover and Lord.

Brigid, the daughter of Duffy, was brought to the court of the King,
(Monarch of Leinster, MacEnda, whose praises the poets would sing).
"Hither, O monarch," said Duffy, "I've come with a maiden
    to sell;   35
Buy her and bind her to bondage— she's needing such
    discipline well!
Ah, but 'twas wise was the King. From the maid to the
    chieftain he turned;
Mildness he saw in her face, in the other 'twas anger that burned;
"This is no bondmaid, I'll swear it, O chief, but a girl of your own.
Why sells the father the flesh of his flesh and bone of his bone?   40

Brigid, the daughter of Duffy, was mute while her father replied—
"Monarch, this maid has no place as the child of a chieftain of pride.
Beggars and wretches whose wounds would the soul of a
    soldier affright,
Sure, 'tis on these she is wasting my substance from morning
    till night!"
Ah, but 'twas bitter was Duffy; he spoke like a man that was vext. 45
Musing, the monarch was silent; he pondered the question perplexed.
"Maiden," said he, "if 'tis true, as I've just from your father
    heard tell,
Might it not be, as my bondmaid, you'd waste all my
    substance as well?"

Brigid, the daughter of Duffy , made answer. " O monarch,"
    she said,

"Had I the wealth for your coffers, and had I the crown from
your head—   50
Yea, if the plentiful yield of the broad breasts of Erin were mine,
All would I give to the people of Christ who in poverty pine."
Ah, but 'twas then that the King felt the heart in his bosom
upleap,
"I am not worthy," he cried, "such a maiden in bondage to keep!
Here's a king's sword for her ransom, and here's a king's
word to decree   55
Never to other than Christ and His poor let her in servitude be!"

FOR THE AMBITIOUS STUDENT

Look up and report to the class the story of some saint
whose name is familiar to you. (Perhaps you live on St.
James Street, or St. Agnes Church is on the next corner,
or your brother goes to St. Olaf College.) If most of the
class are interested in the project, perhaps your teacher
will make this a class exercise and declare an All-Saints
Day. Do you know why November first would be a good
day for an exercise? Did you ever connect Hallowe'en
with saints?

A most interesting report to the class would be an
explanation of the process by which a person is declared
a saint. In any study of this subject you will learn the
correct meaning of such terms as *miracle, devil's
advocate, beatification, canonization.*

---

51. *Erin*: Ireland.
55. *ransom*: sum paid for the release of a captive. The king buys her from her
    father and sets her free to continue her Christian work.

St. Swithin
Daniel Henderson

Do you sometimes wonder how certain superstitions began? I had often heard of St. Swithin's Day, July 15th, and the common belief:

> St. Swithin's Day if it doth rain,
> For forty days rain will remain;
> St. Swithin's Day if it doth not pour
> For forty days 'twill rain no more.

But I never knew how this tradition concerning the weather originated until I read the old legend which is given in the following poem.

"Bury me," the bishop said,
"Close to my geranium bed;
Lay me near the gentle birch.
It is lonely in the church,
And its vaults are damp and chill!   5
Noble men sleep there, but still
House me in the friendly grass!
Let the linnets sing my mass!"

Dying Swithin had his whim
And the green sod covered him.   10

Then what holy celebrations
And what rapturous adorations,
Joy no wordly pen may paint—

Swithin had been made a saint!
Yet the monks forgot that he [15]
Craved for blossom, bird and bee,
And, communing round his tomb,
Vowed its narrow earthen room
Was unworthy one whose star
Shone in Peter's calendar. [20]

"Who," they asked "when we are gone
Will protect this sacred lawn?
What if time's irreverent gust
Should disperse his holy dust?"
Troubled by a blackbird's whistle, [25]
Vexed by an invading thistle,
They resolved to move his bones
To the chaste cathedral stones.
But the clouds grew black and thick
When they lifted spade and pick, [30]
And they feared that they had blundered
By the way it poured and thundered.
Quoth the abbot;"Thus, I deem,
Swithin shows us we blaspheme!
He was fond of wind and rain; [35]
Let him in their clasp remain!"
Forty days the heavens wept,
But St. Swithin smiled and slept.

After reading this poem, I looked up the legend of
St. Swithin and discovered that the tradtional story

---

20. *St. Peter's calendar*: church calendar of saints and saints' days

moves along just as Mr. Henderson wrote it, and that it goes on to say that the monks erected a chapel over the grave of the venerable saint.

According to the encyclopedia, Swithin was a famous bishop of Winchester, England, who taught Alfred the Great. He died in 862; and on July 15, 971, his bones were transferred to a magnificent shrine within the cathedral. But unfortunately for the St. Swithin's Day weather prophets, there is no record that any unusual weather conditions prevailed to denote the good saint's approval or disapproval.

FOR THE AMBITIOUS STUDENT

If you have found this account of the St. Swithin legend interesting, you may enjoy looking up the origin of some other tradition or custom and reporting to the class either orally or in writing. What do you know about Groundhog Day, for instance? Or Twelfth Night? Or St. Valentine's Day?

THE VIZIER'S APOLOGY
Arthur Guiterman

What would you do if by some chance you had to prove that an excuse may be even worse than the crime committed? This poem, with its saucy nonsense, might help you out. The author chose an Oriental setting for his poem, perhaps because the old-time Eastern rulers were so notoriously autocratic that their wrath was no joke—even if the author makes light of it. Don't miss the rich images which build up the impression of grandeur surrounding the monarch.

Sing, Muse, of the anger of Haroun the Caliph
    Aroused by complaints on the Sheik of Irak.
"The scoundrel!" he thundered, "we'll cast him in jail if
    We don't drop him overboard sewn in a sack!

"It seems he has robbed the imperial coffer,   5
    And witnesses charge him with every abuse.
And think of the rascal disdaining to offer
    Our Clemency even a shred of excuse!"

"It might be as well, " said his minister, smiling,
    "To calm the imperial wrath for a time.   10
Excuses, like charges, are framed for beguiling;
    Besides, the excuse might be worse than the crime."

"What nonsense!" cried Haroun, that monarch effulgent,
    "A fault not as bad as the criminal's plea?"

9. *minister: i.e.,* the Vizier

"Perhaps," said the minister, blandly indulgent, 15
"I'll prove to your Highness that such it may be."

The very next morning, superbly attended
    By eunuchs in dozens, and emirs in pairs,
With grandeur befitting the nobly descended
    The Caliph descended the glittering stairs. 20

Then, daring unspeakable woes and disasters
    And rage that devours its prey like pilaff,
The minister reached through the marble pilasters
    And wickedly pinched the imperial calf!

Aghast at an outrage unthinkably sinister, 25
    "Dog!" roared the Autocrat, "what do you mean!"
"What a mischance!" wailed the profligate minister;
    "Pardon, your Highness, I thought 'twas the Queen!"

And so, by another experience wiser,
    The Caliph with graciousnesss truly sublime 30
Admitted the truth that his faithful adviser
    Had made an excuse that was worse than the crime.

FOR YOUR VOCABULARY

"You wouldn't *fool* me, would you?" says Miss Modern; her great-great-grandmother might have said, "Is't they intention to *beguile* me, sir?" Miss Modern says " I don't *get* it"; her ancestress said, "I am certainly *mazed* beyond belief." Maisie says, "I *work* in the 5 and 10"; her great-uncle may have said, "I *moil* in the mines for gold." Johnnie would say Maisie was *good-looking*; his eighteenth-century ancestor called his girl friend a *comely* lass. What are the modern synonyms of the following words; *albeit, clave, doff, dolt, ire, loath, meet, nether, perchance, poll, recked, sooth, springe, swound, visage, wan, wain, yon*?

COLUMBUS

Joaquin Miller

In a few brief stanzas, Joaquin Miller's famous poem depicts the dramatic conflict of emotions which must have existed on Columbus's ships during the fateful voyage of 1492. Remember that to the crew the three frail frigates were headed into shoreless seas, moving farther and farther from charted lands, until the men felt that stars, God, hope successively were blotted out. In the face of increasing and mutinous despair, the brave Admiral had only one answer: "Sail on! sail on!"

Behind him lay the gray Azores,
　　Behind the Gates of Hercules;
Before him not the ghost of shores,
　　Before him only shoreless seas.
The good mate said: "Now must we pray,　　　　5
　　For lo! the very stars are gone.
Brave Admiral, speak, what shall I say?"
　　"Why, say, 'Sail on! sail on! and on!'"

"My men grow mutinous day by day;
　　My men grow ghastly, wan and weak."　　　　10
The stout mate thought of home; a spray
　　Of salt wave washed his swarthy cheek.
"What shall I say, brave Admiral, say,
　　If we sight naught but seas at dawn?"

---

1. *Azores*: a group of islands in the north Atlantic, belonging to Portugal
2. *Gates of Hercules*: the Strait of Gibraltar.

"Why, you shall say at break of day: 15
    'Sail on! sail on! sail on! and on!'"

They sailed and sailed, as winds might blow,
    Until at last the blanched mate said:
"Why, now not even God would know
    Should I and all my men fall dead.   20
These very winds forget their way,
    For God from these dread seas is gone.
Now speak, brave Admiral, speak and say"—
    He said: "Sail on! sail on! and on!"

They sailed. They sailed. Then spake the mate: 25
    "This mad sea shows his teeth tonight.
He curls his lip, he lies in wait,
    He lifts his teeth, as if to bite!
Brave Admiral, say but one good word:
    What shall we do when hope is gone?"   30
The words leapt like a leaping sword:
    "Sail on! sail on! sail on! and on!"

Then, pale and worn, he paced his deck,
    And peered through darkness. Ah, that night
Of all dark nights! And then a speck—   35
    A light! A light! At last a light!
It grew, a starlit flag unfurled!
    It grew to be Time's burst of dawn.
He gained a world; he gave that world
    Its grandest lesson: "On! sail on!"   40

In the last stanza Joaquin Miller deftly leaps three centuries (l.36), carrying us from 1492 to 1776; and finally in the last two lines he brings the lesson of the poem right home to you and me today.

What effect is gained by the personification of the sea in lines 26-28? How does this compare with that in "Sea Lullaby" (page 50)?

What do you make of the metaphor in line 38?

This a good poem to commit to memory.

FOR YOUR VOCABULARY

The word *naught* (sometimes spelled *nought*) which means *nothing*, should not be confused with *aught*, which means *something*: If a column of figures adds up to twenty, put down the *naught* and carry the two."

Other pairs of words like *aught—naught* are *one—none, ever—never, either—neither, willy—nilly*.

POCAHONTAS
William Makepeace Thackeray

Pocahontas ("Playful One") was the daughter of Powhatan, chief of a confederacy of Indians in Virginia in the early 1600's. She is of some importance in American history because of her marriage to John Rolfe, a union which was regarded as a bond of friendship between the two races, and brought a peace which lasted eight years and greatly aided in establishing the Jamestown colony on a firm footing. But to most Americans she is known as the Indian "princess" who saved the life of Captain John Smith, leader of the Jamestown colonists. Since our only account of this episode is the one by John Smith himself, and since the gallant captain is known to be something of a romancer in relating his adventures, some historians question whether or not this famous incident ever really occured. But, true or false, the story has become a firmly established American legend.

The following account of it is by a famous English author, and is related with a romantic flavor that would do credit to John Smith himself.

Wearied arm and broken sword
    Wage in vain the desperate fight:
Round him press a countless horde,
    He is but a single knight.
Hark! a cry of truimph shrill   5
    Through the wilderness resounds,
    As, with twenty bleeding wounds,
Sinks the warrior, fighting still.

Now they heap the fatal pyre,
    And the torch of death they light: 10

Ah! 'tis hard to die of fire!
    Who will shield the captive knight?
Round the stake with fiendish cry
    Wheel and dance the savage crowd,
    Cold the victim's mien, and proud,   15
And his breast is bared to die.

Who will shield the fearless heart?
    Who avert the murderous blade?
From the throng, with sudden start,
    See there springs an Indian maid.   20
Quick she stands before the knight,
    "Loose the chain, unbind the ring,
    I am daughter of the king,
And I claim the Indian right!"

Dauntlessly aside she flings   25
    Lifted axe and thirsty knife;
Fondly to his heart she clings.
    And her bosom guards his life!
In the woods of Powhatan,
    Still, 'tis told by Indian fires,   30
    How a daughter of their sires
Saved the captive Englishman.

THE FIRST THANKSGIVING DAY
Maragret Junkin Preston

It was in 1620 that "a band of exiles moored their bark on the wild New England shore," and "the breaking waves dashed high on a stern and rockbound coast."* On December 21 the Mayflower was anchored in Plymouth harbor, and the Pilgrims landed on Plymouth Rock. The winter was a hard and bitter one. When spring came, more than half their number had died, but those who remained set courageously to work to plow the land and sow the seed in the fields. The virgin soil, the sunshine, and the rain combined to produce a bounteous harvest. When the harvest had been gathered in, Governor Bradford ordered a three days' celebration of feasting and rejoicing.

Thus the first Thanksgiving festival was celebrated in America in 1621. Little by little the custom spread, and its influence deepened; now a day is set aside each year as a national holiday, officially proclaimed by the President and re-proclaimed by the Governors of the various states. The following account of the first Thanksgiving Day recalls to our minds the details of that historic occasion. It also reminds us of the spirit of friendship which existed between the Pilgrims and Massasoit's Indians, united in brotherly love as children of the same great Spirit.

"And now," said the Governor, gazing abroad on the piled-up store
Of the sheaves that dotted the clearings and covered the
      meadows o'er,

---

* Do you know the famous poem from which these lines are quoted? It is
  "The Landing of the Pilgrim Fathers" by Felicia Hemans. The poem ends:
      Aye, call it holy ground,
        The soil where first they trod!
     They have left unstained what there they found—
        Freedom to worship God!
If you do not know this, poem, you should certainly look it up.

"'Tis meet that we render praises because of this yield of grain;
'Tis meet that the Lord of the harvest be thanked for His sun and rain.

"And therefore, I, William Bradford (by the grace of God today,   5
And the franchise of this good people), Governor of
        Plymouth, say,
Through virtue of vested power— ye shall gather with one accord,
And hold, in the month November, thanksgiving unto the Lord.

"He hath granted us peace and plenty, and the quiet we've
        sought so long;
He hath thwarted the wily savage, and kept him from wrack
        and wrong;   10
And unto our feast the Sachem shall be bidden, that he may know
We worship his own Great Spirit who maketh the harvests grow.

"So shoulder your matchlocks, masters: there is hunting of
        all degrees;
And fishermen, take your tackle, and scour for spoil the seas;
And maidens and dames of Plymouth, your delicate crafts
        employ   15
To honor our First Thanksgiving, and make it a feast of joy!

"We fail of the fruits and dainties—we fail of the old home cheer;
Ah, these are the lightest looses, mayhap, that befall us here;
But see, in our open clearings, how golden the melons lie;
Enrich them with sweets and spices, and give us the pumpkin pie!"   20

---

11. *Sachem*: great chief; in this case, Massasoit, chief of the Indians of Cape
    Cod and vicinity. In March, 1621, he made a treaty of peace with the
    Pilgrims, which he never broke, remaining a faithful friend of the English
    throughout his life.

So, bravely the preparations went on for the autumn feast;
The deer and the bear were slaughtered; wild game from the
    greatest to least
Was heaped in the colony cabins; brown home-brew served
    for wine,
And the plum and the grape of the forest, for orange and
    peach and pine.

At length came the day appointed; the snow had begun to fall,   25
But the clang from the meeting-house belfry rang merrily
    over all,
And summoned the folk of Plymouth, who hastened with
    glad accord
To listen to Elder Brewster as he fervently thanked the Lord.

In his seat say Governor Bradford; men, matrons, and maidens fair;
Miles Standish and all his soldiers, with corselet and sword
    were there;   30
And sobbing and tears and gladness had each in its turn the sway,
For the grave of the sweet Rose Standish o'ershadowed
    Thanksgiving Day.

And when Massasoit, the Sachem, sat down with his hundred braves,
And ate of the varied riches of gardens and woods and waves,
And looked on the granaried harvest — with a blow on his
    brawny chest,
He muttered, "The good Great Spirit loves His white children best!"

---

32. *Rose Standish*: the first wife of Miles Standish. Perhaps you have read the
    story of a later—and imaginary—love of Captain Standish in Longfellow's
    "The Courtship of Miles Standish." What is the famous line often quoted
    from that poem?

Stories in Verse

THE MEANS MASSACRE
Robert P. Tristram Coffin

Before the American Revolution, when George II ruled over England, and Louis XV over France, these two nations were frequently at war with each other. Their wars extended to the New World, where each country claimed colonial lands. In the American colonies, the Indians aided the French in opposing the English, and the last of these conflicts is called the French and Indian War.

"The Means Massacre" is an episode from that struggle. The story is dramatic, but not too easy too read. One difficulty is the highly figurative language. The poem abounds in metaphors and similes, some of which I have analyzed in the sidenotes. There is also an unusual characteristic of structure in the poem: Each couplet, or pair of lines, is a complete sentence in itself, and adds a complete new fact or picture to the unfolding tale. The resulting abruptness of style is, of course well suited to the violent, startling nature of the story; but you will need to exert your imagination to establish the connection between these successive couplet-pictures as you read, and thus preserve the continuous flow of the narrative.

King George raised his jewelled pen | In England
And wrote *death* for a thousand men.

King Louis spoke a single word, | In France
And overseas the forest stirred. | In America

Naked bodies through the
      brakes   ⁵
Slid like deadly copper snakes.

a= Indians
b= snakes → stealth and brown color

5. *brakes*: thickets

— 302 —

Thomas Means was hoeing corn,
His wife was lulling her last-born.

The father smiled to hear the tune
Of a lullaby at noon.   10

Chloris, Chloris, wooing doves | Mistress Means sings.
Are the sentries of our loves.

Maquoit Bay was a diamond's shine
Through the branches of the pine.

Jane and Mary, three-feet high,   15
Stared round-eyed at a dragonfly.

Baby James's eyes were tight
As morning-glories are at night.

Every bush along the rise
Held a pair of hungry eyes.   20

All the afternoon the swallows
Clicked their beaks along the hollows.

The afterglow of daytime brought
Peleg Anderson foot-hot.

"The Redskins have been seen at Gorham,   25
Houses are in flame at Shoreham.

---

13. *Maquoit Bay*: on the coast of   25. *Gorham, Shoreham*: neighboring
    Maine.   towns.

"Take your family, Thomas, fly
To the blockhouse, and be spry!"

Thomas looked upon his crop
Fed by sweat in drop on drop.   30

Every cornstalk had its feet
In an alewife plump and sweet.

The Lord had exalted Thomas's horn,   His farm prospered. The corn
His head was roofed in by his corn.   (his wealth) was stored in the
                                       attic.

He had powder and two guns,   35
The Lord would look after his sons!

Thomas folded in his flock,
Dropped the bar and turned the lock.

Thomas sat on the settee,
His rifle lay across his knee.   40

The honey bees that sang all day
In his head still hummed away.   He grew drowsy.

Thomas's chin sank lower, lower,
His heart hammered slower, slower.

Through the grass the snakes crawled nigher,   45
Their eyeballs were red coals of fire.

---

32. *alewife*: a fish. Farmers used to plant fish with the corn, for fertilizer
33. *horn*: horn of plenty, signifying rich yield

A whippoorwill cried hoarse with fright
To the four corners of the night.

A tree was coming up the hill
On twelve legs, stealthily and still. ⁵⁰

> The Indians carry a tree trunk for a battering ram.

Mistress Means was picking may
In Kent three thousand miles away.

> She dreams of her English home.

The night split with the crack of doom,
The tree came through into the room.

Goodman Thomas sprang up
    blind, ⁵⁵
A bob-cat leapt him from
    behind.

a= Indian
b= bobcat
agility and ferocity

Mistress Means came back from dreams
To a world of children's screams.

She caught a brand up with a yell,
She stood upon the brink of hell. ⁶⁰

At her feet a dusky spider
Was busy where a gash grew wider.

> See what she saw: In the dim light of her brand, an Indian—like a spider—scalping her husband.

A horrible red spider spread
His fangs along her husband's head.

---

51. *may*: flowers—hawthorn, spiraea, or other spring-blooming (May) plants.
52. *Kent*: a county in southeastern England.

She brought the brand down on the thing,   65
She smelt the red flesh sundering.

The monstrous insect leapt aside,
The husband's eyes stared upward wide.

The curls were gone from baby's head,
He wore a fearful cap of red.   70

The mother heard a distant gun
And the shout of Peleg Anderson. | Help is on the way.

The serpents melted from the room,
Hissed, and vanished in the gloom.

The neighbor found the mother weeping   75
On son and mate forever sleeping.

She kept saying, "We were five,
And I am all the one alive.

"Father, Mary, James, and Jane —
I shall not hear them speak again."   80

The oven creaked, and Jane came out
And clasped her mother round about.

---

83. *churn's*: and old-fashioned wooden churn, big enough to hide a child. In
other stories of Indian raids, children hid under large iron kettles.

The churn's lid gave a sudden lift,
And Mary sprang out in her shift.

Mistress Means sat by her dead   85
With living tears upon her head.

> She sits on the floor beside
> her husband and baby. The
> girls lean over her, weeping.

Across the ocean dark and broad
King George played his harpsicord.

And Louis sat with mistresses
Leaning on his satin knees.   80

In "The Means Massacre" Mr. Coffin has not merely told a bloody tale; he has expressed a point of view about it, too. A successful reading, then, will make clear not only the story, but also the author's point of view. This is given in the first four and the last four lines. Did these seem clear when you first read them? If not, examine them again. They are not really hard now, are they? Try to state in your own words the point of view which these lines suggest.

---

84. *shift*: chemise, or nightgown
85. *her dead*: her dead husband and baby

Stories in Verse

PAUL REVERE'S RIDE
Henry Wadsworth Longfellow

This poem is the Landlord's tale in Longfellow's famous series, **Tales of a Wayside Inn.** *In his introduction to these poems Longfellow takes us into the parlor of the old Red-Horse Inn at Sudbury, Massachusetts, where "around the fireside at their ease there sat a group of friends": a Student, a young Sicilian (whose tale is the well-known "King Robert of Sicily"), a Spanish Jew, a Theologian, a Poet, a Musician, and — of course — the Landlord. After the Musician had filled the air with magic music from his violin, a silence followed. And then the guests all clamored for the Landlord's tale, "the story promised them of old, they said, but always left untold."*

To read this story effectively, you must imagine yourself the old Landlord, sitting with his friends, "the firelight shedding over all the splendor of its ruddy glow." The story is very real and important to him, one of his proudest possessions being "the sword his grandsire bore in the rebellious days of yore, down there at Concord in the fight." Try to read the story with the sincerity and depth of feeling that must have been in the Landlord's voice as he opened his heart to his friends.

Listen, my children, and you shall hear
Of the midnight ride of Paul Revere,
On the eighteenth of April, in Seventy-five;

---

2. Paul Revere was a Boston silversmith who took an active part in many of the events leading up to the Revolution, including the Boston Tea Party. On April 16, 1775, he rode over to Concord, about twenty miles away, to warn the patriots to move their military stores from that village, and arranged with some friends for lantern signals in the Old North Church if the British should start for Concord. On April 18 the British troops moved, and Paul Revere made his famous ride to rouse the countryside to resistance. Paul Revere was a most interesting and versatile man, and I think you would enjoy reading about his life in some good encyclopedia. From that you could go on to the biography by Esther Forbes, published in 1941.

Hardly a man is now alive
Who remembers that famous day and year.   5
He said to his friend, "If the British march
By land or sea from the town tonight,
Hang a lantern aloft in the belfry arch
Of the North Church tower as a signal light, —
One, if by land, and two, if by sea;   10
And I on the opposite shore will be,
Ready to ride and spread the alarm
Through every Middlesex village and farm,
For the country folk to be up and to arm."

Then he said, "Good-night!" and with muffled oar   15
Silently rowed to the Charlestown shore,
Just as the moon rose over the bay,
Where swinging wide at her moorings lay
The Somerset, British man-of-war;
A phantom ship, with each mast and spar   20
Across the moon like a prison bar,
And a huge black hulk, that was magnified
By its own reflection in the tide.

Meanwhile, his friend, through alley and street,
Wanders and watches with eager ears,   25
Till in the silence around him he hears
The muster of men at the barrack door,
The sound of arms, and the tramp of feet,
And the measured tread of the grenadiers,
Marching down to their boats on the shore.   30

Then he climbed the tower of the Old North Church,
By the wooden stairs, with stealthy tread,
To the belfry-chamber overhead,
And startled the pigeons from their perch
On the somber rafters, that round him made   35
Masses of moving shapes of shade,—
By the trembling ladder, steep and tall,
To the highest window in the wall,

> The rafters (not the pigeons) made the *moving shapes of shade*, as the lantern swung in his hand.

Where he paused to listen and look down
A moment on the roofs of the town,   40
And the moonlight flowing over all.

Beneath, in the churchyard, lay the dead,
In their night-encampment on the hill,
Wrapped in silence so deep and still
That he could hear, like a sentinel's tread,   45
The watchful night-wind, as it went
Creeping along from tent to tent,
And seeming to whisper, "All is well!"
A moment only he feels the spell
Of the place and the hour, and the secret dread 50
Of the lonely belfry and the dead;
For suddenly all his thoughts are bent
On a shadowy something far away,
Where the river widens to meet the bay, —
A line of black that bends and floats   55
On the rising tide, like a bridge of boats.

Meanwhile, impatient to mount and ride,
Booted and spurred, with a heavy stride

On the opposite shore walked Paul Revere.
Now he patted his horse's side, 60
Now gazed at the landscape far and near,
Then, impetuous, stamped the earth,
And turned and tightened his saddle-girth;
But mostly he watched with eager search
The belfry-tower of the Old North Church, 65
As it rose above the graves on the hill,
Lonely and spectral and somber and still.
And lo! as he looks, on the belfry's height
A glimmer, and then a gleam of light!
He springs to the saddle, the bridle he turns, 70
But lingers and gazes, till full on his sight
A second lamp in the belfry burns!

A hurry of hoofs in a village street,
A shape in the moonlight, a bulk in the dark,
And beneath, from the pebbles, in passing, a spark 75
Struck out by a steed flying fearless and fleet;
That was all! And yet, through the gloom and the light,
The fate of a nation was riding that | This is the big line.
        night;
And the spark struck out by that steed, in his flight,
Kindled the land into flame with its heat. 80

He has left the village and mounted the steep,
And beneath him, tranquil and broad and deep,
Is the Mystic, meeting the ocean tides;
And under the alders, that skirt its edge,
Now soft on the sand, now loud on the ledge, 85

Is heard the tramp of his steed as he rides.

It was twelve by the village clock
When he crossed the bridge into Medford town.
He heard the crowing of the cock,
And the barking of the farmer's dog,   90
And felt the damp of the river fog,
That rises after the sun goes down.

It was one by the village clock,
When he galloped into Lexington.
He saw the gilded weathercock   95
Swim in the moonlight as he passed,
And the meeting-house windows, blank and bare,
Gaze at him with a spectral glare,
As if they already stood aghast
At the bloody work they would look upon.   100

It was two by the village clock,
When he came to the bridge in Concord town.
He heard the bleating of the flock,
And twitter of birds among the trees,
And felt the breath of the morning breeze   105
Blowing over the meadows brown.
And one was safe and asleep in his bed
Who at the bridge would be first to fall,
Who that day would be lying dead,
Pierced by a British musket-ball.   110

You know the rest. In the books you have read,
How the British Regulars fired and fled, —
How the farmers gave them ball for ball,
From behind each fence and farm-yard wall,
Chasing the red-coats down the lane,   115
Then crossing the fields to emerge again
Under the trees at the turn of the road,
And only pausing to fire and load.

So through the night rode Paul Revere;
And so through the night went his cry of alarm   120
To every Middlesex village and farm, —
A cry of defiance and not of fear,
A voice in the darkness, a knock at the door,
And a word that shall echo forevermore!
For, borne on the night-wind of the Past,   125
Through all our history, to the last,
In the hour of darkness and peril and need,
The people will waken and listen to hear
The hurrying hoof-beats of that steed,
And the midnight message of Paul Revere.   130

What was Paul Revere's message? Does it have any
significance today? Do you know any modern Paul
Reveres?

Stories in Verse

INDEPENDENCE BELL
Anonymous

*July 4, 1776, is probably the most famous day in American history;
and Independence Hall, the old State House in Philadelphia
sheltering the Liberty Bell, which was rung on that day to signify the
formal adoption of the Declaration of Independence, has become one
of our most revered patriotic shrines. The unknown poet who in the
following verses related the events of that historic day in 1776 was
probably not too accurate in his details, but he caught the spirit of the
occasion and its importance to every American citizen. This old poem
was a favorite in my boyhood, and I still thrill to many of its lines.
Somehow as you read it, you feel as if you were actually there, first
restless and anxious, then breathless with suspense, then exultant with
joy, and finally silent from awe at the significance of the occasion.*

There was tumult in the city,
    In the quaint old Quaker town,
And the streets were thronged with people
    Passing restless up and down —
People gathering at the corners,   5
    Where they whispered lip to ear,
While the sweat stood on their temples,
    With the stress of hope and fear.

As the bleak Atlantic currents
    Lash the wild Newfoundland shore,   10
So they beat about the State House,
    So they surged against the door;
And the mingling of their voices

Swelled in harmony profound,
Till the quiet street of Chestnut   15
    Was all turbulent with sound.

"Will they do it?" "Dare they do it?"
    "Who is speaking?" "What's the news?"
"What of Adams?" "What of Sherman?"
    "Oh, God grant they won't refuse!"   20
"Make some way, there!" "Let me nearer!"
    "I am stifling!" "Stifle then!
When a nation's life's at hazard
    We've no time to think of men!"

So they surged against the State House,   25
    While all solemnly inside
Sat the Continental Congress,
    Truth and reason for their guide;
O'er a simple scroll debating:
    Which, though simple it might be,   30
Yet should shake the cliffs of England
    With the thunders of the free.

Far aloft in the high steeple
    Sat the bellman, old and gray;
He was weary of the tyrant   35
    And his iron-sceptered sway.
So he sat with one hand ready

---

19. *Adams, Sherman*: Samuel Adams of Massachusetts and Roger Sherman of
Connecticut, two prominent members of the Continental Congress.
31. *shake the cliffs of England*: a figure like "the shot heard around the world."
Do you know "The Concord Hymn"?

On the clapper of the bell,
Till his eye should catch the signal,
The expected news to tell.   40

See! See! the dense crowd quivers
As beside the door a boy
Looks forth with hands uplifted,
His eyes alight with joy.
Hushed the people's swelling murmur   45
As they listened breathlessly —
"Ring!" he shouts; "ring, grandpa, ring!
Ring! oh, ring for liberty!"

Quickly at the welcome signal
The old bellman lifts his hand;   50
Forth he sends the good news, making
Iron music through the land.
How they shouted! What rejoicing!
How the old bell shook the air,
Till the clang of freedom echoed   55
From the belfries everywhere.

The old State House bell is silent,
Hushed is now its clamorous tongue,
But the spirit it awakened
Still is living, ever young.   60
And we'll ne'er forget the bellman
Who, that great day in July,
Hailed the birth of Independence,
Which, please God, shall never die.

NATHAN HALE
Revolutionary War Ballad

Nathan Hale, revered as the ideal youthful hero of the Revolution, graduated from Yale in 1773 and for two years taught in the schools of Connecticut. His amazing athletic feats gave him great prestige among men, and his handsome person made him popular with women. When the Revolutionary War began in April, 1775, the patriotism of this engaging young schoolmaster carried him early into the military struggle; and, when Washington called for a volunteer to secure information about the strength and designs of the enemy, Captain Nathan Hale offered himself for this dangerous enterprise.

"You know the rest. In the books you have read" how he entered the enemy's lines disguised as a schoolmaster, secured the desired information, almost reached his own picket lines, was at the last minute captured, was proved to be a spy by the papers found on his person, confessed, and was condemned to be hanged. On the next day (September 22, 1776) he went forth to the gallows, where he made a spirited speech, ending with the memorable words, "I only regret that I have but one life to lose for my country."

The heroic fate of this handsome young patriot has been the subject of many poems and plays. Among these is the following ballad, which appeared anonymously soon after his death.

The breezes went steadily thro' the tall pines,
　　A-saying "Oh! hu-ush!" a-saying "Oh! hu-ush!"
As stilly stole by a bold legion of horse,
　　For Hale in the bush; for Hale in the bush.

"Keep still!" said the thrush as she nestled her young,   5
    In a nest by the road; in a nest by the road.
"For the tyrants are near, and with them appear
    What bodes us no good; what bodes us no good."

The brave captain heard it, and thought of his home,
    In a cot by the brook; in a cot by the brook,   10
With mother and sister and memories dear,
    He so gayly forsook; he so gayly forsook.

Cooling shades of the night were coming apace,
    The tattoo had beat; the tattoo had beat.
The noble one sprang from his dark lurking-place,   15
    To make his retreat; to make his retreat.

He warily trod on the dry rustling leaves,
    As he pass'd thro' the wood; as he pass'd thro' the wood;
And silently gain'd his rude launch on the shore,
    As she play'd with the flood; as she play'd with the flood. 20

The guards of the camp, on that dark, dreary night,
    Had a murderous will; had a murderous will.
They took him and bore him afar from the shore,
    To a hut on the hill; to a hut on the hill.

No mother was there, nor a friend who could cheer,   25
    In that little stone cell; in that little stone cell.
But he trusted in love, from his Father above.
    In his heart, all was well; in his heart, all was well.

10. *cot*: cottage.
14. *tattoo*: a call sounded on drum and bugle shortly before taps.

An ominous owl with his solemn bass voice,
    Sat moaning hard by; sat moaning hard by.   30
"The tyrant's proud minions most gladly rejoice,
    For he must soon die; for he must soon die."

The brave fellow told them, no thing he restrain'd,
    The cruel gen'ral; the cruel gen'ral.
His errand from camp, of the ends to be gain'd,   35
    And said that was all; and said that was all.

They took him and bound him and bore him away,
    Down the hill's grassy side; down the hill's grassy side.
'Twas there the base hirelings, in royal array,
    His cause did deride; his cause did deride.   40

Five minutes were given, short moments, no more,
    For him to repent; for him to repent.
He pray'd for his mother, he ask'd not another,
    To Heaven he went; to Heaven he went.

The faith of a martyr, the tragedy show'd,   45
    As he trod the last stage; as he trod the last stage.
And Britons will shudder at gallant Hale's blood,
    As his words do presage; as his words do presage.

---

31. *tyrant*: King George III of England.
39. *hirelings*: hired soldiers. Many of the soldiers in the British army were hired
    Germans.

"Thou pale king of terrors, thou life's gloomy foe,
    Go frighten the slave; go frighten the slave;   50
Tell tyrants, to you their allegiance they owe.
    No fears for the brave; no fears for the brave."

FOR THE AMBITIOUS STUDENT

Nathan Hale, by Clyde Fitch, is a highly romanticized but most interesting play, giving the whole story of Nathan Hale's famous exploit, and adding a love story for good measure.

---

49. *king of terrors*: death

MOLLY PITCHER
Kate Brownlee Sherwood

Just as Nathan Hale is the ideal young hero of the Revolution, so Molly Pitcher is the ideal heroine.

When John Hays enlisted in the First Pennsylvania Artillery, his wife, Mary, determined to accompany him and do whatever she could to serve her country. It became her regular duty to carry water to the soldiers in the heat and dust of battle; and because she carried it in a pitcher instead of a pail, she became known as "Molly Pitcher." At Monmouth, New Jersey, June 28, 1778, when her husband fell in battle, Molly stepped up beside his cannon, and filled his place ably and heroically for the rest of the fight. For her bravery on this occasion Washington commissioned her a sergeant in the Continental Army (so says tradition).

"'Twas hurry and scurry at Monmouth Town,
　　For Lee was beating a wild retreat;
The British were riding the Yankees down,
　　And panic was pressing on flying feet.

Galloping down like a hurricane   5
　　Washington rode with his sword swung high,
Mighty as he of the Trojan plain
　　Fired by a courage from the sky.

"Halt, and stand to your guns!" he cried.
　　And a bombardier made swift reply.   10

---

2. *Lee*: Charles Lee, a Revolutionary general, no relation to Robert E. Lee.
7. *he of the Trojan plain*: probably Achilles, who, clad in a suit of splendid armor forged for him by the god Vulcan, killed Hector on the plain before Troy.

Wheeling his cannon into the tide,
  He fell 'neath the shot of a foeman nigh.

Molly Pitcher sprang to his side,
  Fired as she saw her husband do,
Telling the king in his stubborn pride   15
  Women like men to their homes are true.

Washington rode from the bloody fray
  Up to the gun that a woman manned.
"Molly Pitcher, you saved the day,"
  He said, as he gave her a hero's hand.   20

He named her sergeant with manly praise,
  While her war-brown face was wet with tears —
A woman has ever a woman's ways,
  And the army was wild with cheers.

ABRAHAM DAVENPORT

John Greenleaf Whittier

Your skill in reading blank verse will be called into action by "Abraham Davenport." You probably will have no difficulty with it after you get safely past the first few very long sentences.

Two things in this poem are of particular interest. One is the theme, which you may recognize before you come to Whittier's specific statement of it in the last line. The other is the picture of a memorable character. Abraham Davenport, a real historic personage, has the earnestness and the stanch sense of duty that characterized the best of the Puritans. It is worth noting that in this respect Whittier, the author of the poem, was like him.

In the old days (a custom laid aside | A sly dig at modern politics.
With breeches and cocked hats) the | Whom do we send now?
    people sent
Their wisest men to make the public laws.
And so, from a brown homestead, where the Sound
Drinks the small tribute of the Mianas,   5
Waved over by the woods of Rippowams,
And hallowed by pure lives and tranquil deaths,
Stamford sent up to the councils of the State
Wisdom and grace in Abraham Davenport.

   'Twas on a May-day of the far old year   10
Seventeen hundred eighty, that there fell | The subject of *fell* is in 1.14.

---

4. *Sound*: Long Island Sound.
5. *Mianas*: a Connecticut stream.
8. *Stamford*: a town in Connecticut, on the *Sound*.

Over the bloom and sweet life of the Spring,

Over the fresh earth and the heaven of noon,

A horror of great darkness, like the night

> Today, when eclipses are announced beforehand, there would be no horror.

In day of which the Norland sagas tell, —   15

The Twilight of the Gods. The low-hung sky

Was black with ominous clouds, save where its rim

Was fringed with a dull glow, like that which climbs

The crater's sides from the red hell below.

Birds ceased to sing, and all the barn-yard fowls   20

Roosted; the cattle at the pasture bars

Lowed, and looked homeward; bats on leathern wings

Flitted abroad; the sounds of labor died;

Men prayed, and women wept; all ears grew sharp

To hear the doom-blast of the trumpet shatter   25

> Judgment Day—a definite part of Puritan belief.

The black sky, that the dreadful face of Christ

Might look from the rent clouds, not as he looked

A loving guest at Bethany, but stern

As Justice and inexorable Law.

Meanwhile in the old State House, dim as ghosts,   30

Sat the lawgivers of Connecticut,

Trembling beneath their legislative robes.

"It is the Lord's Great Day! Let us adjourn,"

Some said; and then, as if with one accord,

All eyes were turned to Abraham Davenport.   35

---

15. *Norland sagas*: hero tales of Scandinavia.
16. *Twilight of the Gods*: a sort of doomsday for the Gods.
28. *Bethany*: Here Jesus visited with Mary, Martha, and Lazarus; and Mary anointed his feet with ointment. See John, chapter 12.

He rose, slow cleaving with his steady voice
The intolerable hush. "This well may be
The Day of Judgment which the world awaits;
But be it so or not, I only know
My present duty, and my Lord's command   40
To occupy till He come. So at the post
Where He hath set me in His providence,
I choose, for one, to meet Him face to face, —
No faithless servant frightened from my task,
But ready when the Lord of the harvest calls;   45
And therefore, with all reverence, I would say,
Let God do His work, we will see to ours.
Bring in the candles." And they brought them in.

Then by the flaring lights the
           Speaker read,

The minor importance of this act *emphasizes Abraham's devotion to duty. It also seems faintly comic.*

Albeit with husky voice and shaking
           hands,   50
An act to amend an act to regulate
The shad and alewive fisheries. Whereupon
Wisely and well spake Abraham Davenport,
Straight to the question, with no

Notice the pun on figures.

           figures of speech
Save the ten Arab signs, yet not without   55
The shrewd dry humor natural to the man:
His awe-struck colleagues listening all the while,
Between the pauses of his argument,
To hear the thunder of the wrath of God

---

41. *To occupy*: to stay at the post of duty.
52. *Shad and alewive*: varieties of fish

Break from the hollow trumpet of the cloud.   60

And there he stands in memory to this day,
Erect, self-poised, a rugged face, half seen
Against the background of unnatural dark,
A witness to the ages as they pass,
That simple duty hath no place for fear.   65

Abraham Davenport appears to have been a shrewd Yankee as well as a good Puritan. What evidence of his Yankee shrewdness do you find in the lines of the poem?

Note the vivid description of the effect on men and animals of the darkening of the sun — all in one sentence. What images can you suggest to add to this passage? (The famous Dark Day of this poem occurred on May 19, 1780.)

Their fear, of course, seems strange in our age of scientific forecasts and of universal communication. But it must have been very real in earlier times. Mark Twain employs this fear with humorous effect in *A Connecticut Yankee in King Arthur's Court*.

THE PIONEER
William B. Ruggles

The most spectacular adventure in American history is that of the westward-pushing pioneers. Through the Cumberland Gap into the great Mississippi Basin, down the rivers in flatboats, across the plains in great prairie schooners — on, on they rolled, to the Western promised land — on, on, to the Great Open Spaces — on, on, to the Pacific and the end of the Western trek.

But this great wave of migration consisted of individual pioneers. What were they like? What made them keep moving on? What did their neighbors think of them? Here is a brief glimpse into the life and heart of one pioneer — one I think the author meant to be typical of the great army of adventurers that made America.

He could not breathe in a crowded place —
He wanted his air and his open space —
He watched while civilization neared
On the path through the wilderness Boone had cleared,
Saw highways hiding the Indian trails: 5
West fled the bear and the elk and the deer —
"I've got to go," said the Pioneer.
He whistled to his dog and called to his wife,
Loaded his rifle and sharpened his knife,
Tossed in his wagon a pan or two —   10
Texas-bound, to a land plumb new.
They watched him go, and shook each head —
"Shiftless fool — better stay," they said.
Not a sign they saw that might denote
That a Nation rode in his coonskin coat.   15

KIT CARSON'S RIDE
Joaquin Miller

*Every schoolboy knows the name and fame of Kit Carson —
trapper, guide, frontiersman, Indian fighter. Having lived constantly
in the open, he was scarcely able to endure the life of cities, loved
the freedom of the West. Joaquin Miller, just thirty years younger,
was also an outdoor man. And each of them married an Indian girl.
This poem suggests that Kit Carson stole his bride; in reality, he
married her "in quiet fashion, with bell and candle."*

*As you may infer from the twelfth line, Joaquin Miller wrote this
poem during a visit to England, where he created a sensation in
London society by wearing chaps and sombrero, indoors and out.
Feeling confined in the crowded city and restricted by the
conventions of society, the Western poet longed intensely for the
freedom of his native land. The lines of the poem breathe this
longing for the spacious western plains, and the love of a horseman
for his mount. As you read them aloud, stress the riding rhythm.*

*Room! room to turn round in, to breathe and be free,
To grow to be giant, to sail as at sea
With the speed of the wind on a steed with his mane
To the wind, without pathway or route or a rein.
Room! room to be free where the white border'd sea*   5
*Blows a kiss to a brother as boundless as he;
Where the buffalo come like a cloud on the plain,
Pouring on like the tide of a storm-driven main,
And the lodge of the hunter to friend or to foe
Offers rest; and unquestion'd you come or you go.*   10

My plains of America! Seas of wild lands!
From a land in the seas in a rainment of foam,
That has reached to a stranger the welcome of home,
I turn to you, lean to you, lift you my hands.

Run? Run? See this flank, sir, and I
   do love him so!   ¹⁵

> Standing beside his blind horse Apache, Kit explains why the horse is dear to him.

But he's blind, badger blind. Whoa, Pache, boy, whoa.
No, you wouldn't believe it to look at his eyes,
But he's blind, badger blind, and it happen'd this wise:

    "We lay in the grass and the sunburnt clover
That spread on the ground like a
   great brown cover   ²⁰

> Note how the plain is parched dry.

Northward and southward, and west and away
To the Brazos, where our lodges lay,
One broad and unbroken level of brown.
We were waiting the curtains of night to come down
To cover us trio and conceal our flight   ²⁵
With my brown bride, won from an Indian town
That lay in the rear the full ride of a night.

    "We lounged in the grass — her eyes were in mine,
And her hands on my knee, and her hair was as wine
In its wealth and its flood, pouring on
   and all over   ³⁰

> Note the many comparisons.

---

16. *badger blind*: as blind as a badger; *i.e.*, completely blind. (The badger isn't really blind, but he burrows in the darkness underground, and blinks in daylight.) *Pache*: Apache—his horse; named after the Apaches, southwestern Indians who were always on the warpath.

22. *Brazos*: a river that runs through Texas to the Gulf.

Her bosom wine red, and pressed never by one.
Her touch was as warm as the tinge of the clover
Burnt brown as it reach'd to the kiss of the sun.
Her words they were low as the lute-throated dove,
And as laden with love as the heart when it beats   35
In its hot, eager answer to earliest love,
Or the bee hurried home by its burthen of sweets.

    "We lay low in the grass on the broad plain levels,
Old Revels and I, and my stolen brown bride;
'Forty full miles if a foot, and the devils   40
Of red Comanches are hot on the | Old Revels speaks.
    track
When once they strike it. Let the sun go down
Soon, very soon,' muttered bearded old Revels
As he peer'd at the sun, lying low on his back,
Holding fast to his lasso. Then he jerk'd at his steed   45
And he sprang to his feet, and glanced swiftly around,
And then dropp'd, as if shot, with an ear to the ground;
Then again to his feet, and to me, to my bride,
While his eyes were like flame, his | More comparisons.
    face like a shroud,
His form like a king, and his beard like a cloud,   50
And his voice loud and shrill, as both trumpet and reed, —
'Pull, pull in your lassoes, and bridle to steed,
And speed you if ever for life you would speed.
Aye, ride for your lives, for your lives you must ride!
For the plain is aflame, the prairie on fire,   55

41. *Comanches*: a Shoshone tribe of Indians, originally in Wyoming, later
    ranging the Southwest.

And the feet of wild horses hard flying before
I heard like a sea breaking high on the shore,
While the buffalo come like a surge of the sea,
Driven far by the flame, driving fast on us three
As a hurricane comes, crushing palms in his ire.'   60

      "We drew in the lassoes, seized saddle and rein,
Threw them on, cinched them on, cinched them over again,
And again drew the girth; and spring we to horse,
With head to the Brazos, with a sound in the air
Like the surge of a sea, with a flash in the eye,   65
From that red wall of flame reaching up to the sky;
A red wall of flame and a black rolling sea
Rushing fast upon us, as the wind sweeping free
And afar from the desert blown hollow and hoarse.

      "Not a word, not a wail from a lip was let fall;   70
We broke not a whisper, we breathed not a prayer;
There was work to be done, there was death in the air,
And the chance was as one to a thousand for all.

Twenty miles!…thirty miles!…a din distant speck…
Then a long reaching line, and the Brazos in sight!   75
And I rose in my seat with a shout of delight.
I stood in my stirrup, and looked to my right —
But Revels was gone; I glanced by my shoulder
And saw his horse stagger; I saw his head drooping
Hard down on his breast, and his naked breast stooping   80
Low down to the mane, as so swifter and bolder
Ran reaching out for us the red-footed fire.

He rode neck to neck with a buffalo bull,
That made the earth shake where he came in his course,
The monarch of millions, with shaggy mane full   85
If smoke and of dust, and it shook with desire
Of battle, with rage and with bellowing hoarse.
His keen, crooked horns, through the storm of his mane,
Like black lances lifted and lifted again;
And I looked but this once, for the fire licked through,   90
And Revels was gone, as we rode two and two.

      "I looked to my left then — and nose, neck, and shoulder
Sank slowly, sank surely, till back to my thighs,
And up through the black blowing veil of her hair
Did beam full in mine her two marvelous eyes,   95
With a longing and love yet a look of despair
And a pity for me, as she felt the smoke fold her,
And flames leaping far for her glorious hair.
Her sinking horse falter'd, plunged, fell, and was gone
As I reach'd through the flame and I bore her still on.   100
On! Into the Brazos, she, Pache, and I —
Poor, burnt, blinded Pache, I love | Back to the scene of II. 15-18.
     him…That's why."

FOR THE AMBITIOUS STUDENT

While Joaquin Miller was in England, he was invited to a fashionable breakfast, where he met Robert Browning. Having in mind the idea of writing a poem about a prairie fire on the Western plains of America, and a horseman's race with the fire, he asked Browning's permission to borrow the rhythm and spirit of "Good News from Ghent" for his poem. Browning replied, "Why not borrow from Vergil, as I did? He is as rich as one of your gold mines, while I am but a poor scribe." Ask your Latin teacher to quote the lines from Vergil that Browning referred to. If you can, read these lines to the class, to see whether they can feel the horse-gallop rhythm.

SKIPPER IRESON'S RIDE

John Greenleaf Whittier

"Skipper Ireson's Ride" is an incident made famous in two separate poems. The first of these is by Whittier, who heard an account of Skipper Ireson from a friend at school. Without checking the facts, he wrote this version, the inaccuracy of which will be apparent to you when you have read the second version by Charles Buxton Going, which follows after. But Whittier's poem, with its catchy refrain, soon became a popular favorite, and for years Floyd Ireson wrongfully served as a horrible example of unworthy behavior. Such is the power of the poet's pen.

Of all the rides since the birth of time,
Told in story or sung in rhyme, —
On Apuleius's Golden Ass,
Or one-eyed Calendar's horse of brass,
Witch astride of a human back,   5
Islam's prophet on Al-Borák, —
The strangest ride that ever was sped
Was Ireson's, out from Marblehead!
    Old Floyd Ireson, for his hard heart,
    Tarred and feathered and carried in a cart   10
    By the women of Marblehead!

3-6. These references are to famous stories of fantastic rides, the first by a
Roman author, the second from *The Arabian Nights*. "Islam's prophet" is
Mohammed, and Al-Borák the wonderful animal on which he rode to the
seventh heaven.

8. *Marblehead*: a famous fishing village near Boston.

Body of turkey, head of owl,
Wings a-droop like a rained-on fowl,
Feathered and ruffled in every part,
Skipper Ireson stood in the cart.   15
Scores of women, old and young,
Strong of muscle, and glib of tongue,
Pushed and pulled up the rocky lane,
Shouting and singing the shrill refrain:
    "Here's Flud Oirson, fur his horrd horrt,   20
    Torr'd an' futherr'd an' corr'd in a corrt
    By the women o'Morble'ead!"

Wrinkled scolds with hands on hips,
Girls in bloom of cheek and lips,
Wild-eyed, free-limbed, such as chase   25
Bacchus round some antique vase,
Brief of skirt, with ankles bare,
Loose of kerchief and loose of hair,
With conch shells blowing and fish horns' twang,
Over and over the Mænads sang: 30
    "Here's Flud Oirson, fur his horrd horrt,
    Torr'd an' futherr'd an' corr'd in a corrt
    By the women o'Morble'ead!"

Small pity for him! — He sailed away
From a leaking ship in Chaleur Bay, —   35

---

26. *Bacchus*: Roman god of wine and dancing, often pictured on antique vases
    with his attendant maidens.
30. *Mænads (mē′ nădz)*: wildly dancing followers of Bacchus. The Marblehead
    girls were "drunk" with excitement.
35. *Chaleur Bay*: a bay in the Gulf of St. Lawrence, near the fishing banks of
    Newfoundland.

Sailed away from a sinking wreck,
With his own town's people on her deck!
"Lay by! lay by!" they called to him.
Back he answered, "Sink or swim!
Brag of your catch of fish again!" 40
And off he sailed through the fog and rain!
　　Old Floyd Ireson, for his hard heart,
　　Tarred and feathered and carried in a cart
　　By the women of Marblehead!

Fathoms deep in dark Chaleur 45
That wreck shall lie forevermore.
Mother and sister, wife and maid,
Looked from the rocks of Marblehead
Over the moaning and rainy sea, —
Looked for the coming that might not be! 50
What did the winds and the sea birds say
Of the cruel captain who sailed away? —
　　Old Floyd Ireson, for his hard heart,
　　Tarred and feathered and carried in a cart
　　By the women of Marblehead. 55

Through the street, on either side,
Up flew windows, doors swung wide;
Sharp-tongued spinsters, old wives gray,
Treble lent the fish horn's bray.
Sea-worn grandsires, cripple-bound, 60
Hulks of old sailors run aground,
Shook head, and fist, and hat, and cane,
And cracked with curses the hoarse refrain:

"Here's Flud Oirson, fur his horrd horrt,
Torr'd an' futherr'd an' corr'd in a corrt   65
   By the women o'Morble'ead!"

Sweetly along the Salem road
Bloom of orchard and lilac showed.
Little the wicked skipper knew
Of the fields so green and the sky so blue.   70
Riding there in his sorry trim,
Like an Indian idol glum and grim,
Scarcely he seemed the sound to hear
Of voices shouting, far and near:
   "Here's Flud Oirson, fur his horrd horrt,   75
   Torr'd an' futherr'd an' corr'd in a corrt
    By the women o'Morble'ead!"

"Hear me, neighbors!" at last he cried, —
"What to me is this noisy ride?
What is the shame that clothes the skin   80
To the nameless horror that lives within?
Waking or sleeping, I see a wreck,
And hear a cry from a reeling deck!
Hate me and curse me, — I only dread
The hand of God and the face of the dead!"   85
   Said old Floyd Ireson, for his hard heart,
   Tarred and feathered and carried in a cart
    By the women of Marblehead!

Then the wife of the skipper lost at sea
Said, "God has touched him! why should we?"   90

Said an old wife mourning her only son,
"Cut the rogue's tether and let him run!"
So with soft relentings and rude excuse,
Half scorn, half pity, they cut him loose,
And gave him a cloak to hide him in,   95
And left him alone with his shame and sin.

    Poor old Floyd Ireson, for his hard heart,
    Tarred and feathered and carried in a cart
      By the women of Marblehead!

THE TRUE STORY OF SKIPPER IRESON
Charles Buxton Going

If Whittier had checked the facts of the story before writing his version of Skipper Ireson's ride, he would have discovered, to his surprise, that Ireson was probably not so much to blame as his men. The truth seems to be that he tried to stay by the sinking vessel, but his crew refused to obey him. When they reached the shore, the crew threw the blame on Skipper Ireson. During his terrible ordeal, Ireson kept silence except to remark, "I thank you for the ride, gentlemen, and you will live to regret it." And they did.

Years later Going, wishing to right what he felt was a cruel wrong, wrote the following version of the story. In this account Skipper Ireson is made as great a hero as Whittier had made him a villain. If you are alert, you will note several other differences between the two accounts. If the nautical details are confusing, you may find help in the Note for the Land-Lubber at the end of the poem.

> *Here's Flood Ireson, for his hard heart*
> *Tarr'd and feather'd and carried in a cart*
> *By the women of Marblehead!*
> — Old Song

I

Out of the fog and the gloom,
    Chased by the lift of the sea,
Dripping with spindrift and spume
    Races the *Betty*, free.

> The boat was running before a heavy gale.

Hold-full of cod to the planks, ⁵

    Staggering under her spread —

Never such luck from the banks

    Sailed into Marblehead!

> She had every sail spread to the wind.

Full — keep her full! Drown her rail —

    Lee-decks awash to the hatch! ¹⁰

While the rest ride out the gale,

    Flood Ireson's home with his catch!

Cape Cod abeam to the south'ard —

    Up sprang the skipper on deck:

What was that hail the wind

      smothered? ¹⁵

    "Wreck, O — to port, there — a wreck!"

> They were driving her hard, racing home with their unusual catch.

> Just before reaching port they are hailed by a sinking vessel.

Logged, and awash in the sea,

    Ready to sink by the head —

"Looks like the *Active* to me —

    Stand by those head sheets!" he said; ²⁰

"Keep your helm up all you can —

    We'll round-to and bring her to

      weather.

Keep her away, I said, man!

    Are you all mad there, together?

> He gave orders to turn and go to the rescue, a dangerous maneuver in such a gale.

"God, men! —" He stopped on the

      word, ²⁵

    Sullen his crew stood, and grim;

Never a man of them stirred,

    Save as if guarding from him

> He realized that no one obeyed his orders.

Halyard and sheet; so he stood,
 One man against the whole ship —   30
Skipper? Ay — what was the good?
 Greed was the captain this trip!

Order, when none would obey?
 Threaten? 'Twas idle, he knew;
Reason? Ay — argue and pray   35
 And plead with a mutinied crew!

"Look at her signals!" he said: —
 "Stand by her! Shall it go down
That seamen of old Marblehead
 Left sinking shipmates to drown?"   40

"Ay!" growled the mate: — "and by God,   The men were unwilling to risk
 What if a story were told   the fortune they were carrying.
How the year's best catch of cod
 Rotted and spoiled in our hold?
Risk such a catch as we've got?   45
 No!...Let them chance it!" said he: —
"Sink or swim...this is the lot
 Of all men who follow the sea!"

Heartsick, Flood Ireson sailed past,
 Helpless to answer their hail.   50
Deaf as the shriek of the blast,
 Blind as the scud of the gale,
Lee-decks awash to the hatch,
 Tearing her way through the foam —

Blood of men's lives on her catch,   ⁵⁵
    On drove the *Betty* for home.

The *blood* of the men they left to drown.

II

The day was cool; white-crested
    ripples sung

Notice the sudden change of rhythm.

      Along the beach, and all the sky was clear
When, safe into the quiet harbor, swung
      The *Betty*, gliding smoothly to her pier.   ⁶⁰

First of the fleet, and welcome as the day —
      A little fortune in her close-filled hold —
Why did her crew, then, seem to turn away
      From friendly greetings? Ireson, too, of old

Kindly of heart, whose brave words often cheered   ⁶⁵
      The poor home-comings of an empty trip —
Why was it he himself had not appeared,
      But sent his crew ashore, and kept his ship?

Then, bit by bit, was forged a black report;
      From mouth to mouth the cruel story spread,   ⁷⁰
And murmurs rose — till, sailing into port
      Like some accuser risen from the dead,
The rescued skipper of the *Active* came,
      And told the angry gossips of the town
How Skipper Ireson, to their lasting shame,   ⁷⁵
      Heedless of signals, left him to go down.

"Heedless of love of man or laws of God,

Or all the brave old honor of the sea,
He sold us, shipmates, for a mess of cod —
    And Marblehead shall bear the shame!" said he.   ⁸⁰

"He left us — and before the | Another boat—
    Swallow came | this one did stop.
    Four of my men were washed away. The dead
Shall haunt your cape, to cry Flood Ireson shame —
    The whole world know the shame of Marblehead!"

The strong men, cursing, swore to purge the town   ⁸⁵
    Of such dishonor; smarting with disgrace,
They dragged Flood Ireson, unresisting, down
    And stripped him in the public market-place.

The rest you know — the tar-and-feather coat,
    The shameful ride they gave him, dragged with jeers ⁹⁰
To Salem village, in a fishing-boat —
    The cruel, lying song that lived for years.

And all he bore, thinking it best the shame
    Should cling to one man, though that man were he,
If that would save the honorable name   ⁹⁵
    Of Marblehead, and of her sons at sea.

III

So Ireson won the day, and no one hears
    His crew's disgrace. Their very names are lost,
While he has borne the blame through all these years
    And paid the cost.   ¹⁰⁰

All they are gone who wronged him — some asleep
    In quiet graveyards, others roving free
Till God shall call by name from out the deep
    Those lost at sea.

For that was all a hundred years ago;   105
    Long is Flood Ireson's rest among the dead;
But still the fishing-schooners come and go
    At Marblehead.

And those who sailed them have been true and brave —
    Heroes of surf and rescue, storm and wreck,   110
Gone, unafraid, to death on shore and wave
    And battle-deck.

Then let the blood and seas blot out the wrong
    Done long ago; we will not judge the dead,
But lay our laurel wreath where thorns pressed long   115
    On Ireson's head.

NOTE FOR THE LAND-LUBBER

The *Betty* was probably headed due west because Cape Cod was sighted *abeam* (off to the side) to the south. And the wind must have been coming from about the northeast, for, although the ship was riding *free* (with a favorable wind), her *lee-decks* (those opposite the direction from which wind was blowing) were *a-wash* (under water); and, if the wind were directly behind the ship, the ship would not be tipping, nor would there be a lee-deck. Moreover, when the

Active is sighted to *port* (to the left; *i.e.*, in this case to the south), the captain orders the helmsman to *keep the helm up, keep her away* (turn the ship more in the direction the wind is blowing). The captain's intention evidently was to turn south and pass the *Active*, then *round-to* and *bring her to weather* (turn completely around and head directly into the wind) and thus come up to the *Active* from the south, stop, and rescue her men. Other nautical terms follow:

> *halyard*: a rope used to raise or lower a sail.
>
> *hatch*: a covering over an opening in the deck of a ship.
>
> *head sheets*: the ropes governing the set of the sails in the forward part of the ship.
>
> *helm:* the steering apparatus.
>
> *keep her full*: keep the sails full of wind; don't ease the strain by changing direction.
>
> *logged*: water-logged.
>
> *mutinied*: refusing to obey the captain's orders.
>
> *ride out the gale*: to take every precaution to stay afloat.
>
> *spindrift*: spray blown from the waves during a gale.
>
> *spume*: foam.

Stories in Verse

HOW CYRUS LAID THE CABLE
John Godfrey Saxe

Here is a simple, easy poem about a notable event by a once-famous American humorous poet. In our day of split-second communication, who remembers how in 1858 Queen Victoria's ninety-word message to the President of the United States was transmitted by trans-Atlantic cable in sixty-seven minutes?

And who among the readers of Ogden Nash and Margaret Fishback and Dorothy Parker remembers John Godfrey Saxe? He was a writer of popular humorous poems when "Cyrus laid the cable." In the following verses, the humorous effect seems to derive not merely from the choice of words, but also in part from the ballad form.

But for all its whimsical tone, the poem has a serious theme. It is the same theme that you will find in "Columbus," and it can be put in one word: Persistence!

Come, listen all unto my song;
    It is no silly fable;
'Tis all about the mighty cord
    They call the Atlantic Cable.

Bold Cyrus Field he said, says he,   5
    "I have a pretty notion
That I can run a telegraph
    Across the Atlantic Ocean."

---

8. Samuel F.B. Morse, inventor of the telegraph, had laid a cable across New York harbor in 1842; and in the 1850's numerous cables were laid in European waters.

Then all the people laughed, and said
  They'd like to see him do it;   10
He might get half-seas over, but
  He never could go through it.

To carry out his foolish plan
  He never would be able;
He might as well go hang himself   15
  With his Atlantic Cable.

But Cyrus was a valiant man,
  A fellow of decision;
And heeded not their mocking words,
  Their laughter and derision.   20

Twice did his bravest efforts fail,
  And yet his mind was stable;
He wa'n't the man to break his heart
  Because he broke his cable.

"Once more, my gallant boys!" he cried; 25
  "*Three times* — you know the fable
(I'll make it *thirty*," muttered he,
  "But I will lay the cable!").

Once more they tried, — hurrah! hurrah!
  What means this great commotion? 30
The Lord be praised! the cable's laid
  Across the Atlantic Ocean!

---

21. *bravest efforts*: Cyrus Field's bravery was a matter of risking reputation and
  money, rather than his skin. He was a financier.

Loud ring the bells — for, flashing through
    Six hundred leagues of water,
Old Mother England's benison   35
    Salutes her eldest daughter!

O'er all the land the tidings speed,
    And soon, in every nation,
They'll hear about the cable with
    Profoundest admiration!   40

Now, long live President and Queen;
    And long live gallant Cyrus;
And may his courage, faith, and zeal
    With emulation fire us;

And may we honor evermore   45
    The manly, bold, and stable;
And tell our sons, to make them brave,
    How Cyrus laid the cable!

FOR THE AMBITIOUS STUDENT

Another interesting theme poem by John Godfrey Saxe is called "The Blind Men and the Elephant." You might read this to the class and explain its theme in your own words.

When I looked up in the encyclopedias the accounts of the origin of the idea of submarine cables, and of the various attempts at laying cables across the

---

35.benison: blessing. Queen Victoria sent congratulations to the United States.

oceans, I found them very entertaining. If you find this information equally entertaining, you may wish to prepare a compelling oral report on it for the class.

FOR YOUR VOCABULARY

Two opposing attitudes toward Cyrus are found in the words *derision* and *emulation*. If we are to *emulate* Cyrus, we must *imitate* his conduct, striving to equal or excel his admirable accomplishments. The people who *derided* him did not admire him; if they imitated him at all, they did so to ridicule him. The poet says they hurled at him "*mocking* words"; these may have been merely *derisive*, or they may have been scornfully *imitative*. *Mockery* sometimes denotes *derision*, at other times scornful *imitation*. Write a story using all of the italicized words.

SIMON LEGREE — A NEGRO SERMON
(To be read in your own variety of Negro dialect)
Vachel Lindsay

Vachel Lindsay won his title, the "American troubadour," by traveling all over the United States — sometimes on foot — and reciting his poems everywhere, in farmhouses, town halls, theaters, schools, colleges. He believed that poetry must be heard, and he recited his poems with definite rhythmic effects. "Simon Legree" shows the author in one of his lighter moments, but even here the oral effects are important. Lindsay read the poem with a marked rhythm; rolled it forth with a swift, oratorical rush; made the chains rattle and Simon Legree snarl; chanted the refrain with great deliberation: "But HE went DOWN to the DEVil." In the last stanza, he would look at various individuals in the audience and shake his finger warningly when he said:

> They are matching pennies — and shooting craps,
> They are playing poker — and taking naps.

And in the last three lines his voice dropped lower and lower till you actually felt that it, too, had gone "down to the devil" with Simon Legree.

Legree's big house was white and green.
His cotton-fields were the best to be seen.
He had strong horses and opulent cattle,
And bloodhounds bold, with chains that would rattle.
His garret was full of curious things: 5
Books of magic, bags of gold,

And rabbits' feet on long twine strings.
But he went down to the Devil.

Legree he sported a brass-buttoned coat,
A snake-skin necktie, a blood-red shirt.   10
Legree he had a beard like a goat,
And a thick hairy neck, and eyes like dirt.
His puffed-out cheeks were fish-belly white,
He had great long teeth, and an appetite.
He ate raw meat, 'most every meal,   15
And rolled his eyes till the cat would squeal.

His fist was an enormous size
To mash poor niggers that told him lies:
He was surely a witch-man in disguise.
But he went down to the Devil.   20

He wore hip-boots, and would wade all day
To capture his slaves that had fled away.
But he went down to the Devil.

He beat poor Uncle Tom to death
Who prayed for Legree with his last breath.   25
Then Uncle Tom to Eva flew,
To the high sanctoriums bright and new;
And Simon Legree stared up beneath,
And cracked his heels, and ground his teeth:
And went down to the Devil.   30

He crossed the yard in the storm and gloom;

He went into his grand front room.
He said, "I killed him, and I don't care."
He kicked a hound, he gave a swear;
He tightened his belt, he took a lamp,   35
Went down cellar to the webs and damp.
There in the middle of the mouldy floor
He heaved up a slab, he found a door —
And went down to the Devil.

His lamp blew out, but his eyes burned bright.   40
Simon Legree stepped down all night —
Down, down to the Devil.
Simon Legree he reached the place,
He saw one half of the human race,
He saw the Devil on a wide green throne,   45
Gnawing the meat from a big ham-bone,
And he said to Mister Devil:

     "I see that you have much to eat —
     A red ham-bone is surely sweet.
     I see that you have lion's feet;   50
     I see your frame is fat and fine,
     I see you drink your poison wine —
     Blood and burning turpentine."

And the Devil said to Simon Legree:
     "I like your style, so wicked and free.   55
     Come sit and share my throne with me,
     And let us bark and revel."
And there they sit and gnash their teeth,

And each one wears a hop-vine wreath.
They are matching pennies and shooting craps,   60
They are playing poker and taking naps.
And old Legree is fat and fine:
He eats the fire, he drinks the wine—
Blood, and burning turpentine —
    Down, down with the Devil;   65
        Down, down with the Devil;
            Down, down with the Devil.

OFF TO THE WAR
(From *John Brown's Body*)
Stephen Vincent Benét

*The nearest approach to a great epic poem in American literature
is* **John Brown's Body**, *a stirring account of the War between the
States. The story is told in episodes by spot-lighting first one person,
then another, who is involved in the great struggle. Each episode is
a little unit in itself, but all are held together by a slim thread of
narrative. In this story of 367 pages Mr. Benét has used many
different styles of poetry to suit the varying moods.*

*In this passage in blank verse two mountain lads from Kentucky
are on the way to join the army — they hardly know which army,
nor who the enemy is. The passage gives you a real insight into
the characteristics of the fast-disappearing mountain folk of
America, and in addition tells a brief incident with suspense —
and, I hope, a chuckle or two at the end.*

Up in the mountains where the hogs are thin
And razorbacked, wild Indians of hogs,
The laurel's green in April — and if the nights
Are cold as the cold cloud of watersmoke
Above a mountain-spring, the midday sun   5
Has heat enough to make you sweat.

They are a curious and most native stock,
The lanky men, the lost, forgotten seeds
Spilled from the first great wave-march toward the West
And set to sprout by chance in the deep cracks   10

Of that hill-billy world of laurel-hells.
They keep the beechwood-fiddle and the salt
Old-fashioned ballad-English of our first
Rowdy, corn-liquor-drinking, ignorant youth;
Also the rifle and the frying-pan,   15
The old feud-temper and the old feud-way
Of thinking strangers better shot on sight
But treating strangers that one leaves unshot
With border-hospitality.

                    The girls
Have the brief-blooming, rhododendron-youth   20
Of pioneer women, and the black-toothed age.
And if you yearn to meet your pioneers,
You'll find them there, the same men, inbred sons
Of inbred sires perhaps, but still the same;
A pioneer-island in a world that has   25
No use for pioneers — the unsplit rock
Of Fundamentalism, calomel,
Clan-virtues, clannish vices, fiddle-tunes
And a hard God.

                They are our last frontier.
They shot the railway-train when it first came,   30
And when the Fords first came, they shot the Fords.
It could not save them. They are dying now
Of being educated, which is the same.
One need not weep romantic tears for them,
But when the last moonshiner buys his radio,   35
And the last, lost, wild-rabbit of a girl

---

13. *our*: America's
27. *Fundamentalism*: a religious attitude which holds that certain traditional
    beliefs are fundamental; opposed to modernism.

Is civilized with a mail-order dress,
Something will pass that was American
And all the movies will not bring it back.

They are misfit and strange in our new day,   40
In Sixty-One they were not quite so strange,
Before the Fords, before the day of the Fords...

Luke Breckinridge, his rifle on his shoulder,
Slipped through green forest-alleys toward the town,
A gawky boy with smoldering eyes, whose feet   45
Whispered the crooked paths like moccasins.
He wasn't looking for trouble, going down,
But he was on guard, as always. When he stopped
To scoop some water in the palm of his hand
From a sweet trickle between moss-grown rocks,   50
You might have thought him careless for a minute,
But when the snapped stick cracked six feet behind him
He was all sudden rifle and hard eyes.
The pause endured a long death-quite instant,
Then he knew who it was.

          "Hi Jim," he said,   55
Lowering his rifle. The green laurel-screen
Hardly had moved, but Jim was there beside him.
The cousins looked at each other. Their rifles seemed
To look as well, with much the same taut silentness.
"Goin' to town, Luke?"

          "Uh-huh, goin' to town,   60
You goin'?"

        "Looks as if I was goin'."

"Looks
As if you was after squirrels."
       "I might be.
You goin' after squirrels?" "I might be, too."
"Not so many squirrels near town."
         "No, reckon there's not."
Jim hesitated. His gaunt hands caressed   65
The smooth guard of his rifle. His eyes were sharp.
"Might go along a piece together," he said.
Luke didn't move. Their eyes clashed for a moment,
Then Luke spoke, casually.
      "I hear the Kelceys
Air goin' to fight in this here war," he said.   70
Jim nodded slowly, "Yuh, I heerd that too."
He watched Luke's trigger-hand.
        "I might be goin'
Myself sometime," he said reflectively
Sliding his own hand down. Luke saw the movement.
"We-uns don't like the Kelceys much," he said.   75
With his eyes down to pinpoints.
       Then Jim smiled.
"We-uns neither," he said.
       His hand slid back.
They went along together after that
But neither of them spoke for half-a-mile,
Then finally, Jim said, half-diffidently,   80
"You know who we air goin' to fight outside?
I heard it was the British. Air that so?'
"Hell, no," said Luke, with scorn. He puckered his brows.
"Dunno's I rightly know just who they air."

He admitted finally, "But 'tain't the British.　　　85
It's some trash-lot of furriners, that's shore.
They call 'em Yankees near as I kin make it,
But they ain't Injuns neither."
　　　　　　　　　　　　"Well," said Jim
Soothingly, "Reckon it don't rightly matter
Long as the Kelceys take the other side."　　　90

FOR THE AMBITIOUS STUDENT

I think if you got *John Brown's Body* in your hands, you would find, as you browsed through the book, passages which you would read with great interest. Try it.

KENTUCKY BELLE
(Told in an Ohio Farm-House; 1868)
Constance Fenimore Woolson

*This story is being told by a woman from the Tennessee
mountains who, after marrying Conrad, a German farmer, had
gone North to make her home among his people in Ohio, just
before the War between the States. During a cavalry raid she felt
called upon to make a great sacrifice, a sacrifice which sprang
from her deep love for her own home-land. You will enjoy the
regular beat of the lines, especially those describing the raid of
Morgan, the famous Confederate cavalry leader.*

Summer of sixty-three, sir, and Conrad was gone away —
Gone to the county-town, sir, to sell our first load of hay;
We lived in the log-house yonder, poor as ever you've seen;
Röschen there was a baby, and I was only nineteen.

Conrad, he took the oxen, but he left Kentucky Belle;   5
How much we thought of Kentuck, I couldn't begin to tell;
Came from the Blue-Grass country, my father gave her to me
When I rode north with Conrad, away from the Tennessee.

Conrad lived in Ohio, — a German he is you know:
The house stood right in the cornfields, stretching on row
      after row;   10
The old folks made me welcome; they were kind as kind could be,
But I kept longing, longing for the hills of the Tennessee!

---

4. *Röschen*: Little Rose (German).
7. *Blue-Grass country*: Kentucky.

Oh! for a sight of water, the shady top of a hill,
The smell of the mountain balsams, a wind that never is still!
But the level land went stretching away to meet the sky,   15
Never a rise from north to south to rest the homesick eye;

From east to west no river to shine out under the moon,
Nothing to make a shadow in the yellow afternoon,
Only the steady sunshine as I looked out all forlorn,
Only the "rustle, rustle," as I walked among the corn.   20

When I fell sick with pining, we didn't wait any more,
We moved away from the cornfields out to this river-shore;
The Tuscarawas it's called, sir, off there's a hill you see —
And now I've got to like it next best to the Tennessee.

I was at work that morning. Some one came riding like mad   25
Over the bridge and up the road — Farmer Rouf's little lad;
Bareback he rode; he had no hat; he hardly stopped to say:
"Morgan's men are coming, Frau, they're galloping straight this way!

"I'm sent to warn the neighbours. He isn't a mile behind!
He sweeps up all the horses, every horse that he can find;   30
Morgan, Morgan the raider, and Morgan's terrible men,
With bowie-knives and pistols are galloping up the glen!"

The lad rode down the valley; and I stood still at the door;
The baby laughed and prattled, playing with spools on the floor;

---

23. *Tuscarawas*: a river in eastern Ohio.
28. *Frau*: Madame (German).

Kentuck was in the pasture; Conrad, my man, was gone; 35
And near and nearer Morgan's men were galloping, galloping on!

Sudden I picked up baby, and ran to the pasture-bar,
"Kentuck," I called, "Kentucky"; she knew me ever so far.
I led her down the gully that turns off there to the right,
And tied her to the bushes; her head was just out of sight. 40

As I ran back to the log-house, my ears they caught a sound,
The ring of hoofs, galloping hoofs, thundering over the ground;
Coming into the turnpike, out from the White-Woman glen,
Morgan, Morgan the raider, and Morgan's terrible men!

I scarce could breathe, and nearly my heart it stopped in alarm, 45
As still I stood in the doorway, with baby on my arm;
They came; they passed; with spur and whip in haste they
swept along,
Morgan, Morgan the raider, and his band, six hundred strong.

Oh! fierce they looked and jaded, riding through night and
through day,
Pushing straight on for the river, many long miles away; 50
They must reach the edge of Virginia where it bends up
toward the West.
They must reach the ford and cross it, before they could stop for rest.

On like the wind they hurried, and Morgan rode in advance,
Bright were his eyes like live coals as he gave me a hasty glance.
And I was just breathing freely, after my choking pain, 55
When the last one of the troopers suddenly drew his rein.

Frightened I was to death, sir; I scarce dared look in his face
As he asked for a drink of water, and glanced about the place;
I gave him a drink; and he smiled; his eyes were soft and blue —
'Twas only a boy; and his tired voice was the dear home-voice I
    knew! 60

Only sixteen he was, sir — a fond mother's only son,
Off and away with Morgan before his life had begun;
The big drops stood on his temples, drawn was the boyish mouth,
And I thought me of that mother, waiting down in the South!

Oh, pluck was he to the backbone, and clear grit through and
    through, 65
Boasted and bragged like a trooper, but the big words wouldn't do!
The boy was dying, sir, dying — as plain as plain could be,
Worn out by his ride with Morgan, up from the Tennessee.

But when I told the laddie that I, too, was from the South,
Water came in his dim eyes and quivers about his mouth; 70
"Do you know the Blue-Grass country?" he wistful began to say,
Then swayed like a willow-sapling, and fainted clean away.

I had him into the log-house, and worked and brought him to: —
I fed him, and I coaxed him, as I thought his mother'd do;
And when the faintness left him, and the noise in his head
    was gone, 75
Morgan's men were miles away, galloping, galloping on.

He tried to go — the laddie! "You've kept me half the day!
Morgan, Morgan is waiting for me! Oh, what will Morgan say?"

But I heard a sound in the distance, and kept him back from
    the door,
The very same sound of horses' hoofs that I had heard before;   80

And on, on, came the soldiers, the Michigan cavalry,
And hard they rode, and black they looked, galloping rapidly;
They had followed hard on Morgan's track; they had followed
    day and night
But of Morgan and Morgan's raiders, they had never caught a sight.

And rich Ohio sat frightened through all those troubled days,   85
For strange wild men were galloping over her broad highways,
Now here, now there, now seen, now gone, now north, now east,
    now west,
Through river valleys, and cornland farms, sweeping away her best.

A bold ride and a long ride! But they were taken at last!
They has almost reached the river by galloping hard and fast,   90
But the boys in blue were upon them or ever they crossed the ford,
And Morgan, Morgan the raider, laid down his terrible sword.

Well — I kept the lad all evening, kept him against his will;
But he was too weak to follow, and sat there pale and still;
Then when his head was better—you'll wonder to hear me tell—   95
I stole down to that gully and brought up Kentucky Belle.

I kissed the star on her forehead — my pretty, gentle lass —
But I knew that she'd be happy, back in the old Blue-Grass;
A suit of clothes of Conrad's, and all the money I had,
And Kentuck, pretty Kentuck, I gave to the worn-out lad.   100

I guided him to the southward as well as I knew how;
The boy rode off with many thanks, and many a backward bow;
Then when the glow had faded, my heart began to swell,
As down the glen away she went, my lost Kentucky Belle!

When Conrad came in the evening, the moon was shining high, [105]
Baby and I were both crying, I couldn't tell him why!
But a battered suit of rebel grey was hanging against the wall,
And a thin old horse with drooping head stood in Kentucky's stall.

Well—he was kind and never once said a harsh word to me—
For he knew I couldn't help it—'twas my love for Tennessee—. [110]
But after the war was over, just think what came to pass —
A letter, sir; and the two were safe, back in the old Blue-Grass!

The lad got across the border, riding Kentucky Belle,
And Kentuck, she was happy, and fat, and hearty, and well,
He kept her, and he petted her, nor touched her with whip
      nor spur — [115]
Well — we've had many horses, but *never* a horse like her!

THE MORMON TRAIL
Elder Saul's Story
Daniel Henderson

One of the greatest sagas of America is that of the Mormon pilgrimage from New York, to Ohio, to Missouri, to Illinois, to Utah. The last phase, the long trek across the plains and mountains to the Salt Lake Valley, achieved truly epic proportions. After the founder of the Church, Joseph Smith, was murdered in Carthage, Illinois, Brigham Young became the second great leader and prophet. He it was who led the "Saints" through battle, famine, plague, Indian attack, to the Promised Land in the Western desert. One of the most dramatic scenes in American history was enacted when Brigham Young, looking down into the desolate Salt Lake Valley, turned to his travel-weary followers, and declared, "This is the place." Not all of the Mormons could see a great future in this desert country, but Brigham Young told them they would "make the desert blossom as the rose," and this the Mormons have done. All America can well be proud of this great accomplishment.

In Henderson's poem the story of the trip from Illinois to Utah is told by "Elder Saul," evidently a Mormon who has made the journey and lived to achieve honor among his people.

I

On Cummorah Hill
The angel of the Lord
Flashed at Joseph Smith
His flaming sword.

---

1. *Cummorah Hill*: a hill near Manchester, New York, where in 1827 Joseph Smith, directed by the angel Moroni, claimed to find the plates of gold upon which was written the history of the "Lost Tribe," later translated and published as *The Book of Mormon*.

Nigh Cummorah Hill   5
Joseph found
The Lost Tribe's golden plates
Hidden in the ground.
He found the golden plates
With their Revelation pages,   10
And the angel bade him read
The mysteries of the ages.

II

Baptist was I —
My father, Gospel George,
Tramped without shoes   15
The snows of Valley Forge.
He prayed — and he swore,
But I gave up kin and kith,
As the Angel Nephi bade,
To follow Prophet Smith!   20

When the Gentiles rose
The saints to destroy;
When our Prophet's blood stained
The earth of Illinois,
Then Angel Nephi said   25
"Anoint Brigham Young."

---

19. *Angel Nephi*: an important character in Mormon history.
21. *Gentiles*: any non-Mormons.
22. *saints*: the Mormons. The official name of the Mormon Church is the Church of Jesus Christ of Latter-Day Saints.
23. *Prophet*: Joseph Smith, murdered at Carthage, Illinois, June 27, 1844.

And we said, "Yea,"
For he had a prophet's tongue;
He had the will of Moses
And the heart of a lion.   30
And the Lord said to him,
"Lead the Saints west to Zion!"

We came to deep rivers —
They wouldn't roll back!
We met the Philistines —   35
God let them attack!
We suffered famine,
But no manna came;
Yet over the plains
Moved our pillar of flame: 40
'Twas Prophet Joseph Smith —
His flesh they might slay,
But his spirit blazed
Our wilderness way.

III

By the North Platte River   45
We prayed and cried,
For with plague and hunger

---

32. *Zion*: the heavenly city of God.
35. *Philistines*: enemies of the ancient Jews; hence, enemies of God's chosen people.
38. *manna*: food miraculously supplied to the Israelites in their journey through the wilderness. (Exod.16)
40. *pillar of flame*: See Exod. 13: 21-2.
45. *North Platte River*: a river five hundred and ten miles long, in Colorado, Wyoming, and Nebraska.

Weak folk died.
Among the cactus,
Amid the wild sage, 50
The mounds of our dead
Marked our pilgrimage.

A new plague rose
In our desert tramp —
Rattlesnakes swarmed 55
Where we made our camp.
They stung the horses,
They poisoned the cattle,
Where we laid our heads
Came the viper's rattle! 60
"Fight them with flame,"   "Set fire to the prairie."
Said Brigham Young,
And we were delivered
From the adder's tongue!

IV

Like a thief in the night — 65
Not a grass-blade stirred —
The wolfish Sioux   The Indians came into the
Entered our herd.   midst of the cattle to cause
                                     a stampede.
We woke to the bellow
And the rush of cattle. 70
We mounted, we went
As Gideon to battle.

---

72. *Gideon*: an Israelitish hero, who with a small band of followers, defeated the
Midianites.

In a thundering race
That endured till morn
We tamed the cyclone   75
Of hoof and horn. | A dynamic metaphor.
We turned the herd
With rifle flame,
And once as I fired
The vision came: 80
The Prophet rode   The spirit of Joseph Smith
To help us smite   was with them.
The skull of the thieving
Midianite!

We were sorely spent,   85
We were wounded or gored,
But the red morning rang
With our praise to the Lord!

V

When we climbed from the prairie
Children ran   90
And plucked gay flowers
For the grim caravan.
Under blue mountains
Capped with snows
They plucked monk's-hood   95
And the evening primrose.
All the hunger
And fright and pain
Of our pilgrimage

On the endless plain,   100
The young forgot
In the green-hill lands
As they clutched shy ferns
In their little moist hands.

We had come to Canaan —   105
Yet it didn't seem
The Paradise
Of the wanderers' dream.
Our eyes were blind
To the hills of grace,   110
But our Captain said:
"This is the place.

Here ends our warfare;
Here ends our woes.
We will make the desert   115
Blossom as the rose!"

> These five lines should be read with the solemn dignity which the occasion merited.

And then we saw
The lilies quiver
In the golden sun
By Jordan River!   120

> Accent *then*. Inspired by Brigham Young's words, the people see in their imaginations the beautiful New Canaan which they will create.

105. *Canaan*: the Promised Land.
120. *Jordan River*: the river in ancient Canaan.

JESSE JAMES
American Myth
A Design in Red and Yellow for a Nickel Library
William Rose Benét

If you had lived fifty or sixty years ago, you would have escaped today's flood of "comic books" filled with the fantastic exploits of Superman, Tarzan, Don Winslow, and the Lone Ranger. But you would doubtless have owned your own "library" of current thrillers, carefully hidden from the prying eyes of disapproving parents. These would have been the nickel weeklies, that related stupendous feats ascribed to Nick Carter, Buffalo Bill, Kit Carson, and other gallant adventurers in the conquest of the West. By calling this poem "A Design in Red and Yellow for a Nickel Library," Mr. Benét seems to promise you an extravagant, sensational story, like the yarns in those old nickel weeklies. And he richly fulfills the promise, for the poem is full of incredible exploits, told with fine gusto. The hero is the Missouri outlaw, Jesse James; and like most men who live by the six-shooter he must have been a rather contemptible sort in real life. But in American legend — and in this poem — he has become a popular idol, like Robin Hood, because he has a heart of gold and robs the rich to help the poor. Thus, have many figures become legendary heroes.

Jesse James was a two-gun man,
  (Roll on, Missouri!)
Strong-arm chief of an outlaw clan.
  (From Kansas to Illinois!)
He twirled an old Colt forty-five,   5
  (Roll on, Missouri!)

---

2. **AUTHOR'S NOTE:** In the refrain the proper native pronunciation of "Missouri" is, of course, "Mizzoura."

They never took Jesse James alive.
>   *(Roll, Missouri, roll!)*

Jesse James was King of the Wes';   10
>   *(Cataracks in the Missouri!)*
He'd a di'mon' heart in his lef' breas';
>   *(Brown Missouri rolls!)*
He'd a fire in his heart no hurt could stifle;
>   *(Thunder, Missouri!)*   15
Lion eyes an' a Winchester rifle.
>   *(Missouri, roll down!)*

Jesse James rode a pinto hawse;
Come at night to a water-cawse;
Tetched with the rowel that pinto's flank;   20
She sprung the torrent from bank to bank.

Jesse rode through a sleepin' town;
Looked the moonlit street both up an' down;
Crack-crack-crack, the street ran flames
An' a great voice cried, "I'm Jesse James!"   25

Hawse an' afoot they're after Jess!
>   *(Roll on, Missouri!)*
Spurrin' an' spurrin' — but he's gone Wes'.
>   *(Brown Missouri rolls!)*
He was ten foot tall when he stood in his boots;
>   *(Lightnin' light the Missouri!)*   30
More'n a match fer sich galoots.
>   *(Roll, Missouri, roll!)*

Jesse James rode outa the sage;
Roun' the rocks come the swayin' stage;
Straddlin' the road a giant stan's   35
An' a great voice bellers, "Throw up yer han's!"

Jesse raked in the di'mon' rings,
The big gold watches an' the yuther things;
Jesse divvied 'em then an' thar
With a cryin' child had lost her mar.   40

The U.S. troopers is after Jess;
        (Roll on, Missouri!)
Their hawses sweat foam, but he's gone Wes';
        (Hear Missouri roar!)
He was broad as a b'ar, he'd a ches' like a drum,   45
        (Wind an' rain through Missouri!)
An' his red hair flamed like Kingdom Come.
        (Missouri down to the sea!)

Jesse James all alone in the rain
Stopped an' stuck up the Eas'-boun' train;   50
Swayed through the coaches with horns an' a tail,
Lit out with the bullion an' the registered mail.

Jess made 'em all turn green with fright,
Quakin' in the aisles in the pitch-black night;
An' he give all the bullion to a pore ole tramp   55
Campin' nigh the cuttin' in the dirt an' damp.

---

56. *cuttin':* a clearing; a piece of land from which the trees have been cut.

The whole U.S. is after Jess;
> *(Roll on, Missouri!)*
The son-of-a-gun, if he ain't gone Wes';
> *(Missouri to the Sea!)*   60
He could chaw cold iron an' spit blue flame;
> *(Cataracks down the Missouri!)*
He rode on a catamount he'd learned to tame.
> *(Hear that Missouri roll!)*

Jesse James rode into a Bank;   65
Give his pinto a tetch on the flank;
Jumped the teller's window with an awful crash;
Heaved up the safe an' twirled his mustache;

He said, "So long, boys!" He yelped, "So long!
Feelin' porely to-day — I ain't feelin' strong!"   70
Rode right through the wall agoin' crack-crack-crack, —
Took the safe home to Mother in a gunny-sack.

They're creepin', they're crawlin', they're stalkin' Jess;
> *(Roll on, Missouri!)*
They's a rumor he's gone much further Wes';   75
> *(Roll, Missouri, roll!)*
They's word of a cayuse hitched to the bars
> *(Ruddy clouds on Missouri!)*
Of a golden sunset that busts into stars.
> *(Missouri, roll down!)*   80

Jesse James rode hell fer leather;
He was a hawse an' a man together;

In a cave in a mountain high up in air
He lived with a rattlesnake, a wolf, an' a bear.

Jesse's heart was as sof' as a woman;   85
Fer guts an' stren'th he was sooper-human;
He could put six shots through a woodpecker's eye
And take in one swaller a gallon o'rye.

They sought him here an' they sought him there,
    (Roll on, Missouri!)   90
But he strides by night through the ways of the air,
    (Brown Missouri rolls!)
They say he was took an' they say he is dead;
    (Thunder, Missouri!)
But he ain't — he's a sunset overhead!   95
    (Missouri down to the sea!)

Jesse James was a Hercules.
When he went through the woods he tore up the trees.
When he went on the plains he smoked the groun'
An' the hull lan' shuddered fer miles aroun'.   100

Jesse James wore a red bandanner
That waved on the breeze like the Star Spangled Banner;
In seven states he cut up dadoes.
He's gone with the buffler an' the desperadoes.

---

103. *cut up dadoes*: played tricks; a commoner word is *didoes* (dī' dōz)
104. *buffler*: buffaloes.

Yes, Jesse James was a two-gun man   105
    (Roll on, Missouri!)
The same as when this song began;
    (From Kansas to Illinois!)
An' when you see a sunset bust into flames
    (Lightnin' light the Missouri!)   110
Or a thunderstorm blaze — that's Jesse James!
    (Hear that Missouri roll!)

The purpose of the refrain in this poem, it seems to me, is to emphasize the rhythm and to speed up the tempo, much as does the hand-clapping of bystanders at a barn dance. If some pupil reads this poem in class, you should all join in chanting the refrain to mark the rhythm and the swing (of course you'll need a leader to keep you on the beat). In fact the refrains should almost be sung. Furthermore, the rhythmic swing should increase with the increasing excitement of the poem. As Jesse's exploits grow more and more astounding, you must show more and more abandon in swinging the lines.

THE MOUNTAIN WHIPPOORWILL
(Or, How Hill-Billy Jim Won the Great Fiddler's Prize)
(A Georgia Romance)
Stephen Vincent Benét

Down in Georgia, where fiddling contests are a cherished entertainment, Hill-Billy Jim came down from the mountains to try his skill at the Essex County Fair. In "The Mountain Whippoorwill" he tells how well he succeeded.

Hill-Billy Jim is a rare character. He glories in his power over the fiddle, and risks a silver dollar on his skill; but he has no false conceit. He is a hill-billy, and admits it; he praises his rivals with sincere generosity; and when awed silence greets his own efforts, he mistakes it for a sign of his defeat.

But there is more than modesty in Jim. He has the soul of a poet. For him the earth lives and breathes; he loves the creatures of the forest, the trees and the flowers, the murmuring rivers and the whispering wind. And when he tells how his rivals fiddled, he expresses himself in remarkable comparisons and exaggerations. He calls his own fiddle a whippoorwill, and talks to it as to a loved child.

Finally, he has an irresistible feeling for rhythm. As you read the poem, swing each line in its own rhythm, for there is great variety. Make each fiddler sound different; and when Jim cuts loose toward the end of each poem, be sure to cut loose, too. Jim treats his fiddle like a living thing; it's up to you to make it come alive.

Up in the mountains, it's lonesome all the time,
(Sof' win' slewin' thu' the sweet-potato vine).

Up in the mountains, it's lonesome for a child,
(Whippoorwills a-callin' when the sap runs wild).

Up in the mountains, mountains in the fog,   5
Everythin's as lazy as an old houn' dog.

Born in the mountains, never raised a pet,
Don't want nuthin' an' never got it yet.

Born in the mountains, lonesome-born,
Raised runnin' ragged thu' the cockleburrs and corn.   10

Never knew my pappy, mebbe never should.
Think he was a fiddle made of mountain laurel-wood.

Never had a mammy to teach me pretty-please.
Think she was a whippoorwill, a-skitin' thu' the trees.

Never had a brother ner a whole pair of pants,   15
But when I start to fiddle, why, yuh | He makes sample strokes
    got to start to dance! | with the bow.

Listen to my fiddle — Kingdom Come — Kingdom Come!
Hear the frogs a-chunkin' "Jug | He plucks the strings.
    o'rum, Jug o'rum!" | (The line is onomatopoetic.)
Hear that mountain-whippoorwill be lonesome in the air,
An' I'll tell yuh how I traveled to the Essex County Fair.   20

Essex County has a mighty pretty fair,
All the smarty fiddlers from the South come there.

Elbows flyin' as they rosin up the bow
For the First Prize Contest in the Georgia Fiddler's Show.

Old Dan Wheeling, with his whiskers | These fellows are worth
   in his ears,   25 | seeing: see them!
King-pin fiddler for nearly twenty years.

Big Tom Sargent, with his blue wall-eye,
An' Little Jimmy Weezer that can make a fiddle cry.

All sittin' roun', spittin' high an' struttin' proud,
(Listen, little whippoorwill, yuh | He talks to his fiddle.
*   better bug yore eyes!)*   30
Tun-a-tun-a-tunin' while the jedges told the crowd
Them that got the mostest claps 'd win the bestest prize.

Everybody waitin' for the first tweedle-dee,
When in comes a-stumblin' — hill-billy me!

Bowed right pretty to the jedges an' the rest,   35
Took a silver dollar from a hole inside my vest,

Plunked it on the table an' said, "There's my callin' card!
An' anyone that licks me—well, he's got to fiddle hard!"

Old Dan Wheeling, he was laughin' fit to holler,
Little Jimmy Weezer said, "There's | "You've lost before you
   one dead dollar!"   40 | begin!"

Big Tom Sargent had a yaller-toothy grin,
But I tucked my little whippoorwill spang underneath my chin,
An' petted it an' tuned it till the jedges said, "Begin!"

Big Tom Sargent was the first in line;
He could fiddle all the bugs off a sweet-potato vine.   45
He could fiddle down a possum from a mile-high tree.
He could fiddle up a whale from the bottom of the sea.

Yuh could hear hands spankin' till they spanked each other raw,
When he finished variations on "Turkey in the Straw."

Little Jimmy Weezer was the next to play;   50
He could fiddle all night, he could fiddle all day.

He could fiddle chills, he could fiddle fever,
He could make a fiddle rustle like a lowland river.

He could make a fiddle croon like a lovin' woman.
An' they clapped like thunder when he'd finished strummin'.   55

Then came the ruck of the bob-tailed fiddlers,
The let's-go-easies, the fair-to-middlers.

They got their claps an' they lost their bicker,
An' settled back for some more corn-licker.

An' the crowd was tired of the no-count squealing,   60
When out in the center steps Old Dan Wheeling.

---

42. *spang*: straight; directly.   56. *ruck of the bob-tailed fiddlers*:
                                                  ordinary crowd of unskilled fiddlers.

He fiddled high and he fiddled low,
(Listen, little whippoorwill; yuh got to spread yore wings!)
He fiddled with a cherrywood bow.
(Old Dan Wheeling's got bee-honey in his strings.)   65

He fiddled the wind by the lonesome moon,
He fiddled a most almighty tune.

He started fiddling like a ghost.
He ended fiddling like a host.

He fiddled north an' he fiddled south,   70
He fiddled the heart right out of yore mouth.

He fiddled here an' he fiddled there.
He fiddled salvation everywhere.

When he was finished, the crowd cut loose,
(Whippoorwill, they's rain on yore breast.)   75
An' I sat there wonderin', "What's the use?"
(Whippoorwill, fly home to yore nest.)

But I stood up pert an' I took my bow,
An' my fiddle went to my shoulder, so.

An' — they wasn't no crowd to get me fazed —   80
But I was alone where I was raised.

> He forgets the crowd,
> thinking of the hills of home.

Up in the mountains, so still it makes yuh skeered.
Where God lies sleepin' in his big white beard.

— 381 —

An' I heard the sound of the squirrel in the pine,
An' I heard the earth a-breathin' thu' the long night-time.   85

They've fiddled the rose, an' they've fiddled the thorn,
But they haven't fiddled the mountain-corn.

They've fiddled sinful an' fiddled moral,
But they haven't fiddled the breshwood-laurel.

They've fiddled loud, an' they've fiddled still,   90
But they haven't fiddled the whippoorwill.

I started off with a *dump-diddle-dump*,
(Oh, hell's broke loose in Georgia!)
Skunk-cabbage growin' by the bee-gum stump,
(Whippoorwill, yo're singin' now!)   95

Starting slow, he works up to a frenzy of rhythmic excitement.

Oh, Georgia booze is mighty fine booze,
The best yuh ever poured yuh,
But it eats the soles right offen yore shoes,
For Hell's broke loose in Georgia.

My mother was a whippoorwill pert,   100
My father, he was lazy,
But I'm Hell broke loose in a new store shirt
To fiddle all Georgia crazy.

Swing yore partners — up an' down the middle!
Sashay now — oh, listen to that fiddle!   105
Flapjacks flippin' on a red-hot griddle,
An' hell broke loose,

104–5. *Swing...Sashay now*: calls in the old square dances.

Hell broke loose,
Fire on the mountains — snakes in the grass.
Satan's here a-bilin' — oh, Lordy, let him pass!   110
Go down Moses, set my people free,
Pop goes the weasel thu' the old Red Sea!
Jonah sittin' on a hickory-bough,
Up jumps a whale — an' where's yore prophet now?
Rabbit in the pea-patch, possum in the pot,   115
Try an' stop my fiddle, now my fiddle's gettin' hot!
Whippoorwill, singin' thu' the mountain hush,
Whippoorwill, shoutin' from the burnin' bush,
Whippoorwill, cryin' in the stable-door,
Sing to-night as yuh never sang before!   120
Hell's broke loose like a stompin' mountain-shoat,
Sing till yuh bust the gold in yore throat!
Hell's broke loose for forty miles aroun'
Bound to stop yore music if yuh don't sing it down.
Sing on the mountains, little whippoorwill,   125
Sing to the valleys, an' slap 'em with a hill,
For I'm struttin' high as an eagle's quill,
An' Hell's broke loose,
Hell's broke loose,
Hell's broke loose in Georgia!   130

They wasn't a sound when I stopped bowin',
(Whippoorwill, yuh can sing no more.)

But, somewhere or other, the dawn was growin',
(Oh, mountain whippoorwill!)

An' I thought, "I've fiddled all night an' lost.   135
Yo're a good hill-billy, but yuh've been bossed."

So I went to congratulate old man Dan,
— But he put his fiddle into my han' —
An' then the noise of the crowd began.

The language in this poem is picturesque; that is, it adds local color to the story. You may be surprised, therefore, to find in *Webster's Dictionary* most of the peculiar words in this poem: *stewin', a-skitin'* (*a-* is a prefix common in dialectal speech; look under *skite*), *a-bilin', spang, ruck, fazed, skunk-cabbage,* etc. Most of these words are classified as "colloquial."

136. *bossed*: mastered; defeated.

PERSHING AT THE FRONT
Arthur Guiterman

*Here is a neat little narrative, with the age-old one-two-three
set of incidents (first-line trench, second-line trench, third-line
trench), and a clever twist at the end. The first two lines ought to
persuade you at once not to take the General's visit to the front
too seriously; read the poem to get a laugh.*

The General came in a new tin hat
To the shell-torn front where the war was at;
With a faithful Aide at his good right hand
He made his way toward No Man's Land,
And a tough Top Sergeant there they found,   5
And a Captain, too, to show them round.

Threading the ditch, their heads bent low,
Toward the lines of the watchful foe
They came through the murk and the powder stench
Till the Sergeant whispered, *"Third-line trench!"*   10
And the Captain whispered, *"Third-line trench!"*
And the Aide repeated, *"Third-line trench!"*
And Pershing answered, —not in French—
"Yes, I see it. Third-line trench."

Again they marched with wary tread,   15
Following on where the Sergeant led
Through the wet and the muck as well,

---

1. *The General*: General John J. Pershing, commander-in-chief of the American
Expeditionary Forces in France, 1917-1919.

Till they came to another parallel.
They halted there in the mud and drench,
And the Sergeant whispered, *"Second-line trench!"*   20
And the Captain whispered, *"Second-line trench!"*
And the Aide repeated, *"Second-line trench!"*
And Pershing nodded: *"Second-line trench!"*

Yet on they went through mire like pitch
Till they came to a fine and spacious ditch   25
Well camouflaged from planes and Zeps
Where soldiers stood on firing steps
And a Major sat on a wooden bench;
And the Sergeant whispered, *"First-line trench!"*
And the Captain whispered, *"First-line trench!"*   30
And the Aide repeated, *"First-line trench!"*
And Pershing whispered, *"Yes. I see.*
How far off is the enemy?"
And the faithful Aide he asked, asked he,
"How far off is the enemy?"   35
And the Captain breathed in a softer key,
"How far off is the enemy?"

The silence lay in heaps and piles
As the Sergeant whispered, *"Just three miles."*
And the Captain whispered, *"Just three miles."*   40
And the Aide repeated, *"Just three miles."*
"Just three miles!" The General swore,
"What in hell are we whispering for?".
And the faithful Aide the message bore,
"What in hell are we whispering for?"   45

And the Captain said in a gentle roar,
"What in hell are we whispering for?"
"Whispering for?" the echo rolled;
And the Sergeant whispered, *"I have a cold."*

When you come to class, you will have more fun
with this poem if you use one boy for narrator and
four others with husky whispers to read Sergeant,
Captain, Aide, and General Pershing, respectively. If
the rhythm has a tendency to carry you away at times,
don't mind that; it needs to be quite prominent in this
poem. The profanity you will have to excuse as
appropriate to a poem of the war.

THE CHRIST OF THE ANDES
Edwin Markham

Mr. Markham's own note to this poem says:
"Chile and Argentine, after quarreling for generations
over their boundary line, submitted the question to
arbitration and settled it in good feeling. As an emblem
of their peace and as a pledge of its permanence, the two
republics united in the erection of an heroic statue of
Christ on the highest Andean peak of the borderline."
The little prayer in the last stanza might well be committed to memory.

Over dead craters, hushed with snows,
Up where the wide-winged condor goes,
Great Aconcagua, hushed and high,
Sends down the ancient peace of the sky.

So, poised in clean Andean air,   5
Where bleak with cliffs the grim peaks stare,
Christ, reaching out his sacred hands,
Sheds his brave peace upon the lands.

There once of old wild battles roared
And brother-blood was on the sword;   10
Now all the fields are rich with grain
And only roses redden the plain.

---

3. *Aconcagua*: mountain peak in Argentina, highest peak in the Western
Hemisphere.

Torn were the peoples with feuds and hates—
Fear on the mountain-walls, death at the gates;
Then through the clamor of arms was heard   15
A whisper of the Master's word.

"Fling down your swords: be friends again:
Ye are not wolf-packs: ye are men.
Let brother-counsel be the Law:
Not serpent fang, not tiger claw."   20

And then the war-torn nations heard;
And great hopes in their spirits stirred;
The red swords from their clenched fists fell,
And heaven shone out where once was hell!

They hurled their cannons into flame   25
And out of the forge the strong Christ came.
'Twas thus they moulded in happy fire
The tall Christ of their heart's desire....

O Christ of Olivet, you hushed the wars
Under the far Andean stars: 30
Lift now your strong nail-wounded hands
Over all peoples, over all lands—
Stretch out those comrade hands to be
A shelter over land and sea!

---

29. *Olivet*: the Mount of Olives, a mountain range just east of Jerusalem. Here
    occurred Christ's ascension, and at the base of one of its peaks is the Garden
    of Gethsemane.

History has now given the "wide-winged condor" of line 2 a significance which the author could hardly have anticipated. In August of the year 1941, which Chileans called "the year of the avalanches," a small village high in the Chilean Andes was buried under one hundred feet of snow. Two aviators of the Chilean Air Force, who were flying food to the rescue workers, were caught in treacherous downdrafts and plunged to death on the Argentine slopes of the range. Argentine Alpine troops delivered the bodies of these two pilots of a "wide-winged condor" to their Chilean comrades in the very shadow of the "Christ of the Andes," giving proof of the friendship between the two nations described in the poem. (Pictures in *Life* for December 8, 1941, show the tragedy and the epic heroism of this event.)

THE LAW OF DEATH
John Hay

So strong is the love with which some persons cling to their dear ones, that when death does strike, it seems to them like a personal injury, a cruel injustice. In the "The Law of Death" an American poet (once President Lincoln's secretary, and, later, President McKinley's Secretary of State) shows how Buddha taught a young mother of India that death is the universal human fate— "the common lot" of all—and thus reconciled her at last to her own child's death.

The song of Kilvani: fairest she
In all the land of Savatthi.
She had one child, as sweet and gay
And dear to her as the light of day.
She was so young, and he so fair,   5
The same bright eyes and the same dark hair;
To see them by the blossomy way,
They seemed two children at their play.

There came a death-dart from the sky,
Kilvani saw her darling die.   10
The glimmering shade his eyes invades,
Out of his cheek the red bloom fades;
His warm heart feels the icy chill,
The round limbs shudder, and are still.
And yet Kilvani held him fast   15
Long after life's last pulse was past,
As if her kisses could restore
The smile gone out forevermore.

But when she saw her child was dead,
She scattered ashes on her head,   20
And seized the small corpse, pale and sweet,
And rushing wildly through the street,
She sobbing fell at Buddha's feet.

"Master, all-helpful, help me now!
Here at thy feet I humbly bow;   25
Have mercy, Buddha, help me now!"
She groveled on the marble floor,
And kissed the dead child o'er and o'er.
And suddenly upon the air
There fell the answer to her prayer: 30
"Bring me tonight a lotus tied
With thread from a house where none has died."

She rose, and laughed with thankful joy,
Sure that the god would save the boy.
She found a lotus by the stream;   35
She plucked it from its noonday dream.
And then from door to door she fared,
To ask what house by Death was spared.
Her heart grew cold to see the eyes
Of all dilate with slow surprise: 40

"Kilvani, thou hast lost thy head;
Nothing can help a child that's dead.
There stands not by the Ganges' side

---

20. *ashes on her head*: a common Oriental mode of expressing uncontrolled grief.
32. *house*: home; family; not merely the literal four walls of a building.
43. *Ganges*: largest river in India.

A house where none hath ever died."
Thus, through the long and weary day, 45
From every door she bore away
Within her heart, and on her arm,
A heavier load, a deeper harm.
By gates of gold and ivory,
By wattled huts of poverty, 50
The same refrain heard poor Kilvani,
The living are few, the dead are many.

The evening came—so still and fleet—
And overtook her hurrying feet.
And, heartsick, by the sacred fane 55
She fell, and prayed the god again.
She sobbed and beat her bursting breast:
"Ah, thou hast mocked me, Mightiest!
Lo! I have wandered far and wide;
There stands no house where none hath died." 60
And Buddha answered, in a tone
Soft as a flute at twilight blown,
But grand as heaven and strong as death
To him who hears with ears of faith:
"Child, thou art answered. Murmur not! 65
Bow, and accept the common lot."

Kilvani heard with reverence meet,
And laid her child at Buddha's feet.

---

67. *reverence meet*: the proper reverence.

Stories in Verse

FOR YOUR VOCABULARY

Kilvani fell by the sacred *fane*, or temple. This is a word almost out of use today; but two other words are pronounced the same, which you will often run across, are *fain* and *feign*. *Fain* is an adverb meaning gladly: "I would *fain* do it." *Feign* means to pretend, as to *feign* death. Such words (*fane, fain, feign*) are called homonyms. Define *homonym*, and give other illustrations. Write five sentences each containing a group of homonyms. Examples:

1. *They're* doing *their* work in *there*.
2. *It's* true that our dog has lost *its* life.
3. Shall we transport this *ore o'er* the lake by *oar or* motor?
4. *Who's* going to find out *whose* book this is?
5. The *principal* of our school is a man of *principle*.
6. The navy *sees* to it that the enemy does not *seize* our ships on the high *seas*. (Note that all three begin with *se—*.)
7. Back and *forth* he went for the *fourth* time.
8. While we *rowed* upstream, he *rode* a horse quietly down the *road*.

PLANTER'S CHARM
Fay M. Yauger

Here is the story of a brave widow farm-woman, whose tragic life is powerfully suggested to us in just a few lines. You will like her fine courage in the face of misfortunes which would crush an ordinary person.

The form of this poem is interesting, too. Its pattern is determined by an old planting song: as the poem proceeds, each line of the charm is used to introduce a new character in the story.

Slowly Nan the widow goes
Up and down the furrowed rows,

Corn-bags chafing her waist, her hips
As the kernels fall from her finger-tips:

     "One for the buzzard—   5
     One for the crow—
     One to rot—and—
     One to grow!"

Once she had dreams (but not of late)
Of another life, of a kinder fate: 10

Of quiet streets in foreign towns,
Of dancing tunes, and men, and gowns.

---

5. She sings this magic charm as she drops four kernels into each hill.

But all of her dreams were dreamed before
Tim Slade drew rein outside her door.

"One for the buzzard"—Tim was dead   15
With a bullet-hole thru his reckless head:

Tim with his cheating ways and words—
Marked from the first for the wart-necked birds:

Tim who had left her sorrowing days,
The farm, and a pair of sons to raise.   20

Lon was her first-born: "One for the Crow!"
Where had he gone? She'd never know,

For there was a price upon his head—
"A chip off the old block," people said.

Then "One to rot!" Her thoughts go back,   25
Like hunting-dogs on an easy track,

To the girl she'd been before she came
To love Tim Slade and bear his name;

And something as stinging and hot as sand
Slides down her cheek and strikes her hand,   30

And she sees the field thru a shimmering blur
For what has marriage meant to her

18. *wart-necked birds*: *i.e.*, the buzzards.

But a heel of bread in a roofless hut,
Or a crawling course thru a mouldy rut?

As if in answer, over the ditch   35
A boy comes riding with a willow switch:

Her second-born of whom no one
Could say in truth, "His father's son,"

For his chin is firm, and his mouth is grave,
And the dreams in his eyes are bright and brave.   40

And she, remembering farm-hand talk,
"You lose three seeds to get one stalk,"

Stands tall and proud and her pale cheeks glow
As she drops a kernel — "One to grow!"

Slowly Nan the widow moves   45
Up and down the furrowed grooves,

Peace in her heart and a smile on her lips
As the kernels fall from her finger-tips:

> *"One for the buzzard—*
> *One for the crow—*   50
> *One to rot—and—*
> *One to grow!"*

BALLAD OF CAP'N PYE
Robert P. Tristram Coffin

On the shore sits an old, white-haired sea captain with a strange glint in his eyes. Around him, eagerly expectant, sit a group of youngsters, watching the clever fingers of the old man as his jackknife fashions a graceful little boat. Sure enough, he's going to begin one of his yarns; and when I say yarns, I mean yarns—pirates, jewels, gold, and "them"—honest-to-goodness nightmare stuff. And can he tell them!

The ancestors of Isaac Pye
    Had the sea for board and bed;
Cap'n Pye had tall ships, too,
    But his ships sailed inside his head.

They would not let him sleep at night,   5
    They poked sly bowsprits through the room;
On their decks he heard men's feet
    Going back and forth like doom.

Isaac sat and whittled boats
    For boys with very wide blue eyes,   10
But his brain was moonshot waves,
    Pirates, and their thin, far cries.

Isaac stood it just so long,
    Then he put the whittling by.
"Listen, sonnies, this is true,   15
    Cross my heart and hope to die!

"I'm the man who's seen the chist
  Of Cap'n Kidd the Buccaneer.
Godfrey Diamonds, what a sight!
  And here I be still setting here!   20

"The tide was up, the moon was full,
  I rowed in under Whaleboat Ledge,
Hitched my painter, climbed the bank
  With my eye-teeth all on edge.

"My shadow crotched just where I did   25
  And went along all dumb with me.
First it was a quag-bog full
  Of lilies cold as Charity.

"Hoot-owls, maybe, nothing else
  But lilies like I never seen...   30
When all at once I heard a sound
  That made my marrowbones turn green.

"Someone opened up and sung,
  My blood run cold as water-glasses,
Sung like a storm wind round the eaves,   35
  No pork and no molasses.

"I edged up on the lonesome tune,
  And then I see a lonesome light
Like a codfish on a shelf
  Shining awful in the night.   40

"Mother of Moses! a little tyke
    Was setting on his bottom there
Astraddle of a kag, and he
    Was letting out the song for fair.

"But the laddie's head was not 45
    Where the laddies's head should be,
He had it like a jacky-lattern
    Down upon his little knee!

"The pirates must have sliced it off
    Even with his little ears 50
And left him there to guard the chist,
    The chist I've looked for all the years.

"And sure as preaching, there it was,
    With a ring upon the top,
Three steps going down to it. 55
    My old heart went skip-a-hop!

"I see the boy wan't mad at me,
    And so down two of the steps went I,
But you can bet your sweet big-toes
    The third was not for Cap'n Pye. 60

"I knowed them third steps and their ways,
    When you step on them, they cave
Into the bowels of the earth,
    And you won't never need no grave!

---

41. *tyke*: boy.

"And you can bet your Sunday boots 65
    I was not the man to dare
To put my fingers on that ring
    For Kingdom Come to find them there.

"I jist stood still and reached a hand,
    I fetched a stone of cranium size, 70
I threw it smack upon the box,
    Up flew the lid, out went my eyes!

"Godfrey! what a sight I see!
    A million ruby-stones and pearls,
Lapis Lazuruses, too, 75
    Shavings of gold like baby curls.

"Jacinths, hyacinths, and beads
    And turcusses to make you croon,
Emeralds and dollars bright
    And yaller as the harvest moon. 80

"And in the middle of them all
    A skull the proper size for kings....
Joshua Jehoshaphat!
    I hankered for them shiny things!

"I took a stick and pocked it through 85
    A ring to fit a grown-man's leg
With a diamond-stone ablaze
    Bigger'n any goose's egg.

---

78. *turcusses*: turquoises.

"I'd hardly rigged it on my stick
  When that boy let out a screech,
I sat down hard and dented earth
  With the two butts of my breech.

"Then I heard the hemlocks stir
  With a hungry kind of humming,
They was hopping, hopping mad,
  They was loose, and *they* was coming!

"I never see *them* then, and I
  Hope to die I never do.
Two-hundred-foot-high pines were crashing,
  And the moon was coming through!

"The old bull-spruces bent that low
  Their trunks were bowed into a noose,
Golly Mighty, wan't *they* mad,
  Hell and all was broken loose!

"I guess I didn't want no ring,
  I left that chist right then and there,
I put my toes longside my ears,
  I wan't a-touching nought but air!

"I ran the rabbits out of breath,
  I reached my skiff as fast as spit,
When all the water in that bay
  Hissed and run right out of it.

"Jist like steam out of a kittle,
    And left me high and dry on shore.
Thunderation! — but I shoved 115
    Fit to split the pants I wore!

"I shoved that skiff like greasy lightning
    Over that whole blasted bay,
I heard *them* snorting still and churning,
    But, my lads, I got away. 120

"I got away, boys, but my hair
    Was white as any span-new sail....
I'm the man that's seen Kidd's chist,
    And I'm still here to tell the tale!"

FAITHLESS NELLY GRAY

A Pathetic Ballad

Thomas Hood

"But still a pun I do detest;
'Tis such a paltry, humbug jest;
They who've least wit can make them best."
                    —William Combe: "Dr. Syntax in
                            Search of the Picturesque"

*Whenever any one of our friends makes a pun, we are apt to groan
disdainfully and make a great show of our disapproval. But the seeds
of punning are in all men, and when they shoot up and blossom forth
in ourselves, we generally think our own puns, at least, are pretty
clever. Some puns have become more or less famous:*

His death, which happened in his berth
At forty-odd befell;
They went and told the sexton, and
The sexton tolled the bell.

                    —Thomas Hood:
                        "Faithless Sally Brown'

My sense of sight is very keen,
My sense of hearing weak.
One time I saw a mountain pass,
But could not hear its peak.

                    —Oliver Herford:
                        "My Sense of Sight"

We wanted Li Wing
But we winged Willie Wong,
A sad but excusable
Slip of the tong.
                    — Keith Preston: "Lapsus Linguae"

The Reverend Henry Ward Beecher
Called a hen a most elegant creature.
The hen, pleased with that,
Laid an egg in his hat,—
And thus did the hen reward Beecher.
                    — Oliver Wendell Holmes:
                          "An Eggstravagance"

Now, if you are in the mood for more puns —

Ben Battle was a soldier bold,
        And used to war's alarms;
But a cannon-ball took off his legs,
        So he laid down his *arms*!

Now as they bore him off the field,
        Said he, "Let others shoot,
For here I leave my second leg,
        And the Forty-second *Foot*!"

The army-surgeons made him limbs:
Said he, "They're only pegs;

5

10

But there's as *wooden members* quite
    As represent my legs!"

Now Ben he loved a pretty maid,
    Her name was Nelly Gray;
So he went to *pay* her his *devoirs*   15
    When he'd *devoured* his *pay*!

But when he called on Nelly Gray,
    She made him quite a scoff;
And when she saw his wooden legs,
    Began *to take them off*!   20

"O Nelly Gray! O Nelly Gray!
    Is this your love so warm?
The love that loves a scarlet coat,
    Should be more *uniform*!"

She said, "I loved a soldier once,   25
    For he was blithe and brave;
But I will never have a man
    With *both feet in the grave*!

"Before you had those timber toes,
    Your love I did allow,   30
But then, you know, you stand upon
    Another *footing* now!"

---

11. *wooden members*: wooden-headed members of Parliament, representing the people.
15. *devoirs (de-vwärz´)* : respects.
20. *take off*: make fun off; imitate (see *scoff*, 1. 18.).

"O Nelly Gray! O Nelly Gray!
 For all your jeering speeches,
At duty's call I left my legs
 In Badajoz's *breaches*!"   35

"Why, then," said she, "you've lost the *feet*
 Of legs in war's alarms,
And now you cannot wear your shoes
 Upon your *feats* of *arms*!"   40

"Oh, false and fickle Nelly Gray,
 I know why you refuse: —
Though I've no feet, some other man
 Is *standing in my shoes*!

"I wish I ne'er had seen your face;   45
 But now a long farewell!
For you will be my death: — alas!
 You will not be my *Nell*!"

Now when he went from Nelly Gray,
 His heart so heavy got,   50
And life was such a burthen grown,
 It made him take a *knot*!

So round his melancholy neck
 A rope he did entwine,

---

36. *Badajoz's breaches*: breaks in the fortified wall at Badajoz, a Spanish city
 where a great battle occurred in 1811.
48. *be my Nell*: be my death *knell*.
52. *a knot*: a porter's knot, a shoulder pad used for carrying loads.

And, for his second time in life,   55
    Enlisted in the Line!

One end he tied around a beam,
    And them removed his pegs,
And, as his *legs were off*, — of course
    He soon was *off his legs*!   60

And there he hung till he was dead
    As any nail in town, —
For though distress had *cut* him *up*,
    It could not cut him down!

A dozen men sat on his corpse,   65
    To find out why he died —
And they buried Ben at four cross-roads,
    With a *stake* in his inside!

---

56. *Enlisted in the Line*: joined the regular army. The pun, of course, involves
the "line" of rope.
65. *sat on his corpse*: held deliberations concerning the corpse. The reference is
to the coroner's jury.
68. *stake*: steak (for the pun). In England suicides were buried at a crossroad,
with a stake driven through the body.

FOREST FIRE
Edna Davis Romig

*Would you like to experience a terrific forest fire? If your
imagination is alert, you may see the flames, smell the pines and
the bitter smoke, and actually hear the progress of the flames as
they roar through the forest, all as if you were right there. And
when you have seen the fire finally extinguished, you learn, in a
single line, the staggering cost of such a catastrophe, so often the
result of someone's thoughtlessness.*

Whispers of little winds low in the leaves,
Rustle of warm winds through tall green trees,
A full resinous fragrance, rich, warm, sweet,
A sharp acrid odor, a hint of heat,
Snap, hiss, crackle, a faint blue smoke,   5
A whirl of black swept by tawny flame —
Deep in the forest the wild wind broke;
Fast in the wild wake the fire-wind came,
A soughing of branches swept sudden and strong
Like the rush and crash when the storm winds meet: 10
Crimson streams of fire flowed quickly along
The tall grey grasses and the spruce needles deep;
Red tongues of fire licked the tall pine trees,
Grey twigs fell as though shrivelled by disease;
Broad orange streamers floated everywhere   15
And bulging puffs of copper smoke filled the molten air.
A pitiable squeaking came from little furry creatures,
Chipmunks and marmots as they scurried helter-skelter;
Mountain sheep and mountain goats leaping to some shelter,

Warned by their instincts — grim, sure teachers — 20
And the suffocating stenches from the red relentless thing;
Like a plummet dropped a blue-jay with a burning broken wing;
The eagles screamed in anger from the smoke-beclouded skies;
A sudden rush of slender deer, dumb fright in liquid eyes ...
Now burning brands seem missiles sent, 25
Projectiles hurled through space,
Now and then a chuckle, like mirth malevolent,
A sweeping beauty sinister, a dread and treacherous grace;
And conflagration with the sound of thunder
Has pulled a thousand tall trees under. 30
But men have come in purpose bent
To halt the fire's fierce race.
They fell great trees and dig deep lanes,
They smother out small flames;
With tools and chemicals and wit 35
At last they curb, they conquer it.
But the fire that raged for half a day
Has burned a hundred years away.

Make three lists: one of color words, one of words
suggesting smells, and one of onomatopoetic words.
Find three good figurative comparisons.

HAYING
Ethel Romig Fuller

This poem is an unusually effective example of blank verse. It will give you a realistic picture of farm life, will show you how good sports react to the call of duty, and will detail for you in wonderful imagery the loveliness that so moves the boy telling the story. In the short space of time between leaving a field and reaching a hayloft, as the beauty of a summer evening enters into his soul, this sensitive farm boy grows to manhood.

The supper bell was ringing as Neill strode —
A bucket of warm milk in either hand,
The cat and her five kittens at his heels —
Down through the yellow tansy from the barn,
Where Tod and I were washing the trough —   5
We laid the pipe that summer from the hills —
And said, his weather eye cocked toward the south,
We're in for rain by morning. The wind has changed;
So we'll be finishing hay tonight.
Tod lifted his black curly head from which   10
The bright drops splashed, and glared at Neill —
Aw, have a heart, he said. *I've worked enough*
For two farm hands today, and there's a dance
At Mary's Corners. Neill, I have a date ....
The crickets fiddled in the dusty grass   15
I looked away. What could a fellow do?
And Nancy'd promised she would go with me....
Neill turned and went on slowly to the house.
His shirt was stained across the back by sweat;

He looked dog-tired. We all were; we'd been up 20
And in the hay fields since before the dawn —
How endless long the murky day had seemed!
How hot! And how the green deer-flies had stung!
And then I was remembering the drought —
The dreadful years with scarce a drop of rain, 25
And Neill had almost lost Glenacres, and
Had shot his herd of starving blooded stock.
And we'd gone hungry too. *We'd better stand*
By Neill, I said. *A crop of hay means cash;*
And cash is mighty hard come by these days. 30
But Tod was mad — you couldn't blame him much —
Don't be a fool, he snapped. *Neill thinks because*
We're kids that he can run us. Then Maurine,
Neill's wife — who's kind of little-like and thin
From over-work and worry, but sure good 35
To Tod and me — we'd lived with her and Neill
Since Dad and Mother died — Maurine then called,
Your supper's hot and waiting. Better hurry, boys!
So when we'd wiped upon the roller-towel
Beside the kitchen door, we dragged our chairs 40
Up to the table where already Neill
Was eating. He piled our plates with new fried spuds,
Thick salt pork gravy, cobs of early corn
And passed the blue glass dish of fireweed honey —
We kept our hives far up the old hill-burn — 45
Hot biscuits, and sweet butter churned that day —
Our butter gets blue ribbons at the Fair —
And no one talked, till, belts let out a notch,
Our chairs tipped back against the wall, Neill said,
Be sports, you kids! Hay means more meals like this.... 50
Maurine's blue eyes were pleading, *go with him* —
Not even Tod could quite withstand that glance;

45. *hill-burn*: brook.

So like bull yearlings bunting at a fence,
We charged the telephone. Tod got there first.
When he'd called off his date, I rung up Nancy — 55
Nan's pretty as crab apple blossoms, and as slim
As any alder tree. She dances too
Like willows swaying in the April wind —
But Nancy Saunders comes of farmer-stock.
Next week, then, Karl, she said, *when haying's done.* 60

Neill had the big greys hitched up to the rick
When we ran to the barn. So Tod and I
Climbed in the back and sat with dangling heels
As Prince and Nelly ambled down the lane
Between the daisies and the bouncing-bet. 65
It was a different world from afternoon,
The air as yellow-cool as buttercups;
The sun had set; the sky, no longer fiery-blue
Was fleeced with lamb's wool clouds, and these
Were fringed with wild rose pink. I looked at Tod 70
And Neill, and wondered if they noticed too.
I couldn't see Neill's features, but his back
Looked rested-like. Tod sort of sighed and chewed
A clover stalk...and when at last we slid
The creaking gate bars out and rattled in 75
The west-end meadow — the sightliest spot
In all Glenacres any hour of the day —
It was so beautiful now in the dusk
That something caught me in the throat
Like Christmas carols on the radio.... 80

Long purple shadows from the fir trees lay
Across the cocks and stubble. It was so still

---

53. *bunting*: butting.

That we could hear the falls of Cedar Creek....
A wood thrush in the hazel bushes piped
One sweet high note; an owl called to its mate;   85
White foxgloves glowed like candles by the fence;
In place of choking dust, there now was dew.
As Tod and I forked up the hay to Neill,
Who stacked as fast as two could pitch,
The fragrance made me think of Nancy's hair....   90

With every load the magic grew. A star
Rose in the west...we worked with scarce a word.
Oh, it was like our church with hymns and prayers
On Sundays when the riding parson comes.
Then as we took the last load in, the moon   95
Came up behind the hill, and Tod and Neill
And I, the horses and the meadow, all
Were silvered with its light, and suddenly
I was as far away from Tod, as if
I swam alone across the lake and left him,   100
My own brother, on the farther shore.
My heart cried out, but there was no reply....
Between a field and hayloft, I grew up....
Toward morning I half-wakened to a sound
Of rain drops pelting on the attic roof....   105

FOR THE AMBITIOUS STUDENT

Read *The Yearling*, a best-seller by Marjorie Kinnan
Rawlings. It describes the growing up of a young boy
who lives on a farm in the Florida backwoods.

SWIMMERS
Louis Untermeyer

Rarely will you find a poem so filled as this one with the unquenchable joy of sheer living—that zest for life which goes with youth and abounding physical vigor. Even the spectacle of death could not, except for a moment, dampen the spirits of the young swimmer. This poem should appeal to every warm-blooded young reader, and especially to those who have themselves felt the keen joy of battling a heavy surf.

I took the crazy short-cut to the bay;
Over a fence or two and through a hedge,
Jumping a private road, along the edge
Of backyards full of drying wash it lay.
And now, the last set being played and over,   5
I hurried past the ruddy lakes of clover;
I swung my racket at astonished oaks,
My arm still tingling from aggressive strokes.
Tennis was over for the day —
I took the leaping short-cut to the bay.   10

Then quick plunge into the cool, green dark,
The windy waters rushing past me, through me;
Filled with sense of some heroic lark
Existing in a vigor clean and roomy.
Swiftly I rose to meet the cat-like sea   15
That sprang upon me with a hundred claws,
And grappled, pulled me down and played with me.
Then, held suspended in the tightening pause
When one wave grows into a toppling acre,

I dived headlong into the foremost breaker,   20
Pitting against a cold and turbulent strife
The feverish intensity of life.
Out of the foam I lurched and rode the wave,
Swimming, hand over hand, against the wind;
I felt the sea's vain pounding, and I grinned   25
Knowing I was its master, not its slave.
Back on the curving beach I stood again,
Facing the bath-house, when a group of men,
Stumbling beneath some sort of weight, went by.
I could not see the heavy thing they carried;   30
I only heard: "He never gave a cry —"
"Who's going to tell her?" "Yes, and they just married —"
"Such a good swimmer, too…" And then they passed,
Leaving the silence throbbing and aghast.

A moment there my frightened heart hung slack,   35
And then the rich, retarded blood came back
Singing a livelier tune; and in my pulse
Beat the great wave that endlessly exults.
Why I was there and whither I must go,
I did not care. Enough for me to know   40
The same persistent struggle and the glowing
Waste of all spendthrift hours, bravely showing
Life, an adventure perilous and gay,
And death, a long and vivid holiday.

FOR THE AMBITIOUS STUDENT

If you have witnessed some calamitous occurrence, such as a drowning, write a story of the experience in which you try to convey to the reader your feeling of excitement or dismay or horror.

SHAMEFUL DEATH
William Morris

Revenge is an ancient human error. In his Sermon on the Mount, Jesus condemned revenge: "You have heard the saying, an eye for an eye and a tooth for a tooth. *But I tell you, you are not to resist an injury:*

Whoever strikes you on the right cheek,
   turn the other to him as well;
Whoever wants to sue you for his shirt,
   let him have your coat as well;
Whoever forces you to go one mile,
   go two miles with him." (Matthew 5: 38-41)

Observation suggests that this Christ-like point of view has made little headway in the world. Certainly it was not the customary view in the bygone day of "Shameful Death." On the contrary, in that harsh day of feuds and violence, revenge was thought a sacred duty, a duty the more pressing in this instance because the murdered man had died by the most shameful of all ways to die — by hanging. So the knight tells his story calmly; he does not find it strange to take pride in having killed two men, and in the same breath to ask our prayers for his brother and sister. To appreciate his point of view is to advance your understanding of the age we call "medieval," an age when the duty of revenge was a part of the code of a man of honor.

There were four of us about that bed;	The old man is recalling his brother's death a long time ago.
The mass-priest knelt at the side,	
I and his mother stood at the head,	
Over his feet lay the bride;	

We were quite sure that he was dead,   5
    Though his eyes were open wide.

He did not die in the night,
    He did not die in the day,
But in the morning twilight
    His spirit pass'd away,   10
When neither sun nor moon was bright,
    And the trees were merely gray.

He was not slain with the sword,
    Knight's axe, or the knightly spear,
Yet spoke he never a word   15
    After he came in here;
I cut away the cord
    From the neck of my brother dear.

He did not strike one blow,
    For the recreants came behind,   20
In a place where the hornbeams grow,
    A path right hard to find,
For the hornbeam boughs swing so,
    That the twilight makes it blind.

They lighted a great torch then,   25
    When his arms were pinion'd fast,
Sir John the knight of the Fen,
    Sir Guy of the Dolorous Blast,

---

27. *Fen*: marshy country in Lincolnshire, England.
28. *Dolorous Blast*: moaning wind. See line 41.

With knights threescore and ten,
    Hung brave Lord Hugh at last.   30

I am threescore and ten, | Shift to present time.
    And my hair is all turn'd gray,
But I met Sir John of the Fen
    Long ago on a summer day,
And am glad to think of the moment when   35
    I took his life away.

I am threescore and ten,
    And my strength is mostly pass'd,
But long ago I and my men,
    When the sky was overcast,   40
And the smoke roll'd over the reeds of the fen,
    Slew Guy of the Dolorous Blast.

And now, knights all of you,
    I pray you pray for Sir Hugh,
A good knight and a true,   45
    And for Alice, his wife, pray too.

THE LADY OF SHALOTT
Alfred, Lord Tennyson

"The Lady of Shalott" is rich in all the fundamental elements of verse stories presented in this book — narrative, word music, imagery.

The story itself is a fine example of pure romance, set in the days when King Arthur ruled at Camelot. A young girl, for fear of a mysterious curse, stays in her tower, never daring to look at the outside world except in her mirror. By her tower the river flows to Camelot; all the movement of boats and horses and people flows toward many-towered Camelot, too; and so do the Lady's thoughts. So when one day her mirror shows Lancelot passing by, she turns to gaze at this hero of the great world, and the curse strikes. When autumn comes, she lies down in her boat and dies, drifting down toward Camelot.

The word-music of this poem is worthy of Tennyson, who was one of the greatest masters of music in poetry. The stanza form, though somewhat unusual, is attractive; the multiple rimes reinforce the rhythm with pleasing effect; the refrains, with the constantly recurring "Shalott" and "Camelot," are like a lullaby; alliteration and onomatopoeia speak subtly to the ear. All these things tend to hypnotize you into accepting the highly romantic story.

Finally, there is gorgeous imagery. From the vantage point of the tower window, you see and hear the world go by — a vivid pageant, remarkable for its symphony of color. I have often advised you to try, in reading poetry, to see the images clearly, as if a film were unrolling before your mind's eye; now I merely add that this time you will get the full fun only if your film is in Technicolor.

PART I

On either side the river lie
Long fields of barley and of rye,
That clothe the wold and meet the sky;
And thro' the field the road runs by
    To many-tower'd Camelot;   5
And up and down the people go,
Gazing where the lilies blow
Round an island there below,
    The island of Shalott.

Willows whiten, aspens quiver,   10
Little breezes dusk and shiver
Thro' the wave that runs for ever
By the island in the river
    Flowing down to Camelot.
Four gray walls, and four gray towers,   15
Overlook a space of flowers,
And the silent isle imbowers
    The Lady of Shalott.

By the margin, willow-veil'd
Slide the heavy barges trail'd   20
By slow horses; and unhail'd
The shallop flitteth silken-sail'd
    Skimming down to Camelot;
But who hath seen her wave her hand?
Or at the casement seen her stand?   25
Or is she known in all the land,
    The Lady of Shalott?

---

3. *wold*: upland plain.
22. *shallop*: a light open river-boat, with oars or sails or both.

Only reapers, reaping early
In among the bearded barley,
Hear a song that echoes cheerly   30
From the river winding clearly,
  Down to tower'd Camelot;
And by the moon the reaper weary,
Piling sheaves in uplands airy,
Listening, whispers, "'Tis the fairy   35
  Lady of Shalott."

PART II

There she weaves by night and day
A magic web with colors gay.
She has heard a whisper say,
A curse is on her if she stay   40
  To look down to Camelot.
She knows not what the curse may be,
And so she weaveth steadily,
And little other care hath she,
  The Lady of Shalott.   45

And moving thro' a mirror clear
That hangs before her all the year,
Shadows of the world appear.
There she sees the highway near
  Winding down to Camelot;   50
There the river eddy whirls,
And there the surly village-churls,
And the red cloaks of market girls,
  Pass onward from Shalott.

Sometimes a troop of damsels glad, [55]
An abbot on an ambling pad,
Sometimes a curly shepherd-lad,
Or long-hair'd page in crimson clad,
    Goes by to tower'd Camelot;
And sometimes thro' the mirror blue [60]
The knights come riding two and two:
She hath no loyal knight and true,
    The Lady of Shalott.

But in her web she still delights
To weave the mirror's magic sights, [65]
For often thro' the silent nights
A funeral, with plumes and lights
    And music, went to Camelot;
Or when the moon was overhead,
Came two young lovers lately wed; [70]
"I am half sick of shadows," said
    The Lady of Shalott.

PART III

A bow-shot from her bower-eaves,
He rode between the barley-sheaves,
The sun came dazzling thro' the leaves, [75]
And flamed upon the brazen greaves
    Of bold Sir Lancelot.
A red-cross knight for ever kneel'd
To a lady in his shield,

---

56. *ambling pad*: a horse with a gentle, easy pace.
71. *shadows*: images in the mirror. These reflections no longer satisfy her.
76. *greaves*: armor to cover the lower leg; shin-guards.

That sparkled on the yellow field,   80
    Beside remote Shalott.

The gemmy bridle glitter'd free,
Like to some branch of stars we see
Hung in the golden Galaxy.
The bridle bells rang merrily   85
    As he rode down to Camelot;
And from his blazon'd baldric slung
A mighty silver bugle hung,
And as he rode his armor rung,
    Beside remote Shalott.   90

All in the blue unclouded weather
Thick-jewell'd shone the saddle-leather,
The helmet and the helmet-feather
Burn'd like one burning flame together,
    As he rode down to Camelot;   95
As often thro' the purple night,
Below the starry clusters bright,
Some bearded meteor, trailing light,
    Moves over still Shalott.

His broad clear brow in sunlight glow'd;   100
On burnish'd hooves his war-horse trode;
From underneath his helmet flow'd
His coal-black curls as on he rode,
    As he rode down to Camelot.

84. *Galaxy*: the Milky Way.

From the bank and from the river 105
He flash'd into the crystal mirror,
"Tirra lirra," by the river
  Sang Sir Lancelot.

She left the web, she left the loom,
She made three paces thro' the room, 110
She saw the water-lily bloom,
She saw the helmet and the plume,
  She look'd down to Camelot.
Out flew the web and floated wide;
The mirror crack'd from side to side; 115
"The curse is come upon me," cried
  The Lady of Shalott.

PART IV

In the stormy east-wind straining,
The pale yellow woods were waning,
The broad stream in his banks complaining, 120
Heavily the low sky raining
  Over tower'd Camelot;
Down she came and found a boat
Beneath a willow left afloat,
And round about the prow she wrote 125
  The Lady of Shalott.

And down the river's dim expanse
Like some bold seër in a trance,
Seeing all his own mischance —
With a glassy countenance 130

Did she look to Camelot.
And at the closing of the day
She loosed the chain, and down she lay;
The broad stream bore her far away,
        The Lady of Shalott.   135

Lying, robed in snowy white
That loosely flew to left and right —
The leaves upon her falling light —
Thro' the noises of the night
        She floated down to Camelot;   140
And as the boat-head wound along
The willowy hills and fields among,
They heard her singing her last song,
        The Lady of Shalott.

Heard a carol, mournful, holy,   145
Chanted loudly, chanted lowly,
Till her blood was frozen slowly,
And her eyes were darken'd wholly,
        Turn'd to tower'd Camelot.
For ere she reach'd upon the tide   150
The first house by the water-side,
Singing in her song she died,
        The Lady of Shalott.

Under tower and balcony,
By garden-wall and gallery,   155
A gleaming shape she floated by,
Dead-pale between the houses high,
        Silent into Camelot.
Out upon the wharfs they came,
Knight and burgher, lord and dame,   160

And round the prow they read her name,
    The Lady of Shalott.

Who is this? and what is here?
And in the lighted palace near
Died the sound of royal cheer;   165
And they cross'd themselves for fear,
    All the knights at Camelot:
But Lancelot mused a little space;
He said, "She has a lovely face;
God in his mercy lend her grace,   170
    The Lady of Shalott."

    I said at the start that this poem is especially rich in images. Many of these are given directly; many others by means of comparisons. If you are not sure you saw these comparisons clearly as you read the poem, go back now, spot them, and analyze them. Perhaps you could choose four committees for the four parts of the poem. You will be surprised to see how often, and how naturally, Tennyson uses metaphors and similes.

FOR THE AMBITIOUS STUDENT
    Tennyson's Lady of Shalott was the same as the lovely Elaine, who fell in love with Lancelot, told him of it, and grieved herself to death. Tennyson told this latter story in one of his *Idylls of the King*, a collection of long narrative poems based on the old legends of King Arthur and the Round Table knights. If you were moved to sympathy by "The Lady of Shalott," I think you would enjoy reading "Lancelot and Elaine."

THE VISION OF SIR LAUNFAL
James Russell Lowell

If you have read the famous stories of King Arthur and his Round Table, you are familiar with the knight's search for the Holy Grail, the wine-cup used by Christ at the Last Supper. According to tradition, the Grail was eventually brought to England for safekeeping. Its keepers having become sinful, it disappeared, and the thereafter became the object of search by many knights.

In "The Vision of Sir Launfal" Lowell pictures a knight, Sir Launfal, who has vowed that he, too, will search for the Holy Grail. But before starting, Sir Launfal lies down on a bed of rushes to sleep, hoping that some dream will direct him in his search. He does have a dream, and the dream shows him where to find the Holy Grail. In this story Lowell created the greatest of the many poems teaching the age-old truth: "Inasmuch as ye have done it unto one of the least of these my brethren, ye have done it unto me."

"The Vision of Sir Launfal" is related in two Parts, each Part preceded by a long "Prelude," much like orchestra music before the acts of a play, or an overture before an opera. In the Prelude to Part First, Lowell describes in beautiful lines the joy and happiness of the coming of Spring:

> And what is so rare as a day in June?
>   Then, if ever, come perfect days;
> Then Heaven tries earth if it be in tune,
>   And over it softly her warm ear lays....

In the Prelude to Part Second, we find an equally effective description of the wonders of Winter. Although the Preludes are beautiful descriptive poetry, I have omitted them from this book because for your first reading of "Sir Launfal" I want you to concentrate on the story. This is such a famous poem that you will be sure to run across it again; then you may read it in its entirety.

PART FIRST

I

"My golden spurs now bring to me, | Sir Launfal speaks.
    And bring to me my richest mail,
For to-morrow I go over land and sea
    In search of the Holy Grail;
Shall never a bed for me be spread,   5
Nor shall a pillow be under my head,
Till I begin my vow to keep;
Here on the rushes will I sleep,
And perchance there may come a vision true
Ere day create the world anew."   10
    Slowly Sir Launfal's eyes grew dim;
    Slumber fell like a cloud on him,
And into his soul a vision flew.

II

The crows flapped over by twos and | This is the first line of the
    threes, | vision.
In the pool drowsed the cattle up to their knees,   15
    The little birds sang as if it were
    The one day of summer in all the year,
And the very leaves seemed to sing on the trees:

---

2. *mail*: armor made of interlinked metal rings.

The castle alone in the landscape lay
Like an outpost of winter, dull and gray: 20
'Twas the proudest hall in the North Countree,
And never its gates might opened be,
Save to lord or lady of high degree;
Summer besieged it on every side,
But the churlish stone her assaults | The forbidding coldness of
    defied;   25 | the castle withstood all the
                    attacks of summer's warmth.
She could not scale the chilly wall,
Though around it for leagues her pavilions tall
Stretched left and right,
Over the hills and out of sight;
    Green and broad was every tent,   30
    And out of each a murmur went
Till the breeze fell off at night.

III

The drawbridge dropped with a surly | [The vision continues. Sir
    clang, | Launfal sees himself in his
                    dream.
And through the dark arch a charger sprang,
Bearing Sir Launfal, the maiden knight,   35
In his gilded mail, that flamed so bright
It seemed the dark castle had gathered all
Those shafts the fierce sun had shot over its wall
    In his siege of three hundred summers long,
And, binding them all in one blazing sheaf,   40
    Had cast them forth: so, young and strong,
And lightsome as a locust-leaf,

---

27. *pavilions*: tents; here, the forests.
35. *maiden knight*: a knight that has never been tried in battle.

Sir Launfal flashed forth in his maiden mail,
To seek in all climes for the Holy Grail.

IV

It was morning on hill and stream and tree,   45
    And morning in the young knight's heart;
Only the castle moodily
Rebuffed the gifts of sunshine free,
    And gloomed by itself apart;
The season brimmed all other things up   50
Full as the rain fills the pitcher-plant's cup.

V

As Sir Launfal made morn through the darksome gate,
    He was 'ware of a leper, crouched by the same,
Who begged with his hand and moaned as he sate;
    And a loathing over Sir Launfal came;   55
The sunshine went out of his soul with a thrill,
    The flesh 'neath his armor 'gan shrink and crawl,
And midway its leap his heart stood still
    Like a frozen waterfall;
For this man, so foul and bent of stature,   60
Rasped harshly against his dainty nature,
And seemed the one blot on the summer morn, —
So he tossed him a piece of gold in scorn.

VI

The leper raised not the gold from the dust:
"Better to me the poor man's crust,   65
Better the blessing of the poor,

Though I turn me empty from his door;

That is no true alms which the hand can hold;

> Mere money, which can be held in the hand, is not true charity.

He gives only the worthless gold

     Who gives from a sense of duty; [70]

But he who gives but a slender mite,

And gives to that which is out of sight,

    That thread of the all-sustaining

      Beauty

> He gives as to a brother, impelled by the love in his heart—that unseen thread of God's spirit which makes all men brothers.

Which runs through all and doth unite,—

The hand cannot clasp the whole of his alms, [75]

The heart outstretches its eager palms,

For a god goes with it and makes it store

To the soul that was starving in darkness before."

PART SECOND

I

There was never a leaf on bush or tree,

The bare boughs rattled shudderingly; [80]

> This is still the vision. The season changes from spring to winter—in the dream.

The river was dumb and could not speak,

    For the weaver of Winter its shroud had spun;

A single crow on the tree-top bleak

    From his shining feathers shed off the cold sun;

Again it was morning, but shrunk and cold, [85]

As if her veins were sapless and old,

And she rose up decrepitly

For a last dim look at earth and sea.

---

77. *store*: an abundance of good things.

II

Sir Launfal turned from his own hard
    gate,

Still the vision. Many years have passed—in the dream only.

For another heir in his earldom sate;   90
An old, bent man, worn out and frail,
He came back seeking the Holy Grail;
Little he recked of his earldom's loss,
No more on his surcoat was blazoned the cross,
But deep in his soul the sign he wore,   95
The badge of the suffering and the poor.

III

Sir Launfal's raiment thin and spare
Was idle mail 'gainst the barbèd air,
For it was just at the Christmas time;
So he mused, as he sat, of a sunnier
    clime,   100
And sought for a shelter from cold
    and snow

In his dream, Sir Launfal tries to keep warm by thinking about his long-past travels in desert countries.

In the light and warmth of long-ago;
He sees the snake-like caravan crawl
O'er the edge of the desert, black and small,
Then nearer and nearer, till, one by one,   105
He can count the camels in the sun,
As over the red-hot sands they pass
To where, in its slender necklace of grass,
The little spring laughed and leapt in the shade,
And with its own self like an infant played,   110
And waved its signal of palms.

IV

"For Christ's sweet sake, I beg an alms;"
The happy camels may reach the spring,
But Sir Launfal sees only the
    grewsome thing,
The leper, lank as the rain-blanched bone,   115
That cowers beside him, a thing as lone
And white as the ice-isles of Northern seas
In the desolate horror of his disease.

Sir Launfal's meditation is interrupted by the leper, and the camels fade from his mind. This is still part of his dream.

V

And Sir Launfal said, "I behold in thee
An image of Him who died on the
    tree;   120
Thou also hast had thy crown of thorns,
Thou also hast had the world's buffets and scorns,
And to thy life were not denied
The wounds in the hands and feet and side:
Mild Mary's Son, acknowledge me;   125
Behold, through him, I give to thee!"

This time the beggar does not move him to loathing, but to true Christian charity. Sir Launfal is a changed man. (See II. 95-6.)

He speaks to Christ. "Through the leper I give to Christ."

VI

Then the soul of the leper stood up in his eyes
    And looked at Sir Launfal, and straightway he
Remembered in what a haughtier guise
    He had flung an alms to leprosie,   130
When he girt his young life up in gilded mail
And set forth in search of the Holy Grail.
The heart within him was ashes and dust;
He parted in twain his single crust,

Sir Launfal is ashamed of his former treatment of the leper. Ashes and dust signify shame and humility.

He broke the ice on the steamlet's brink,   135

And gave the leper to eat and drink,

'Twas a mouldy crust of coarse brown bread,

    'Twas water out of a wooden bowl, —

Yet with fine wheaten bread was the leper fed,

    And 'twas red wine he drank with his thirsty soul.   140

VII

As Sir Launfal mused with a downcast face,

A light shone round about the place;

The leper no longer crouched at his side,

But stood before him glorified,

Shining and tall and fair and straight   145

As the pillar that stood by the Beautiful Gate, —

Himself the Gate whereby men can

Enter the temple of God in Man.

> The leper is transformed into Christ, who said of himself, "I am the way, the truth, and the life" (John 14:6).

VIII

His words were shed softer than leaves from the pine,

And they fell on Sir Launfal as snows on the brine,   150

That mingle their softness and quiet in one

With the shaggy unrest they float down upon;

And the voice that was softer than silence said,

"Lo, it is I, be not afraid!

In many climes, without avail,   155

Thou hast spent thy life for the Holy Grail;

Behold, it is here, — this cup which thou

Didst fill at the streamlet for me but now;

This crust is my body broken for thee,

---

146. *Beautiful*: the name of one of the gates of the temple at Jerusalem (Acts 3:2).

This water his blood that died on the tree; 160

The Holy Supper is kept, indeed,

In whatso we share with another's need;

Not what we give, but what we share,

For the gift without the giver is bare;

Who gives himself with the alms feeds three, 165

Himself, his hungering neighbor,
      and me."

The next six lines contain the theme of the story.

End of vision.

IX

Sir Launfal awoke as from a swound:

"The Grail in my castle here is found!

Hang my idle armor up on the wall,

Let it be the spider's banquet-hall; 170

He must be fenced with stronger mail

Who would seek and find the Holy
      Grail."

This is the same young Sir Launfal who went to sleep in I. 12

To find the Holy Grail one must be armed with spiritual qualities, like brotherly love.

X

The castle gate stands open now,

    And the wanderer is welcome to the hall

As the hangbird is to the elm-tree bough; 175

    No longer scowl the turrets tall,

The Summer's long seige at last is o'er;

When the first poor outcast went in at the door,

She entered with him in disguise,

And mastered the fortress by surprise; 180

There is no spot she loves so well on ground,

She lingers and smiles there the whole year round;

The meanest serf in Sir Launfal's land

Has hall and bower at his command;
And there's no poor man in the North
   Countree
But is lord of the earldom as much as he.

A democratic spirit now
prevails on Sir Launfal's lands.

185

"The Vision of Sir Launfal" is a theme poem; and in reading it you must, first of all, grasp the details of the story and the lesson it teaches. But it would be too bad if you should miss the beautiful imagery: the siege of summer against the castle, an "outpost of winter"; the flaming beauty of the maiden knight springing into sight over the drawbridge with its "surly clang" (did you hear it?); the castle "glooming" by itself apart; the "sapless and old" morning rising up decrepitly "for a last dim look at earth and sea" — and many other really exquisite bits of poetic artistry. Perhaps for class discussion your teacher will let sixteen members of the class concentrate on the imagery, each on a different stanza, and point it out in detail to the class.

THE REVENGE OF HAMISH
Sidney Lanier

You would look long to find a more dramatic poem than "The Revenge of Hamish." Maclean is a cruel Scotch lord who lived in the days when masters had absolute power over their servants; Alan is his huntsman; and Hamish, his cringing servant. With fine suspense the poem tells what happened when Maclean went out for a day of hunting (he would do the killing: his servants would do the footwork). As the story unfolds, love and hate, pride and fear mount to almost unbearable tension. Finally the dramatic climax is reached; the violent passions have spent their force; and in the last stanza the flying shadow of a wind-driven cloud passes over like a symbol of tragedy, and the sun begins to shine.

It was three slim does and a ten-tined buck in the bracken lay;
　　And all of a sudden the sinister smell of a man,
　　Awaft on a wind-shift, waved and ran
Down the hill-side and sifted along through the bracken and
　　passed that way.

Then Nan got a-tremble at nostril; she | She smells danger.
　　was the daintiest doe;　　⁵ |
　　In the print of her velvet flank on the velvet fern
　　She reared, and rounded her ears in turn.
Then the buck leapt up, and his head as a king's to a crown
　　did go | Read right on.

---

1. *ten-tined buck*: A buck with ten-pointed antlers would be a fine specimen.
   bracken: a thicket of ferns.

Full high in the breeze, and he
stood as if Death
had the form of a
deer;

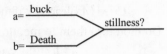

And the two slim does long
lazily stretching arose, 10

> The words stretch lazily
> too, with their liquid *l*'s.

For their day-dream slowlier came to a close,

Till they woke and were still, breath-bound with waiting and
wonder and fear.

> Note the alliteration.

Then Alan the huntsman sprang over the hillock, the hounds
shot by,

The does and the ten-tined buck made a marvellous bound,

The hounds swept after with never a sound, 15

But Alan loud winded his horn in sign that the quarry was nigh.

For at dawn of that day proud Maclean of Lochbuy to the
hunt had waxed wild,

And he cursed at old Alan till Alan fared off with the hounds

For to drive him the deer to the lower glen-grounds:

"I will kill a red deer," quoth Maclean, "in the sight of the
wife and the child." 20

So gayly he paced with the wife and the child to his chosen
stand;

But he hurried tall Hamish the henchman ahead: "Go
turn," —

---

12. *breath-bound*: holding their breath; not breathing.
16. *winded (winded)*: blew, as a signal to the other hunters.
17. *to the hunt had waxed wild*: had grown impatient to hunt.

Cried Maclean — "if the deer seek to cross to the burn,
Do thou turn them to me: nor fail,
　　　　　lest thy back be
　　　　　red as thy hand."

Maclean threatens a lashing.

Now hard-fortuned Hamish, half blown of his breath with the
　　　　　height of the hill,　　　　　　　　　　　　　25
　　　　Was white in the face when the ten-tined buck and the does
　　　　Drew leaping to burn-ward; huskily rose
His shouts, and his nether lip twitched, and his legs were o'er-
　　　　　weak for his will.

So the deer darted lightly by Hamish and bounded away to the burn.
　　　　But Maclean never bating his watch tarried waiting below. 30
　　　　Still Hamish hung heavy with
　　　　　fear for to go

He is afraid to face his master.

All the space of an hour; then he went, and his face was
　　　　　greenish and stern,

And his eye sat back in the socket,

From what he has seen before, he knows what to expect

　　　　　and shrunken the eye-balls shone,
　　　　As withdrawn from a vision of deeds it were shame to see.
　　　　"Now, now, grim henchman, what is't with thee?"　　　35
Brake Maclean, and his wrath rose red as a beacon the wind
　　　　　hath upblown.

"Three does and a ten-tined buck made out," spoke Hamish,
　　　　　full mild,

23. *burn*: brook; stream.
25. *hard-fortuned*: unlucky.
30. *never bating his watch*: never relaxing his watchfulness.
35. *what is't with thee?* What's the matter with you?
37. *made out*: broke away.

"And I ran for to turn, but my breath it was blown, and
they passed;
I was weak, for ye called ere I broke me my fast."
Cried Maclean: "Now a ten-tined buck in the sight of the
wife and the child   40 | Don't stop.

I had killed if the gluttonous kern had | He calls Hamish a snail
not wrought me a | because, climbing on an
| empty stomach, he could
snail's own wrong!" | not overtake the deer!
Then he sounded, and down came the kinsmen and
clansmen all:
"Ten blows, for the ten tine, on his back let it fall,
And reckon no stroke if the blood follow not at the bite of thong!"

So Hamish made bare, and took him his strokes; at the last
he smiled.   45
"Now I'll to the burn," quoth Maclean, "for it still may be,
If a slimmer-paunched henchman will hurry with me,
I shall kill the ten-tined buck for a gift to the wife and the child!"

Then the clansmen departed, by this path and that; and over
the hill
Sped Maclean with an outward wrath | A common reaction—
for an inward shame; 50 | shamed inside, you show
| anger outside.
And that place of the lashing full quiet became;
And the wife and the child stood sad; and bloody-backed
Hamish sat still.

---

38. *turn*: head them off.
39. *ere I broke me my fast:* before I had breakfast.
41. *had killed*: would have killed. *Gluttonous kern*: heavy-eating peasant.
42. *sounded*: blew the horn.
47. *slimmer-paunched*: less potbellied.

But look! red Hamish has risen; quick about and about turns he.
> "There is none betwixt me and the crag-top!" he
> > screams under breath.
> Then, livid as Lazarus lately from death,   55
He snatches the child from the mother, and clambers the crag
> > toward the sea.

Now the mother drops breath; she is dumb, and her heart
> > goes dead for a space,
> > Till the motherhood, mistress of death, shrieks, shrieks
> > > through the glen,
> > And that place of the lashing is live with men,
And Maclean, and the gillie that told him, dash up in a
> > desperate race.   60

Not a breath's time for asking; an eye-glance reveals all the
> > tale untold.
> > They follow mad Hamish afar up the crag toward the sea,
> > And the lady cries: "Clansmen, run for a fee! —
Yon castle and lands to the two first hands that shall hook
> > him and hold | Don't stop.

Fast Hamish back from the brink!" — and ever she flies up
> > the steep,   65
> > And the clansmen pant, and the sweat, and they jostle
> > > and strain.

---

55. *livid as Lazarus lately from death*: In the eleventh chapter of the Gospel of
John, you may read how Lazarus, brother of Martha and Mary, was raised
from the dead by Jesus.

58. *motherhood, mistress of death*: Her mother love overcomes the
breathlessness and the temporary pause ("death") of her heartbeat.

60. *gillie*: a servant, especially a man serving a Scottish chieftain or hunter.

But, mother, 'tis vain; but, father 'tis vain;
Stern Hamish stands bold on the brink, and dangles the child
o'er the deep.

Now a faintness falls on the men that run, and they all stand
still.   70
And the wife prays Hamish as if he were God, on her knees,
Crying: "Hamish! O Hamish! but please, but please
For to spare him!" and Hamish still | Hamish wrestles with
dangles the child, with | conflicting emotions.
a wavering will.

On a sudden he turns; with a sea-hawk scream, and a gibe, and a song,
Cries: "So; I will spare ye the child if, in sight of ye all, 75
Ten blows on Maclean's bare | This was a shocking proposal
back shall fall, | from a humble servant.
And ye reckon no stroke if the blood follow not at the bite of
the thong!"

Then Maclean he set hardly his tooth to his lip that his tooth
was red,
Breathed short for a space, said: "Nay, but it never shall be!
Let me hurl off the damnable hound in the sea!"   80
But the wife: "Can Hamish go fish us the | Now Maclean wrestles
child from the sea, if dead? | with conflicting emotions.

Say yea! — Let them lash *me*, Hamish?" | Watch the quotes!
— "Nay!" — "Husband, the lashing will heal;
But, oh, who will heal me the bonny sweet bairn in his grave?

---

77. *hardly*: firmly; violently; hard.
82. *bairn*: child (Scotch).

Could ye cure me my heart with the death of a knave?   85
Quick! Love! I will bare thee — so — kneel!" then Maclean
    'gan slowly to kneel

With never a word, till presently downward he jerked to the earth.
    Then the henchman — he that smote Hamish —
        would tremble and lag;
    "Strike, hard!" quoth Hamish, full stern, from the crag;
Then he struck him, and "One!" sang Hamish, and danced
        with the child in his mirth.   90

And no man spake beside Hamish; he counted each stroke
        with a song.
    When the last stroke fell, then he moved him a pace
        down the height,
    And he held forth the child in the heartaching sight
Of the mother, and looked all pitiful | Is he acting?
        grave, as repenting a wrong.

And there as the motherly arms stretched out with the
        thanksgiving prayer —   95
    And there as the mother crept up with a fearful swift pace,
    Till her finger nigh felt of the bairnie's face —
In a flash fierce Hamish turned round and lifted the child in the air,

And sprang with the child in his arms from the horrible
        height in the sea,
    Shrill screeching, "Revenge!" in the wind-rush; and
        pallid Maclean   100

---

83. *knave*: servant.
90. *moved him*: moved himself; moved.

Age-feeble with anger and impotent pain,
Crawled up on the crag, and lay flat, and locked hold of dead
    roots of a tree —

And gazed hungrily o'er, and the blood from his back drip-
    dripped in the brine,
    And a sea-hawk flung down a skeleton fish as he flew,
    And the mother stared white on the waste of blue,   105
And the wind drove a cloud seaward, and the sun began to shine.

The last stanza of this poem is a highly effective ending. After the whirlwind of violence, the silence and the bleak sunshine returning make a horribly desolate scene. And the dripping blood, the skeleton fish, and the passing cloud-shadow seem grimly suggestive.

Maclean and Hamish are both interesting characters, skillfully revealed. What are the evidences of Maclean's intolerance? Of his cruelty? Of his pride? What sort of man is Hamish? Is his repentance genuine (line 92)? Is his final act of revenge due to the triumph of evil will, or to fear of what will happen to him if he relents?

Lanier, a Southern poet, was a master of word-music in poetry. This particular poem is rich in alliteration; pick out instances that seem especially effective.

In spite of the unusual stanza form, this poem may be called a ballad. Point out its ballad characteristics.

Stories in Verse

THE LABORATORY
Robert Browning

*This story takes you far back into the past to a medieval town
and into the shop of a druggist. The sinister excitement of this
episode will be heightened for the reader who knows that, at that
time, most chemists were bootleggers of drugs, working in well-
hidden shops, making and selling their illegal medicines and
their poisons, and searching endlessly for a magic formula which
would enable them to change base metals into pure gold.*

*Into such a shop, reeking with arsenic fumes, has stolen a well-
dressed aristocratic lady, to secure poison with which to murder
her rival in love. As she waits for the chemist to fill her murderous
order, she thinks and talks aloud. And gradually the whole story
becomes clear, bit by bit. A story told by this method is called a
dramatic monologue — a play with only one speaker.*

Now that I, tying thy glass-mask
    tightly,
> He has given her a mask to
> protect her from the fumes.

May gaze thro' these faint smokes curling whitely,
As thou pliest thy trade in this devil's smithy —
Which is the poison to poison her, prithee?

He is with her; and they know that I
    know
> Her sweetheart is with her
> rival. They think she is in
> 5 church, but—

Where they are, what they do; they believe my tears flow
While they laugh, laugh at me, at me fled to the drear
Empty church, to pray God in, for them! — I am here.

Grind away, moisten and mash up thy paste,

Pound at thy powder, — I am not in haste!   10
Better sit thus, and observe thy strange things,
Than go where men wait me and dance at the King's.

That in the mortar — you call it gum?
Ah, the brave tree whence such gold oozings come!
And yonder soft phial, the exquisite blue,   15
Sure to taste sweetly, — is that poison too?

Had I but all of them, thee and thy treasures,
What a wild crowd of invisible pleasures!
To carry pure death in an earring, a casket,
A signet, a fan-mount, a filigree-basket!   20

Soon, at the King's, a mere lozenge to give
And Pauline should have just thirty | Apparently she has several
    minutes to live! | rivals.
But to light a pastille, and Elise, with her head,
And her breast, and her arms, and her hands, should drop dead!

Quick — is it finished? The color's | She is afraid that the color
    too grim!   25 | of this poison in the wine
Why not soft like the phial's, enticing | will repel, rather than
    and dim? | attract, her victim.
Let it brighten her drink, let her turn it and stir,
And try it and taste, ere she fix and prefer!

What a drop! She's not little, no | Now she's afraid it won't
    minion like me — | be enough to kill such a
That's why she ensnared him. This never will free | vital, "masculine" woman.   30

The soul from those strong, great eyes, say "no!"
To that pulse's magnificent come-and-go.

For only last night, as they
  whispered, I brought
My own eyes to bear on her so, that I thought
Could I keep them one half minute fixed, she would fall,   35
Shrivelled; she fell not; yet this does it all!

> If looks could have killed, she wouldn't need the poison.

Not that I bid you spare her pain!
Let death be felt and the proof remain;
Brand, burn up, bite into its grace —
He is sure to remember her dying face!   40

> Let the agony of death destroy the beauty of her rival's face.

It is done? Take my mask off! Nay, be not morose,
It kills her, and this prevents seeing it
  close:
The delicate droplet, my whole fortune's fee —
If it hurts her, beside, can it ever hurt me?

> Eager to see this fatal drop, she ignores the risk to herself.

Now, take all my jewels, gorge gold to your fill,   45
You may kiss me, old man, on my mouth if you will!
But brush this dust off me, lest horror
  it brings
Ere I know it — next moment I dance at the King's.

> There must be no warning of her intentions.

FOR THE AMBITIOUS STUDENT

This poem makes a wonderful recital piece for a reader gifted with acting ability and imagination. As you read it, try to imagine the lady talking, and follow her changes of mood.

If you have enjoyed reading this difficult poem, I should like to recommend two more dramatic monologues by Browning: "My last Duchess" and "Andrea del Sarto." They are not easy reading, but well worth the effort.

MORGIANA DANCES
(An Arabian Night)
William Rose Benét

Ali Baba, a poor Persian woodcutter, accidentally discovered the place where a band of robbers hid the treasure which they and their ancestors had amassed by plunder and murder. When the robbers realized that their hiding-place was known, they set out at once to capture the man who possessed their secret. Two of the robbers found their man, and marked the door of Ali Baba's house with chalk, expecting to enter his house and strike him down later, but both times they were foiled by Morgiana, a female slave, who put the same mark on a number of neighboring houses. Later Hoseyn, the leader of the robbers, disguised himself as an oil merchant, secreted his men in large jars carried on the backs of mules, and thus sought shelter in Ali Baba's house. Again the wily Morgiana discovered the plot, and killed the robbers by pouring hot oil into the jars. Finally Hoseyn disguised himself as a rich merchant, and once more gained access to Ali Baba's house, as a guest. But because he refused salt in his food (to eat salt would have bound him to loyalty to his host), Morgiana became suspicious and again discovered his identity, also perceiving a dagger hidden under his vest. So she dressed herself as a dancing girl, with suitable head-dress, and a girdle of silver, to which she fastened a dagger. To the music of the tabor (a tambourine without the jingles) she danced before Ali Baba and his guest. In her final routine she held the dagger in her hand, and pretended to strike sometimes herself, at other times one of her audience. At the very last, with her left hand she held out her tabor to Hoseyn, asking for wine and a gift of money. As he was taking a coin from his purse, with her right hand she plunged the dagger into his heart.

Mr. Benét's remarkable poem, written to the rhythm of Morgiana's dance recounts the whole story as it passes through the mind (not the lips) of the dancing Morgiana. The so's and ho's indicate particularly strong beats upon the tabor. If, as you read, you can see the Oriental room with its red lights and purple shadows — if you can hear the rhythm of the dance as Morgiana sways, and whirls, and spins — if you can sense the tremendous drama of the tense situation — then, this poem will become one of your favorites, as it is one of mine.

Aha! A guest, —
Within my master's house, a guest, —
To eat
With his meat
No salt?   5
Say you so?
His vest — his vest —
What glitters through his merchant's vest?
Fast and fleet, tabor, beat, —
Round again we go!   10
Scarves about my head — so!
Silver girdle, flash —ho!
Round again, again we go;
Round again, again we go.
Chalk on the lintel lies,   15
Oil on the pave dries.
A guest ho! A guest, ho!

15. *lintel*: top of doorframe.
16. *pave*: pavement

A strange guest, ho!
Laden mules, laden mules
Clattered in the court there.   20
Who boil
In their oil?
The thieves?
Say you so?
Fools, — frantic fools,—   25
The moon saw the sport there.
Spin, spin, — tabor din, —
Round again we go!
Thieves' beards be red — so!
Poniard, forth and flash — ho!   30
Round again, again we go;
Round again, again we go;
Ali, only I divine
'Tis Hoseyn
Drinks your wine!   35
Mazed master, a guest — ho!
A sly guest, ho!
For treasure, for pleasure
Stabbed and plotted many men;
The fox   40
Picked the locks;
The springe
Snapped — so!
Pour measure, full measure,
Your purse for my dance then!   45
Purple are the shadows,
The lamps red and low.

The thieves were clever,
but at last they were caught

The blade at my breast — so!
The blade at my breast — ho!
Round again, again we go;   50
Round again, again we go…
Plunge, poniard!
Ha! — see,
Here's salt for villainy!
A guest ho! A guest, ho!   55
A dead guest—ho!

A dagger thrust is proper
seasoning for a villain who
refused salt.

THE BALLAD OF EAST AND WEST
Rudyard Kipling

Hard riding, proud words, singing bullets, defiance of death, admiration for courage, and rivalry in gift-giving — all are in this stirring poem. Truly, as Kipling says, a gallant spirit is a measure of man's worth that sets aside consideration of race, geography, nationality — "Border, Breed, and Birth."

The setting of this poem is northwestern India, which Kipling knew well. Here the British colonial administration had stationed border garrisons to maintain the peace, for there were bands of native marauders who continually threatened the property and safety of the inhabitants. In this poem the relation between the British troops and outlaw bands is presented as a rather sporting, but nonetheless deadly, hostility.

Do not make the error of supposing that all the native fighters were outlaws. Many of them were loyal British soldiers: there is a native commander of a British cavalry unit in this poem (the "Ressaldar"). But the chief character, Kamal, is an outlaw chieftain, with a curious point of view. He looks upon his theft of the Colonel's mare as a proof of professional skill, and a successful feat of border strife, rather than a crime. And I think Kipling wants you to regard it in the same way, because he soon gives you abundant reason to admire Kamal.

As the title asserts, this poem is a ballad. Even the form is the true ballad form, as you may see at a glance if it is printed thus:

> O, East is East and West is West,
>> And never the twain shall meet,
> Till Earth and Sky stand presently
>> At God's great Judgment seat.

Now go ahead and enjoy this thrilling ballad, with its long,

rhythmic swing, so well tuned to the steady gallop of a long
pursuit. There are certain difficulties of geography and
vocabulary (terms of horsemanship, for example): in the notes I
have given you as many helps as I was able to give. Use them.

O, East is East and West is West, and never the twain shall meet,
Till Earth and Sky stand presently at God's great Judgment Seat;
But there is neither East nor West, Border, nor Breed, nor Birth,
When two strong men stand face to | This is the theme.
face, tho' they come from the
ends of the earth!

Kamal is out with twenty men to raise the Border side,   5
And he has lifted the Colonel's mare that is the Colonel's pride:
He has lifted her out of the stable-door between the dawn and the day,
And turned the calkins upon her feet, and ridden her far away.
Then up and spoke the Colonel's son that led a troop of the Guides:
"Is there never a man of all my men can say where Kamal hides?"   10
Then up and spoke Mahommed Khan, the son of the Ressaldar,
"If ye know the track of the morning-mist, ye know where his
        pickets are.
"At dusk he harries the Abazai — at dawn he is into Bonair,
"But he must go by Fort Bukloh to his own place to fare,
"So if ye gallop to Fort Bukloh as fast as a bird can fly,   15

---

5. *raise*: excite to riot or unrest.
6. *lifted*: stolen; carried off.
8. *turned the calkins upon her feet*: fastened cleats on her shoes, for surefooted
   going over rough ground.
11. *Ressaldar*: title of the chief of a troop of native cavalry in the British Indian
    force. His son's name, *Mahommed Khan*, means "praiseworthty prince."
14. *Fort Bukloh*: evidently an outpost of the British occupation. The *Tongue of
    Jagai* is no doubt a pass through the hills, leading into the "grisly plain"
    beyond the British patrols. Don't worry about the other geographical names.

"By the favor of God ye may cut him off, ere he win to the
      Tongue of Jagai,
"But if he be passed the Tongue of Jagai, right swiftly
      turn ye then,
"For the length and the breadth of that grisly plain is sown with
      Kamal's men.
"There is a rock to the left, and rock to the right, and low lean
      thorn between,
"And ye may hear a breech-bolt snick where never a man is seen." 20
The Colonel's son has taken a horse, and a raw rough dun was he,
With the mouth of a bell and the heart of Hell, and the head of
      the gallows-tree.
The Colonel's son to the Fort has won, they bid him stay to eat —
Who rides at the tail of a Border thief, he sits not long at his meat.
He's up and away from Fort Bukloh as fast as he can fly,   25
Till he was aware of his father's mare in the gut of the Tongue of
      Jagai,
Till he was aware of his father's mare with Kamal upon her back,
And when he could spy the white of her eye, he made the pistol crack.
He has fired once, he has fired twice, but the whistling ball went wide.
"Ye shoot like a soldier," Kamal said. "Show now if ye can ride."   30
It's up and over the Tongue of Jagai, as blown dust-devils go,
The dun he fled like a stag of ten, but the mare like a barren doe.
The dun he leaned against the bit and | The dun is exhausted, the
      slugged his head above, | red mare still fresh.

---

20. *hear a breech-bolt snick*: hear the click of rifles being loaded and cocked.
    Snick is an onomatopoetic word.
26. *gut*: narrow passage; gully or defile.
31. *dust-devils:* sand-spouts; moving columns of sand carried along by small
    whirlwinds.

But the red mare played with the snaffle-bars, as a maiden plays
    with a glove.
There was rock to the left and rock to the right, and low lean
    thorn between,   35
And thrice he heard a breech-bolt snick tho' never a man was seen.
They have ridden the low moon out of the sky, their hoofs drum
    up the dawn,
The dun he went like a wounded bull, but the mare like a new-
    roused fawn.
The dun he fell at a water-course — in a woeful heap fell he,
And Kamal has turned the red mare back, and pulled the
    rider free.   40
He has knocked the pistol out of his hand — small room was
    there to strive,
"'Twas only by favor of mine," quoth he, "ye rode so long alive:
"There was not a rock for twenty mile, there was not a clump of
    tree,
"But covered a man of my own men with his rifle cocked on his
    knee.
"If I had raised my bridle-hand, as I have held it low,   45
"The little jackals that flee so fast were feasting all in a row:
"If I had bowed my head on my breast, as I have held it high,
"The kite that whistles above us now were gorged till she could
    not fly."
Lightly answered the Colonel's son: "Do good to bird and beast,
"But count who come for the broken meats before thou makest a feast.   50

| "But count who come for the broken meats before thou makest a feast. 50 | "Don't forget: my death would be avenged." |

---

34. *snaffle-bars*: a bridle bit made in links.
46. *were*: would be. So also in lines 48,52.
48. *kite*: a bird of the hawk family, that feed on dead bodies, like a buzzard.

— 457 —

"If there should follow a thousand swords to carry my bones away,

"Belike the prince of a jackal's meal were more than a thief
could pay.

"They will feed their horse on the standing crop, their men on
the garnered grain,

"The thatch of the byres will serve their fires when all the cattle
are slain.

"But if thou thinkest the price be fair, —
thy brethren wait to sup,   55

> Kamal is called a brother of
> jackals and kites.

"The hound is kin to the jackal-spawn, — howl, dog, and call
them up!

"And if thou thinkest the price be high, in steer and gear
and stack,

"Give me my father's mare again, and I'll fight my own way back!"

Kamal has gripped him by the hand and set him upon his feet.

"No talk shall be of dogs," said he, "when wolf and gray wolf
meet.   60

"May I eat dirt if thou hast hurt of me in deed or breath;

"What dam of lances brought thee forth
to jest at dawn with Death?"

> "What mother of soldiers
> gave birth to you, who
> laugh at death?"

Lightly answered the Colonel's son: "I hold by the blood of my clan:

"Take up the mare for my father's gift — by God, she has
carried a man!"

The red mare ran to the Colonel's son, and nuzzled against his
breast;   65

---

52. *Belike*: perhaps, probably.
53. *They*: the troops that would come to avenge his death.
54. *byres*: cowsheds.
57. *steer and gear and stack*: cattle and equipment and grain.
61. *if thou hast hurt*: if you receive a hurt, or injury.
63. *I hold by the blood of my clan*: What I am doing is characteristic of my
people.
64. *Take up*: accept.

"We be two strong men," said Kamal then, "but she loveth the
    younger best.

"So she shall go with a lifter's dower, my turquoise-studded rein,

"My broidered saddle and saddle-cloth, and silver stirrups
    twain."

The Colonel's son a pistol drew and held it muzzle-end,

"Ye have taken the one from a foe," said he; "will ye take the
    mate from a friend?"   70

"A gift for a gift," said Kamal straight; "a limb for the risk of a
    limb.

"Thy father has sent his son to me, I'll send my son to him!"

With that he whistled his only son, that dropped from a
    mountain-crest —

He trod the ling like a buck in spring, and he looked like a lance
    in rest.

"Now here is thy master," Kamal said, "who leads a troop of the
    Guides,   75

"And thou must ride at his left side as shield on shoulder rides.

"Till Death or I cut loose the tie, at camp and board and bed,

"Thy life is his — thy fate it is to guard him with thy head.

"So thou must eat the White Queen's meat, and all her foes are thine,

"And thou must harry thy father's hold for the peace of the
    Border-line,   80

"And thou must make a trooper tough and hack thy way to power —

"Belike they will raise thee to Ressaldar when I am hanged in Peshawur."

---

67. *lifter's dower*: thief's gift. Kamal gives the gear along with the mare, as a
    father would give a money present (dower) along with his daughter in
    marriage—in some countries!

74. *trod the ling*: walked through the heather.

79. *White Queen's*: Queen Victoria of the Empire.

80. *harry thy father's hold*: raid your father's (Kamal's) stronghold.

They have looked each other between the eyes, and there they
    have found no fault,

They have taken the Oath of the Brother-in-Blood on leavened
    bread and salt:

They have taken the Oath of the Brother-in-Blood on fire and
    fresh-cut sod,   85

On the hilt and the haft of the Khyber knife, and the Wondrous
    Names of God.

The Colonel's son he rides the mare and Kamal's boy the dun,

And two have come back to Fort Bukhoh where there went forth
    but one.

And when the drew the Quarter-Guard, full twenty swords flew
    clear—

There was not a man but carried his feud with the blood of the
    mountaineer.   90

"Ha' done! ha' done!" said the Colonel's son. "Put up the steel at
    your sides!

"Last night ye had struck at a Border thief —tonight 'tis a man
    of the Guides!"

O, East is East and West is West, and never the twain shall meet,

Till Earth and Sky stand presently at God's great Judgment Seat;

But there is neither East nor West, Border, nor Breed, nor Birth,   *95*

When two strong men stand face to face, tho' they come from the
    ends of the earth.

---

86. *Khyber*: natives living about the Khyber Pass between India and
   Afghanistan; much celebrated in romantic stories.
89. *Quarter Guard*: sentries at the British post.
92. *had struck*: would have struck

RIZPAH*

Alfred, Lord Tennyson

In this dramatic monologue an old woman dying in poverty speaks to another woman—perhaps a social worker or a member of some religious order—who has come to pray with her in her last hours. The entire poem is spoken by the old woman; sometimes she speaks to herself, sometimes to her dead son Willy, but most of the time to her visitor.

The story which the old woman tells is a pathetic one: her son, unable to resist a dare, robbed the mail and was hanged; his body was left hanging where "all the ships of the world could stare at him, passing by"; the mother became insane; but later released from the insane asylum, she gathered up her boy's bones for the foot of the gallows and secretly buried them in the holy ground of a Christian cemetery.

This is not an easy poem, but it is one most boys and girls enjoy thoroughly, once they understand it. You must dramatize it line by line, and never for a moment forget the dying woman and her changing emotions.

I

Wailing, wailing, wailing, the wind | To herself
      over the land and sea—
And Willy's voice in the wind, "O mother, come out to me!"
Why should he call me tonight, when he knows that I cannot go?
For the downs are as bright as day, and the full moon stares
      at the snow.

---

* *Rizpah*: the name of a woman in the Old Testament whose two sons were hanged. "And Rizpah suffered neither the birds of the air to rest on them by day, nor the beasts of the field by night." (II Samuel 21.) But Tennyson got his material from a magazine story, borrowing only the name from the Bible.

II

We should be seen, my dear; they would | To the dead Willy.
    spy us out of the town.   5
The loud black nights for us, and the storm rushing over the down,
When I cannot see my own hand, but am led by the creak of the
    chain,
And grovel and grope for my son till I find myself drenched
    with the rain.

III

Anything fallen again? nay—what | She imagines herself
    was there left to fall? | *groping for her son.*
I have taken them home, I have number'd the bones, I have
    hidden them all.   10
What am I saying? and what are *you*? | She sees the other woman
    do you come as a spy? | and fears she has said too
                                   much.
Falls? what falls? who knows? As the tree falls so must it lie.

IV

Who let her in? how long has she been? you—what have
    your heard?
Why did you sit so quiet? you never have spoken a word.
O—to pray with me— yes —a lady—none of their spies— 15
But the night has crept into my heart, and begun to darken my eyes.

V

Ah—you, that have lived so soft, what | To the visitor.
    should *you* know of the night,
The blast and the burning shame and the bitter frost and the
    fright?

I have done it, while you were asleep—you were only made
    for the day.
I have gather'd my baby together—and now you may go
    your way.   ²⁰

VI

Nay — for it's kind of you, Madam, to sit by an old dying wife.
But say nothing hard of my boy, I have only an hour of life.
I kiss'd my boy in the prison, before he went out to die.
"They dared me to do it," he said, and he never has told me a lie.
I whipt him for robbing an orchard once when he was but a
    child—   ²⁵
"The farmer dared me to do it," he said; he was always so wild—
And idle — and couldn't be idle — my Willy — he never
    could rest.
The King should have made him a soldier, he would have
    been one of the best.

VII

But he lived with a lot of wild mates, and they never would
    let him be good;
They swore that he dare not rob the mail, and he swore that
    he would;   ³⁰
And he took no life, but he took one purse, and when all was done
He flung it among his fellows — "I'll none of it," said my son.

VIII

I came into court to the Judge and the lawyers. I told them
    my tale,
God's own truth — but they kill'd him, they kill'd him for

robbing the mail.

They hang'd him in chains for a show — we had always
borne a good name—   35

To be hang'd for a thief — and then put away — isn't that
enough shame?

Dust to dust — low down — let us hide! but they set him so high

That all the ships of the world could stare at him, passing by.

God 'll pardon the hell-black raven and horrible fowls of the air,

But not the black heart of the lawyer who kill'd him and
hang'd him there.   40

IX

And the jailer forced me away. I had bid him my last good-bye;

They had fasten'd the door of his cell. "O mother!" I heard him cry.

I couldn't get back tho' I tried, he had something further to say,

And now I never shall know it. The jailer forced me away.

X

Then since I couldn't but hear that cry of
my boy that was dead,   45 | She became insane.

They seized me and shut me up: they fastened me down on my bed.

"Mother, O mother!" — he call'd in the dark to me year after year—

They beat me for that, they beat me — you know that I
couldn't but hear;

And then at last they found I had grown stupid and still

They let me abroad again — but the
creatures had worked their will. 50 | The raven and *horrible fowls* had eaten the body.

— 464 —

XI

Flesh of my flesh was gone, but bone of my bone was left—
I stole them all from the lawyers — and you, will you call it
    a theft?—
My baby, the bones that had suck'd me, the bones that had
    laugh'd and cried —
Theirs? O no! they are mine — not theirs — they had moved
    in my side.

XII

Do you think I was scared by the bones? I kiss'd 'em, I
    buried 'em all—   55
I can't dig deep, I am old — in the night by the churchyard wall.
My Willy 'll rise up whole when the trumpet of judgment 'll sound;
But I charge you never to say that I
    laid him in holy ground.

> She had broken the law by burying the bones of a criminal in consecrated ground.

XIII

They would scratch him up — they would hang
    him again on the cursed tree.
Sin? O yes — we are sinners, I know — let all that be,   60
And read me a Bible verse of the Lord's good will toward men—
"Full of compassion and mercy, the Lord" — let me hear it again;
"Full of compassion and mercy — long suffering." Yes, O yes!
For the lawyer is born but to murder — the Saviour lives but to bless.
He'll never put on the black cap except for the worst of the worst,   65
And the first may be last — I have heard it in church — and
    the last may be first.
Suffering — O, long-suffering — yes, as the Lord must know,
Year after year in the mist and the wind and the shower and
    the snow.

XIV

Heard, have you? what? they have told
　　you he never repented his sin.

Still to the visitor.

How do they know it? are *they* his mother? are *you* of his kin? [70]

Heard! have you ever heard, when the storm on the downs began,

The wind that'll wail like a child and the sea that'll moan
　　like a man?

XV

Election, Election and Reprobation—
　　it's all very well.

But I go tonight to my boy, and I
　　shall not find him in Hell.

For I cared so much for my boy that
　　the Lord has look'd into my care,

She brushes aside these theological terms, which are used by those who believe that God selects certain persons to be saved and others to be condemned regardless of personal merits or faults.

[75]

And He means me I'm sure to be happy with Willy, I know
　　not where.

XVI

And if *he* be lost — but to save *my*
　　soul, that is all your desire:

Do you think that I care for *my* soul if
　　my boy be gone to the fire?

The visitor, who believes that the son's soul has been lost, wishes the woman to think about her own salvation.

I have been with God in the dark — go, go, you may leave
　　me alone—

You never have borne a child — you are just as hard as a
　　stone. [80]

---

78. *fire*: hell

XVII

Madam, I beg your pardon! I think that you mean to be kind,
But I cannot hear what you say for my Willy's voice in the wind—
The snow and the sky so bright — he used but to call in the dark,
And he calls to me now from the church and not from the
     gibbet — for hark!
Nay — you can hear it yourself — it is coming — shaking
     the walls—   85
Willy — the moon's in a cloud — | She dies.
     Good-night. I am going. He calls.

FOR THE AMBITIOUS STUDENT

A dramatic monologue is considered especially good if the speaker, unconsciously revealing his own character, in some way enlarges our understanding of human nature. After you are sure you understand the narrative details in this poem, try to state clearly what truths of human nature it illustrates.

THE MAN HUNT
Madison Cawein

The tense excitement of a lynching party is vividly felt in "The Man Hunt." The author wisely uses few adjectives, trusting to his material to make its own impression. Note how wonderfully effective the short, sharp phrases are in conveying the stark horror and the strain of this grisly pursuit.

The woods stretch deep to the mountain-side,
And the brush is wild where a man may hide.

They have brought the bloodhounds up again
To the roadside rock where they found the slain.

The have brought the bloodhounds up, and they   5
Have taken the trail to the mountain way.

Three times they circled the trail and crossed,
And thrice they found it and thrice they lost.

Now straight through the trees and the underbrush
They follow the scent through the forest's hush.   10

And their deep-mouthed bay is a pulse of fear
In the heart of the wood that the man must hear.

The man who crouches among the trees
From the stern-faced men who follow these.

A huddle of rocks that the ooze has mossed —
And the trail of the hunted again is lost.

An upturned pebble, a bit of ground
A heel has trampled — the trail is found.

And the woods re-echo the bloodhound's bay
As again they take to the mountain way.

A rock, a ribbon of road, a ledge,
With a pine-tree clutching its crumbling edge.

A pine, that the lightening long since clave,
Whose huge roots hollow a ragged cave.

A shout, a curse, and a face aghast,
And the human quarry is laired at last.

The human quarry with clay-clogged hair
And eyes of terror who waits them there.

That glares and crouches and rising then
Hurls clods and curses at dogs and men.

Until the blow of a gun-butt lays
Him stunned and bleeding upon his face.

A rope; a prayer; and an oak-tree near,
And a score of hands to swing him clear.

A grim, black thing for the setting sun
And the moon and the stars to look upon.

GAMESTERS ALL
Du Bose Heyward

Races, lotteries, elections, games, slot machines — on one thing or another at one time or another most of us join the great army of gamesters, those who get a certain thrill from taking a chance. But there are some who can never resist taking a long chance, no matter how high the stake. This is a poem about two such men: a Negro crap-shooter, and a Marshal — "an honest sportsman, as they go." The wager is the Negro's speed against the Marshal's skill with a gun on a moving target at fifty feet. And the stake is the Negro's life. This poem is like an episode from a motion picture, so vivid is the imagery, so swift and dramatic the action.

The river boat had loitered down its way;
The ropes were coiled, and business for the day
Was done. The cruel noon closed down
And cupped the town.
Stray voices called across the blinding heat,   5
Then drifted off it shadowy retreat
Among the sheds.
The waters of the bay
Sucked away
In tepid swirls, as listless as the day.   10
Silence closed about me, like a wall,
Final and obstinate as death.
Until I longed to break it with a call,
Or barter life for one deep, windy breath.

A mellow laugh came rippling 15
Across the stagnant air,
Lifting it into little waves of life.
Then, true and clear,
I caught a snatch of harmony;
Sure lilting tenor, and a drowsing bass, 20
Elusive chords to weave and interlace,
And poignant little minors, broken short,
Like robins calling June —
And then the tune:
"Oh, nobody knows when de Lord is goin ter call, 25
Roll dem bones.
It may be in de Winter time, and maybe in de Fall,
Roll dem bones.
But yer got ter leabe yer baby an yer home an all—
So roll dem bones, 30
Oh my brudder,
Oh my brudder,
Oh my brudder,
Roll dem bones!"

There they squatted, gambling away 35
Their meager pay;
Fatalists all.
I heard the muted fall
Of dice, then the assured,
Retrieving sweep of hand on roughened board. 40

I thought it good to see
Four lives so free

From care, so indolently sure of each tomorrow,
And hearts attuned to sing away a sorrow.

Then, like a shot   45
Out of the hot
Still air, I heard a call:
"Throw up your hands! I've got you all!
It's thirty days for craps.
Come, Tony, Paul!   50
Now, Joe, don't be a fool!
I've got you cool."

I saw Joe's eyes, and knew he'd never go.
Not Joe, the swiftest hand in River Bow!
Springing from where he sat, straight, cleanly made,   55
He soared, a leaping shadow from the shade
With fifty feet to go.
It was the stiffest hand he ever played.
To win the corner meant
Deep, sweet content   60
Among his laughing kind;
To lose, to suffer blind,
Degrading slavery upon "the gang,"
With killing suns, and fever-ridden nights
Behind relentless bars   65
Of prison cars.

He hung a breathless second in the sun,
The staring road before him. Then, like one

---

63. "the gang": Convicts are sometimes sentenced not to jail, but to work on
the roads, chained together in "chain gangs."

Who stakes his all, and has a gamester's heart,
His laughter flashed. 70
He lunged — I gave a start.
God! What a man!
The massive shoulders hunched, and as he ran
With head bent low, and splendid length of limb,
I almost felt the beat 75
Of passionate life that surged in him
And winged his spurning feet.

And then my eyes went dim.
The Marshal's gun was out.
I saw the grim 80
Short barrel, and his face
Aflame with the excitement of the chase.
He was an honest sportsman, as they go.
He never shot a doe,
Or spotted fawn, 85
Or partridge on the ground.
And, as for Joe,
He'd wait until he had a yard to go.
Then, if he missed, he'd laugh and call it square.
My gaze leapt to the corner — waited there. 90
And now an arm would reach it. I saw hope flare
Across the runner's face.
Then, like a pang
In my own heart,
The pistol rang. 95

---

77. *spurning*: dashing; flying (an unusual meaning for the word).

The form I watched soared forward, spun the curve.
"By God, you've missed!"
The Marshal shook his head.
No, there he lay, face downward in the road.
"I reckon he was dead   100
Before he hit the ground,"
The Marshal said.
"Just once, at fifty feet,
A moving target too.
That's just about as good   105
As any man could do!
A little tough;
But, since he ran,
I call it fair enough."
He mopped his head, and started down the road.   110
The silence eddied round him, turned and flowed
Slowly back and pressed against the ears.
Until unnumbered flies set it to droning,
And, down the heat, I heard a woman moaning.

    This poem should start a good discussion in class.
Here are several questions to argue about:

    1. Where does the responsibility for Joe's death lie?

    2. Was the penalty for gambling fair?

    3. Was Joe right in trying to escape?

    4. Was the Marshal concerned particularly in
       upholding the law?

    5. Does the theme of the poems "Bête Humaine" and
       "Buck Fever" apply to this incident?

FOR YOUR VOCABULARY

How many of you have ever felt the *point* of a *poniard*? When we want to say that some remark was keen enough to make us suffer, we call that remark *poignant*. When an odor is so bitter that it hurts our noses we say it is *pungent*. All these words are derived originally from an old Latin word, *pungere*, meaning *to prick* or *to pierce*. *Poignancy, pounce, punch* are other words which are also derived from this word. Make a list of words derived from *audi-* (hear), *ambula-* (walk), *port-* (carry). Or perhaps you know some other root you would prefer to investigate.

THE TWO BROTHERS

Isaac Leib Peretz
Translated from the Yiddish by Jacob Robbins

Since the building of the pyramids — even before — human history has recorded sad stories of man's inhumanity to man: the slave-driver wielding his whip in the field — in the mine — in the mill; the profiteer creating for himself wealth and luxury from the sweat and tears and blood of his fellowmen. In a famous Yiddish play, "The Wedding Gown," one of the characters tells this story of two brothers, whose love and happiness were destroyed when the elder brother learned he could become rich through the suffering of the younger.

The story is an **allegory** *(that is, a prolonged metaphor, in which the actions are symbols of other actions, and the characters represent qualities or types, as in* **Pilgrim's Progress***). The elder brother represents all greedy, ruthless exploiters who achieve success through the toil and suffering of their fellowmen; the younger brother represents the great masses of the poor, exploited and beaten down by the masters of the world. The snake is, of course, the Biblical serpent. It is significant that at the end of the poem the elder brother is as unhappy as the younger: "Two brothers are breaking their hearts."*

On the other side of the wide blue sea
Stood a house that was simple and pretty and wee.
In hid in the valley, a humble cot
Of logs and clay in a hidden spot.
Each day the sun would flush with gold   5
A little window quaint and old.
And the moon would rise,
And its clear, pure eyes
Would paint the panes with silver.

And love was the blessing that Heaven sent   10
To the brothers who lived there in content.
Two hearts were true to each other's need
In thought and word and look and deed.
The work was hard, but the hands that worked
Were brothers' hands, and they never shirked.   15
They lived in love,
The while Time wove
The weft of the web of Fate.

But once a snake came before the door
To flaunt the dress of gold it wore,   20
In beauty clad, with jewels bright.
The older brother beholds the sight —
"There is wondrous wealth in the world, it seems,
Such wealth as I never knew in dreams.
One jewel sold,   25
And the yellow gold
Would buy a pretty milch cow."

The snake, she knows a human's heart —
She calls the older brother apart.
"Ah, foolish man, if you only knew —   30
Barrels of gold would belong to you.
Corals, diamonds, rubies, gems
Worth more than a thousand diadems.
I mean what I say,
At the end of the day   35
Come to the edge of the wood."

When the snake had gone, the younger thought,
"What a wealth of things the Lord has wrought,
What is the use of asking why?"
But passion flames in the older's eye —
"Corals, rubies, diamonds ...God —   40
That she has not deceived this foolish clod!"
Temptation thrills
And away he steals
From his brother to the snake.

The sun goes down, and the west is red   45
Like a flaming world where the sun has bled.
And under a tree sit snake and man
Deep in words that the snake began.
She wraps him round with her body smooth,
And talks of riches without ruth,   50
Of round red gold,
Gems manifold —
"All will be yours, your own.

"Look at your brother. He toils all day,
And he sweats and sweats in the self-same way.   55
The sweat rolls down from his ruddy face,
And the drops stand out on every place,
And he wipes them away with his garment hem.
Don't let him. Each drop is a costly gem.
You make him work,   60
Don't let him shirk,
You will gather barrels of diamonds.

"You think that tear is less than sweat?
Fool, you think it is water because it is wet?
You comfort, caress him, and help him rise,   65
And kiss the tears away from his eyes.
You make yourself poorer with each lost tear.
Let him weep. Take each drop, for each drop is dear,
A tear, understand,
Will ransom a land.   70
You will be rich as a king.

"Your brother has a delicate skin,
Take a needle, and stick it in.
You think it is only blood you draw?
It is greater wealth than ever you saw.   75
Each drop is a coral, a ruby red.
Go, gather the blood your brother has shed.
Out of his pain,
Coin your gain,
You are stronger, and know the secret."   80

His lips compressed, and his fists clenched tight,
The older brother comes home at night.
His eyes are fire, and his looks are black.
Yet love of his brother holds him back.
But he says in his heart — "My brother must weep.   85
I will prick him gently, and not too deep.
My brother? I know —
But it must be so,
For tears and sweat are diamonds."

On the self-same night the pale moon knows   90
The younger's cries at the older's blows,
The trembling stars look in and see
The younger weeping bitterly.
When daylight breaks, the golden sun
Is amazed to see the evil done.   95
And river and tree
Wonder mightily
At the things that go on in the house.

And the Lord hath cursed the brethren twain,
One with fear, the other with pain.   100
And joy is dead, and sleep is done,
And love is away and forever gone.
One cried — "My wealth, my dream of years!"
The other — "My blood, my sweat, my tears."
Over the sea,   105
The wide blue sea,
Two brothers are breaking their hearts.

FOR THE AMBITIOUS STUDENT

In connection with this poem read "The Man With the Hoe" by Edwin Markham.

Isaac L. Peretz, the author of this poem, is generally considered the foremost man of Yiddish letters. The facts about the Yiddish language and literature may interest you. Look them up and report to the class. Yiddish is quite different from Hebrew. It is spoken by ten million Jews throughout the world. "Kibitzer" is a Yiddish word; do you know its meaning?

FLANNAN ISLE
Wilfrid Wilson Gibson

*A door ajar, and an untouched meal, and an overtoppled chair
— this was all they found to indicate the fate of the three men who
dwelt "on Flannan Isle to keep the lamp alight." But they saw
three birds — three queer black, ugly birds — that plunged from
sight into the ocean without a sound or spurt of water. Could
these have solved the mystery for them? And how about the other
tragedies which had befallen all who kept the Flannan Light?*

*This poem is one of the best I have ever seen for the "suggested
story." From the receipt of the message given in the first stanza,
a tragic mood pervades the lines; but at the end the poet leaves
you to solve the mystery of the tragedy yourself — if you can.*

Though three men dwell on Flannan Isle
To keep the lamp alight,
As we steered under the lee we caught
No glimmer through the night.

A passing ship at dawn had brought
The news, and quickly we set sail
To find out what strange thing might ail
The keepers of the deep-sea light.

The Winter day broke blue and bright
With glancing sun and glancing spray
While o'er the swell our boat made way,
As gallant as a gull in flight.

But as we neared the lonely Isle
And looked up at the naked height, 14
And saw the lighthouse towering white
With blinded lantern that all night
Had never shot a spark
Of comfort through the dark,
So ghostly in the cold sunlight
It seemed that we were struck the while 20
With wonder all too dread for words.

And, as into the tiny creek
We stole, beneath the hanging crag
We saw three queer black ugly birds —
Too big by far in my belief 25
For cormorant or shag —
Like seamen sitting bolt-upright
Upon a half-tide reef:
But as we neared they plunged from sight
Without a sound or spirt of white. 30

And still too mazed to spreak,
We landed and made fast the boat
And climbed the track in single file,
Each wishing he were safe afloat
On any sea, however far, 35
So it be far from Flannan Isle:
And still we seemed to climb and climb
As though we'd lost all count of time
And so must climb for evermore;

---

28. *half-tide reef*: a ridge of rocks or sand which is part of the land at low tide and
completely covered at high tide, thus appearing as a reef only at half-tide.

Yet all too soon we reached the door — ⁴⁰

The black sun-blistered lighthouse door,

That gaped for us ajar.

As on the threshold for a spell

We paused, we seemed to breathe the smell

Of limewash and of tar, ⁴⁵

Familiar as our daily breath,

As though 'twere some strange scent | This line modifies *to*
    of death; | *breathe* (l.44).

And so yet wondering side by side

We stood a moment still tongue-tied,

And each with black foreboding eyed ⁵⁰

The door ere we should fling it wide

To leave the sunlight for the gloom:

Till, plucking courage up, at last

Hard on each other's heels we passed

Into the living-room. ⁵⁵

Yet as we crowded through the door

We only saw a table spread

For dinner, meat and cheese and bread,

But all untouched and no one there;

As though when they sat down to eat, ⁶⁰

Ere they could even taste,

Alarm had come and they in haste

Had risen and left the bread and meat,

For at the table-head a chair

Lay tumbled on the floor. ⁶⁵

---

48. *yet*: still.

We listened, but we only heard
The feeble cheeping of a bird
That starved upon its perch;
And, listening still, without a word
We set about our hopeless search.   70
We hunted high, we hunted low,
And soon ransacked the empty house;
Then o'er the Island to and fro
We ranged, to listen and to look
In every cranny, cleft or nook   75
That might have hid a bird or mouse:
But though we searched from shore to shore
We found no sign in any place,
And soon again stood face to face
Before the gaping door,   80
And stole into the room once more
As frightened children steal.
Ay, though we hunted high and low
And hunted everywhere,
Of the three men's fate we found no trace   85
Of any kind in any place
But a door ajar and an untouched meal
And an overtoppled chair.

And as we listened in the gloom
Of that forsaken living-room—   90
A chill clutch on our breath—
We thought how ill-chance came to all
Who kept the Flannan Light,

83. *ay (i)*: yes.

And how the rock had been the death
Of many a likely lad—   95
How six had come to a sudden end
And three had gone stark mad,
And one, whom we'd all known as friend,
Had leapt from the lantern one still night
And fallen dead by the lighthouse wall—   100
And long we thought
On the three we sought,
And on what might yet befall.

Like curs a glance has brought to heel | Supply *which* after *curs*.
We listened, flinching there,   105
And looked and looked on the untouched meal
And the overtoppled chair.
We seemed to stand for an endless while,
Though still no word was said,
Three men alive on Flannan Isle   110
Who thought on three men dead.

FOR THE AMBITIOUS STUDENT

Here again you are offered an opportunity to try
your hand at the "suggested story." Or you may find
greater appeal in one of the stories suggested in lines
94-100, or even in "what might yet befall."

FOR YOUR VOCABULARY

The word *foreboding* (line 50) is a word of *ominous* suggestion. It brings to mind the universal — though perhaps not very wise — human tendency to look into the future, to wish to know what it will bring. In the olden days the *soothsayer* (sayer of truth) used to *interpret* the *omens* (signs) in nature and *prophesy* (foretell) what would happen. Later, if these *prophecies* turned out to be true, he was looked upon as an *oracle* (someone supposed to have the right to give out messages from the gods). Just let some of his *auguries* (prophecies) prove wrong, however, and thereafter his *oracular* powers were credited no more than some people today trust the daily *prognostications* (advance notices) of the weatherman. *Forebodings*, *premonitions*, *ominous*, *seer*, *presage*, *mage*, *sage* are all words related to those above. Write a paragraph or story using all of these words correctly.

THE LISTENERS
Walter de la Mare

No modern poet knows better than Walter de la Mare how to fill a poem with the spirit of the unknown, how to create a mood or mystery out of shadowy things, experienced only through imaginations, spurred by fantasy or fear. Read it as you should, and "The Listeners" will be an unforgettable experience. But don't be too literal-minded about it. It isn't fair to insist on pinning down the "listeners" to an exact identification; as a sensitive reader, knowing that the very silence sometimes seems to have ears, you accept the listeners, shall we say, as a sort of personification of the dark emptiness of night. (Or are they the ghosts of all the people who have ever dwelt in the house?) But the traveler is real: there is his waiting horse to prove it; and the horse's champing, the bird's fluttering, and the man's sharp calls serve to accentuate the silence. The auditory images, especially in the last four lines, are superb.

Tune your senses, then, for keen reception, and read this poem for mood.

"Is there anybody there?" said the Traveller,
    Knocking on the moonlit door;
And his horse in the silence champed the grasses
    Of the forest's ferny floor:
And a bird flew up out of the turret,   5
    Above the Traveller's head:
And he smote upon the door again a second time;
    "Is there anybody there?" he said.
But no one descended to the Traveller;
    No head from the leaf-fringed sill   10
Leaned over and looked into his grey eyes,

Where he stood perplexed and still.
But only a host of phantom listeners
    That dwelt in the lone house then
Stood listening in the quiet of the moonlight 15
    To that voice from the world of men:
Stood thronging the faint moonbeams on the dark stair,
    That goes down to the empty hall,
Hearkening in an air stirred and shaken
    By the lonely Traveller's call. 20
And he felt in his heart their strangeness,
    Their stillness answering his cry,
While his horse moved, cropping the dark turf,
    'Neath the starred and leafy sky;
For he suddenly smote on the door, even 25
    Louder, and lifted his head: —
"Tell them I came, and no one answered,
    That I kept my word," he said.
Never the least stir made the listeners,
    Though every word he spake 30
Fell echoing through the shadowiness of the still house
    From the one man left awake:
Ay, they heard his foot upon the stirrup,
    And the sound of iron on stone,
And how the silence surged softly backward, 35
    When the plunging hoofs were gone.

There are in this poem some fine effects achieved by alliteration. Point out two or three places where you feel the alliteration is pleasing. Note also the onomatopoetic trick in line 31: the echoes stretch out the line to make it the longest in the poem.

FOR THE AMBITIOUS STUDENT

If you can decide who the listeners were, what the rider's errand was, and why he wanted it known that he had come, write out the story in your own way, explaining there things. It should be an interesting story!

Surely you've read Robert Louis Stevenson's *A Child's Garden of Verses*. Another classic of children's poetry is Mr. de la Mare's *Peacock Pie*. And there's no finer collection of poems for young people than the anthology he prepared and called *Come Hither*! Ask for it at the library.

THE ROMNEY
Harriet Monroe

*A baffled art-dealer from London, two aristocratic but poverty-
stricken old Southern spinsters, a practical young nephew for the
University of Southern California, and a valuable portrait by
Romney are the elements of this account of a bitter, yet amusing,
family crisis. The two little old ladies, with their queerly twisted
ideas of right and wrong, would rather starve than sell a family
portrait. It is fun to watch them repulse the crafty buyer and then
to see them argue themselves into believing that it is all right to
sell it after all. And it is interesting that they had long owned a
valuable art treasure without ever appreciating its worth or
enjoying its beauty.*

They lived alone
Under the portraits of their ancestors —
Two elderly spinsters slowly graying away.
They cooked thin little meals,
And ate them on Lowestoft china   5
At the banquet-table no longer served | This was once a very
    by slaves. | wealthy family.
Year by year
Their shadowy income dwindled.

One portrait was a Romney —
Two brave young lads in velvet.   10
A London dealer heard of it and came over,

5. *Lowestoft*: valuable antique English chinaware.
9. *Romney*: a portrait painted by George Romney, famous English portrait
   painter (1734-1802).

And politely, insinuatingly, asked to see.
Reluctantly they showed the stranger in.

Their poverty embarrasses them.

Twenty thousand dollars he offered,
Sure of the prize —   15
Were they not visibly starving, these ladies,
In the ashes of grandeur?

He is trying to take advantage of them.

The sisters stirred a little
In pained surprise.
"You quite mistake us," the elder said; 20
"We cannot sell our family portraits."
And the dealer, in pained surprise,
Bowed himself out.

They are pained *at the mere idea of selling a family picture; he is* pained *by his disappointment and bewilderment.*

A few days later came a letter
Offering thirty thousand.   25
But the dealer waited in vain for an
        answer.

He doesn't realize the reason for their refusal, so he continues the only tactics he understands

Then forty thousand.
A young nephew,
Blowing in from the U. of S.C.,
Was paying a duty call on his aunts.   30
"By the Lord, I'd take it!" he said.

He has no silly ideas about family portraits.

The ladies shrank like gray moths frosted,
And the elder said:
"Great-aunt Millicent, whose name I bear,
Left the picture to Father.   35

They were stepsons of old Simeon Hugea,
Her grandfather —
His wife had been the widow of an Italian."

"Yes, and so not of our line —
They don't belong here."   40

> The nephew argues that they aren't really in the family.

The younger sister turned her eyes inward:
"Old Simeon could make nothing of those boys.
He gave them the grand tour
And ordered this portrait,
And they never came back —   45
Took to fiddling and painting like their father.
Millicent, do you think —"

> The younger sister is weakening—but not Millicent: they were part of the family.

"I am in doubt," said the elder sister;
"They were collateral."

So a family council gathered in the ashen-coated drawing-room, 50
And argued acrimoniously.
And it was decided that the half-Italian collaterals,
Who were not of the blood,
Might well be sold and forgotten.
And the deal was closed.   55

"It is a great deal of money," said the
        elder sister,
"But I am not quite sure —"

> To these sisters a picture was valuable only because it was of some one in the family, not because it was an artistic masterpiece.

---

43. *the grand tour*: an extended trip through Europe formerly taken by wealthy youth as a part of their education.
49. *collateral*: belonging to the same family but not in a direct line of descent.

And the younger,
"Who was this Romney?"

Each of the characters in this narrative represents a type of person. Can you characterize each by a single phrase? (Consider the two old ladies as one person.) Do you think it is reasonable that people would be unaware of the value of such a possession? Why?

Another version of this poem has the following last line:

"Was Romney a gentleman, I wonder?"

Which ending do you prefer?

"CONCERNING THE ECONOMIC INDEPENDENCE OF WOMEN"
John V.A. Weaver

*This poem with the imposing title is a dramatic monologue
written in blank verse. You may find it something of a shock. In
the first place the language will sound extremely crude, because
the poet is trying to employ the language that would actually be
used by the speaker. (His volume of poems is called* **In
American**.*) The subject-matter may also seem unusual for
poetry. But poetry can be written around the everyday lives of the
people; in this case we get a scene that is being enacted tonight
in thousands of American homes. A mother, not well educated but
intensely earnest, is at her wits' end about her daughter — not a
bad daughter, perhaps, just independent and rather short-sighted.
So Mother talks it over this evening with Dad. You cannot read
this very modern poem without taking sides. I wonder whom you
will think right — the mother or the daughter.*

"And after all," she says, "and after all,
Daughter or not, I got my life to live,
And there ain't no one elset can live it, see?
So if I wanta do the way I wanta,
You nor nobody elset is gointa stop me.   5
I'm getting' twenty per, down to the office,
And that's enough to live on, if I hafta;
Either you cut this always jawin' out,
Or either I takes my little trunk to Jane's....
I just as lief to anyways, and rather,   10
Only I know how lonely you would be

With only Pa to talk to, and him tired
So's that he lays around and snores all evenin',
And you wore out with sewin' all day long.
But if I wanta go out twicet a week,   15
Or three or four times, why, that's my own business;
And where I go, and who I go there with …
That's my own business, too. And so, that's that!"

And then I says a awful foolish thing….
I says, "Look out, Miss, or I tell your Pa."   20

Oh, Jim, you should of ought to see the look
She give me then, and her eyes all on fire.

"That's swell!" she says. "Yeh, I just wish you try it.
Now listen, Ma, you better get this straight:
If you sic Pa on me, and he starts in   25
To bawl me out, too, that's the end for sure.
Him bawl me out! Not neither of you won't."

I seen she meant it, too. So don't you never,
Not never, say a word….Then I got frantic,
Seein' her standin' there, so independent   30
And sassy, and so beautiful, and foolish….

I just broke down and cried, and tried to beg her
To not be quite so wild and act so crazy.
"Why don't you find some nice boy, and get married?"
She drawed herself up, awful proud and fierce.   35
"Get married! Me? Aw, Ma, don't make me laugh!

Me only nineteen, and get tied for life
To some poor fish that thinks he's gointa own me,
And tell me what to do?…Not for this girlie!
Nobody runs me, and nobody will.   40
Men is all right to fool around and play with,
But they's too many nice ones in the world
To ever stick to one. I know 'em, too,
And I can handle 'em. So you should worry."

What could I do? I begs her, I just begs.   45
"Helen, my darlin' kiddie, can't you see?
I ain't a-scoldin', I'm just tryin' to show you.
I know you ain't a bad girl, nor you won't be.
But all this runnin' to cabarets and dancin',
And takin' drinks, I guess, and auto-ridin' …   50
It all seems fine and lively and excitin'.
"'This is the life!' you says and the other day.
And kissin' ain't no harm, so far as that goes,
Nor anything — not anything that's real.
But that ain't real — that stuff all you is doin' … 55
It's cheap — just cheap, I tell you, and it wastes you.
Them pretty cheeks 'll fade and in a while
You'll get so sick and tired of excitement
It won't excite no more. And all the mystery
From everything 'll go. And even moonlight …   60
Oh, I know how it is, I can remember….
Even the moonlight 'll look pale and sick-like.
And then, the things that might have meant so much,…
Real love, and pretty things, 'll be all stale
And tiresome — just stale. Oh, won't you see?   65

For God's sake, have you got to eat your cake
All in one bite, and not have nothin' left?
Those is the rules — they ain't no way to beat 'em....
You sure can't eat your cake, and have it, too!"
Oh, Jim, she turns away, and humps her shoulders,   70
And says, "Well, Ma, you said your speech, I hope?
Old people always thinks and talks that way.
I'm sorry, but you know it's my own life.
And don't belong to nobody but me.
So long, and don't set up too late to-night....   75
I guess I won't be back till two or three."...

COUNTER-ATTACK
Siegfried Sassoon

Perhaps you will not like this poem. But I want you to see at least one example of the grim realism some of our modern poets are writing. Siegfried Sassoon, a brave British soldier in World War I, has written many poems portraying the war in all its shocking brutality. The war he knew was a matter of artillery duels and digging of trenches and "going over the top," rather than battles between vast fleets of tanks or planes. In this account of an unsuccessful attempt by the Germans to regain a line of trenches captured by the British, you will discover vivid imagery quite different from anything else in this book.

"Counter-Attack" is written in blank verse. As you read, don't lose either the rhythm or the thought.

We'd gained our first objective hours before
While dawn broke like a face with blinking eyes,
Pallid, unshaved and thirsty, blind with smoke.
Things seemed all right at first. We held their line,
With bombers posted, Lewis guns well placed,   5
And clink of shovels deepening the shallow trench.
     The place was rotten with dead; green clumsy legs
     High-booted, sprawled and grovelled along the saps;
     And trunks, face downward, in the sucking mud,
     Wallowed like trodden sand-bags loosely filled;   10
     And naked sodden buttocks, mats of hair,
     Bulged, clotted heads slept in the plastering slime.

---

5. *bombers*: men with bombs. Lewis guns: machine guns.
8. *saps*: trenches made by digging away the earth from within the trench itself.

And then the rain began, — the jolly old rain!
A yawning soldier knelt against the bank,
Staring across the morning blear with fog;   15
He wondered when the Allemands would get busy;
And then, of course, they started with the five-nines
Traversing, sure as fate, and never a dud.
Mute in the clamor of shells he watched them burst
Spouting dark earth and wire with gusts from hell,   20
While posturing giants dissolved in drifts of smoke.
He crouched and flinched, dizzy with galloping fear,
Sick for escape, — loathing the strangled horror
And butchered, frantic gestures of the dead.
An officer came blundering down the trench: 25
"Stand-to and man the fire-step!" On he went ...
Gasping and bawling, "Fire-step...counter-attack!"

     Then the haze lifted. Bombing on the right
     Down the old sap: machine-guns on the left;
     And stumbling figures looming out in front.   30

     "O Christ, they're coming at us!" Bullets spat,
And he remembered his rifle...rapid fire...
And started blazing wildly...then a bang
Crumpled and spun him sideways, knocked him out
To grunt and wiggle. None heeded him; he choked   35
And fought the flapping veils of smothering gloom,
Lost in a blurred confusion of yells and groans ...
Down, and down, and down, he sank and drowned,
Bleeding to death. The counter-attack had failed.

---

16. *Allemands*: the Germans (the French word).
17. *five-nines*: a term denoting the size of the shell.
18. *traversing*: turning from side to side so as to point in any direction.
26. *fire-step*: firing step.

THE BATTLE OF BLENHEIM
Robert Southey

Until very recent times poets tended to glorify war and battle, to praise the bravery and the sacrifice, and to regard these as exalted expressions of patriotism, whatever the purpose or the results of the wars. The following poem, ironical in tone, is a famous exception.

I

It was a summer evening;
    Old Kaspar's work was done,
And he before his cottage door
    Was sitting in the sun,
And by him sported on the green   5
His little grandchild Wilhelmine.

She saw her brother Peterkin
    Roll something large and round,
Which he beside the rivulet
    In playing there had found;   10
He came to ask what he had found,
That was so large, and smooth, and round.

Old Kaspar took it from the boy,
    Who stood expectant by; | Expecting what?
And then the old man shook his head,   15
    And with a natural sigh,
"'Tis some poor fellow's skull," said he,
"Who fell in the great victory.

---

18. *the great victory*: In 1704, during the War of the Spanish Succession, the English under Marlborough and the Austrians under Prince Eugene won a decisive victory over the French and their allies at the Bavarian village of Blenheim.

"I find them in the garden,
  For there's many here about;   20
And often, when I go to plow,
  The plowshare turns them out!
For many thousand men," said he,
"Were slain in that great victory."

"Now tell us what 'twas all about,"   25
  Young Peterkin, he cries;
And little Wilhelmine looks up
  With wonder-waiting eyes;
"Now tell us all about the war,
And what they fought each other for."   30

It was the English," Kaspar cried,
  "Who put the French to rout;
But what they fought each other for,
  I could not well make out;
But everybody said," quoth he,   35
"That 'twas a famous victory.

"My father lived at Blenheim then, | Who is speaking?
  Yon little stream hard by;
They burnt his dwelling to the ground,
  And he was forced to fly;   40
So with his wife and child he fled,
Nor had he where to rest his head.

"With fire and sword the country round
  Was wasted far and wide,

---

38. *Yon little stream hard by*: hard by (*i.e.*, near) yonder little stream
42. *where*: a place in which.

And many a childing mother then 45
    And new-born baby died;
But things like that, you know, must be
At every famous victory.

"They say it was a shocking sight
    After the field was won; 50
For many thousand bodies here
    Lay rotting in the sun;
But things like that, you know, must be
After a famous victory.

"Great praise the Duke of Marlbro' won, 55
    And our good Prince Eugene."
"Why, 'twas a very wicked thing!"
    Said little Wilhelmine.
"Nay . . nay . . my little girl," quoth he, | Could both be right?
"It was a famous victory. 60

"And everybody praised the Duke
    Who this great fight did win."
"But what good came of it at last?"
    Quoth little Peterkin.
"Why, that I cannot tell," said he, 65
"But 'twas a famous victory."

There are three clearly defined attitudes in this poem, one for each character. State these points of view precisely. Are they contradictory? Which one appears repeatedly in the refrain? Does this repetition necessarily indicate that the author favored that view? What is meant by saying that the poem is ironical in tone?

45. *childing*: with child.

DUNKIRK
Robert Nathan

However much we hate war, the long tradition of famous fights has a power over our imaginations that we cannot deny. We cannot help thrilling at the thought of human bravery and fortitude brought to mind by the names of such battles as those of Thermopylae, Trenton, Trafalgar, Waterloo, Gettysburg, Jutland, the Marne. And World War II has added names to this long tradition. Surely men will long remember the evacuation of Dunkirk, the bombing of Coventry, the pursuit of the Bismarck, and the defense of Bataan.

But even if our memories were short, the poets would not let us forget. Here is a poem which memorializes Dunkirk by showing what it meant to one English boy and girl. And somehow their exploit is made a part of the tradition of gallantry of the British navy. For the spirits of the two famous admirals, Nelson and Drake, in their flagships, the **Victory** *and the* **Golden Hind**, *are shown as guiding Will and Bess in their perilous flight across the channel.*

Here, then, you see how tradition grows and how the events of today provide the materials for poetry.

Will came back from school that day
And he had little to say.
But he stood a long time looking down
To where the gray-green Channel water
Slapped at the foot of the little town, 5
And to where his boat, the *Sarah P*,
Bobbed at the tide on an even keel,
With her one old sail, patched at the leech,

---

8. *leech*: edge of the sail.

Furled like a slattern down at heel.

He stood for a while above the beach;   10
He saw how the wind and current caught her.
He looked a long time out to sea.
There was steady wind and the sky was pale,
And a haze in the east that looked like smoke.

Will went back to the house to dress.   15
He was half way through when his sister Bess,
Who was near fourteen and younger than he
By just two years, came home from play.
She asked him, "Where are you going, Will?"
He said, "For a good long sail."   20
"Can I come along"?
                      "No, Bess," he spoke.
"I may be gone for a night and a day."
Bess looked at him. She kept very still.
She had heard the news of the Flanders rout,
How the English were trapped above Dunkirk,   25
And the fleet had gone to get them out —
But everyone thought that is wouldn't work.
There was too much fear, there was too much doubt.

She looked at him and he looked at her.
They were English children, born and bred.   30
He frowned her down, but she wouldn't stir.
She shook her proud young head.
"You'll need a crew," she said.
They raised the sail on the *Sarah P*,

Like a penoncel on a young knight's lance,   35
And headed *Sarah* out to sea,
To bring their soldiers home from France.

There was no command, there was no set plan,
But six hundred boats went out with them
On the gray-green waters, sailing fast,   40
River excursion and fisherman,
Tug and schooner and racing M,
And the little boats came following last.

From every harbor and town they went
Who had sailed their craft in the sun and rain,   45
From the South Downs, from the cliffs of Kent,
From the village street, from the country lane.
There are twenty miles of rolling sea
From coast to coast, by the seagull's flight,
But the tides were fair and the wind was free,   50
And they raised Dunkirk by the fall of night.
They raised Dunkirk with its harbor torn
By the blasted stern and the sunken prow;
They had raced for fun on an English tide,
They were English children bred and born,   55
And whether they lived or whether they died,
They raced for England now.

---

35. *penoncel*: a small narrow flag or streamer fastened at the lance head.
42. *racing M*: a class of racing boat.
46. *South Downs*: treeless, chalk uplands along the southeast English Coast.
51. *raised*: brought into view above the horizon; came in sight of.
53. *stern...prow*: The harbor had already been bombed, and choked with wrecked ships.

Bess was as white as the *Sarah's* sail,
She set her teeth and smiled at Will.
He held his course for the smoky veil   60
Where the harbor narrowed thin and long.
The British ships were firing strong.

He took the *Sarah* into his hands,
He drove her in through fire and death
To the wet men waiting on the sands.   65
He got his load and he got his breath,
And she came about, and the wind fought her.

He shut his eyes and he tried to pray.
He saw his England where she lay,
The wind's green home, the sea's proud daughter,   70
Still in the moonlight, dreaming deep,
The English cliffs and the English loam —
He had fourteen men to get away,
And the moon was clear and the night like day
For planes to see where the white sails creep   75
Over the black water.
He closed his eyes and he prayed for her;
He prayed to the men who had made her great,
Who had built her land of forest and park,
Who made the seas an English lake;   80
He prayed for a fog to bring the dark;
He prayed to get home for England's sake.
And the fog came down on the rolling sea,
And covered the ships with Englist mist.
The diving planes were baffled and blind.   85

---

77. *Her*: England.

For Nelson was there in the *Victory*,
With his one good eye, and his sullen twist,
And guns were out on *The Golden Hind*,
Their shots flashed over the *Sarah P.*
He could hear them cheer as he came about.   90

By burning wharves, by battered slips,
Galleon, frigate, and brigantine,
The old dead Captains fought their ships,
And the great dead Admirals led their line.
It was England's night, it was England's sea.   95

The fog rolled over the harbor key.
Bess held to the stays and conned him out.
And all through the dark, while the *Sarah's* wake
Hissed behind him, and vanished in foam,
There at his side sat Francis Drake,   100
And held him true and steered him home.

FOR THE AMBITIOUS STUDENT

John Masefield, present poet laureate of England, has written a prose account of the withdrawal from Dunkirk, which he called *The Nine Days' Wonder*. The book contains a number of pictures of English troops massed on the beach, waiting for transport. Perhaps someone could prepare an interesting report, based on this book.

---

86. *Lord Nelson*: England's greatest naval hero (1758-1805). He lost first the sight of one eye, then an arm. The *Victory* was his ship at the battle of Trafalgar, where he died.
87. *sullen twist*: empty, twisted sleeve.
88. *The Golden Hind*: flagship of Sir Francis Drake, who circumnavigated the globe in it, at the close of the sixteenth century.
92. *Galleon, frigate, and brigantine*: types of sailing vessels used by the "old dead Captains."
97. *conned*: superintended the steering; watched the course and directed the helmsman.

THE RIME OF THE ANCIENT MARINER
In Seven Parts
Samuel Taylor Coleridge

It is fitting to close a volume like this one with a masterpiece. So as a grand climax to your study of narrative poetry, you are hereby offered "The Rime of the Ancient Mariner." It has everything a great poem should possess: its story is dramatic and enthralling; its music, rich and haunting; its imagery, gorgeous; its lesson, well worth while. Since no helps except footnotes are provided (the sidenotes are the author's own), the poem will serve as a gauge to measure the appreciation you have developed from your study and reading in this text. May you richly enjoy it, and may you go on to gain that wealth of new pleasure which awaits you in all the great poetry that lies outside the covers of this slim volume.

ARGUMENT

How a Ship having passed the Line was driven by storms to the cold country toward the South Pole; and how from thence she made her course to the Tropical Latitude of the Great Pacific Ocean; and of the strange things that befell; and in what manner the Ancyent Marinere came back to his own country.

PART I

It is an ancient Mariner,
And he stoppeth one of three.
"By thy long gray beard and
    glittering eye,
Now wherefore stopp'st thou me?

An ancient Mariner meeteth three Gallants bidden to a wedding-feast, and detaineth one.

The Bridegroom's doors are open wide,   5
And I am next of kin;
The guests are met, the feast is set:
May'st hear the merry din."

He holds him with his skinny hand,
"There was a ship," quothe he.   10
"Hold off! Unhand me, gray-beard loon!"
Eftsoons his hand dropt he.

He holds him with his glittering eye —
The Wedding-Guest stood still,
And listens like a three years' child: 15
The Mariner hath his will.

> The Wedding-Guest is spellbound by the eye of the old sea-faring man, and constrained to hear his tale.

The Wedding-Guest sat on a stone:
He cannot choose but hear;
And thus spake on that ancient man,
The bright-eyed Mariner.   20

"The ship was cheered, the harbor
        cleared,
Merrily did we drop
Below the kirk, below the hill.
Below the lighthouse top.

> The Mariner tells how the ship sailed southward with a good wind and fair weather till it reached the Line.

The Sun came up upon the left,   25
Out of the sea came he!

---

12. *Eftsoons*: at once.
23. *kirk*: church.

And he shone bright, and on the right
Went down into the sea.

Higher and higher every day,
Till over the mast at noon —"   30
The Wedding-Guest here beat his breast,
For he heard the loud bassoon.

The bride hath paced into the hall;
Red as a rose is she;
Nodding their heads before her goes   35
The merry minstrelsy.

> The Wedding-Guest heareth
> the bridal music; but the
> Mariner continueth his tale.

The Wedding-Guest he beat his breast,
Yet he cannot choose but hear;
And thus spake on that ancient man,
The bright-eyed Mariner.   40

"And now the Storm-Blast came, and he
Was tyrannous and strong:
He struck with his o'ertaking wings,
And chased us south along.

> The ship driven by a storm
> toward the south pole.

With sloping masts and dipping prow,   45
As who pursued with yell and blow
Still treads the shadow of his foe,
And forward bends his head,
The ship drove fast, loud roared the blast,
And southward aye we fled.   50

And now there came both mist and snow,
And it grew wondrous cold:
And ice, mast-high, came floating by,
As green as emerald.

The land of ice, and of fearful sounds, where no living thing was to be seen; 55

And through the drifts the snowy clifts
Did send a dismal sheen:
Nor shapes of men nor beasts we ken —
The ice was all between.

The ice was here, the ice was there,
The ice was all around: 60
It cracked and growled, and roared and howled,
Like voices in a swound!

At length did cross an Albatross,
Thorough the fog it came;
As if it had been a Christian soul, 65
We hailed it in God's name.

Till a great sea-bird called the Albatross, came through the snow-fog, and was received with great joy and hospitality.

It ate the food it ne'er had eat,
And round and round it flew.
The ice did split with a thunder-fit;
The helmsman steered us through! 70

And a good south wind sprung up behind;
The Albatross did follow,
And every day, for food or play,
Came to the mariners' hollo!

And lo! the Albatross proveth a bird of good omen, and followeth the ship as it returned northward, through fog and floating ice.

---

57. *ken*: know.   64. *thorough*: through.

In mist or cloud, on mast or shroud,   75
It perched for vespers nine;
Whiles all the night, through fog-smoke white
Glimmered the white Moonshine."

"God save thee, ancient Mariner,
From the fiends that plague thee
      thus! —   80
Why look'st thou so?" — "With my cross-bow
I shot the Albatross.

> The ancient Mariner inhospitably killeth the pious bird of good omen.

PART II

The Sun now rose upon the right:
Out of the sea came he,
Still hid in mist, and on the left   85
Went down into the sea.

And the good south wind still blew behind,
But no sweet bird did follow,
Nor any day for food or play
Came to the mariners' hollo!   90

And I had done a hellish thing,
And it would work 'em woe;
For all averred, I had killed the bird
That made the breeze to blow.
'Ah, wretch!' said they, 'the bird to slay,   95
That made the breeze to blow!'

> His shipmates cry out against the ancient Mariner, for killing the bird of good luck.

---

76. *vespers nine*: nine evenings.

Nor dim nor red, like God's own head,
The glorious Sun uprist:
Then all averred, I had killed the bird
That brought the fog and mist.
''Twas right,' said they, 'such birds to slay,
That bring the fog and mist.'

> But when the fog cleared off they justify the same, and thus make themselves accomplices in the crime.
>
> 100

The fair breeze blew, the white foam flew,
The furrow followed free;
We were the first that ever burst   105
Into that silent sea.

> The fair breeze continues; the ship enters the Pacific Ocean and sails northward, even till it reaches the Line.

Down dropt the breeze, the sails dropt down,
'Twas sad as sad could be;
And we did speak only to break
The silence of the sea!   110

> The ship hath been suddenly becalmed.

All in a hot and copper sky,
The bloody Sun, at noon,
Right above the mast did stand,
No bigger than the Moon.

Day after day, day after day,
We stuck, nor breath nor motion;
As idle as a painted ship
Upon a painted ocean.

115

Water, water, everywhere,
And all the boards did shrink;

> And the Albatross begins to be avenged.
>
> 120

---

98. *Uprist*: rose up.

Water, water, everywhere,
Nor any drop to drink.

The very deep did rot: O Christ!
That ever this should be!
Yea, slimy things did crawl with legs   125
Upon the slimy sea.

About, about, in reel and rout
The death-fires danced at night;
The water, like a witch's oils,
Burnt green, and blue, and white.   130

And some in dreams assured were
Of the Spirit that plagued us so;
Nine fathom deep he had followed us
From the land of mist and snow.

A spirit had followed them; one of the invisible inhabitants of this planet, neither departed souls nor angels; concerning whom the learned Jew Josephus and the Platonic Constantinopolitan, Michael Psellus, may be consulted. They are very numerous, and there is no climate or element without one or more.

And every tongue, through utter drought,   135
Was withered at the root;
We could not speak no more than if
We had been choked with soot.

The shipmates in their sore distress would fain throw the whole guilt on the ancient Mariner; in sign whereof they hang the dead sea-bird round his neck.

Ah! well-a-day! what evil looks
Had I from old and young!   140
Instead of the cross, the Albatross
About my neck was hung.

PART III

There passed a weary time. Each throat
Was parched, and glazed each eye.
A weary time! a weary time!   145
How glazed each weary eye,
When looking westward, I beheld
A something in the sky.

The ancient Mariner beholdeth a sign in the element afar off.

At first it seemed a little speck,
And then it seemed a mist;   150
It moved, and moved, and took at last
A certain shape, I wist.

A speck, a mist, a shape, I wist!
And still it neared and neared:
As if it dodged a water-sprite,   155
It plunged and tacked and veered.

At its nearer approach, it seemeth him to be a ship; and at a dear ransom he freeth his speech from the bonds of thirst.

With throats unslaked, with black lips baked,
We could nor laugh nor wail;
Through utter drought all dumb we stood!
I bit my arm, I sucked the blood,   160
And cried, 'A sail! a sail!'

With throats unslaked, with black lips baked,
Agape they heard me call:
Gramercy! they for joy did grin,   *A flash of joy;*
And all at once their breath drew in,   165
As they were drinking all.

152. *wist*: knew.
164. *Gramercy*: great thanks.

'See! see!' I cried, 'she tacks no more!
Hither to work us weal,
Without a breeze, without a tide,
She steadies with upright keel!'

And horror follows. For
can it be a *ship* that comes
onward without wind of tide?

170

The western wave was all a-flame,
The day was well-nigh done!
Almost upon the western wave
Rested the broad bright Sun;
When that strange shape drove suddenly
Betwixt us and the Sun.

175

And straight the Sun was flecked
    with bars,
(Heaven's Mother send us grace!),
As if through a dungeon-grate he peered,
With broad and burning face.

It seemeth him but the
skeleton of a ship.

180

Alas! (thought I, and my heart beat loud)
How fast she nears and nears!
Are those *her* sails that glance in the Sun
Like restless gossameres?

Are those *her* ribs through which the Sun

185

Did peer, as through a grate?
And is that Woman all her crew?
Is that a Death? and are there two?
Is Death that Woman's mate?

And its ribs are seen as bars
on the face of the setting Sun.
The Specter-Woman and her
Deathmate , and no other on
board the skeleton-ship.

---

168. *weal*: good.
184. *gossamers*: filmy cobwebs.

Her lips were red, her looks were free,   190
Her locks were yellow as gold;
Her skin was as white as leprosy,
The Nightmare Life-in-Death was she,
Who thicks man's blood with cold. | Like vessel, like crew!

The naked hulk alongside came,   195
And the twain were casting dice;   Death and Life-in-Death
'The game is done! I've won! I've won!'   have diced for the ship's
                                          crew, and she (the latter)
Quoth she, and whistles thrice.   winneth the ancient Mariner.

The Sun's rim dips; the stars rush out.
At one stride comes the dark;   200   No twilight within the
                                           courts of the Sun.
With far-heard whisper, o'er the sea,
Off shot the specter-bark.

We listened and looked sideways up!
Fear at my heart, as at a cup,
My life-blood seemed to sip!   205
The stars were dim, and thick the night,
The steersman's face by his lamp | At the rising of the Moon,
        gleamed white;

From the sails the dew did drip —
Till clomb above the eastern bar
The hornèd Moon, with one bright star   210
Within the nether tip.

One after one, by the star-dogged Moon, | One after another
Too quick for groan or sigh,

---

209. *clomb*: climbed.

Each turned his face with a ghastly pang,
And cursed me with his eye. ²¹⁵

Four times fifty living men
(And I heard nor sigh nor groan),
With heavy thump, a lifeless lump,
They dropped down one by one.

His shipmates drop down dead.

The souls did from their bodies fly— ²²⁰
They fled to bliss or woe!
And every soul, it passed me by,
Like the whizz of my crossbow!"

But Life-in-Death begins her work on the ancient Mariner.

PART IV

"I fear thee, ancient Mariner!
I fear thy skinny hand! ²²⁵
And thou art long, and lank, and brown,
As is the ribbed sea-sand.

The Wedding-Guest feareth that a Spirit is talking to him.

I fear thee and thy glittering eye,
And thy skinny hand, so brown" —
"Fear not, fear not, thou Wedding-
Guest! ²³⁰
This body dropt not down.

But the ancient Mariner assureth him of his bodily life, and proceedeth to relate his horrible penance.

Alone, alone, all, all alone,
Alone on a wide, wide sea!
And never a saint took pity on
My soul in agony. ²³⁵

The many men, so beautiful!
And they all dead did lie;
And a thousand thousand slimy things
Lived on; and so did I.

He despiseth the creatures
of the calm,

I looked upon the rotting sea,   240
And drew my eyes away;
I looked upon the rotting deck,
And there the dead men lay.

And envieth that they
should live and so many lie
dead,

I looked to Heaven, and tried to pray;
But or ever a prayer had gusht,   245
A wicked whisper came, and made
My heart as dry as dust.

I closed my lids, and kept them close,
And the balls like pulses beat;
For the sky and the sea, and the sea and the sky   250
Lay like a load on my weary eye,
And the dead were at my feet.

The cold sweat melted from their limbs,
Nor rot nor reek did they:
The look with which they looked on me   255
Had never passed away.

But the curse liveth for him
in the eye of the dead men.

An orphan's curse would drag to hell
A spirit from on high;
But oh! more horrible than that
Is a curse in a dead man's eye!   260

Seven days, seven nights, I saw that curse,
And yet I could not die.

The moving Moon went up the sky,
And nowhere did abide;
Softly she was going up, 265
And a star or two beside —

In his loneliness and fixedness he yearneth toward the journeying Moon, and the stars that still sojourn, yet still move onward; and everywhere the blue sky belongs to them, and is their appointed rest and their native country and their own natural homes, which they enter unannounced, as lords that are certainly expected and yet there is silent joy at their arrival.

Her beams bemocked the sultry
    main,
Like April hoar-frost spread;
But where the ship's huge shadow lay,
The charmèd water burnt alway 270
A still and awful red.

Beyond the shadow of the ship,
I watched the water-snakes;
They moved in tracks of shining white,
And when they reared, the elfish light
Fell off in hoary flakes.

By the light of the Moon he beholdeth God's creatures of the great calm,
275

Within the shadow of the ship
I watched their rich attire:
Blue, glossy green, and velvet black
They coiled and swam; and every track
Was a flash of golden fire.

Their beauty and their happiness.
280

O happy living things! no tongue
Their beauty might declare:
A spring of love gushed from my heart,

And I blessed them unaware: ²⁸⁵ | He blesseth them in his heart.
Sure my kind saint took pity on me,
And I blessed them unaware.

The self-same moment I could pray; | The spell begins to break.
And from my neck so free
The Albatross fell off, and sank   ²⁹⁰
Like lead into the sea.

PART V

Oh, sleep! it is a gentle thing,
Beloved from pole to pole!
To Mary Queen the praise be given!
She sent the gentle sleep from Heaven,   ²⁹⁵
That slid into my soul.

The silly buckets on the deck, | By grace of the holy Mother, the ancient Mariner is refreshed with rain.
That had so long remained,
I dreamt that they were filled with dew;
And when I awoke, it rained.   ³⁰⁰

My lips were wet, my throat was cold,
My garments all were dank;
Sure I had drunken in my dreams,
And still my body drank.

I moved, and could not feel my limbs: ³⁰⁵
I was so light — almost
I thought that I had died in sleep,
And was a blessèd ghost.

---

297. *silly*: useless; or perhaps "blessed."

And soon I heard a roaring wind:
It did not come anear;   310
But with its sound it shook the sails,
That were so thin and sear.

He heareth sounds, and seeth strange sights and commotions in the sky and the element.

The upper air burst into life!
And a hundred fire-flags sheen;
To and fro they were hurried about!   315
And to and fro, and in and out,
The wan stars danced between.

And the coming wind did roar more loud,
And the sails did sigh like sedge;
And the rain poured down from one black cloud;   320
The Moon was at its edge.

The thick black cloud was cleft, and still
The Moon was at its side:
Like waters shot from some high crag,
The lightning fell with never a jag,   325
A river steep and wide.

The loud wind never reached the ship,
Yet now the ship moved on!
Beneath the lightning and the Moon
The dead men gave a groan.   330

The bodies of the ship's crew are inspired, and the ship moves on.

They groaned, they stirred, they all arose,
Nor spake, nor moved their eyes;
It had been strange, even in a dream,

To have seen those dead men rise.

The helmsman steered, the ship moved on; 335
Yet never a breeze up-blew;
The mariners all 'gan work the ropes,
Where they were wont to do;
They raised their limbs like lifeless tools —
We were a ghastly crew. 340

The body of my brother's son
Stood by me, knee to knee:
The body and I pulled at one rope,
But he said nought to me."

"I fear thee, ancient Mariner!" 345
"Be calm, thou Wedding-Guest!
'Twas not those souls that fled in pain,
Which to their corses came again,
But a troop of spirits blest:

> But not by the souls of the men, nor by demons of earth or middle air, but by a blessed troop of angelic spirits, sent down by the invocation of the guardian saint.

For when it dawned — they dropped their arms, 350
And clustered round the mast;
Sweet sounds rose slowly through their mouths,
And from their bodies passed.

Around, around, flew each sweet sound,
Then darted to the Sun; 355
Slowly the sounds came back again,
Now mixed, now one by one.

Sometimes a-dropping from the sky
I heard the sky-lark sing;
Sometimes all little birds that are,   360
How they seemed to fill the sea and air
With their sweet jargoning!

And now 'twas like all instruments,
Now like a lonely flute;
And now it is an angel's song,   365
That makes the heavens be mute.

It ceased; yet still the sails made on
A pleasant noise till noon,
A noise like of a hidden brook
In the leafy month of June,   370
That to the sleeping woods all night
Singeth a quiet tune.

Till noon we quietly sailed on,
Yet never a breeze did breathe:
Slowly and smoothly went the ship,   375
Moved onward from beneath.

Under the keel nine fathom deep,
From the land of mist and snow,
The spirit slid: and it was he
That made the ship to go.   380
The sails at noon left off their tune,
And the ship stood still also.

> The lonesome Spirit from the south pole carries on the ship as far as the Line, in obedience to the angelic troop, but still requireth vengeance.

The Sun, right up above the mast,
Had fixed her to the ocean:
But in a minute she 'gan stir,   385
With a short uneasy motion —
Backwards and forwards half her length
With a short uneasy motion.

Then like a pawing horse let go,
She made a sudden bound: 390
It flung the blood into my head,
And I fell down in a swound.

How long in that same fit I lay,
I have not to declare;
But ere my living life returned,   395
I heard and in my soul discerned
Two voices in the air.

'Is it he?' quoth one, 'Is this the man?
By Him who died on cross,
With his cruel bow he laid full low 400
The harmless Albatross.

The spirit who bideth by himself
In the land of mist and snow,
He loved the bird that loved the man
Who shot him with his bow.'   405

The other was a softer voice,
As soft as honey-dew:

The Polar Spirit's fellow demons, the invisible inhabitants of the element, take part in his wrong; and two of them relate, one to the other, that penance long and heavy for the ancient Mariner hath been accorded to the Polar Spirit, who returneth southward.

Quoth he, 'The man hath penance done
And penance more will do.'

PART VI

FIRST VOICE

'But tell me, tell me! speak again,   410
Thy soft response renewing —
What makes that ship drive on so fast?
What is the ocean doing?

SECOND VOICE

'Still as a slave before his lord,
The ocean hath no blast;   415
His great bright eye most silently
Up to the Moon is cast —

If he may know which way to go;
For she guides him smooth or grim.
See, brother, see! how graciously   420
She looketh down on him.'

FIRST VOICE

'But why drives on that ship so fast,
Without or wave or wind?'

> The Mariner hath been cast into a trance; for the angelic power causeth the vessel to drive northward faster than human life could endure.

SECOND VOICE

'The air is cut away before,
And closes from behind.   425

Fly, brother, fly! more high, more high!

Or we shell be belated:
For slow and slow that ship will go,
When the Mariner's trance is abated.'

I woke, and we were sailing on   430
As in a gentle weather:
'Twas night, calm night, the Moon
    was high;
The dead men stood together.

The supernatural motion is retarded; the Mariner awakes, and his penance begins anew.

All stood together on the deck,
For a charnal-dungeon fitter: 435
All fixed on me their stony eyes,
That in the Moon did glitter.

The pang, the curse, with which they died,
Had never passed away:
I could not draw my eyes from theirs,   440
Nor turn them up to pray.

And now this spell was snapt: once more | *The curse is finally expiated.*
I viewed the ocean green,
And looked far forth, yet little saw
Of what had else been seen —   445

Like one, that on a lonesome road
Doth walk in fear and dread,
And having once turned round, walks on,
And turns no more his head;

---

435. *charnal-dungeon*: burial vault.

Because he knows, a frightful fiend   450
Doth close behind him tread.

But soon there breathed a wind on me,
Nor sound nor motion made:
Its path was not upon the sea,
In ripple or in shade.   455

It raised my hair, it fanned my cheek
Like a meadow-gale of spring —
It mingled strangely with my fears,
Yet it felt like a welcoming.

Swiftly, swiftly flew the ship,   460
Yet she sailed softly too:
Sweetly, sweetly blew the breeze —
On me alone it blew.

Oh! dream of joy! is this indeed
The light-house top I see?   465
Is this the hill? is this the kirk?
Is this mine own countree?

And the ancient Mariner beholdeth his native country.

We drifted o'er the harbor-bar,
And I with sobs did pray —
'O let me be awake, my God!   470
Or let me sleep always.'

The harbor-bay was clear as glass,
So smoothly it was strewn!

And on the bay the moonlight lay,
And the shadow of the Moon.   475

The rock shone bright, the kirk no less,
That stands above the rock:
The moonlight steeped in silentness
The steady weathercock.

And the bay was white with silent   The angelic spirits leave
    light,   480   the dead bodies,
Till rising from the same,
Full many shapes, that shadows were,
In crimson colors came.

A little distance from the prow   And appear in their own
Those crimson shadows were: 485   forms of light.
I turned my eyes upon the deck —
Oh, Christ! what I saw there!

Each corse lay flat, lifeless and flat,
And, by the holy rood!
A man all light, a seraph-man,   490
On every corse there stood.

This seraph-band, each waved his hand:
It was a heavenly sight!
They stood as signals to the land,
Each one a lovely light;   495

---

489. rood: cross.

This seraph-band, each waved his hand,
No voice did they impart —
No voice; but oh! the silence sank
Like music on my heart.

But soon I heard the dash of oars,   500
I heard the Pilot's cheer;
My head was turned perforce away
And I saw a boat appear.

The Pilot, and the Pilot's boy,
I heard them coming fast: 505
Dear Lord in Heaven! it was a joy
The dead men could not blast.

I saw a third — I heard his voice:
It is the Hermit good!
He singeth loud his godly hymns   510
That he makes in the wood.
He'll shrieve my soul, he'll wash away
The Albatross's blood.

PART VII

This Hermit good lives in that wood | The Hermit of the wood
Which slopes down to the sea.   515
How loudly his sweet voice he rears!
He loves to talk with mariners
That come from a far countree.

---

512. shrieve: shrive (see Glossary).

He kneels at morn, and noon, and eve —
He hath a cushion plump: ⁵²⁰
It is the moss that wholly hides
The rotted old oak-stump.

The skiff-boat neared: I heard them talk,
'Why, this is strange, I trow!
Where are those lights so many and fair, ⁵²⁵
That signal made but now?'

'Strange, by my faith!' the Hermit
    said —

> Approacheth the ship with wonder.

'And they answered not our cheer!
The planks look warped! and see those sails,
How thin they are and sear! ⁵³⁰
I never saw aught like to them,
Unless perchance it were

Brown skeletons of leaves that lag
My forest-brook along;
When the ivy-tod is heavy with snow, ⁵³⁵
And the owlet whoops to the wolf below,
That eats the she-wolf's young.'

'Dear Lord! it hath a fiendish look' —
The Pilot made reply,
'I am a-feared' — 'Push on, push on!' ⁵⁴⁰
Said the Hermit cheerily.

---

535. *ivy-tod*: ivy-bush.

The boat came closer to the ship,
But I nor spake nor stirred;
The boat came close beneath the ship,
And straight a sound was heard.   545

The ship suddenly sinketh.

Under the water it rumbled on,
Still louder and more dread:
It reached the ship, it split the bay;
The ship went down like lead.

Stunned by that loud and dreadful sound,   550
Which sky and ocean smote,
Like one that hath been seven days drowned
My body lay afloat;   The ancient Mariner is
But swift as dreams, myself I found   saved in the Pilot's boat.
Within the Pilot's boat.   555

Upon the whirl, where sank the ship,
The boat spun round and round;
And all was still, save that the hill
Was telling of the sound.

I moved my lips — the Pilot shrieked   560
And fell down in a fit;
The holy Hermit raised his eyes,
And prayed where he did sit.

I took the oars; the Pilot's boy,
Who now doth crazy go,   565
Laughed loud and long, and all the while

His eyes went to and fro.
'Ha! ha!' quoth he, 'full plain I see,
The Devil knows how to row.'

And now, all in my own countree, 570
I stood on the firm land!
The Hermit stepped forth from the boat,
And scarcely he could stand.

'O shrieve me, shrieve me, holy man!'
The Hermit crossed his brow.   575
'Say quick,' quoth he, 'I bid thee say —
What manner of man art thou?'

The ancient Mariner earnestly entreateth the Hermit to shrieve him; and the penance of life falls on him.

Forthwith this frame of mine was wrenched
With a woful agony,
Which forced me to begin my tale; 580
And then it left me free.

Since then, at an uncertain hour,
That agony returns:
And till my ghastly tale is told,
This heart within me burns.

And ever and anon throughout his future life an agony constraineth him to travel from land to land,
585

I pass, like night, from land to land;
I have strange power of speech;
That moment that his face I see,
I know the man that must hear me:
To him my tale I teach. 590

What loud uproar bursts from that door!
The wedding-guests are there:
But in the garden-bower the bride
And bride-maids singing are:
And hark the little vesper bell,   595
Which biddeth me to prayer!

O Wedding-Guest! this soul hath been
Alone on a wide wide sea:
So lonely 'twas, that God himself
Scare seemèd there to be.   600

O sweeter than the marriage-feast,
'Tis sweeter far to me,
To walk together to the kirk
With a goodly company! —

To walk together to the kirk,   605
And all together pray.
While each to his great Father bends,
Old men, and babes, and loving friends
And youths and maidens gay!

> And to teach, by his own example, love and reverence to all things that God made and loveth.

Farewell, farewell! but this I tell   610
To thee, thou Wedding-Guest!
He prayeth well, who loveth well
Both man and bird and beast.

He prayeth best, who loveth best
All things both great and small;   615

For the dear God who loveth us,
He made and loveth all."

The Mariner, whose eye is bright,
Whose beard with age is hoar,
Is gone: and now the Wedding-Guest 620
Turned from the bridegroom's door.

He went like one that hath been stunned,
And is of sense forelorn:
A sadder and a wiser man,
He rose the morrow morn. 625

Now That You Have Finished the Book

POSTSCRIPT FROM THE EDITOR

If you have enjoyed the poems in this volume, the reason perhaps is—at least in part—that you have learned enough about the poet's craft to appreciate good workmanship in a poem. If this book has not missed its aim, you have now learned to experience pleasure in sheer story-telling skill, in the various kinds of word music, in poetic imagery; in short, you have begun to know a good narrative poem when you see one. I should like now to express the further hope that your reading of poetry will not stop here, but that you will continue to read and enjoy poems as you grow older.

With that hope in mind, I am adding a few pages to tell you a little about some other narrative poems and to describe some other forms of poetry that you are now prepared to enjoy. It may even be that for some of you this section will become the most rewarding part of your work with the book.

To discuss even very briefly the whole field of poetry, I shall have to make a few formal classifications—and, for those who want such things, there are included some formal definitions, which are kept as simple as may be. But the purpose I cherish most is to name some poets and some titles of poems which are not included in this book, that may give you dependable directions toward further hours of absorbing reading.

The real purpose of this postscript is to remind you that you haven't yet exhausted the pleasure—or the profit—that poetry has to offer. Indeed, you have only just begun what we may call, in the words of Mr. de la Mare, your "travels and adventures in the rich, strange, scarce-imaginable regions of romance."

Types of Poetry

Poetry is usually divided into three great classes: narrative, lyric, dramatic. As this book has been limited to narrative poetry, you have still before you the whole fields of lyric and dramatic poetry to explore for enjoyment.

LYRIC POETRY

*A lyric poem is a poem which voices the author's own thoughts or feelings on some subject,** as love, death, patriotism, nature. The *Psalms* in the Bible ("The Lord is my shepherd"; "Bless the Lord, O my soul") are perhaps the greatest lyrics in the world. Some other famous lyrics with which you may be familiar are "Trees," "Crossing the Bar," "America," "In Flanders Fields," "Annie Laurie." Since a lyric poem has no story in it, lyric poetry is often spoken of as "pure poetry."

Before you complete your high-school education, you will surely have the opportunity to learn more about lyric poetry. The ability to read lyrics intelligently will increase your pleasure in the music

---

* In this postscript, definitions have been italicized.

of poetry and in poetic imagery, to both of which *Stories in Verse* has introduced you. And you will learn that the reading of lyric poetry has some rewarding pleasures of its own. See to it that you don't miss them.

DRAMATIC POETRY

A dramatic poem is a play written in poetic form. Almost all early drama was poetic: the old Greek plays; the Spanish drama of Lope de Vega and Calderon; the plays of Shakespeare, Marlowe, Ben Jonson. Although the tendency to realism has placed most modern drama in the realm of prose, occasionally even today plays are written as poetry; Maxwell Anderson in particular has experimented successfully in this literary form. In this book we have three examples of a special type of dramatic poetry, the *dramatic monologue.* In this type, as the name signifies, there is but one speaker. (See pages 446,461, and 494.) Sometimes in your school course you will surely have a chance to study the drama; when you do, I hope you will not neglect the great plays written in poetic form.

NARRATIVE POETRY

A narrative poem is a non-dramatic poem which tells a story. Narrative poetry is usually divided into four classes: (1) great epics, (2) metrical romances, (3) ballads, and (4) metrical tales. In this book I have had to limit the poems to ballads and metrical tales; I have been unable to include the great epics and the metrical romances because of their length.* But these two latter kinds of poetry, especially the epics, are exceedingly important parts of literature.

EPICS

A great epic is a long narrative poem, majestic in tone and mighty in scope, characterized by:

a. A majestic hero, usually of supernatural origin.

b. Events of national or international importance.

c. Supernatural characters.

d. Episodes rather loosely connected.

e. Many long speeches.

f. Heroic verse.

The epic is the greatest of the types of narrative poetry. It is to the other types as the novel is to the short story or the fairy tale. In it may be found the essential elements of the civilization of a whole race, or nation, or religion. Some of the great epics seem to have grown out of folk legends and stories, which at first circulated orally, sung by minstrels. At last some poet, not always known to us by name, joined these old legends together and made them into a single poem which expressed the significance of a whole

---

*Exceptions are represented in the cases of "Achilles' Revenge" (page 134) and "Off to the War (page 354), which are selections from great epics, although by itself each selection is similar to a metrical tale.

heroic age. Other epics, unlike these folk poems, are the conscious work of poets who deliberately chose to imitate the old epic form of their poems; these are sometimes called "literary epics."

There are not many great epics in all the world's literature, probably not more than twenty really important ones. Of these, most were written in languages other than English; therefore those of us who are not linguists must read them in translation. For many of them there are English prose versions written for young people, and in almost every case these versions are by far the best introduction to the original epics. In fact, many of them tell stories so spiritedly and catch the flavor of the originals so well that by reading them you can become quite familiar with nearly all the great epics of the world and can appreciate to a surprising degree why these poems rank among the world's greatest literature. Because I hope that you will want to read some of these epics, I am going to tell you about them and recommend to you the particular version of each story that I like best. Perhaps at least one pupil will read each epic and report on it to the class.

THE ILIAD AND THE ODYSSEY

The greatest poems ever written are the epics of ancient Greece, the *Iliad* and the *Odyssey*. These poems, ascribed to Homer, relate incidents of the siege of Troy (Ilium) and the wanderings of Ulysses (Odysseus) after the war. In them we find the ageless stories of Achilles and Hector, the Lotus-Eaters, the Cyclops Polyphemus, the enchantress Circe, Scylla and Charybdis, and the rapid, fiery, tragic description of the slaying of Penelope's wooers. ("Achilles' Revenge," page 134, is from the *Iliad*.) Even in translation these stories retain much of their sweep, imaginative beauty, and human appeal; and even from a translation you may learn much of the customs and ideals of the ancient Greeks, the fathers of our modern civilization.

There are many English versions of these two poems. One of my favorites—and the one I recommend for your first reading—is *the Adventures of Odysseus* and the *Tale of Troy* by Padraic Colum. Mr. Colum dedicates his book as follows:

For Hughie and Peter
the telling of the world's greatest story
because their imaginations
rise to deeds and wonders

If you, like Hughie and Peter, have an imagination which rises to deeds and wonders, you are sure to thrill to these ancient tales as related with Mr. Colum's fire and spirit.

THE AENEID

The *Aeneid* is the great epic of ancient Rome, written in Latin by Virgil in imitation of the *Iliad* and the *Odyssey*. It relates the story of Aeneas, a Trojan prince, who after the fall of Troy had many adventures by land and sea, finally reaching Italy, where he founded a nation which in time became the commonwealth of Rome. The purpose of the poem is to glorify Rome and her emperors by pointing out the nobility and heroism of the founder of the race. The best introduction to the *Aeneid* which I have been able to find is *The Aeneid for Boys and Girls*, edited by Alfred J. Church. Rolfe Humphries says of his *The Aeneid of Virgil, a Verse Translation*: "It is better, no doubt, to read Virgil in his own Latin, but still—I hope some people may have some pleasure of him, some idea of how good he was, through this English arrangement." Some of you, however, will, I hope, read this epic in the original in your high-school Latin class.

THE LUSIADS

The great epic of Portugal is *The Lusiads*, written by Luis de Camoens in the sixteenth century. The title means the sons of Lusus, mythical first settler of Portugal, a country sometimes referred to as Lusitania.

This poem relates the adventures of Vasco de Gama, who in 1497-8 sailed around the Cape of Good Hope and opened a new route to India, an event of more immediate importance to European trade than Columbus's discovery of America in 1492.

A good English prose translation of this poem is the Penguin Classic by William C. Atkinson.

THE CID

One of the best of the medieval folk epics is the Spanish *Poema de Mio Cid*, which recounts the heroic adventures of "The Cid" (the lord), sometimes also called *El Campeador* (the champion, or warrior).

The Cid of history was Rodrigo Diaz de Bivar (c. 1040-1099), the greatest Spanish warrior in the long struggle between Christians and Mohammedans for the possession of Spain. The title, "The Cid," was given to Rodrigo by five Moorish kings whom he conquered in one battle and who then acknowledged him as their lord (El Cid). The Cid of romance is not only an invincible warrior, but also the model of knightly virtue, the mirror of patriotic duty, the flower of all Christian grace—the perfect cavalier of old Spanish tradition. *The Tale of the Warrior Lord* by Merriam Sherwood is a good prose translation.

THE SONG OF ROLAND

In medieval France the troubadours sang of the illustrious deeds of Charlemagne and his knights, the greatest of whom was his nephew Roland. The gallant adventures of this legendary hero are incorporated in the finest epic of old chivalric France, the *Chanson de Roland* (*Song of Roland*). This greatest hero of the Middle Ages is presented in *The Story of Roland*, by James Baldwin, who takes much of his material from the old epic, but freely borrows from other legendary stories in the romances of the troubadours. In this book you will read of the famous friendship of Roland

and Oliver, the exciting adventures of Ogier the Dane, and the last fight and heroic death of the valiant Roland. This is one of the greatest of the hero stories, and Mr. Baldwin has written an interesting account of it. (Be sure to get the edition containing Peter Hurd's beautiful colored pictures.) A thrilling poetic translation is *The Song of Roland* by Frederick Bliss Luquiens.

SIEGFRIED (SIGURD, THE VOLSUNG)

Out of medieval Germany come the great *Nibelungenlied* (*Songs of the Nibelungs*). This epic is a poetic account of the exploits of Siegfried, including his adventures among the Nibelungs, guardians of a great treasure in the land of fog and mist. The stories of the *Nibelungenlied* have been immortalized by Richard Wagner in his four great operas known collectively as *The Ring of the Nibelungs*: *Das Rheingold* (*The Rhinegold*), *Die Walküre* (*The Valkyrie*), *Siegfried*, and *Götterdämmerung* (*The Twilight of the Gods*). For this epic I again recommend a book by James Baldwin, illustrated in color by Peter Hurd, *The Story of Siegfried*.

The *Nibelungenlied* is based on old legends which flourished for years in all Scandinavian and Germanic countries. The usual name for the hero was not Siegfried, but Sigurd. In Icelandic literature we find another famous account of the adventures of Sigurd, the prose *Volsunga Saga*. William Morris has translated this old Norse story into noble English poetry in his *Sigurd, the Volsung*.

THE KALEVALA

For many hundreds of years the people of Finland have listened to legends and folk-tales of their heroes, chanted by wandering singers before the chiefs of clans and even in the huts of the poor. About a hundred years ago Dr. Elias Lönnrot painstakingly collected these old songs and wove them into a great epic poem which he called *Kalevala*, or "Land of Heroes." The three most important heroes are Vainamoinen (the oldest magician), Lemminkainen (an Arctic Don Juan), and Ilmarinen (the cunning smith who forged the Sampo, the wonderful mill which ground corn, salt, and money). This is one of my favorite epic stories, and I am glad to have a really satisfactory version of it to recommend to you: *Heroes of the Kalevala*, by Babette Deutsch.

One interesting fact about the *Kalevala* is that Longfellow used its unusual rhythm in *The Song of Hiawatha*. So, if you wish to know how the *Kalevala* sounds in the original, read Longfellow's poem. It (the *Kalevala*) ought to go something like this:

> Louhi said to Ilmarinen:
> "If you wish to wed my daughter,
> You must plough the field of vipers,
> Catch the great Bear of Tuoni,
> Bring to me the great Wolf muzzled,
> Grasp within your naked fingers
> The great Pike, so fierce and scaly."

BEOWULF

When the Germanic tribes overran the Roman Empire in the fourth and fifth centuries A.D., it was the Angles and Saxons, ancestors of the modern English, who first took possession of Britain. These peoples gave us the first English literature. Among the few Anglo-Saxon manuscripts which have been preserved is one poem which at least approaches epic proportions, the story of *Beowulf.* Beowulf is a hero prince of an ancient European country called Geatsland, who rids the neighboring Danes of the man-devouring monster Grendel, and then tracks Grendel's revengeful mother to a cavern at the bottom of the sea and slays her. *The Story of Beowulf* by Stafford Riggs is a book I can recommend to you with real enthusiasm. Mr. Riggs has caught the spirit of the original to an extraordinary degree, and the illustrations by Henry A. Pitz are just exactly right. I promise a thrill to every reader from the description of Beowulf's fight with Grendel; and I think most of you will like the entire story, from "Once upon a time" to the fateful end, "Thus passed to his own gods Beowulf, King of Geatsland, in the North."

KING ARTHUR

The greatest legendary hero of English literature, however, is not Beowulf but King Arthur, who led the Knights of his Round Table: Lancelot, Galahad, Gawain, Gareth, Tristram, and the rest. Unfortunately the chivalrous deeds of these gallant knights have never been incorporated into an epic poem. In the fifteenth century Thomas Malory gathered the legendary stories together into a book of English prose, which he called *Le Morte d'Arthur* (The Death of Arthur). And in the nineteenth century Alfred Tennyson wrote his poetic *Idylls of the King*, which just missed achieving epic proportions. But these great old stories have all the epic ingredients, and they should be on your *must* list. There are many good versions for young people. One quite generally liked is Sidney Lanier's *The Boys' King Arthur*.

ROBIN HOOD

Another popular Englishman who might well have been the hero of an epic is Robin Hood. You are already familiar with him and have read one of the ballads relating his adventures. (See page 164.) Although no poet ever wove the Robin Hood ballads into a great epic, I am mentioning him here because, like the Arthur stories, the cycle of Robin Hood poems is the stuff of which epics are made. The best-known prose account of these tales is Howard Pyle's *The Merry Adventures of Robin Hood*, of which there are several editions, prepared for boys and girls of various ages.

CUCHULAIN

The greatest hero of ancient Irish legend is Cuchulain (koo kŭl'ĭn), whose heroic adventures are recorded in many old Gaelic stories, the chief of which is "The Cattle-Raid of Cooley." This epic story relates how Queen Maeve of Connaught tried to carry off from Ulster the famous brown bull of Cooley and how Cuchulain, single-handed, defended the frontier against her whole army.

THE SHAH NAMAH

The *Shah Namah* (*Book of Kings*) is the national epic of Persia (now called Iran). It was written by Firdausi, greatest of the Persian poets, who spent thirty years of his life in composing it. Among the heroes of these ancient stories the greatest is the mighty Rustam, a leader of strength, valor, and barbaric courage. Of his many thrilling adventures, the best-known is his fight with his son, Sohrab. (This is the subject matter of Matthew Arnold's narrative poem called "Sohrab and Rustum.")

The *Shah Namah* is one of the masterpieces of the world's literature. In *Rustum, Lion of Persia*, by Alan Lake Chidsey, which is the version I like best, the author has preserved much of the fire, imagery, and daring fancy of the original.

THE ROMANCE OF ANTAR

Even better known in Arabia than *The Thousand and One Nights* is the collection of stories known as *The Romance of Antar*. About their campfires on the desert or in their colorful market places the Arabs gather today and listen in rapt attention to their professional storytellers (most of whom are blind), telling of "the hero Antar, warrior, lover, poet, whom none might conquer in battle, whom none might equal in love." The Arabic original is in thirty-four volumes, in alternate poetry and prose. *The Romance of Antar* by Eunice Tietjens is an excellent English account of this little-known but truly epic hero, whose "terrible war-cry still sighs in the gusty desert."

EPICS OF INDIA

In India and the Indies the *Ramayana* and the *Mahabharata* occupy about the same place as the *Iliad* and the *Odyssey* do in Greece and Western Europe. I have already told you about Dhan Gopal Mukerji's *Rama, the Hero of India* (page 271). So far as I know, there is no simple English version of the *Mahabharata*. But I do recommend that you make the acquaintance of Rama; then, if your interest is stirred, you may care to investigate the other great story of the Hindus.

AMERICAN EPICS

The literature of the American Indians includes no great epic. The poet Longfellow tried to remedy this omission by writing *The Song of Hiawatha*. In this poem, as I have told you before, he used the rhythmic pattern of the epic *Kalevala*; and he included as well as he could the legends, customs, and religious beliefs of the Indians. Of course, no white man could possibly give to an Indian epic the sense of reality that we find in the true folk epics which have come right out of the hearts of the people, but *The Song of*

Hiawatha is, nevertheless, an important and interesting poem. It is not difficult for you to read in the original.

Another American John G. Neihardt, has written a series of five poems which together, under the title *A Cycle of the West*, make something very near to a great epic. The names of these poems are: *The Song of Three Friends*, *The Song of Hugh Glass*, *The Song of the Indian Wars*, *The Song of Jed Smith*, and *The Song of the Messiah*. The material of these stories comes from early accounts of Western hunters and Indian fighters who performed the mighty feats of courage and endurance which crowd Mr. Neihardt's pages. These stories, of course, can be found in prose form, but the Neihardt poems themselves make easy reading. I think many of you will thrill to these American hero stories, as I do.

A third American epic which I hope you will read some day, and to part of which you have been introduced in this book, is Stephen Vincent Benét's *John Brown's Body*. (See page 354.)

THE GAUCHO MARTIN FIERRO

The most famous South American epic is that of the Argentine gaucho, Martin Fierro, written in the 1870's by José Hernández. The gaucho has disappeared from the pampas of Argentina, but in the great epic he loved and whose verses he sang to the strains of his guitar, he still lives. If you can locate a copy of Walter Owen's delightful version, "adapted into English verse," you will have a wonderful time reading about the stirring adventures of this "strange mixture of virtues and vices, of culture and savagery."

TWO GREAT LITERARY EPICS

Of the great epics for which there is no young people's version I shall mention only two: *Paradise Lost* and *The Divine Comedy*.

Paradise Lost, by John Milton, is the great epic of Puritanism. It relates in noble English blank verse the story of the Fall of Man, based on the account in Genesis.

The Divine Comedy, written by the Italian poet Dante, is the great epic of medieval Christianity. In it Dante describes his visionary journey through Hell, Purgatory, and Paradise.

Perhaps some day you will read these magnificent poems. In the meantime, if you can find a copy of either illustrated by the great Frenchman Gustave Doré, look it through; the pictures will give you some idea of the epic scope of the narrative.

METRICAL ROMANCES

The metrical romance is a long, rambling, highly imaginative narrative poem featuring love, chivalry, and religion. The older romances flourished among the troubadours of the Middle Ages, "when knighthood was in flower." They are full of romantic adventure, color and pageantry, heroic deeds, supernatural incidents. As I have already told you, many of them were about Charlemagne and his followers or about King Arthur and the Knights of the Round Table.

Among the later literary imitations of the old metrical romances probably the most famous are Tennyson's *Idylls of the King* (which you must surely read some day) and Sir Walter Scott's three poems: *The Lady of the Lake*, *Marmion*, and *The Lay of the Last Minstrel*. Of these three, *The Lady of the Lake* is perhaps the most interesting and the best known. But *Marmion* contains the popular ballad "Lochinvar"; and *The Lay of the Last Minstral* is, you will probably recall, the book which Philip Nolan, the "man without a country," tossed overboard when he came to the now famous lines:

> Breathes there the man with soul do dead
> Who never to himself hath said,
> This is my own, my native land?

BALLADS

A ballad is a short narrative folk poem, often characterized by:

a. Crude diction and verse

b. Superstition

c. Stirring events

d. Much dialogue

e. Repetition and refrain

f. Tragic ending

Stories in Verse

In this book you have read many of the old ballads, and a number of "imitation ballads" written by poets known by name. These are, of course, only a few of the well-known ballads of our literature. Some other interesting ballads or the names of the compilers and titles of books in which they may be found are as follows:

Old Ballads

 Baby Livingstone
 The Bailiff's Daughter of Islington
 The Demon Lover
 Fair Margaret and Sweet William
 Get Up and Bar the Door
 The Golden Vanity, or The Little Cabin Boy
 Kemp Owyne
 Kinmount Willie
 Lord Lovel
 The Riddling Knight
 Robin Hood and Alan-a-Dale
 Robin Hood and Guy of Gisborne
 Robin Hood and the Monk
 Robin Hood's Death and Burial
 The Twa Corbies
 The Wee Wee Man
 Young Waters

Native American Ballads

 Casey Jones
 Noah's Ark

Stories in Verse

The Old Chisholm Trail
The Shanty Boy and the Farmer's Son
Yankee Doodle
Young Charlotte
Lomax, J.A. and Alan ....*American Ballads and Folk Songs*
Sandburg, Carl ....*The American Songbag*

Imitation Ballads

Benét, Stephen Vincent ....The Ballad of William
Sycamore
Benét, William Rose ....The Horse Thief
Campbell, Thomas......................Lord Ullin's Daughter
Chesterton, G.K. ....The Ballad of the White Horse
Lepanto
Cowper, William ....John Gilpin's Ride
Hay, John.......................Jim Bludso of the Prairie Belle
Hemans, Felicia Dorothea............................Casabianca
Hopkinson, Francis....................The Battle of the Kegs
Keats, John ....La Belle Dame Sans Merci
Kipling, Rudyard.....................................Danny Deever
Fuzzy Wuzzy
Gunga Din
Mandalay
Lowell, James Russell....................The Singing Leaves
Macaulay, Thomas Babington ....Horatius at the Bridge
Masefield, John ....A Ballad of John Silver
Millay, Edna St. Vincent........The Ballad of the Harp-
Weaver
Scott, Sir Walter ....The Eve of St. John
Jock o'Hazeldean

METRICAL TALES

The metrical tale is hard to define. In classifying narrative poetry, we find three types with certain definite characteristics: epics, metrical romances, ballads. The rest are just lumped together—somewhat by the process of elimination—into this fourth class. Therefore, you see, *a metrical tale is any narrative poem which is not an epic, a metrical romance, or a ballad.* Most metrical tales (but not all) are comparatively short and usually (but not always) less fanciful—more realistic—than the metrical romances and the ballads. The metrical tale is to poetry what the short story is to prose. You know from your reading in this volume how varied in form, style, and subject matter these poems are. In this book all the poems which are not ballads are metrical tales (excepting, of course, the three dramatic monologues and the two excerpts from epics). Some other metrical tales I think you may like are in the following list:

Arnold, Matthew........................The Forsaken Merman
　　　　　　　　　　　　　　　Sohrab and Rustum
Benét, Stephen Vincent ....Portrait of a Boy
Benét, William Rose ....Merchants from Cathay
Browning, Robert ....Hervé Riel
　　　　　　　　　　An Incident of the French Camp
Burns, Robert...Tam o'Shanter
Byron, George Gordon.............The Prisoner of Chillon
Clark, Badger ....The Glory Trail
Gibson, Wilfrid W. ....The Blind Rower
　　　　　　　　　　　　　　　　　The Brothers

Stories in Verse

Stories in Verse

Glossary

This glossary contains (1) words from the editorial material which seem likely to be new to you, and (2) the same kind of words from the poems themselves, provided these appear to be *useful* additions to your vocabulary. You will find here the spelling, pronunciation, part of speech, and meaning of each word; but remember that those from a poem are given according to the use to which the word is put in the poem. Some of these words are used as other parts of speech, or with other meanings, on other occasions.

Only the preferred pronunciation of each word is given here. For explanation of the markings used in giving the pronunciation, and for fuller information about the words, consult *Webster's New International Dictionary*, published by G. and C. Merriam Company, which has been used as authority in the compilation of this glossary.

accord (ă kôrd'), *n.*: agreement.
acrid (ăk'rĭd), *adj.*: bitterly irritating.
acrimoniously (ăk rĭ mō'nĭ ŭs lĭ), *adv.*: bitterly.
aghast (å gåst'), *adj.*: terrified.
albeit (ôl bē'ĭt), *conj.*: although, even though.
alewife (āl'wĭf), *n.*: an Atlantic coast fish, 8 or 10 inches long, used mainly as a fertilizer.
anonymous (å nŏn' ĭ mŭs), *adj.*: bearing no name; of unknown authorship.

Glossary

antagonism (ăn tăg'ô nĭz'm), *adj.*: resistance; opposition; action against.

anthropomorphic (ăn thrô pô môr'fĭk), *adj.*: in the shape of a man; having human physical characteristics.

askance (á skăns'), *adv.*: sideways; with a side glance; with an indirect meaning.

augur (ô'gẽr), *n.*: a prophet; a soothsayer.

avert (á vûrt'), *v.*: to turn away; to ward off; to prevent.

awaft (á wâft'), *adj.*: adrift; afloat; floating.

bailiff (bāl'ĭf), *n.*: an overseer; an officer or agent of a ruler.

baldric (bôl'drĭk), *n.*: a belt for sword or bugle, worn over one shoulder, across the breast, and under the opposite arm, often richly adorned.

bar (bär), *n.*: bank of sand or gravel at the mouth of a river or harbor, hindering entrance and exit.

barrack (băr'ák), *n.*: a building for lodging soldiers.

barter (bär'tẽr), *v.*: to exchange. *n.*: the art of exchanging.

bask (básk), *v.*: to warm oneself, as in sunshine or before an open fire.

beacon (bē'k'n), *n.*: a signal fire on a high place.

beguiled (bê gīld'), *adj.*: charmed.

beguiler (bê gīl'ẽr), *n.*: one who deceives; a charmer.

beguiling (bê gīl'ĭng), *n.*: deceiving.

bereft (bê rĕft'), *adj.*: deprived; dispossessed.

bicker (bĭk'ẽr), *n.*: ill-tempered quarrel; tendency to wrangle.

billow (bĭl'ō), *n.*: a wave.

blanch (blánch), *v.*: to take the color out of; to turn pale.

blaspheme (blăs fēm'), *v.*: to commit an act of irreverence toward anything sacred.

blazon'd (blā'z'nd), *adj.*: adorned with bright colors, or with heraldic devices or coats-of-arms.

blear (blẽr), *adj.*: dim; misty.

bouchal (bōō'kál), *n.*: young man (Irish).

brake (brāk), *n.*: a thicket; a dense growth of brushwood or shrubs.

brand (brănd), *n.*: a stick or piece of wood partly burned; a torch.

buck (bŭk), *n.*: a male deer.

bullion (bŏŏl′yŭn), *n.*: uncoined gold or silver.

burgess (bûr′jĕs), *n.*: a person elected to represent a borough, or city; a leading citizen.

burgher (bûr′gēr), *n.*: an inhabitant of a town having the privilege of voting; a substantial citizen.

burnish'd (bûr′nĭsht), *adj.*: polished; rubbed to a high luster.

caliph (kā′lĭf), *n.*: successor; ruler.

calomel (kăl′ŏ mĕl), *n.*: a common medicinal drug used as a cure-all.

caravan (kăr′à văn), *n.*: a company of travelers, pilgrims, or merchants on a long journey through perilous country.

casement (kās′mĕnt), *n.*: a window.

casket (kàs′kĕt), *n.*: a small box for jewels.

catamount (kăt′à mount), *n.*: a species of wild cat; a cougar.

cataract (kăt′à răkt), *n.*: a large waterfall; an overwhelming rush or downpour of water.

cerulean (sĕ rōō′lê ăn), *adj.*: blue; colored like the sky.

champ (chămp), *v.*: to bite and chew noisily.

churl (chûrl), *n.*: a man without any rank; a peasant; a base fellow.

churlish (chûr′lĭsh), *adj.*: surly; ungracious.

cinch (sĭnch), *v.*: to fasten the belly-strap, or cinch, of a saddle.

cite (sīt), *v.*: to quote, for authority or proof or example.

clan (klăn), *n.*: a group of people held together by their common family name.

clave (klāv), *v.*: split. (The present tense is *cleave*; *clave* is an old-fashioned past tense.)

cleft (klĕft), *adj.*: split; separated. (This is the past participle of *cleave*; *cleft* is also now used as the past tense.)

clemency (klĕm′ĕn sĭ), *n.*: mercy.

cock (kŏk), *n.*: a small cone-shaped pile of hay.

cockatoo (kŏk à tōō′), *n.*: an Australian parrot.

cockleburr (kŏk″l bûr), *n.*: a plant with prickly pods that cling to the clothing; or the burrs (pods) themselves.

coffer (kŏf′ēr), *n.*: a treasure chest.

colleague (kŏl′ēg), *n.*: an associate or partner in employment, or in office.

Glossary

combatant (kŏm'bȧ tȧnt), *n.*: one who engages in combat.

comely (kŭm'lĬ), *adj.*: beautiful.

concede (kŏn sēd'), *v.*: to yield; to acknowledge.

consonant (kŏn'sŏ nȧnt), *n.*: one of a class of speech sounds characterized by some kind of stoppage in the breath channel; any letter of the alphabet except the vowels *a, e, i, o, u.*

consume (kŏn sūm'), *v.*: to destroy, as by fire; to use up.

convulsively (kŏn vŭl'sĬv lĬ), *adv.*: in a manner characterized by convulsions or spasms; jerkily; in a violently abrupt manner.

cormorant (kôr'mŏ rȧnt), *n.*: a large sea bird that devours fish greedily.

counsel (koun'sĕl), *n.*: advice; interchange of opinions.

covet (kŭv'ĕt), *v.*: to want something belonging to another.

cranium (krā'nĬ ŭm), *n.*: skull.

craven (krā'vĕn), *adj.*: cowardly; fainthearted.

cremation (krē mā'shŭn), *n.*: practice or process of burning the dead.

crone (krōn), *n.*: a withered old woman, especially a poor one.

crop (krŏp), *v.*: to bite off the tops of.

cursory (kûr'sŏ rĬ), *adj.*: rapid or careless; without attention to detail.

dastard (dăs'tērd), *n.*: a coward.

dauntless (dônt'lĕs), *adj.*: fearless.

decapitate (dē kăp'Ĭ tāt), *v.*: to cut off the head of; to behead.

demur (dē mûr'), *v.*: to object.

deprivation (dĕp'rĬ vā'shŭn), *n.*: a loss.

derelict (dĕr'ĕ lĬkt), *n.*: a vessel abandoned on the high seas and constituting a menace to navigation.

derision (dē rĬzh'ŭn), *n.*: the act of holding up to scorn or ridicule; contemptuous laughter.

desecrated (dĕs'ē krāt ĕd), *adj.*: put to shameful or unworthy use; profaned.

desolation (dĕs ŏ lā'shŭn), *n.*: gloominess; ruin.

diadem (dī'ȧ dĕm), *n.*: a crown; an emblem of regal power or dignity.

dialect (dī'ȧ lĕkt), *n.*: a local or provincial form of a language.

dilate (dī lāt'), *v.*: to expand; to enlarge.

dirk (dûrk), *n.*: a short sword or dagger.

dissemble (dĬ sĕm'b'l), *v.*: to pretend; to conceal; to disguise.

distorted (dĭs tôr′tĕd), *adj.*: twisted out of the natural or regular shape.

divine (dĭ vīn′), *adj.*: Godlike; heavenly. *v.*: to perceive; to detect.

doe (dō), *n.*: a female deer.

doff (dŏf), *v.*: to put off, as dress; to remove or lift (the headgear).

dolorous (dŏl′ĕr ŭs), *adj.*: sorrowful; grievous.

dolt (dōlt), *n.*: a blockhead; a numbskull.

dower (dŏw′ĕr), *n.*: the property a bride brings to her husband; a dowry; a ceremonial gift.

down (doun), *n.*: a tract of open upland.

drastic (drăs′tĭk), *adj.*: violent; harsh.

draught (drȧft), *n.*: a drink.

dun (dŭn), *n.*: a horse of dun color (dingy or dull grayish brown).

dusk (dŭsk), *v.*: to grow dusk; to darken.

dust-devil (dŭst′dĕv′l), *n.*: a sand spout; a moving column of sand supported by the wind.

eerie (ē′rĭ), *adj.*: weird; uncanny; serving to inspire fear, as of ghosts.

effulgent (ĕf fŭlj′ĕnt), *adj.*: radiant.

elfin (ĕl′fĭn), *adj.*: magic; pertaining to an elf.

emir (ĕ mēr′), *n.*: a Turkish official or dignitary.

emulation (ĕm û lā′shŭn), *n.*: ambitious rivalry; the endeavor to equal or excel someone else.

ermine (ûr′mĭn), *n.*: a kind of weasel, valued for its fine white fur.

eunuch (û′nŭk), *n.*: a court chamberlain.

evasive (ê vā′sĭv), *adj.*: deceitful; shifty; sly.

fagot (făg′ŭt), *n.*: a bundle of branches for firewood.

fain (făn), *adv.*: gladly.

fane (făn), *n.*: a temple; a shrine.

fatalist (făt′ȧl ĭst), *n.*: a person who believes everything is determined by fate or chance.

fathom (fath′ŭm), *n.*: a measure of length containing six feet.

Glossary

feign (fān), *v.*: to pretend; to invent.

fen (fĕn), *n.*: marsh.

feud (fūd), *n.*: a quarrel; bitter mutual ill-feeling, especially between families.

filigree (fĭl'ĭ grē), *n.*: delicate ornamental work fashioned out of fine wire.

flawed (flôd), *adj.*: cracked; broken.

flippant (flĭp'ănt), *adj.*: treating something serious with undue lightness.

fold (fōld), *n.*: a pen, or enclosure, for sheep.

foreboding (fōr bōd'ĭng), *n.*: a feeling of approaching evil.

franchise (frăn'chīz), *n.*: a political privilege; especially, the right to vote.

frescoe (frĕs'kō), *n.*: a drawing or painting on plaster.

fretting (frĕt'ĭng), *n.*: ornamental work in relief.

furled (fûrld), *adj.*: taken in; wrapped around the mast, stay, or yard.

galleon (găl'ê ŭn), *n.*: a large sailing vessel of the fifteenth, sixteenth, and seventeenth centuries, usually a treasure ship or a man-of-war.

galoot (gà lōōt'), *n.*: a queer chap.

garnered (gär'nĕrd), *adj.*: gathered; harvested.

garnished (gär'nĭsht), *adj.*: richly decorated.

gear (gēr), *n.*: goods; things.

gemmy (jĕm'ĭ), *adj.*: bedecked with gems; glittering like gems.

ghastly (gàst'lĭ), *adj.* or *adv.*: like a ghost.

gibbet (jĭb'ĕt), *n.*: a gallows, where criminals were hung in chains and allowed to remain as a warning.

gibe (jĭb), *n.*: an expression or shout of sarcastic scorn.

glutinous (glōō'tĭ nŭs), *adj.*: gluey.

gluttonous (glŭt''n ŭs), *adj.*: greedy in taking food.

goose-tick (gōōs'tĭk), *n.*: a mattress filled with goose feathers.

gored (gōrd), *adj.*: pierced with the horns of an animal.

grenadier (grĕn à dēr'), *n.*: soldier.

grisly (grĭz'lĭ), *adj.*: inspiring fear.

grovel (grŏv''l), *v.*: to crawl on the earth.

Stories in Verse

gruesome (grōō'sŭm), *adj*.: inspiring fear or horror.

guilder (gĭl'dēr), *n*.: any of various obsolete German coins (of both gold and silver), varying in value.

guile (gĭl), *n*.: deceit.

haft (hăft), *n*.: handle; hilt.

hazel (hā'z'l), *adj*.: brown.

hench (hĕnch), *n*.: henchman; servant.

henchman (hĕnch'mŭn), *n*.: an attendant; a right-hand man; a trusted follower.

hoar (hōr), *adj*.: white or light gray, as with frost or age.

hollow (hŏl'ō), *n*.: a valley; a low spot surrounded by elevations.

hornbeam (hôrn'bēm), *n*.: a tree with smooth gray bark, hard white wood, and leaves like birch leaves.

husky (hŭs'kĭ), *n*.: an Eskimo dog.

hypnotic (hĭp nŏt'ĭk), *adj*.: tending to produce sleep.

imbower (ĭm bŏw'ēr), *v*.: to shelter or place in a bower, or arbor.

immerse (ĭ mûrs'), *v*.: to dip or plunge into a fluid.

impetuous (ĭm pĕt'ŭ ŭs), *adj*.: rushing violently; hastily energetic.

implication (ĭm plĭ kā'shŭn), *n*.: that which is implied.

impotent (ĭm'pŏ tĕnt), *adj*.: powerless.

inbred (ĭn'brĕd), *adj*.: produced by marriages between close relations, with no new blood coming into the family.

incessantly (ĭn sĕs'ănt lĭ), *adv*.: unceasingly; continually.

indolently (ĭn'dŏ lĕnt lĭ), *adv*.: lazily.

indomitable (ĭn dŏm'ĭ tă b'l), *adj*.: unconquerable; not to be subdued.

indulgent (ĭn dŭl'jĕnt), *adj*.: yielding to the wishes of others; lenient.

inexorable (ĭn ĕk'sŏ rá b'l), *adj*.: unyielding; relentless.

inexpedient (ĭn ĕks pē'dĭ ĕnt), *adj*.: not serving to promote a purpose; not advantageous.

infamous (ĭn'fá mŭs), *adj*.: having a bad reputation.

infidel (ĭn'fĭ dĕl), *n*.: an unbeliever.

inquisitive (ĭn kwĭz'ĭ tĭv), *adj*.: prying; improperly curious.

insalubrious (ĭn sá lū'brĭ ŭs), *adj*.: unwholesome.

Glossary

insinuatingly (ĭn sĭn'ů āt ĭng lĭ), *adv*.: by winning favor and confidence, little by little.

interdicted (ĭn tēr dĭk'tĕd), *adj*.: forbidden.

intolerable (ĭn tŏl'ēr à b'l), *adj*.: unbearable.

intricate (ĭn'trĭ kĭt), *adj*.: complicated.

ire (ĭr), *n*.: anger.

irony (ĭ'rŏ nĭ), *n*.: a kind of sarcastic use of language, in which the intended meaning is the opposite of the literal meaning.

jackals (jăk'ŏls), *n*.: cowardly wild dogs that feed on carrion.

jaded (jād'ĕd), *adj*.: worn out; exhausted.

jargoning (jär'gŏn ĭng), *n*.: unintelligible talk.

joyance (joi'ăns), *n*.: gaiety, festivity.

king-pin (kĭng'pĭn), *n*.: the chief person in a group or undertaking.

knell (nĕl), *n*.: a death signal sounded by a bell.

laggard (lăg'ērd), *n*.: a slow-poke.

lair (lâr), *v*.: the bed or couch of a wild beast.

lapis lazuli (lăp'ĭs lăz'û lĭ), *n*.: a rich blue stone.

lavishly (lăv'ĭsh lĭ), *adv*.: profusely, abundantly.

league (lēg), *n*.: a measure of distance varying from 2.4 to 4.6 miles.

lee (lē), *n*.: a place sheltered from the wind.

linnet (lĭn'ĕt), *n*.: a common songbird of England.

literal (lĭt'ēr ăl), *adj*.: according to the "letter"; unimaginative.

livid (lĭv'ĭd), *adj*.: ashy pale.

loath (lōth), *adj*.: unwilling.

low (lō), *v*.: to make the calling sound of cows; to moo.

lozenge (lŏz'ĕnj), *n*.: a piece of candy.

lug (lŭg), *n*.: a bar in a fireplace on which kettles are hung.

lugubrious (lû gū'brĭ ŭs), *adj*.: mournful.

mage (māj), *n*.: a magician.

main (mān), *n*.: the high sea; ocean.

malevolent (mà lĕv'ŏ lĕnt), *adj*.: showing ill-will.

marmot (mär′mŭt), *n.*: a woodchuck.

massive (măs′ĭv), *adj.*: bulky; heavy.

mattock (măt′ŭk), *n.*: an implement for digging and grubbing; a combination of pick, ax, and heavy hoe.

mazed (māzd), *adj.*: bewildered.

meet (mēt), *adj.*: suitable; proper.

mellowing (mĕl′ô ĭng), *adj.*: soothing.

metamorphose (mĕt á môr′fōz), *v.*: to change into a different form.

mien (mēn), *n.*: manner; air.

milch cow (mĭlch), *n.*: a milk-giving cow.

minion (mĭn′yŭn), *n.*: a dainty darling; a fawning favorite.

ministration (mĭn ĭs trā′shŭn), *n.*: a service.

minor (mīn′ēr), *n.*: a musical chord.

moil (moil), *v.*: to toil.

mollified (mŏl′ĭ fīd), *adj.*: pacified; calmed.

monk's-head (mŭngks′hĕd), *n.*: the dandelion.

monkshood (mŭngks′hŏŏd), *n.*: a poisonous plant. The name is suggested by the shape of the flower.

monotony (mô nŏt′ô nĭ), *n.*: wearisome sameness.

moonshiner (mōōn′shĭn ēr), *n.*: one who unlawfully distills liquor at night.

morose (mô rōs′), *adj.*: sullen; gloomy.

mortar (môr′tēr), *n.*: a strong vessel in which chemical substances are pounded or rubbed with a pestle.

murky (mûr′kĭ), *adj.*: dark; gloomy.

mush (mŭsh), *v.*: to travel on foot across the snow with dogs.

musty (mŭs′tĭ), *adj.*: having a rank, pungent, offensive odor.

muted (mūt′ĕd), *adj.*: muffled; deadened.

mutinous (mū′tĭ nŭs), *adj.*: rebellious; unruly.

nether (nĕth′ēr), *adj.*: lower.

night-rack (nīt′răk), *n.*: night fog or mist; wind-driven mass of clouds.

obeisance (ô bā′sǎns), *n.*: a gesture of respect; a bow.

obese (ō bēs′), *adj.*: very fat.

Glossary

omen (ō′měn), *n.*: a sign foretelling future events.

ominous (ŏm′ĭ nŭs), *adj.*: threatening; foreshadowing evil or disaster.

opulent (ŏp′û lěnt), *adj.*: wealthy; excessively liberal.

ostensibly (ŏs těn′sĭ blĭ), *adv.*: avowedly; professedly (often used as opposed to *actually*).

ostler (ŏs′lēr), *n.*: a stableman; a hostler.

pallid (păl′ĭd), *adj.*: pale.

pallor (păl′ēr), *n.*: paleness.

parable (păr′á b′l), *n.*: a short narrative of life from which a moral or spiritual principle is drawn.

parka (pär′ká), *n.*: an outer garment formerly made of skins; a shirt with a hood.

pastille (păs těl′), *n.*: a small cone of incense.

paunch (pônch), *n.*: potbelly.

penance (pěn′áns), *n.*: repentance; sorrow for wrongdoings; a hardship or punishment undergone for some sin.

pensive (pěn′sĭv), *adj.*: dreamy; sadly thoughtful.

perchance (pēr châns′), *adv.*: perhaps.

persecutor (pûr′sê kū tēr), *n.*: one who causes another to suffer.

pert (pûrt), *adj.*: lively; sprightly.

phantom (făn′tŭm), *n.*: an imagined appearance, not real; a specter or apparition.

phenomenon (fê nŏm′ê nŏn), *n.*: an extraordinary or remarkable occurrence or thing.

piebald (pī′bôld), *adj.*: of different colors.

pilaff (pĭ läf′), *n.*: an Oriental dish of rice, meat, etc.

pilaster (pĭ lăs′tēr), *n.*: a pillar.

pillage (pĭl′ĭj), *n.*: plunder, especially in war; the act of plundering or laying waste.

pinto (pĭn′tō), *n.*: a pony with patches of different colors.

piteous (pĭt′ê ŭs), *adj.*: full of pity; tending to excite pity.

pliable (plĭ′á b′l), *adj.*: easy to be bent or influenced; flexible.

plowshare (plŏw′shâr), *n.*: the blade of the plow.

plummet (plŭm′ět), *n.*: a heavy piece of lead used to measure the depth of water.

pocked (pŏkt), *adj*.: marked with pocks or skin blemishes.

poignant (poin′yănt), *adj*.: piercingly effective.

poll (pōl), *n*.: head; scalp.

poniard (pŏn′yĕrd), *n*.: a kind of dagger.

portmanteau (pôrt măn′tō), *n*.: a traveling bag.

presage (prĕ sāj′), *v*.: to predict.

primitive (prĭm′ĭ tĭv), *adj*.: of or pertaining to the earliest period; simple or undeveloped; uncivilized.

profligate (prŏf′lĭ gât), *adj*.: immoral.

providence (prŏv′ĭ dĕns), *n*.: divine guidance or care.

psaltery (sôl′tĕr ĭ), *n*.: an ancient stringed instrument resembling a harp.

puncheon (pŭn′chŭn), *n*.: a large cask.

purge (pûrj), *v*.: to clear of guilt.

pyre (pīr), *n*.: a heap of wood or other fuel on which a dead body is to be burned.

quaff (kwåf), *v*.: to drink.

quagmire (kwăg′mīr), *n*.: soft, wet, miry land.

quarry (kwôr′ĭ), *n*.: game; prey; the pursued animals.

quip (kwĭp), *n*.: a joke.

rack (răk), *n*.: a strain.

ramped (rămpt), *v*.: advanced with forelegs raised in anger.

rear (rēr), *v*.: to raise up; to rise up.

recked (rĕkt), *v*.: took heed; cared.

reckon (rĕk′ŭn), *v*.: to count; to compute.

recreant (rĕk′rĕ ŏnt), *n*.: cowardly wretch; betrayer; deserter.

re-creation (rĕ krē ā′shŭn), *n*.: act of creating, or making again.

recurring (rĕ kûr′ĭng), *adj*.: occurring again, usually according to some rule.

reek (rēk), *v*.: to smell bad.

rendezvous (rän′dĕ vōō), *n*.: a meeting by appointment.

repair (rĕ pâr′), *v*.: to go.

repiner (rĕ pīn′ĕr), *n*.: a complainer.

reprehensibly (rĕp rĕ hĕn′sĭ blĭ), *adv*.: in a manner deserving blame.

resinous (rĕz′ĭ nŭs), *adj*.: full of resin (gum).

Glossary

ribald (rĭb′ʌld), *adj.*: coarsely offensive.

rosary (rō′zȧ rĭ), *n.*: a string of beads used in counting prayers.

rout (rout), *n.*: total defeat or repulse; the disorganized state of an army in retreat or flight.

rowel (rou′ĕl), *n.*: a little wheel on some spurs, having a number of sharp points.

rueful (rōō′fŏŏl), *adj.*: mournful; sorrowful.

ruth (rōōth), *n.*: pity; mercy.

sable (sā′b'l), *adj.*: black in color.

sanctorium (săngk tō′rĭ ŭm), *n.*: a shrine.

scud (skŭd), *n.*: loose, vapory clouds driven swiftly by the wind.

sear (sēr), *adj.*: worn out; threadbare.

sedge (sĕj), *n.*: marsh grass.

seer (sē′ēr), *n.*: one who foresees events; a prophet or crystal gazer.

sentinel (sĕn′tĭ nĕl), *n.*: a guard.

shag (shăg), *n.*: a large sea bird.

sheathing (shēth′ĭng), *n.*: a covering; a garment.

sheaves (shēvs), *n., pl. of* **sheaf**: a bundle of grain, straw, or other plants.

shoat (shōt), *n.*: a pig; a young hog.

shrive (shrīv), *v.*: to confess one's sins. The word now means to hear confession.

shroud (shroud), *n.*: a rope or wire stay to support the mast; the dress for the dead.

signet (sĭg′nĕt), *n.*: a small seal, as in a ring.

sinew (sĭn′ū), *n.*: a muscle; a tendon.

sinister (sĭn′ĭs tēr), *adj.*: indicating hidden evil or harm.

slattern (slăt′ērn), *n.*: an untidy, slovenly woman.

sloe (slō), *n.*: a black wild plum.

smarty (smär′tĭ), *adj.*: unpleasantly clever; tricky.

somnolent (sŏm′nŏ lĕnt), *adj.*: sleepy.

sooth (sōōth), *n.*: truth.

spangle (spăng′g'l), *v.*: to sprinkle with small glittering bodies.

spawn (spŏn), *n.*: product; offspring; numerous issue.

spectral (spĕk′trǎl), *adj.*: ghostly.

speculate (spĕk′ û lāt), *v.*: to consider attentively; to ponder.

spheroid (sfēr′oid), *n.*: an object like a sphere, but not absolutely spherical.

sprat (sprăt), *n.*: a herring.

springe (sprĭnj), *n.*: a snare; a trap.

squall (skwôl), *n.*: a sudden violent windstorm, often bringing rain or snow.

stagnant (stăg′nǎnt), *adj.*: motionless.

staved (stāvd), *adj.*: broken open.

stealthily (stĕl′thĭ lĭ), *adv.*: in a secret, hidden, furtive manner.

stimulus (stĭm′û lŭs), *n.*: something that incites to activity.

sublime (sŭb lĭm′), *adj.*: noble; exalted.

subtle (sŭt″l), *adj.*: ingenious; clever; nicely discriminating.

suffered (sŭf′ērd), *v.*: permitted.

sumptuous (sŭmp′tû ŭs), *adj.*: costly; splendid.

sundering (sŭn′dēr ĭng), *adj.*: separating; coming apart.

surcoat (sûr′kōt), *n.*: a tunic or cloak worn over armor.

surly (sûr′lĭ), *adj.*: ill-natured; cross; crabbed.

swarthy (swôr′thĭ), *adj.*: of a dark color.

swound (swound), *n.*: swoon; fainting fit.

tabor (tā′bēr), *n.*: a sort of tambourine without jingles.

tansy (tăn′zĭ), *n.*: an herb with a bitter taste.

tarry (tăr′ĭ), *v.*: to wait; to delay; to linger.

tawny (tô′nĭ), *adj.*: a dusky, brownish yellow; tan.

tell (tĕl), *v.*: to count; to reckon up or calculate the total amount of.

teocalli (tē ô kăl′ĭ), *n.*: an ancient Mexican temple.

tepid (tĕp′ĭd), *adj.*: lukewarm.

tether (tĕth′ēr), *n.*: a rope or chain used to limit an animal's freedom.

thong (thŏng), *n.*: a strip of leather, used as a rein or whip lash.

tine (tīn), *n.*: a tooth, spike, or prong, as of an antler.

treble (trĕb″l), *n.*: a high-pitched sound.

turbulent (tûr′bû lĕnt), *adj.*: tempestuous; stormy.

turquoise (tûr′koiz), *n.*: a blue green.

Glossary

twain (twān), *adj.*: two.

vain (vān), *adj.*: proud.

verify (vĕr′ĭ fī), *v.*: to prove to be true.

vermin (vûr′mĭn), *n.*: mischievous or disgusting insects or small animals.

vesture (vĕs′t̲ū̲r), *n.*: garment; apparel.

vicariously (vĭ kā′rĭ *us* lĭ), *adv.*: by substitution; by putting oneself in another's place.

visage (vĭz′ȧj), *n.*: the face; the appearance.

wallow (wŏl′ō), *v.*: to roll about in mire.

wan (wŏn), *adj.*: pale.

wattled (wŏt′'l'd), *adj.*: roofed or floored with a network of interwoven twigs.

weft (wĕft), *n.*: a thing woven.

whet (hwĕt), *v.*: to make sharp or eager.

wont (wŭnt), *adj.*: accustomed; used.

wrench (rĕnch), *n.*: a sudden twist or jerk.

writhing (rĭt̲h̲′ĭng), *adj.*: twisting violently, as in pain.

wrought (rôt), *adj.*: fashioned; formed (old form of *worked*).

yeoman (yō′mȧn), *n.*: a member of the Yeomanry, a British volunteer cavalry force; a man free-born.

yon (yŏn), *adj.*: yonder; that (one) over there.

zealous (zĕl′*ŭ*s), *adj.*: devoted.

Index

Subject entries are set in roman type; *title entries* in *italics*; and *author entries* in CAPITALS.

Index

Stories in Verse

Index

Stories in Verse

Index

Index

Stories in Verse

Index